Right Center Left

Right Center Left

Essays in American History

LEO P. RIBUFFO

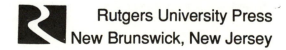

Rutgers University Press
New Brunswick, New Jersey

Library of Congress Cataloging-in-Publication Data

Ribuffo, Leo P.
  Right center left : essays in American history / Leo P. Ribuffo.
    p.   cm.
  Includes bibliographical references and index.
  ISBN 0-8135-1775-3 (cloth)   ISBN 0-8135-1776-1 (pbk.)
  1. United States—Civilization—20th century. I. Title.
  E169.1.R53   1992   91-5030
  973.9—dc20   CIP

British Cataloging-in-Publication information available

Six of these essays have appeared earlier in slightly or very different form
and sometimes with different titles:

Chapter 1: "Nativism and Religious Prejudice," in Charles Lippy and
Peter W. Williams, eds., *Encyclopedia of the American Religious
Experience* (New York: Charles Scribner's Sons, 1987), 3:1525–1546.
Copyright © 1988 by Charles Scribner's Sons, an imprint of Macmillan
Publishing Company.

Chapter 2: "Henry Ford and *The International Jew*," *American Jewish
History* 69 (June 1980), 437–477.

Chapter 3: "Jesus Christ as Business Statesman: Bruce Barton and the
Selling of Corporate Capitalism," *American Quarterly* 33 (Summer 1981),
206–231.

Chapter 4: "Communism and Anti-Communism in America," *Humanities*
5 (April 1984), 8–9.

Chapter 6: "Is Poland a Soviet Satellite? Gerald Ford, the Sonnenfeldt
Doctrine, and the Election of 1976," *Diplomatic History* 14 (Summer
1990), 385–403.

Chapter 7: "God and Jimmy Carter," in M. L. Bradbury and James B.
Gilbert, eds., *Transforming Faith: The Sacred and the Secular in Modern
American History* (Westport, Conn.: Greenwood Press, 1989), 141–159.

FOR MY GREAT TEACHERS

School 4, Paterson, New Jersey
Frances Torzella

Warren Point School, Fair Lawn, New Jersey
Lynne Langberg
Anthony Ardis

Memorial Junior High School, Fair Lawn, New Jersey
Helen Ryerson

Fair Lawn High School, Fair Lawn, New Jersey
Virginia Anastassoff
Frederick M. Binder
Robert Masterman

Rutgers University
Lloyd C. Gardner
Eugene D. Genovese
Warren I. Susman

Yale University Graduate School
Sydney E. Ahlstrom
John William Ward

Contents

Acknowledgments

Usually it helps to throw money at problems. While working through the intellectual problems discussed in this book, I was fortunate to receive research grants from the National Endowment for the Humanities, the Gerald R. Ford Foundation, and the George Washington University Committee on Research.

At various stages, the essays revised for publication here have benefited from the criticism and advice of many busy scholars and archivists. I want to thank Henry Abelove, David Alsobrook, JoAnn Argersinger, James Banner, Miles Bradbury, Barton Bernstein, Peter Carroll, David Crippen, Emmett Curran, Robert Dallek, Leonard Dinnerstein, Justus Doenecke, Noralee Frankel, James Gilbert, Cynthia Harrison, Barbara Kraft, Barry Machado, Barbara Melosh, Phyllis Palmer, Otis Pease, Irving Richter, Diana Rodriguez, Howard Sachar, Gaddis Smith, Geoffrey Smith, Werner Steger, Richard Tedlow, Jon Wakelyn, Peter Williams, and James Yancey. Lorraine Brown generously invited me to present an earlier version of chapter 5 to a conference on New Deal Culture at George Mason University in 1981. Cyndy Donnell expertly transferred to disk several of these chapters begun before I entered the computer age.

For a decade or more I have borrowed ideas and received moral support from Muriel Atkin, Bill Becker, Ed Berkowitz, and Jim Horton, fellow historians at George Washington University. Other debts go back even further. It sometimes seems that I have discussed—usually several dozen times—every intellectual, ethical, and educational issue of the past quarter century with Lee Fleming, Dan Guttman, Bruce Kuklick, Ken O'Brien, Mike Perlin, John Rosenberg, Sid Rosenzweig, Bob Schulzinger, Mike Sherry, Dan Singal, Sarah Stage, Jerry Winchell, and Leila Zenderland. No one could ask for more loyal friends.

September 1991

Right Center Left

Introduction:
The Complexity of American History

There are two basic ways to approach an understanding of the past. Some people try to understand it, or at least significant parts of it, seriously and thoroughly; others do not. Most though not all professional historians fall into the first category; most journalists, politicians, and ordinary citizens do not. Since the mid-1960s historians have not only fought among themselves about the best ways to understand the past, but also worried increasingly about their relations with the other Americans for whom this is not a pressing matter or even a noticeable issue. All of the essays collected here have been affected by my profession's recent intellectual opportunities and problems as well as by my own interests and idiosyncrasies.

When I began graduate school in 1966, one creative phase in the study of American history was coming to an end and another was just beginning. The first phase, usually described in the shorthand phrase "consensus history," represented an attempt, in the inescapable context of the Cold War, to deal with the intellectual legacy of Charles A. Beard, Frederick Jackson Turner, Carl Becker, and other "old progressive" historians. The second phase, usually described in equally problematic terms as the rise of "new left" history, represented an attempt, in the inescapable context of the Vietnam War, to question "consensus" orthodoxy without necessarily retreating to old progressive assumptions.

Both of these creative phases were embedded in broader cultural developments. The signal motifs of American social thought in the 1950s and early 1960s derived as much from memories of the Great Depression and World War II as from the ongoing reality of the Cold War. Contrary to the hopes of many intellectuals, the economic crisis of the 1930s had produced no revolution. Contrary to the fears of many more, the restoration of peace produced no renewed economic crisis. The war itself brought the inconceivable horror of the Holocaust, intimations of nuclear apocalypse, and Soviet domination of Eastern Europe. In this context, social thinkers as diverse as Daniel Bell, C. Wright Mills, and Arthur Schlesinger, Jr., questioned the central premises that, with some modification during the 1930s, had dominated social thought since the progressive era.

Indeed, the term "counterprogressive," coined by Gene Wise in 1973, captures the main concerns of the leading historians from the late 1940s to the early 1960s. Whereas progressive historians had emphasized class, group, regional, and (occasionally) racial conflict, counterprogressives perceived a general national unity of values and behavior. Especially suspicious of economic interpretations, they discovered the unconscious and experimented with psychological explanations. Chiding their predecessors for reducing ideas to social symptoms, they emphasized the importance of evaluating thoughts and thinkers on their own terms. Unlike progressive historians, who typically conceptualized politics as a fierce battle between forward-looking liberals and reactionaries, counterprogressives invariably conceptualized a responsible "vital center" (to recall Schlesinger's famous phrase) in which pragmatists argued amicably within broad bounds of agreement while irresponsible "extremists" harassed them from the far left and far right.[1]

Counterprogressives pointedly rejected an ethos as well as a world view. Celebration of "the people," a hallmark of the progressive era and Great Depression, yielded to fears of "mass man." Counterprogressives distrusted both passionate actors in history itself and passionate prose by historians. Similarly, they warned against interpreting past events according to contemporary standards. As early as 1948, Roy F. Nichols derided the progressives' "slavery to present-mindedness." Indeed, the label "present-minded," a term earlier used without rancor by Carl Becker, became a standard denigration.

According to the counterprogressives, partisanship and present-mindedness had fostered intellectual *and* moral oversimplification; specifically, the progressive historians had misunderstood human motives, missed history's paradoxes, and too neatly divided heroes from villains. Looking back in 1968, Richard Hofstadter, the foremost counterprogressive, summarized his generation's accomplishment as the "rediscovery of complexity in American history."[2]

Although most scholars in the 1950s remained content with using the progressive historians as targets in their monographs, some of them explicitly reevaluated the whole progressive legacy. Hofstadter in particular felt a need to come to terms with his "intellectual forebears." In 1968 he concluded that the progressive historians suffered from a "simple faith . . . in the sufficiency of American liberalism." Turner had lacked the "profound ambiguity" characteristic of the "most fruitful and interesting minds." In short, he was not the sort of self-consciously cosmopolitan intellectual admired after World War II. Beard's mind was tougher but his "excessive preoccupation with the motives and methods" of the powerful had produced a "fundamental misconception of the way in which history works."[3]

Curiously, the counterprogressives both claimed greater intellectual sophistication and evaded epistemological issues that had increasingly troubled progressive historians in the 1930s. What is usually called the problem of "relativism" had simmered in American intellectual life since the late nineteenth century. Was there an objective way to explain or even to describe a world that was, in William James's phrase, a "booming buzzing confusion?" While James, John Dewey, and other philosophers had wrestled with relativism during the early 1900s, the progressive historians, impressed by the claims of social science and feeling superior to *their* predecessors, whom they thought mere men of letters, had initially slighted the problem too. After World War I and the Great Depression had eroded their optimism, however, the most reflective scholars among them wondered whether written history was, in Charles Beard's phrase from 1933, largely an "act of faith."[4]

Beard distinguished between history as "past actuality" and history as "thought about past actuality." All history in the latter sense represented an "act of choice, conviction and interpretation," and all historians were influenced by their "time and cultural setting" whether they admitted it or not. Without surrendering his commitment to accuracy—indeed, as a way of making history more truthful—every historian needed to examine, clarify, and enlarge his own "frame of reference." Carl Becker made a similar distinction between past events, which remained "absolute and unchanged," and our memories of those events, which were "always changing in response to the increase or refinement of knowledge." Historians try to make the correspondence between these two histories "as exact as possible." In doing so, however, they must abandon the illusion that facts spoke for themselves and acknowledge the temporary nature of their contribution to knowledge.[5]

The mixture of epistemological modesty and professional humility that characterized Beard and Becker during the Great Depression had virtually evaporated among historians by 1960. The 1950s were an incongruously productive and prosperous time for intellectuals, especially for young intellectuals pursuing academic careers. Federal programs ranging from the G.I. bill of rights to the National Defense Education Act made graduate degrees accessible to some students from nonelite backgrounds, expanding colleges and universities needed new faculty, and prejudices against hiring Catholics and Jews diminished. Moreover, even before the Cold War rendered all economic interpretations suspect, the old progressive assumptions in several disciplines had run their creative course. "If we were to have any new insight into American history," Hofstadter later remembered, the postwar generation needed to examine the past "from another angle."[6]

Buoyed by intellectual challenges, rising status, and an academic bull market, scholars in the humanities or social sciences worried little about ethical—let alone epistemological—relativism. For their part, though counterprogressive historians ritualistically called attention to ambiguity, complexity, and irony, they never doubted their own ability to penetrate the ambiguity, analyze the complexity, and sort out the ironies.[7]

Confident counterprogressive historians thought that the differences between themselves and their progressive predecessors were stark. Yet two continuities now look as striking as the divergences. First, the search for hidden meanings beneath the surface of things that Hofstadter criticized in Beard and recognized as a central motif of progressive era social thought became with slight modification a characteristic motif of post–World War II social thought. Counter-progressive historians and pluralist social scientists showed an excessive preoccupation with the motives and methods of the powerless, especially if the powerless were classified as political or cultural extremists. Accordingly, the ideas of Populists, Communists, and fundamentalists were rarely explicated in their own terms even as a prelude to further analysis. On the contrary, their beliefs and behavior were reduced to symptoms of social status anxiety or personal neurosis.

Second, postwar intellectuals believed in progress in spite of themselves. The counterprogressive dismissal of Populists, fundamentalists, and other "backward-looking" Americans betrayed their belief that they knew not only where history had been, but also where it was going and where it should go. It was supposed to move toward "modernization" and "secularization," and conveniently enough that was the way it seemed to be going. Presumably all ironies and paradoxes along the way would stop short of cataclysm. Indeed, intimations of apocalypse were sure signs of status anxiety and a paranoid style. Although noted counterprogressives proclaimed pro forma pessimism and cultivated world-weariness, none of them sounded as troubled as Turner when he imagined the United States without an open frontier or Beard when he anticipated unrestrained presidential power.

Despite prosperity and underlying optimism, the historical profession in the 1950s, like American society as a whole, was not devoid of contentiousness or controversy. Aspiring academics from white ethnic and working class backgrounds still encountered snobbery and suspicion; by and large African-Americans were ostracized or patronized. Methodological disputes persisted despite the ebbing of epistemological malaise. For example, whereas many counterprogressives borrowed from the social sciences, skeptics agreed with Samuel Eliot Morison that such "jargon" threatened "history as a literary art." John Higham, C. Vann Woodward, and Arthur M. Schlesinger, Jr., chided their fellow centrist liberals for exaggerating the American consensus. Further left, the University of Wisconsin nurtured Marxists and unreconstructed progressive historians. Faculty and graduate students there took the lead in founding an important dissident journal, *Studies on the Left,* in 1959.[8]

By late 1967 critics of counterprogressive premises were sufficiently numerous and prominent to elicit a full-fledged response in the *American Historical Review*. Irwin Ungar's interpretation of the "'New Left' and American History" was vintage counterprogressivism in frame of reference and polemical technique. After arbitrarily placing Christian socialists, left liberals, and diverse Marxists under the rubric of "new left historians," Ungar then marveled at their disagreements. Nevertheless, he thought "present-mindedness" distinguished these scholars as a group from their centrist colleagues. Following standard counterprogressive practice, Ungar offered a psychological explanation of their deviant beliefs and behavior. An "excessive" sense of persecution fueled their attacks on "senior men" in the profession, and their critique of the New Deal resembled an "adolescent rebellion." Although most of the historians in question were almost as old as Ungar himself—forty—he persistently described them as "young" and the word was no compliment. He ended with a classic counterprogressive convention, an ostentatious claim to open-mindedness. Because new left historians provided a "useful antidote" to previous exaggerations of consensus, they deserved the attention of senior men after all.[9]

Although less reductionist than Ungar, Hofstadter saw in "new left" historiography a "culpable present-mindedness" reminiscent of that of the old progressives. The ironies, paradoxes, and "moral complexity" that Hofstadter thought intrinsic to history were considered impediments to activism by the "most feverishly committed" historians emerging in the late 1960s. Hence, he predicted that the "very idea of complexity will itself come under fire once again, and that it will become important for a whole generation to argue that most things in life and history are not complex but really quite simple."[10]

The "new left" label, which passed quickly into professional discourse, was problematical from the outset. Some historians wore the term as a badge of pride, yet most used it critically to separate dissidents from "regular" or "real" historians. Moreover, many "new left" historians were neither new to the left nor sympathetic to the Students for a Democratic Society (SDS) or other groups within the new left as a social movement. The term unfortunately persists in the 1990s even though the social movement collapsed twenty years ago, so-called new left scholars have reached middle age, and many of their interpretations are now commonplace.

Problems of terminology aside, we need to appreciate that the radical and left liberal historians who had achieved prominence by the early 1970s were at least as diverse as their counterprogressive predecessors and probably more diverse. For example, whereas Gabriel Kolko attributed American expansion to capitalism's objective need for foreign markets, William Appleman Williams stressed the pervasive but perhaps mistaken *belief* that foreign markets were essential. Williams and Eugene D. Genovese not only agreed with the counterprogressives that most Americans shared basic values but also respected sophisticated "corporate liberals" who defended the capitalist consensus and principled conservatives who tried to move the consensus rightward. Conversely, Herbert Gutman, Norman Pollack, and Eric Foner discerned impressive radical challenges to capitalism, and Caroll Smith-Rosenberg pointed to an autonomous women's culture. Most important for subsequent historiography, although Kolko, Williams, Genovese, Barton Bernstein, and others influenced by classic Marxism or C. Wright Mills closely examined the actions of powerful planters, businessmen, and public officials, this approach ultimately acquired fewer constituents than the study of "history from the bottom up" (a phrase popularized by Jesse Lemisch). A plurality of historians who entered graduate school in the late 1960s preferred to study blacks, women, radicals, native Americans, antebellum artisans, industrial workers, sharecroppers, and ethnic minorities, groups whose ideas, hopes, and efforts had previously been ignored or caricatured.

Although most radical and left liberal historians remained content to use counterprogressives as targets in their monographs, some of them explicitly reevaluated the whole counterprogressive legacy. Lemisch in particular felt the need to come to terms with his intellectual forebears. Writing in 1969, he documented academic acquiescence in the Red Scare of the 1950s, highlighted the scant attention paid to the "inarticulate," and contrasted the historiographical dismissal of dissenters with the generous treatment of the rich, famous, and influential. In short, Lemisch demolished the notion that "American historiography since World War II has been politically neutral." The major professional journals summarily rejected his article and commissioned no reviews when an expanded version appeared as a book in 1975.[11]

Some radical and left liberal historians pointedly repudiated the counterprogressive ethos as well as the main counterprogressive premises. At least a large minority among them asserted that social activism in the present enriched our understanding of the past; except for Schlesinger and Morison, no major historian had championed this position in the 1950s. Howard Zinn, a veteran of the old left, was present-minded without apology. He wrote history in order to promote "justice and brotherhood," not to display "empathy with the dead." Introspective scholars struggled, in Martin Duberman's words, to combine "historical data with personal reflection." Considering the medium of expression an important part of the message, a handful of historians played with new literary forms. Warren Susman sought a new vocabulary to fit the special "logic" of cultural history. William Appleman Williams's books, *Some Presidents* and *Empire as a Way of Life,* read like a mixture of Pascalian *pensées* and the musings of a cracker-barrel sage. These stylistic experiments, which went unappreciated even by Williams's admirers, highlighted his visceral populism and epistemological relativism.[12]

Embattled radical and left liberal historians thought the differences between themselves and their counterprogressive predecessors were stark. Yet several similarities now look as striking as the divergences.

First, the search for hidden meanings beneath the surface of things became, with slight modification, a characteristic motif of social criticism in the 1960s. Radical and left liberal historians uncovered Cold War covert operations, government disruption of protest movements, and secret machinations by businessmen trying to ride out several ages of reform. This renewed emphasis on the motives and methods of the powerful resembled but did not simply replicate progressive historiography. Rather, revisionists had learned from the counterprogressives that hidden motives were not always narrowly economic or even fully conscious. The results were mixed. Some writers subtly analyzed the world views of statesmen and slaveholders. Others offered another round of psychological reductionism, this time directed at racists, imperialists, and fundamentalists instead of Populists, Communists, and fundamentalists.

Second, though counterprogressives and their detractors usually disagreed about the significance of class, both groups exaggerated the impact of ethnicity. In a curious reversal, however, counterprogressives stressed conflict while their critics from the left slighted it. Hofstadter wrote that American life was "saturated" with ethnic and religious conflict, a view shared by Daniel Bell, Seymour Martin Lipset, and other pluralist social scientists. In addition, they regarded a contemporary manifestation of that conflict, jealousy of established white Protestants by upwardly mobile Catholics, as the key to the postwar Red Scare. Radicals and left liberals, in numerous local studies of immigrant and ethnic communities, modified such sweeping generalizations about Jews and Catholics. Unfortunately, they too overstated the persistence of ethnic identity. In addition, they slighted clashes between groups from the "new immigration" that had arrived at the turn of this century. Catholics and Jews typically appeared in revisionist scholarship as common victims of prejudice by an undifferentiated mass of Protestants or as common combatants against the corporate elite.[13]

Certainly ethnic diversity has influenced American life. Indeed, discussions of ethnicity and nativism dominate several chapters of this book. Yet the notion that the United States contained either particularly fierce religious conflict or especially unmelted ethnic groups would surprise residents of Belfast, Belgrade, Beirut, Buenos Aires, New Delhi, Lagos, Montreal, and Moscow. Making their case for diversity, left liberals and radicals ignored international comparisons; making their case for conflict, counterprogressives often compared the United States to something called Europe, but Europe meant for them primarily the cosmopolitan parts of Paris, London, Oxford, and Cambridge. In both instances historians who disagreed about much else shared a common provincialism.

Third, no more than the counterprogressives did their early critics from the left doubt their own ability to explain the past. The few exceptions stand out. While Williams ruminated on relativism, Bruce Kuklick tried to combine a revisionist approach to foreign policy with a systematic study of the philosophy of history. Among prominent left liberals and radicals, only Gene Wise worried in ways reminiscent of Beard and Becker that the problem of relativism might invalidate all historical explanation. Conversely, Howard Zinn found relativism liberating. Since there was "no one true picture of any historical situation," Zinn felt justified in emphasizing those facts that helped the oppressed. In the early 1970s few historians on the left saw a conflict between their politics and matter-of-fact empiricism. On the contrary, most believed with Lemisch that they were "finding out how things actually were."[14]

Fourth, despite Hofstadter's fears, left liberal and radical historians did not repudiate complexity in principle. On the contrary, David Montgomery admitted his perplexity before the "peculiarly opaque character of working class life," Linda Gordon rejected theories of status anxiety and comparable "one-dimensional" interpretations of human behavior, and Herbert Gutman believed that an understanding of the past transformed "historical givens into historical contingencies." Looking back in 1989, Lawrence Levine, who had been one of Hofstadter's graduate students in the 1950s, concluded that *his* generation had increased "acceptance of the complexities of the past."[15]

* * *

Since the mid-1970s, when I received my Ph.D., several historiographical trends begun during the 1960s have accelerated whereas others have subsided or changed direction. Three decades after diplomatic historians denounced Williams's book, *The Tragedy of American Diplomacy,* revisionist approaches to American expansion and the Cold War are respectable and perhaps dominant within the field. Nor is the notion that some sort of "power elite" makes life-and-death decisions for the rest of us any longer a shock. Curiously, however, examination of the motives and methods of the powerful has fallen from fashion. Rather, historians of my generation preferred (in the famous phrase of British historian E. P. Thompson) to rescue from oblivion those men and women who had previously suffered the "enormous condescension of posterity." While political history fell into eclipse, black history, labor history, and women's history emerged as major areas of study.[16]

The "new social history" became the premier field of the late 1970s and 1980s. There was no reason in principle why social historians could not investigate the rich, famous, and influential. Indeed, present-minded scholars in the 1980s might have found ample inspiration to write about such people. Yet the most celebrated—and in many cases the best—recent scholarship has dealt with lost causes: antebellum artisans and turn-of-the-century Populists, whose ethic of "republicanism" was destroyed by industrial capitalism; the Socialist party, which elected a total of two members of Congress; and Communists, whose ephemeral political influence ended abruptly with the Cold War.[17]

Proponents of a "new intellectual history," though less numerous than the new social historians, were equally convinced that they represented a major methodological advance. In the early 1970s, two kinds of "old" intellectual history warily coexisted. The smaller group, typified by Murray Murphey, Bruce Kuklick, and David Hollinger, thought of themselves primarily as "historians of ideas," and they concentrated on explicating the thought of such first-rank thinkers as William James, John Dewey, and Josiah Royce, while paying minimal attention to social and biographical influences. The larger group, typified by John Higham, Christopher Lasch, and Dorothy Ross, concentrated on less impressive but socially more influential thinkers—popular psychologists, political theorists, and clergy—whose ideas they placed in biographical and ideological context.

Dissatisfied with "contextualism" as well as the formal explication of ideas, proponents of the new intellectual history offered broad generalizations about cultures or "*mentalités.*" They sought fresh approaches in anthropology, the sociology of knowledge, and various versions of European cultural theory, especially poststructuralist literary criticism. The concept of cultural hegemony, borrowed from the Italian Marxist Antonio Gramsci, proved particularly attractive to those intellectual historians who wanted not only to explain the weakness of American radicalism but also to incorporate findings from the new social history. With varying sophistication they argued that a capitalist elite used ideas to legitimate its power, and analyzed advertising, films, television shows, and popular fiction to show hegemony in action.[18]

Intense interest in language soon became the trademark of the new intellectual historians. They began "scrutinizing the words on the page harder than new criticism ever had," as French poststructuralist Jacques Derrida advised. They also studied texts that the new critics of the 1950s, self-conscious defenders of high art, would have scorned. Combining close readings with the premise that aesthetic judgments were social products, they typically repudiated the distinctions between "high" and "low" art and denied that any text was "privileged." Then, moving beyond aesthetics, many of them argued that other ostensibly timeless categories, notably those relating to race, class, and gender, were invented by ruling elites. But what had been socially constructed could be deconstructed. As literary historian Sacvan Bercovitch wrote, "language has the capacity to break free of social restrictions and through its own dynamics to undermine power structures it seems to reflect."[19]

Furthermore, the confidence that had characterized both the counterprogressives in their prime and their early critics from the left steadily dissipated. This loss of confidence resulted from economic conditions (as any self-respecting Beardian could see) and status anxiety (as any self-respecting counterprogressive would add). When I began graduate school in 1966, one of my undergraduate professors, Eugene Genovese, warned me not to expect too much from my chosen profession. "History," he said, "isn't a business like other businesses—but it's a business." By the mid-1970s it was a business gone bust. A reserve army of unemployed Ph.D.s glutted the market, real income steadily declined, and colleges and universities took advantage of the situation by reasserting prerogatives lost during the 1960s. Meanwhile, Americans showed strong interest in various kinds of nonacademic history: breezy biographies of famous or infamous men and women, swashbuckling and bodice-ripping fiction, earnest television docudramas, multimedia exhibits at museums and historic sites, actors on tour impersonating dead presidents, and satirical treatments of the American past.

Professors of history responded to the combined economic and spiritual slump in ways in which twentieth-century Americans usually react to depressions and recessions. They blamed themselves for unemployment, pursued ostensibly rational strategies to outwit an irrational market, and hunkered down in their own communities—in this case, their fields of specialization—for mutual support. Inevitably there were nostrums and exhortations. By the late 1980s, diverse historians insisted in monographs, memoirs, speeches, and symposiums that our profession was in a deep crisis. Discussion centered on three issues: the politics of history, the epistemology of history, and the business of history.

While American society moved rightward during the late 1970s and 1980s, the historical profession resisted the trend. Marxists, militant African-Americans, and radical feminists held high office in the American Historical Association, Organization of American Historians, and American Studies Association. The editorial boards of the *Journal of American History* and the *American Quarterly* stood significantly left of vital center. There were countercurrents or at least countereddies. Some prominent historians completed the journey, begun during the 1960s, from left liberalism or democratic socialism to conservatism or neoconservatism, and a few followed the familiar trajectory from dogmatic left sectarianism to dogmatic right sectarianism. Staunch political conservatives and libertarians remained staunch political conservatives and libertarians. Protestant evangelical scholars transformed our understanding of modern American religion, but their work is hardly known outside that specialty. Indeed, in the early 1990s, political and cultural conservatives exert virtually no influence on the main course of American historiography.

Historians disagreed among themselves about the meaning of what Jonathan Wiener called the "institutionalization of radical history." Speaking for most of the left, Wiener saw a triumph of good scholarship over elite suppression. Others on the left discerned a pyrrhic victory. According to Christopher Lasch, leftists found a place in the historical profession "when they began to write books as narrow and irrelevant as those produced by their opponents." Russell Jacoby chided radicals for losing their bite and even their bark after settling into academia. Conversely, centrist liberal Carl Degler feared a new intolerance imposed by the left. Many conservative historians agreed with journalist Roger Kimball that "tenured radicals" were degrading humanistic learning and corrupting vulnerable undergraduates.[20]

For conservative Gertrude Himmelfarb, the issue at stake was "nothing less than the restoration of reason to history." In Himmelfarb's view, practitioners of the "old history" like herself concentrated on notable events, individuals, and institutions, and regarded the men and women who make history as rational political actors. Practitioners of the "new history" not only slighted the study of high politics and diplomacy, but also emphasized emotions and masses instead of ideas and elites. Along with many other conservatives, Himmelfarb disliked the major intellectual trends of the past century, especially the emphasis on the unconscious and the rise of the social sciences. Accordingly, what she derided as the new history was nearly as old as the professional study of history, and she almost admitted as much. Still, she thought that recent developments marked a change for the worse. Himmelfarb deplored feminist, black, ethnic, oral, statistical, psychoanalytical, and—above all—social history as threats to a "meaningful past."[21]

A few historians suggested that the past was so complex that it could not be explained at all. The long-dormant epistemological debate was resumed in the 1980s and took a decidedly pessimistic turn. Beard and Becker, concerned primarily with the problem of ethical relativism, had no doubt that some explanations were better than others. Beard specifically reaffirmed what he called the "scientific method" and urged "no abandonment of the tireless inquiry into objective realities." Now some historians influenced by deconstructionist literary criticism doubted that they had any access to objective realities—if in fact objective realties existed. These cognitive relativists said that all historical evidence consisted of endlessly problematical texts. Indeed, life itself might be just another text subject to countless equally true—or equally false—interpretations. Epistemological questions bothered intellectual historians in particular, but their esoteric debates, featured in major journals, were symptomatic of wider concerns. Once again rank and file historians were wondering, as Becker had asked, "What is the good of history?"[22]

Unlike colleagues concentrating on professional politics or epistemology, historians concerned with the business of history agreed on the cause of the problem—the absence of customers. To be sure, they worried about different sectors of the shrinking market: undergraduates who preferred psychology or accounting majors, officials who lacked any understanding of the past, pundits who cited sociologists instead of historians, and the proverbial intelligent general readers who got their history from novels and docudramas. A handful of historians blamed the mass media for shortening the national attention span. By and large, however, market analysts within the profession blamed historians themselves for the underconsumption of history. They urged historians to create demand by lobbying on Capitol Hill, consulting for television networks, studying public policy and perhaps advising government officials, or cultivating high school teachers, museum curators, journalistic popularizers, and other formerly neglected consumers. Above all, scholars as diverse as Himmelfarb and Jacoby urged historians to attract audiences with lucid prose. Increasingly history resembled a business like other businesses.

* * *

From one perspective, we should not be surprised that problems, controversies, and doubts surround the study of history. After all, what historians do is counterintuitive. To begin with, we must show our students or readers that people now dead were once as fully alive as they are. Fortunately for specialists in United States history, George Washington and Abraham Lincoln seem more lifelike than Muhammad and Charlemagne. Yet such familiarity compounds one of the hardest problems historians face, measuring continuity and change. We try to understand and then to show how dead people both resembled and differed from men and women currently going about their business. Contemporary Americans resist the notion that their ancestors were as smart, brave, or sexy as they are. It is even harder to convince them that intelligence, bravery, and sex appeal did not always mean the same thing. Furthermore, specialists in very recent history soon discover that nobody considers anyone else's rendition of the past, no matter how serious and thorough, as reliable as his or her own memories. Finally, while anticipating an open-ended future, Americans look back with a visceral sense of determinism. According to Ahlstrom's Law, propounded tongue-in-cheek by my dissertation advisor, Sydney E. Ahlstrom, "History had to happen the way it happened or it wouldn't have happened that way."

Viewed from another perspective, however, the pervasive sense of crisis among historians is surprising. The intellectual challenges afflicting our counterintuitive craft are hardly new. Moreover, history as an intellectual pursuit—a calling rather than a business—has improved considerably since the early 1960s. Those who think otherwise typically contrast run-of-the-mill recent books with a few well-remembered masterpieces. Yet a review of ordinary scholarship from the 1950s should give pause even to Gertrude Himmelfarb. Not only were important subjects ignored, but sloppy research and slap-dash analysis characterized many studies of topics then in vogue. For every classic like Hofstadter's *The Age of Reform,* there were dozens of formulaic attributions of status anxiety and crude dichoto-mies between diplomatic "idealists" and "realists."

This acknowledgment of intellectual progress is not intended as a celebration. As I reread and revised these essays, which were origi-nally written between 1980 and 1989, I saw how much I had been influenced by the dominant historiographical trends. But I was even more impressed by the ways in which these pieces diverge from the historiographical mainstream.

On the one hand, I often criticize the New Deal and American foreign policy, sympathetically observe leftist lost causes, playfully use evidence from popular culture, and deny that facts speak for themselves. In chapter 5, I use the Federal Theatre Project to illus-trate the limitations of the Roosevelt administration. Chapter 4 contains my entry into the bitter battle about the lost cause of American Communism. In chapter 2 the analysis of Henry Ford's anti-Semitic series, *The International Jew,* illustrates the value of closely reading even pernicious texts.

On the other hand, these chapters also reveal greater interest in the powerful than in the powerless, an empathic approach to rightist lost causes, and a commitment to the old, contextualist intellectual history. Chapters 6 and 7 focus on Presidents Gerald Ford and Jimmy Carter. In chapter 3, Bruce Barton, who is usually presented by historians as a naive positive thinker, appears instead as a shrewd corporate capitalist. In chapter 1 I rescue diverse nativists from the condescension (though not the condemnation) of posterity.

My divergence from the historiographical mainstream partly re-flects my temperament, age, and place of employment. David Potter said that historians are either "lumpers," who stress the similarities of the people and ideas they study, or "splitters," who stress the differences. Although I sometimes lump and sometimes split, I con-sider myself primarily a smoother. That is, I tend to see continuities along political or cultural spectrums and over time. In addition to this idiosyncracy, I have always considered villains more interesting than heroes. Furthermore, having entered college in 1962, I am at least as much a product of the "fifties" as the "sixties." Finally, I teach in Washington, D.C., where my colleagues, students, and friends pay more attention to elections than to epistemology.

* * *

Despite—or because of—my amorphous sense of being a historiographical outsider, I remain unconvinced that the problems, controversies, and doubts currently surrounding the study of history constitute a crisis. This introduction nevertheless provides an irresistible opportunity to comment on these issues. My central premise is that the latest new histories that began to emerge in the mid-1960s share one final feature with progressive and counterprogressive orthodoxy: they too have ceased to be intellectually innovative.

Although radicals and left liberals now dominate departments at several prestigious universities and routinely sit on editorial boards, polemicists from all sides have caricatured the changing politics of history. Notwithstanding Jonathan Wiener's Whiggish interpretation, contemporary historians on the left, like their counterprogressive predecessors, are not immune to insularity, cronyism, and the promotion of tendentious arguments by citing books promoting the same tendentious arguments. Nevertheless, the historical profession has become more diverse and less pompous, and procedures for hiring faculty and evaluating manuscripts are fairer now than they were twenty-five years ago.

Notwithstanding Gertrude Himmelfarb's Tory condemnation, relatively few rank and file historians are radicals. Perhaps Himmelfarb is misled by her customary concentration on elites. Nor is the social history vogue as subversive as it seems to advocates and opponents alike. To be sure, many historians celebrate "the people" in general or confine their investigation to people they deem admirable. Yet both the focus on private lives and the tendency toward celebration derive less from European Marxist influences, as Himmelfarb contends, than from contemporary trends that are hardly radical. For example, declining voter turnout and the rise of "apolitical" politicians signal a broader disaffection from public affairs. Similarly, the mass media have expanded their coverage of personalities and "lifestyles"; *People,* founded in 1974, now draws the highest circulation of any magazine. Amid this *Zeitgeist* of self-absorption, the study of everyday life seems relevant to historians of my generation in ways that high policy does not; few of us sign treaties but all of us have families and most of us played or watched baseball. Then too, unlike their precursors in the 1930s, contemporary historians live at a time when almost everybody celebrates "the people." Indeed, political conservatives cultivating the common man sound more like Henry Wallace than Robert Taft.

Even so, Himmelfarb is not entirely wrong. As was the case in the early 1960s, a dull orthodoxy has settled over the study of American history. Once again journals publish sterile debates structured as arbitrary dichotomies. Were slaves docile or rebellious? Were women oppressed or active in "separate spheres?" Did the working class accept capitalism or struggle against it? Once again historians strain to magnify the slight differences they discover. Did Italian-Americans in Brooklyn make more money, join more strikes, or attend more ball games than Italian-Americans in Boston? Once again, debates of this kind take on lives of their own and obscure deeper questions. For instance, why did many Italian-American strikers from Brooklyn and Boston ultimately identify with the common men and women in Richard Nixon's "silent majority?"

Ironically, though detractors still accuse historians on the left of present-mindedness, their scholarship is largely irrelevant to explaining the contemporary United States. Twenty-five years ago, Professor Dean Albertson complained that historians knew more about the Socialist party than the Republican party; the same is true today, only now we also know more about SDS than the Republican party. As American politics has moved rightward, proliferating accounts of lost causes have served the left as a literature of consolation and positive thinking. In addition, while the kind of committed history championed most articulately by Howard Zinn has recovered the lost lives of the oppressed, it has obscured conflict among victims of oppression and presented oppressors as stick figures. To apply David Potter's distinction, historians on the left typically split heroic social movements to highlight their complexity while lumping conservatives into derogatory categories to highlight their perfidy.

The historiographical trends of the last two decades have "privileged" some specialties while rendering others underprivileged. Like their counterparts in religious studies, military historians have done important work without influencing the mainstream. In a remarkable reversal, historians of public policy, who now concentrate on past government as well as past politics, lead the list of the underprivileged. Consequently, historians in general know less about the exercise of power than they knew twenty-five years ago. A few continue systematically to examine social institutions, but many more simply postulate "capitalist hegemony." Perhaps no one should be allowed to use the phrase "capitalist hegemony" unless he or she can explain how the Federal Reserve Board works.[23]

To some extent the debate over epistemology is a continuation of politics by other jargon. Cultural historians on the left who deconstruct such categories as class, race, and gender are chided for playing trivial word games by ideological allies in social history. Other radicals and left liberals, while finding this approach valuable, join George Lipsitz in repudiating the "fetishing of texts." Conservatives prefer blanket denunciations of deconstruction as a bastard child of relativism, though there is no logical reason why they could not use this technique themselves to demystify "justice" and "brotherhood." A far right deconstructionist might even argue that the anti-Semitic version of history in Henry Ford's series, *The International Jew,* is as good as any other.[24]

Other critics of what John Toews calls the "linguistic turn" in historiography fear just such a descent into cognitive relativism. Toews, for instance, condemns the "intellectual hubris" of those who reduce "experience to the meanings that shape it." Meanwhile, rank and file historians who have never read Derrida continue to deconstruct politically suspect categories as zealously as their counterprogressive predecessors discovered rampant status anxiety without reading Max Weber. Indeed, much as Molière's *bourgeois gentilhomme* belatedly discovered that he had been speaking prose all his life, anyone who rejects worn-out categories may find himself a deconstructionist unawares. Evidently I became one by questioning the usefulness of "McCarthyism."[25]

At the highest level of erudition, the epistemological debate represents yet another artificial controversy powered by its own momentum. When acrimony subsides, cognitive relativists usually concede that some interpretations of texts are better than others, their critics usually admit that reality is too complex to be described fully, and both sides agree that historians should think more clearly about their counterintuitive craft. Although the terminology has changed, the bottom line differs little from Gene Wise's advocacy of a "perspectivistic model" twenty years ago or, for that matter, from Beard and Becker's advice in the 1930s.[26]

Fortunately for most historians, our subject matter does not require operation at the highest levels of erudition. By and large, those who made the linguistic turn started out studying complicated texts and subsequently applied the technique of very close reading to simpler stuff. Moreover, these new intellectual historians usually write books about other books, whether masterpieces or popular literature, rather than about what people do (or what people read and then do). In the case of William Faulkner's masterpiece, *Absalom, Absalom,* or even of Ginny Haymond's steamy romance novel, *Someone Special,* both the authors' intentions and the readers' responses may be irrelevant or indeterminant. The same cannot be said of social security checks and draft notices. Except in rare instances, recipients know enough respectively to cash and obey (or evade) these texts.

In short, historians need not despair of explaining human thinking and doing. Still, the revived epistemological debate reminds us that our evidence is problematical, our significant generalizations gross, and our conclusions fragile. In addition, practitioners of the new intellectual history have renovated a valuable tool, close reading, that can also help political and diplomatic historians, most of whom pay scant attention to the slippery quality of language. Indeed, sometimes they pay less attention to these nuances than did the policy-makers they study. No deconstructionist examined texts more seriously than President John F. Kennedy pored over conflicting Soviet messages during the Cuban missile crisis.

Discussion of the business of history centers on the necessity and legitimacy of popularization. The whole debate sounds peculiar because most American historians are popularizers already. That is, we are paid to teach undergraduates and our classroom presentations typically lack the complexity of our writings; often they contain more ham than historiography. Russell Jacoby to the contrary, most of us want wider audiences. I would cheerfully appear on *The Tonight Show* whenever Jay Leno needs to banter about the origins of the Cold War or *The Will to Believe.*

The real issue is not whether but how to popularize history. Our guiding rule should be to present the past in as complex a fashion as any given audience can accept—and we should push at the margins. Professors might emulate their fellow performers from Broadway and Hollywood, most of whom entertain diverse audiences and often play both comedy and tragedy. One distinguished veteran of the Federal Theatre Project, E. G. Marshall, subsequently starred in *National Lampoon's Christmas Vacation* (1989) as well as the American premiere of Samuel Beckett's *Waiting for Godot*.

Still, popularization of history beyond a captive classroom audience entails problems that the profession's market analysts rarely acknowledge. To adapt Carl Becker's famous phrase, every man or woman is his or her own historian in ways that he or she is not, for instance, his or her own astrophysicist. As Becker observed in 1931, not only does everyone possess some "memory of things said and done" which he or she applies to daily life, but everyone also acquires "from a thousand unnoted sources . . . a mass of unrelated and related information and misinformation, of impressions and images, out of which he somehow manages, undeliberately for the most part, to fashion a history, a patterned picture of remembered things said and done in past times and distant places." Today powerful communications media, some of which did not exist when Becker wrote "Everyman his own Historian," may occasionally cover quarks and comets, but they constantly disseminate impressions and images of the past.[27]

During the last decade academic historians' fear for their craft merged with a broader controversy over the state of American culture. For instance, according to well-publicized reports by Diane Ravitch, a neoconservative historian, and Lynne Cheney, chair of the National Endowment for the Humanities, pervasive ignorance of our past reflected intellectual flabbiness and lowered educational standards. Their arguments relied on survey data showing that many high school students could not recognize notable names and dates. Because these questions were not posed to a control group of adults, we cannot assume that the current level of misinformation signals a decline. We should also doubt that recollection of names and dates serves as a fair test of historical understanding and question whether teenagers should store up enough of them to last a lifetime.[28]

Despite their notoriety, the conservative educational critics share little common ground either with most professional historians or with the other Americans who continue to create their own versions of the past from a thousand unnoted sources. Whereas historians increasingly acknowledge that facts do not speak for themselves, lay men and women often recall that so many facts made history in high school or college much less interesting than it turned out to be in swashbuckling or bodice-ripping novels, television docudramas, and multimedia museum exhibits. Perhaps Cheney and Ravitch focus on the captive audience of adolescents because they sense that adults have developed a resistance, not only to complex interpretations of parts of the past, but also to the idea that understanding the past in general is a complex process. This resistance crosses class lines and spans the political spectrum. Conservative Supreme Court nominees solemnly vow to interpret the Constitution according to the intent of the founders, whatever that means. Radical activists claim special knowledge of the 1960s because they were there, wherever that was. National leaders (including Lynne Cheney's husband, Secretary of Defense Richard Cheney) justify wars against distant tyrants by invoking the "lessons of history," however tendentious these may be. Cosmopolitan theater audiences mull over *Waiting for Godot* but shun comparably difficult history books because they do not make the past "come alive." That is, they do not deal with people in the *People* sense.

Most mass media presentations of the past strengthen this resistance. For instance, *Atomic Cafe* (1982), a documentary satirizing civil defense in the 1950s, is present-minded in the worst sense. The film trivializes serious issues by highlighting the peculiar cultural styles in which they were expressed—peculiar, of course, because they now seem "old-fashioned." But however silly jingles telling children to "duck and cover" sound in retrospect, civil defense was plausible during the 1950s, when nuclear arsenals were small and delivery systems unreliable. At the showing I attended the audience also condescended toward the past. They laughed when President Harry S Truman appeared on screen to report the bombing of Hiroshima—not because nuclear war made them nervous but because Truman wore a boxy suit and sounded overwrought to a later generation accustomed to cooler announcements of apocalypse.

Popular resistance to a complex past has many sources, not the least of which is bad teaching. Yet schools have less impact than educational reformers think and, in the case of history, teachers and textbooks exert less influence than widespread provincialism and faith in progress. Americans feel comfortable supposing that their forebears essentially resembled themselves, just as they feel comfortable believing that Russians, Japanese, or Nigerians think and act as they do (or at least are trying to think and act as they do). They also like to believe that progress has rendered them better than their forebears, including recent forebears who made them duck and cover. Although nostalgia sometimes leavens this sense of superiority, few Americans would return to the "good old days" unless, like visitors to Davy Crockett's cabin at Disneyland, they could bring along contemporary amenities.

Resistance to a complex past is not uniquely American. British geographer David Lowenthal finds comparable "voyeuristic empathy" on both sides of the Atlantic. Specifically, lay men and women rarely conceive of history as "contingent and unpredictable, or the past as a cluster of realms distinct from the present, each with its own mentalities and sociocultural determinants." While acknowledging in relativist fashion that professional historians, on the one hand, and lay persons, on the other, both "fabricate" the past on "frameworks erected by intervening generations," he sees little possibility of bridging the "chasm" between their attitudes.[29]

Lowenthal is too pessimistic. Psychologist Jerome Bruner argues that the underlying principles of any discipline can be "taught effectively in some intellectually honest form" at any level. Whether or not Bruner's hypothesis fits astrophysics, it does apply to history. Indeed, after we break through the conception of history as easy entertainment or ponderous heritage, everyone's propensity to be his or her own historian can be advantageous. Anyone who remembers an argument with friends or family can sense what Becker called the "malleable" nature of facts. Anyone who listens to representatives of several generations discuss their respectively "swell," "cool," and "awesome" teenage years can understand that world views vary across time and that these differences are embedded in language. Anyone whose high hopes were smashed by a bad break can doubt that history had to happen the way it happened because it happened that way. Even mass media need not inculcate a simplistic past. *The Sorrow and the Pity* (1970), Marcel Ophuls's brilliant documentary of French resistance and collaboration during World War II, illustrates the problematic nature of history as well as any academic book.[30]

If professional historians abandoned the general audience, Becker and Beard warned during an earlier academic depression, they risked sinking into hermetic irrelevance and arrogance. They also might begin to wonder, Beard added with characteristic economic emphasis, "why society provides a living." Current market analysts of the history business fear that society will stop providing a living— or at least a comfortable living. These fears are probably exaggerated and should not, in any event, affect the practice of history as a calling. Americans devote only a small portion of their gross national product to free-floating inquiry of any sort, and scholars in the humanities and social sciences comprise a tiny fraction of the information industry. Accordingly, just as historians should be able to popularize without guilt, they should not feel guilty about investigating esoteric topics in abstruse ways. And we must never confuse the historiographical equivalent of *National Lampoon's Christmas Vacation* with the historiographical equivalent of *Waiting for Godot*.[31]

* * *

Recovery from the academic depression in the 1990s may facilitate another creative phase in the study of American history. As economic pressures diminish, at least some historians will cease hunkering down in their fields of specialization and investigate ideas from across the academic barbed wire. This revival of creativity should involve both an extension of current interests and a recovery of lost agendas. For example, except for students of slavery, few historians write the explicitly comparative history they recommend. International perspectives would both advance our understanding of specific issues—immigration, industrialization, religious pluralism, and development of the welfare state come to mind—and also refurbish an old question: in what ways is the United States unique? Similarly, we need to come to terms with the unconscious. Judging from the proliferation of self-help guides in this century, historians use psychology less to understand the American people than the American people use psychology to understand themselves. And national politics must be rescued from the historiographical doldrums. Pimps, prostitutes, and pitchers are fun to study, but no pimp, prostitute, or pitcher ever ordered Americans into combat.

Perhaps this time tolerance will accompany creativity. Participants in the epistemological debate inadvertently served the cause of good manners by highlighting the problematical nature of evidence. Now historians should be especially wary of accusing one another of bad faith, let alone deliberate deception. In addition, all factions might agree to discard the epithet "present-minded" and admit that passionate involvement with a subject can be as valuable in some cases as detachment is in others. Recent scholarship would be the poorer if political radicals and theological conservatives had not struggled to rediscover the complexity of their respective traditions.

Tolerance should extend to methods of inquiry and modes of expression as well as ideological positions. Historians often write as if they expect their audience to read only one book, or at least only one kind of book. Quantifiers, relativists, nitpickers, cracker-barrel sages, and storytellers should no longer nag each other to change their ways. This sort of badgering, though useful for self-promotion in the history business, is intellectually useless. History, like literature, comes in genres. Historians should be able to learn from reading—and perhaps from writing—in more than one of them. Other authors try their hands at plays, poetry, film scripts, short stories, and novels of various shapes and sizes without any sense of methodological apostasy, and literary critics rarely indict sonnets for containing less character development than trilogies.

Perhaps this time, too, intellectual modesty will accompany creativity. As Carl Becker admitted, study of the past is not the only way to understand human experience. If approached seriously and thoroughly, however, there is still much good to history, and I hope that these essays show some of it.

1

The Complexity of American Religious Prejudice

Being an American means many things, but the meaning has always included the prerogative of calling others un-American. "Nativist" movements—movements dedicated to protecting the United States from allegedly dangerous foreign influences—have marked American history for more than two centuries. Often these manifestations have been inspired by religious beliefs or expressed in religious language. Following contemporary usage, the term "nativism" in this chapter encompasses hostility to both immigrants and "alien" ideas. Similarly, anti-Semitism receives special attention as a particularly revealing form of nativism. However, unlike most other histories of religious prejudice, in which Catholics and Jews appear largely as victims of Protestant harassment, this discussion also considers clashes between these two minorities as well as their treatment of less influential faiths. In a further departure from standard practice, religious prejudice here includes rationalist prejudice against religion in general or against individual religions.

Religious prejudice has rarely appeared in pure form. Rather, it has been mixed with disputes over class, ethnic, and denominational power and prestige, as well as with nationalism, imperialism, racism, rationalism, opportunism, and personal animosity. Moreover, the terms "prejudice," "nativism," and "anti-Semitism" carry enormous negative connotations. "Nativism" was first circulated in the 1840s by foes of "native American" political parties that specialized in attacking Catholics. "Anti-Semitism," coined abroad, was first used in 1879 by Wilhelm Marr, a proponent of Jewish disenfranchisement in imperial Germany. Marr wore the label openly, but Jew-baiters in the United States have often denied their anti-Semitism. Indeed, although various kinds of religious bias survive in the United States, few Americans defend prejudice in principle.

*   *   *

An understanding of American religious prejudice, nativism, and anti-Semitism requires a sense of the very different world of mid-sixteenth-century Europe. Inhabitants of that world could not conceive of the current American creed in which all religions stand equal before the law and all "mainline" faiths deserve equal esteem. In sixteenth-century Spain and France, Roman Catholicism was synonymous with patriotism. In sixteenth-century England, members of the established church divided on many issues but agreed that the Pope was, in William Tyndale's words, the "devil's vicar." Antipathy to Catholicism and enthusiasm for English imperial ambitions reinforced one another. Songs, plays, books, and engravings portrayed Spain as a bastion of autocracy, ignorance, and cruelty worthy of the Turks. In his *Discourse on Western Planting* (1584), Richard Hakluyt, an influential advocate of English expansion, urged colonization in order to save the New World from the Spanish "demie Saracine" and the Roman Antichrist.

"Plantings" first took root in Virginia, but the New England colonies developed faster, left larger legacies to nativist descendants, and better illustrate the danger of imposing modern conceptions of prejudice on previous eras. The Separatists who founded Plymouth in 1620 and their fellow Puritans who established Massachusetts Bay ten years later agreed that Roman Catholicism bore the "mark of the Beast." They considered the Church of England only slightly less tainted in the "image of the Beast." Believing their own holy commonwealths among Satan's favorite targets, the Puritans vigilantly guarded against Catholic infiltrators, "popish" ideas, and other heresies. In 1647 Massachusetts Bay ordered "perpetual imprisonment" for any priest who entered the colony. Although Catholics rarely appeared, the Puritans found it difficult to maintain orthodoxy. The thriving New England settlements, "mixt assemblies" from the time of their founding, quickly attracted Anglicans, Baptists, and such unconventional Puritans as Roger Williams and Anne Hutchinson. In response Puritan leaders restricted the franchise to "visible saints" and banished, harassed, or executed the worst malcontents. When Baptists petitioned for religious toleration in 1681, Samuel Willard accused them of misunderstanding the "design of our first Planters, whose business was not Toleration; but were professed enemies of it, and could leave the world professing they died *no libertines.*" Puritan organizers of communities that developed into New Hampshire, New Jersey, and Connecticut agreed.

Quakers seemed especially dangerous. They not only allowed women to preach but also sanctioned antinomian appeals to an "inner light," which John Higginson, a prominent Puritan, described as a "stinking Vapor of Hell." Stubborn and economically successful, the Quakers were hard to ignore. Between 1658 and 1661 Massachusetts Bay hanged four of them who had persisted in spreading their doctrines. Revulsion against this harsh punishment produced a brief respite. Starting in the 1670s, however, the Puritans reaffirmed their commitment to orthodoxy, partly in response to threats from local Indians and French Catholics in the North. Along with other religious dissidents, Quakers were frequent targets during the witch trials of the 1690s. Cotton Mather linked incongruous theological foes when he claimed that a bewitched girl unable to recite Scripture easily read a "Quaker or Popish book."

Quakers, Baptists, and heterodox Puritans found refuge in settlements that eventually coalesced into Rhode Island. Practices in this "haven" illustrate how little seventeenth-century conceptions of tolerance resemble our contemporary ideal. On the one hand, founder Roger Williams believed that coercion of orthodoxy corrupted true faith; on the other hand, he denounced Quakers for doctrinal error, favored a moral code based on the Ten Commandments, and considered Catholics foreign agents. Thus, although the charter Williams acquired in 1663 promised liberty of conscience, the colony restricted activity on the sabbath and prevented Catholics and Jews from voting. Nevertheless, Jews began to arrive in 1658 and acquired the right to worship in public by the end of the century.

Only Pennsylvania and, briefly, Maryland and New York rivaled Rhode Island as enclaves of relative tolerance. In Pennsylvania, as in Rhode Island, tolerance did not mean liberty of conscience. Under the charter of 1692 Catholics were forbidden to vote, hold office, or celebrate mass in public. Jews, similarly disfranchised, also faced commercial restrictions. Like Pennsylvania's Quaker founder, William Penn, the Catholic founders of Maryland understood that tolerance of their own minority faith required tolerance of other faiths as well as considerable prudence. In 1663 proprietor Caecillus Calvert warned the first Catholic settlers against giving "offense" to Maryland Protestants. Within a decade disputes between Catholic governors and the largely Protestant assembly erupted into violence. The Toleration Act of 1649 embraced all Christians except non-Trinitarians. Temporarily gaining full control in the mid-1650s, the Puritans executed at least four Catholics and banned "popery, prelacy, and licentiousness of opinion." In 1648 a Jewish physician was indicted, but not convicted, for denying the Trinity.

In New York the Dutch legacy and the lenient first English proprietor, James, Duke of York (later King James II), undermined Anglican supremacy. Establishment of the Dutch Reformed Church in the New Netherlands had not prevented settlement by Quakers, Lutherans, and Jews. In several instances Dutch superiors had overruled Governor Peter Stuyvesant, who wanted to bar Jews, a "deceitful race" of "Christ's enemies," from trade if not from the colony itself. The treaty transferring the New Netherlands to England in 1664 provided religious freedom for Dutch Reformed Protestants. In 1683 the predominantly Dutch assembly allowed tax-supported churches in localities where two-thirds of the voters agreed but forbade persecution of any believers "in God by Jesus Christ." Governors appointed by James after his ascension to the throne in 1685 allowed Catholics to vote, hold office, and openly celebrate mass; lifted lingering restrictions on Jewish merchants; and welcomed Huguenot refugees. New Jersey and Delaware shunned such explicit experiments in tolerance. Nonetheless, obliged to accommodate diverse populations, these colonies allowed liberty of conscience to most Protestants.

Throughout the seventeenth century the Anglicans who had settled Virginia managed to exclude all but a handful of Congregationalists, Baptists, Quakers, Catholics, and Jews. Even so, the understaffed Church of England hardly constituted a formidable establishment. In the early eighteenth century Scots-Irish Presbyterians became a powerful presence in the back country. Many Presbyterians also settled in the Carolinas, where the Church of England was even weaker than in Virginia. Georgia, chartered in 1732 as a buffer against Spanish Florida, established Anglicanism but accepted German pietists, Jews, and virtually anyone else willing to settle in this beleaguered outpost.

England's long and tumultuous Reformation decisively influenced religious relations in the colonies. To govern the doctrinally divided Commonwealth established in 1649, Oliver Cromwell acquiesced in liberty of conscience for most Protestants. While the Crown and Parliament harassed their respective religious foes during the subsequent Stuart Restoration, odd alliances flourished among theologically incongruous groups. Edmund Andros, governor of the consolidated Dominion of New England, used tolerance as a weapon against the durable Puritan elite and even allowed George Keith, a leading Quaker, to denounce Puritan "degeneracy" from the Boston Common. According to Cotton Mather, the "Bloody Devotoes of Rome had in their design and Prospect nothing less than the Extinction of the Protestant Religion." Flirtation with Rome ended when William and Mary supplanted James II in 1688–1689. Although the subsequent Toleration Act allowed freedom of conscience, Catholics, Jews, and Protestant dissenters remained second- or third-class subjects. New England Puritans lost much of their power, and Catholics faced imprisonment even in Maryland for openly celebrating mass. As late as 1742 New York executed two suspected Catholics, one of whom was actually a nonjuring Anglican.

The patterns of belief and behavior created by the English Reformation long outlived the specific theological controversies of the time. Indeed, these controversies shaped the contours of American nativism almost a century before there was an independent United States. For example, seventeenth-century Americans, like their more diverse descendants, feared that alien ideas might infiltrate their communities even if aliens themselves were barred. Similarly, when Cotton Mather discerned Catholic and Quaker elements in witchcraft, he illustrated the tendency, still strong in the twentieth century, to conflate incongruous adversaries. Since the seventeenth century, too, apocalyptic rhetoric and expansive categories like "popery" have coexisted with fine distinctions in the measurement of virtue. Nevertheless, students of nativism and religious prejudice must beware of pronouncing ideas absurd or fears groundless simply because they are expressed in archaic or inflated language. In the seventeenth century Quakers did disrupt the Massachusetts social order, Spanish and French Catholic troops did encircle British North America, and occasional "papal plots" did arise in England.

Furthermore, in the seventeenth century and afterwards, words offer only imperfect indications of behavior. Massachusetts Quakers, granted freedom of worship under the charter of 1692, still faced persecution for the next twenty years. Conversely, Jews and Catholics in many colonies evidently fared better than legal codes suggest. Lax enforcement allowed New York Jews to build a synagogue in 1685 and vote until 1737; elsewhere some Catholics voted and held local office after the Revolution of 1689. Incipient rationalism, which eroded the significance of theological issues, mitigated religious conflict in Philadelphia. Chronic labor shortages required concessions everywhere. In general, standards for naturalization were looser in the colonies than in England. By the early eighteenth century British North Americans enjoyed greater religious freedom than any other people in the Western world.

* * *

The religious equilibrium was disrupted by immigration, the first Great Awakening, and the struggle between Britain and France. Roughly a quarter of a million Scots-Irish Presbyterians, two hundred thousand German pietists and Lutherans, and sixty thousand French Huguenots immigrated before the War for Independence. Typically, cultural rather than theological differences between immigrants and the native-born prompted complaints that German and French settlers clung to their foreign ways. Benjamin Franklin underestimated the capacity of the dominant culture to absorb newcomers when he accused "Palatine Boors" of transforming Pennsylvania, "founded by *English* [into] a colony of *Aliens*." In some respects, however, immigrants were changing the dominant culture. Perhaps most important, the influx of non-Anglicans strengthened the constituency seeking freedom of conscience. Paradoxically, after polemics between New Light advocates of the revival and their Old Light foes subsided, the Great Awakening also furthered diversity and toleration among Protestants. Men and women spiritually reborn during the Awakening felt a bond across denominational lines. In New England the dominant Congregationalists became factionalized, and Presbyterians and Separate Baptists strengthened their positions.

The French and Indian War intensified anti-Catholic sentiment and fostered Protestant militancy. Adapting earlier invective against Spain, ministers associated France with the Antichrist, papal power, and the scarlet whore of the Book of Revelation. Sometimes they added that British victory might usher in God's kingdom. Less apocalyptic than the clergy, George Washington suspected Catholics of aiding the enemy and prohibited Catholic troops from celebrating Pope Day. In several colonies Catholics were disarmed.

Fear of "popery," which the colonists interpreted with characteristic expansiveness, helped the movement for independence. As historian Bernard Bailyn has shown, various revolutionaries viewed British efforts to govern the colonies as signs of a vast conspiracy intended to undermine colonial liberty. From this point of view the prospect of a resident Anglican bishop looked like "ecclesiastical slavery." Indeed, many dissenting clergy still viewed the Church of England as an example of thinly disguised "popery." The British cabinet prudently declined to dispatch a bishop but then erred by seeking accommodation with actual "papists." The Quebec Act of 1774 extended French Canadian influence into the Ohio Valley and granted freedom of religion to Catholic settlers there who swore allegiance to the Crown. Many colonists shared Alexander Hamilton's fear that "priestly tyranny may hereafter find as propitious soil in America as it ever had in Spain or Portugal." John Adams fused traditional Protestant antipathy with Enlightenment disdain for the Catholic "horror of letters and learning."

Ultimately the War for Independence created few clear divisions along sectarian lines. Anglicans were disproportionately loyalist, especially in the north, while New Light evangelicals—Presbyterians, Congregationalists, and to some extent Baptists—were disproportionately revolutionary. Although religious and cultural minorities tended to side with the Crown, the Jewish population of roughly two thousand provided an exception to this generalization.

Two Jews acted as aides to General Washington. A Roman Catholic also served on Washington's staff, yet most Catholics probably preferred the Crown to a prospective evangelical republic. Similarly, Quebec declined to join the United States, even though a delegation from the Continental Congress promised religious freedom (a delegation including John Carroll, who later became the first Catholic bishop in the United States). Vital assistance from France further challenged the colonists' ritual allegations of Catholic ignorance, tyranny, and disloyalty. Conversely, Quakers, German pietists, and other pacifists who refused to pay war taxes or swear allegiance to the new government faced arrest, loss of political rights, or seizure of property.

Overall the revolutionary era accelerated the momentum toward religious toleration and liberty. On the eve of independence a majority of the thirteen colonies still retained religious establishments. As John Adams said in defense of Massachusetts, however, these were "very slender" establishments. In the five southern states Protestant dissenters usually voted, held office, attended their own services, and escaped taxation for the Anglican Church. Under New York's multiple establishment most non-Anglicans could apply tax money to their own clergy. Massachusetts, Connecticut, and New Hampshire required each local jurisdiction to support a minister—a system that benefited the Congregationalist majority and highlighted the burdens imposed even by slender establishments. Baptists who refused on theological grounds to seek exemptions were badgered or imprisoned; Quakers and some Anglicans also suffered.

Isaac Backus, a leading Baptist pastor, challenged state authorities by asking, in effect: if the Revolution opposed "ecclesiastical slavery," then how could the state favor one religion over another? Such ideological inconsistency would have produced few legal changes if dissenters like Backus, allied with Enlightenment deists, had not pressed the point. Political, economic, and demographic factors also encouraged disestablishment. Southern Anglican establishments, tainted by Toryism, fell more easily than their Congregationalist counterparts in New England. Moreover, numerous Scots-Irish southerners joined Thomas Jefferson in scorning Anglicanism and its American successor, the Episcopal church, as "truly the religion of the rich."

During or soon after the War for Independence, some states abolished established churches, others forbade their creation, and still others moved from single to dual or from dual to multiple establishment. The new state constitutions implementing these changes undeniably advanced the cause of freedom of conscience. Nevertheless, just as prewar establishments were weaker than the term implies, so, too, did disestablishment fall short of religious equality. Significantly, disestablishment did not necessarily prevent general assessments to support Christian—most often Protestant—churches. A majority of states still barred or restricted office holding by Catholics, and only New York placed no such limitation on Jews. Even Pennsylvania and Delaware, which had never established churches, required officials to affirm the Trinity.

The federal Constitution written in 1787 was much more liberal than those of most states. No delegate to the Philadelphia Convention proposed any sort of religious establishment. Article VI, section 3, banning religious tests for office, passed easily despite a handful of objections by delegates from North Carolina, Connecticut, and Maryland. A few speakers at state ratifying conventions agreed with Rev. David Caldwell, who told the North Carolina meeting that the Constitution invited "Jews and pagans of every kind to come among us." A more common complaint, that there was no bill of rights protecting religious and other freedoms, soon found remedy.

The First Amendment prohibited Congress from enacting any law "respecting an establishment of religion, or prohibiting the free exercise thereof." At minimum, this amendment bars the federal government from requiring compulsory church attendance or directly aiding any one denomination at the expense of the others. After two centuries of debate, however, scholars and jurists still have not reached a consensus on what else the First Amendment means. Although James Madison guided the measure through Congress, his own belief in the "perfect separation" of church and state probably represented a minority opinion among his fellow legislators and countrymen at large. Discussion of the amendment in Congress and the state legislatures revealed little concern for the protection of infidels. Debate focused instead on the potential threat to religion, and some proponents saw the amendment as a way to protect state establishments from federal encroachment.

The federal Constitution set a powerful example. In the decade following ratification, Georgia and South Carolina abandoned preferential treatment for Christians, while Pennsylvania and Delaware dropped their respective New Testament and Trinitarian requirements for office. No state after the original thirteen required a religious test. Yet some faiths remained legally inferior to others. Multiple Protestant establishments lingered in Vermont until 1807, Connecticut until 1818, New Hampshire until 1819, and Massachusetts until 1833. New Jersey Catholics remained ineligible for high office until 1844; restrictions in New Hampshire lasted until 1876. In Maryland and Rhode Island analogous curbs on Jews survived until 1826 and 1842, respectively. North Carolina excluded Jews from the executive branch until Reconstruction. Even where these measures affected few if any citizens, they imposed a stigma, as a Catholic proponent of Jewish equality told the North Carolina constitutional convention in 1835. Campaigns to abolish religious tests often entailed bitter battles. Foes of Maryland's "Jew bill" denounced its foremost advocate, a Protestant, as "Judas Iscariot."

Viewed in isolation, the controversy over religious tests exaggerates prejudice against Catholics and Jews during the early national period. For the most part these restrictions reflected pro forma affirmation of Protestant virtue or concessions to clerical suspicion rather than fervent hostility to Catholics and Jews. Thus evasions and adjustments could and did occur. The Massachusetts Constitution of 1780 permitted Catholics to hold office if they rejected papal authority "in any matter civil, ecclesiastical, or spiritual." New York dropped the ban on Catholic legislators when the first one was elected in 1806. Dismissing tales of the "sordid ignorance" of "popery," some Protestants sent their children to Catholic schools. In the 1790s the Adams administration attempted to curb entry by Jeffersonian "wild Irish" (a category that included Protestants as well as Catholics), but thereafter immigration remained dormant as a national issue until the late 1820s. Similarly, rivalry between Protestant and Catholic clergy simmered without reaching a boil.

Restrictions on Jews were less the product of anti-Semitism in particular than wariness of non-Christians in general. Typical in this respect, a delegate to the Massachusetts constitutional convention in 1820 grouped "jews, mahamedans, deists and atheists" among enemies of the "common religion of the Commonwealth." As early as 1809 the North Carolina legislature bent the law to seat a Jew. Although Maryland barred Jews from state office, one served as United States attorney in Baltimore. These incongruities symbolize a larger ambivalence. On the one hand, since the days of Cotton Mather and Roger Williams, Protestants had viewed Jews as living links with Old Testament prophets; on the other hand, they held Jews responsible for crucifying Christ and rejecting His message. Nor were American Protestants and Catholics immune to the stereotypes long held in Europe of Jews as unusually greedy, cunning, and clannish.

* * *

The two decades following the War for Independence were probably the least devout in United States history. Indeed, Protestant ministers fought to retain state support partly because voluntary contributions declined. Not only were many Americans unchurched, but a significant minority experimented with "rational religion." Enlightenment deists, whose intellectual contribution to the Revolution had eclipsed that of the clergy, held a broad spectrum of beliefs. For example, Washington remained within the Episcopal church, John Adams drifted toward Unitarianism, and Elihu Palmer, Ethan Allen, and Thomas Paine explicitly attacked Christianity. Nor were these attacks the only unsettling consequences of what Bernard Bailyn calls the "contagion of liberty." The lower classes began to refuse deference even to their creditors.

These trends disrupted the coalition among evangelical, enlightened, and impious revolutionaries. The clergymen who favored separation of church and state had never doubted that the United States must remain stable, moral, and, broadly speaking, Christian. Responding to the apparent decline of religious belief, they led a second Great Awakening whose consequences dwarfed those of the first. By the time the last state-supported churches had been disestablished in 1833, interdenominational evangelical Protestantism was already becoming, in Professor William G. McLoughlin's phrase, a "new form of establishment." Until the eve of the Civil War this second Awakening energized movements to uplift strivers or incarcerate malcontents, to abolish war or invade Mexico, to end slavery or extend its boundaries. Participants in such movements played variations on the central theme of the revolutionary ideology —that hidden conspiracies threatened American freedom.

As early as 1798 militant Federalist ministers assailed what Rev. Jedidiah Morse, a New England Congregationalist, called a "secret plan" to destroy American "liberty and religion." According to Morse, this conspiracy, which had begun in 1736 with the creation of the Bavarian Society of Illuminati, an international Enlightenment fraternity, had already spread through European Masonic lodges and precipitated the French Revolution. Morse adapted English charges against the Illuminati to fit American circumstances. Prominent Protestant clergy and at least one Roman Catholic priest echoed his claims. Although these polemicists hesitated to condemn all Masons, they quickly concluded that Jeffersonian Republican political clubs were the main source of domestic danger.

These allegations were only slightly more farfetched than others routinely exchanged by Federalists and Democratic Republicans in the 1790s. Morse and his allies correctly believed that the foremost Republicans, Thomas Jefferson and James Madison, favored strict separation of church and state. Nevertheless, the notion of a conspiracy stretching from Bavaria to Monticello never took hold as a central issue in national politics. President John Adams hedged on the validity of Morse's claims, and the Masons enhanced their reputation by advertising George Washington as one of their own.

By 1830, however, fear of Masonic subversion had inspired a potent social movement and promising political party, the Anti-Masons. In 1826 Masons in Canandaigua, New York, apparently abducted and murdered William Morgan, one of the order's loudest critics. Masons impeded investigation of the crime, secured light sentences or acquittals for indicted brethren, and threatened newspapers covering the story. Incensed critics interpreted Masonic cronyism as grand conspiracy. To expose the conspiracy, they ran candidates for the New York legislature and spread warnings to nearby states. Profiting from a political spectrum in flux since the Federalist collapse in the 1810s, the Anti-Masonic party influenced —and occasionally dominated—the politics of New York, Massachusetts, Vermont, Pennsylvania, and Rhode Island during the early 1830s.

Anti-Masonry grew strongest in New England, where Jedidiah Morse's message had seeped into political lore, and among transplanted New Englanders elsewhere. Unlike Morse's small band of elite Federalist clergy, Anti-Masons promoted their movement in the name of the common man. As Pennsylvania leader Thaddeus Stevens complained, Masonry fostered "hatred of democracy" while securing "unmerited advantage to members of the fraternity over the honest and industrious uninitiated farmer, mechanic, and laborer." Faith as well as fortune seemed at stake. Baptists, Methodists, and Presbyterians shunned Masonry as a rationalist replacement for religion. Quakers and German pietists objected to the order's secret oaths, which sounded especially sinister in their retelling by apostate Masons. Certainly jealousy of the very successful Masons aided party recruitment. Nonetheless, Anti-Masons included prosperous townspeople as well as poor farmers. Nor did such Anti-Masonic leaders as Thurlow Weed, William Seward, and John Quincy Adams emerge from society's fringes.

Although Masonry constituted no "secret government," as Seward contended, Anti-Masons had plausible reasons for viewing it with suspicion. The order had grown rapidly in size and influence since the War for Independence. Investigations of Morgan's disappearance were thwarted because two-thirds of New York state officials were members. The Masons' prominence and influence, combined with their deviance from the prevailing democratic ethos, made them appealing targets. Consistent with their Enlightenment heritage, Masons purported to select their members from a natural aristocracy instead of celebrating the common man. At a time when many middle-class men considered play a threat to discipline, they also sanctioned what a Connecticut Anti-Mason called "extravagant mirth." Middle-class women formed an important auxiliary to the Anti-Masonic party, prompted by their awareness that such playful sessions drew husbands away from the home. Above all, Masonry, which even conducted funeral services for members, looked suspiciously like a rival religion to devout Protestants in the midst of an awakening. In short, Anti-Masonic polemics were no less rooted in the contentious realities of the 1830s than analogous denunciations of a southern "slavocracy," an international abolitionist "conspiracy," or the "Hydra-headed monster" (as President Andrew Jackson called the Second Bank of the United States).

Anti-Masonry achieved greater success as a social movement than as a party. The congressional delegation never exceeded twenty-five. Although several state legislatures investigated the Masons, revoked lodge charters, or banned "extrajudicial oaths," enforcement was lax. Former Attorney General William Wirt, the reluctant presidential candidate in 1832, won roughly 3 percent of the vote and carried only Vermont. Scorning his supporters as "fanatical fools," Wirt failed to see that party managers had become less interested in uprooting Masonry than in opposing Jacksonian Democrats. By 1840 almost all the leaders as well as most of the rank and file had joined the Whig coalition that elected President William Henry Harrison. Anti-Masonry became a victim not only of its own success as a social movement but also of the successful re-creation of a two-party system. At the grass roots level Masons were excluded from congregations and juries, rejected as suitors, and otherwise stigmatized. Verging on collapse, the order no longer looked sufficiently threatening to justify an Anti-Masonic party.

The Church of Jesus Christ of Latter-Day Saints (Mormons) faced much harsher persecution than the surrogate religion of Masonry. This offshoot of evangelical Protestantism offered earthly community, an accessible afterlife, and the strong leadership of founder Joseph Smith, Jr. Mormonism immediately attracted adherents and enemies. Within a year of the church's founding in April 1830 the main body of Mormons moved from upstate New York to Ohio, while a second large contingent settled in Missouri. In both places Mormons suffered physical abuse, destruction of property, and occasional murders. Complying with the governor's declaration that they must be "exterminated" or driven from Missouri, militia massacred a Mormon settlement in 1838. Illinois provided temporary sanctuary. After Smith's arrival in 1839, Mormons transformed a swampy river town into a flourishing, nearly sovereign city of fifteen thousand, which they renamed Nauvoo. Non-Mormons denounced Nauvoo's freedom from state control, Smith's autocratic rule, and the church's drift toward polygamy. In 1844 Smith suppressed a newspaper published by apostate Mormons. After complicated legal and paramilitary maneuvers, Smith and his brother Hyrum were indicted for treason, jailed in Carthage, Illinois, and murdered by a militia turned mob on 27 June 1844. Brigham Young reluctantly led the Mormons west from Nauvoo during the winter of 1845–1846.

Within three years the Mormons built a prosperous enclave around the Great Salt Lake, wrote a constitution, and sought admission to the Union. In 1850 a hostile Congress granted only territorial status to Utah, though President Millard Fillmore prudently appointed Young governor. There followed six years of acrimony between church leaders and non-Mormon Indian agents, federal judges, and surveyors. Embittered officials convinced President James Buchanan that the Mormon hierarchy fostered "open rebellion" against the United States. In 1857 Buchanan ordered the army to escort a new, non-Mormon governor to Utah, expecting most Mormons to welcome this liberation from ecclesiastical tyranny. Instead, the Mormons, fearing another campaign of extermination, fortified mountain passes, raided army supply wagons, and, allying with Indians at Mountain Meadows, murdered settlers bound for California. After federal troops encamped near Salt Lake City, the ignoble "Mormon War" ended in an ambiguous truce.

Antebellum persecution of Mormons was not limited to idiosyncratic agitators. The deadliest mobs consisted of militia acting with government sanction or acquiescence; mob leaders were often merchants or professionals. Economic grievances frequently fueled religious animosity. For instance, a Mormon bank in Ohio failed during the panic of 1837, Mormon migration to Illinois raised land prices, and church members preferred to conduct business among themselves. Some assailants were prompted by the prospect of plunder. Victims of a characteristic nativist double bind, Mormons found that their current prosperity elicited envy while their humble origins prompted scorn.

Anti-Mormon tracts, speeches, and press accounts appealed to Americans who had never met—let alone competed with—a Mormon. Affirming democracy and condemning secrecy, the main themes in this literature overlapped with earlier attacks on Masonry. Mormons were accused of treason, terrorism, importation of foreign "serfs," and a "grand conspiracy" with Indians to destroy white settlements. Even by antebellum standards anti-Mormon rhetoric displayed an unusually high proportion of misunderstanding, envy, and psychological projection. After all, though Brigham Young may have dreamed of divine judgment on the United States, he never seriously considered secession. With few exceptions, such as the Mountain Meadows killings, Mormons resorted to violence only in self-defense. Mormon immigration totaled twenty-two thousand by 1855, a small fraction of the nation's newcomers. To their credit, most Mormons agreed with Young that it was cheaper and more humane to feed Indians than to kill them. Nonetheless, anti-Mormon sentiment was so pervasive during the disintegrating 1850s that, as the *New York Times* editorialized, few Americans would have complained if they were "utterly exterminated."

Roman Catholics were too numerous and well-connected to exterminate. Yet, during the three decades before the Civil War, Catholics encountered worse treatment than at any other time in United States history. The immigration of more than one million Catholics beginning in the late 1820s raised simmering controversy to a boil. The new arrivals, who came primarily from the German states and Ireland, typically drank alcohol, supported urban political machines, slighted the sabbath, and disproportionately filled jails, asylums, and relief rolls. Appalled Protestants denounced "popery" in sermons, speeches, periodicals, novels, and children's books. Leaders of anti-Catholic movements included distinguished clergy, prominent politicians, and unemployed workmen as well as renegade priests, opportunists, and thugs. Their activities ranged from proselytism to arson.

Polemicists renewed traditional accusations that Catholicism fostered false faith, political tyranny, and sexual immorality. Although allusions to the "scarlet whore" were no longer de rigueur, the Presbyterian Assembly of 1835 declared Catholicism "essentially apostasized from the religion of our Lord." Seventh Day Adventists, a new religion that emerged from the apocalyptic fervor of the era, held Catholics responsible for the sin of Sunday worship. Patrician historians presented the Catholic church as the prototypical enemy of liberty and progress. *Awful Disclosures of the Hotel Dieu Nunnery of Montreal* (1836) stands out among tracts alleging priestly lechery; ostensibly the confessions of "Maria Monk," a runaway nun, it actually combined the fantasies of a young woman who had never taken vows with the prose of several Protestant ministers. The traditional motifs of anti-Catholicism sometimes gave way to condemnation of

41

immigrants who failed to meet evangelical standards of honesty, diligence, independence, and sobriety. The invective used by nativist skilled workers mixed economic self-interest with snobbery; Philadelphia carpenter Jacob Teck told a trades convention in 1847 that the glut of Catholic immigrants on the labor market threatened the American artisan's "boasted respectability and moral standing." According to *A Plea for the West,* a nativist classic published in 1835 by Rev. Lyman Beecher, European monarchs deliberately flooded the United States with docile immigrants who, dominated by their priests, were virtually soldiers in a foreign army.

The creators of public school systems in the antebellum era usually conflated morality, patriotism, and Protestantism. The King James Bible was used in opening exercises and sometimes served as a textbook. Catholics protested that their children should be allowed to use the Douay Bible and requested public funds for their own schools. Sometimes they secured considerate treatment for Catholic pupils in Protestant districts, local control in Catholic neighborhoods, and state funds for their own academies. Usually they were thwarted by countercampaigns to save the classroom and state treasury from "popery." Moreover, the creation of two hundred Catholic academies by 1840 reinforced Protestant fears that the church intended to conquer the West.

Anti-Catholic sentiment sometimes went beyond words. In 1834 solid citizens burned an Ursuline convent outside Boston. That same year a mob drove Irish Catholic workmen from New Hampshire. In Philadelphia a dispute over Bible reading in public schools exacerbated conflicts between unskilled Irish immigrants and evangelical artisans. Riots in July 1844 left two churches destroyed and twelve persons dead. Assaults on priests and Catholic laymen were legion throughout the 1830s and 1840s. In California harassment forced Hispanics from the gold fields. Although attacks on Catholics were less likely to receive official sanction than attacks on Mormons, militia in Philadelphia sacked churches or stood aside while others did so.

Catholics answered their foes in print, debated them in public, and heckled, slugged, and sometimes killed them. Bishops in council formally repudiated political meddling for themselves and urged Catholics to refute nativist "babbling" by obeying the law. John

Hughes, the militant archbishop of New York, cultivated both Whigs and Democrats, accused Protestant clergy of denouncing Catholics in order to "extort" money from gullible audiences, and rallied armed parishioners to protect his churches. Catholic officials sometimes banned nativist meetings; a handful of priests publicly burned Protestant Bibles. Waging intermittent war, urban Protestant and Catholic gangs were less interested in theology than in wages, self-esteem, and turf.

The late 1840s brought a partial remission of anti-Catholic sentiment, partly because eleven hundred Catholics served in the Mexican War. During the 1850s anti-Catholic acts spread again, prompted by increased Catholic immigration, an economic recession, a general decline of political civility, and blunders committed by church leaders. No more tolerant than his evangelical enemies, Bishop Hughes in 1850 proclaimed the "decline of Protestantism." When Pope Pius IX dispatched Bishop Gaetano Bedini to America in 1853 to settle controversies between laymen and clergy over church trusteeship, the visit drew attention not only to the volatile issue of parish control, but also to the question of Vatican authority. Dubbed the "bloody butcher of Bologna," where he had served as governor, Bedini was physically attacked in Wheeling and nearly shot in Baltimore. Elsewhere during the 1850s, mobs burned a dozen Catholic churches, beat priests, and sank into the Potomac River the marble block donated by Pope Pius IX for the Washington Monument.

Significantly, the 1850s produced a national political movement centered on opposition to Catholicism: the American party, or, as its members were generally called, the Know-Nothings. As early as the 1830s local "native American" parties had won control of several cities. Many of their constituents later filled Know-Nothing ranks. The Know-Nothing movement began in 1853 when the Order of the Star-Spangled Banner, energized by new recruits from lesser nativist groups, entered a militant new phase and began secretly to back political candidates. Members used secret handshakes, passwords, and rituals; pledged to vote only for native-born Protestants "without regard to party predilections"; and responded to inquiries about their activities with an enigmatic "I know nothing." Such inquiries mounted as the order's covert support swung many elections in 1853 and 1854. By the time the Know-Nothings surfaced and held a national convention as the American Party in 1855, they had already elected at least seventy members to Congress.

The Know-Nothing party was comparable to the Anti-Masonic party a generation earlier. It flourished briefly in the midst of a disintegrating party system, disproportionately attracted young voters and nonvoters alienated from ordinary politics, nonetheless fell into the hands of political professionals, left a slim legislative record, and ultimately merged with a sturdier party—in this case, the Republicans. In several states Know-Nothing legislatures investigated convents and prohibited Catholic bishops from owning church property. Catholics continued to vote despite the efforts of Know-Nothing rowdies and notable Election Day riots in St. Louis, New Orleans, and Louisville. The congressional delegation lacked the power to limit immigration or extend the period of naturalization. Ultimately the Know-Nothings divided over the issue of slavery. Millard Fillmore, the presidential nominee in 1852, won only 21 percent of the vote, running strongest in the South and border states but carrying only Maryland.

In retrospect the antebellum anti-Catholic upsurge is easier to understand than the parallel crusades against Masonry and Mormonism. Hundreds of thousands of Catholic immigrants were changing what it meant to be an American. Since some states allowed immigrants to vote before their naturalization, Catholic ballots may have provided Democratic President Franklin Pierce's margin of victory in 1852. Not only did the midcentury papacy stand firmly for reaction, but also a majority of American bishops had been born abroad. It is hardly surprising, therefore, that Protestant heirs to suspicion of "popery" placed such facts into the omnipresent framework of conspiracy. In so doing, they underestimated the ways in which the United States was changing Catholic immigrants. The church hierarchy—ethnically divided, understaffed, and wary of the Vatican—could not effectively control their behavior. Most Catholic immigrants voted Democratic because the other major party, the Whigs, was hospitable to nativism, not because priests told them to do so. Indeed, the bishops themselves preferred the culturally conservative Whigs to the Democrats.

Jews faced no comparable persecution before the Civil War. Immigrants from Europe, who swelled the Jewish population to one hundred fifty thousand by 1860, seemed less threatening than their Catholic counterparts partly because they were more prosperous. Nonetheless, insensitivity to Jewish beliefs was commonplace. Governors alluded to Christ in Thanksgiving proclamations and at least one treaty protected only Christian clergy abroad. Two national groups spawned by the second Great Awakening, the American Society for Evangelizing the Jews and the American Society for Meliorating the Condition of the Jews, tried to convert them. Along with Seventh Day Adventists and militant freethinkers, Jews were prosecuted for violating Sunday blue laws. Beyond insensitivity, notable cases of discrimination and prejudice also occurred. By the 1830s the infinitive "to Jew" connoted sharp dealing. Sermons, tracts, and Bible school lessons routinely held Jews responsible for Christ's crucifixion. Although Jews prospered in finance, none received a partnership in a gentile banking house. During the early 1800s Federalists, including John Adams and John Quincy Adams, scorned "alien Jew" Jeffersonians. Fifty years later, Judah P. Benjamin, senator from Louisiana, and August Belmont, chairman of the Democratic National Committee, encountered similar slurs.

Any brief account of nativism and religious prejudice in the tumultuous antebellum era risks making the past look too neat. In practice, conspiratorial motifs overlapped; for example, comparisons of Brigham Young and the Pope became commonplace. Despite their interdenominational alliances, evangelical Protestants continued to disagree about theology, church polity, and prospective converts; Seventh Day Adventists and Campbellites (later known as the Disciples of Christ) faced particularly fierce opposition. Yet cooperation and even friendship sometimes transcended religious differences, especially where economic rivalry was minimal. Know-Nothings fared poorly in states from the old Northwest Territory where Protestants and Catholics lived in roughly equal numbers.

Above all, the antebellum era shows that victims of prejudice in one context often practice it in another. James Gordon Bennett, the Catholic editor of the *New York Herald*, flayed "Austrian Jew banker" August Belmont. Representative Lewis C. Levin, the premier Jewish nativist, defended anti-Catholic rioters. Strained relations between Catholic and Jewish leaders worsened during the 1850s as the result of an international controversy over Edgar Mortara, an Italian Jewish child apparently baptized in secret against his parents' wishes and forcibly raised as a Catholic.

Finally, the second Great Awakening failed to eradicate anti-clericalism, rational religion, and militant unbelief. Impious mobs occasionally disrupted revivals. Senator Richard M. Johnson led the fight for Sunday mail delivery, a government service anathema to evangelical Protestants, but nonetheless managed to win the vice-presidency in 1836. Less fortunate, free thinker Abner Kneeland served a prison term for blasphemy.

* * *

In general, the Civil War and Reconstruction marked no drastic transition in the history of nativism and religious prejudice. Representative Thaddeus Stevens, an Anti-Mason turned Republican, feared that the "invisible powers" of Masonry might save Andrew Johnson from impeachment in 1868. Although animosity to Mormons and Catholics declined from prewar peaks, neither faith was regarded yet as fully American. President Abraham Lincoln ended the military occupation of Utah, but Congress, upholding a Republican platform that paired polygamy and slavery, forbade plural marriage in the territories. The influx of non-Mormons into Utah produced new clashes, which in turn prompted renewed hostility in the East. From the 1870s to the 1890s the State Department urged foreign governments to end emigration by "ignorant classes" drawn to Mormonism, army officers blamed Mormons for Indian uprisings, and Protestant clergy condemned Utah as the national "brothel." Congress tightened control over the territory and refused to grant statehood until 1896, six years after the Mormon Church had forbidden new plural marriages. Then the House of Representatives refused to seat the polygamous Brigham Roberts, and the Senate investigated allegations of sub-rosa polygamy before seating monogamous Reed Smoot.

During the 1860s supporters of the Union ominously noted Pope Pius IX's tilt toward the Confederacy, most Know-Nothings found homes in the Republican party, and foes of William Marcy Tweed's Democratic machine in New York routinely conflated Catholicism and corruption. From Reconstruction through the 1890s clashes persisted over Bible reading in public schools, government appropriations to parochial schools, and denominational education of American Indians. Several states banned voting by noncitizens or vigorously enforced laws already on the books. Bigots were not the only Americans concerned about these issues, but even debates among responsible citizens almost always touched on nativist themes. In 1886 Rev. Josiah Strong published *Our Country,* the premier nativist tract of the late nineteenth century, which updated old motifs to fit the social gospel. According to Strong, Catholicism prevented immigrants from understanding representative government, a system that came naturally to Protestants. If these newcomers were evangelized and assimilated, however, Strong thought that they could help the United States become the "elect nation" of the emerging era.

Foes of "Romanism" less complicated than Strong revitalized venerable nativist organizations or built new ones during the late 1880s. The most important group was the American Protective Association (APA), founded by Henry L. Bowers in 1887. APA members pledged not to vote for, strike with, or hire Catholics if non-Catholics were available. Former priests, ersatz nuns, and lurid tracts (including fresh editions of the *Awful Disclosures* of "Maria Monk") helped to spread the secret order's nativist message. By early 1895 the APA had attracted one hundred thousand members and many more allies in proliferating patriotic societies. Although leaders of the APA sometimes suspected the Catholic church of plotting insurrection, they were less likely than their Know-Nothing forebears to sanction violence. Compared to the 1850s, the 1890s produced few interfaith shoot-outs. But when violence did occur, recent immigrants were once again the favorite targets.

The war for and against the Union heightened evangelical fervor and catalyzed a rise in anti-Semitism. Jews served disproportionately in both armies, but were often accused of profiting from the conflict rather than contributing to the fight. In the South, some Jewish merchants suffered boycotts. Judah P. Benjamin, first Secretary of War and then Secretary of State for the Confederacy, faced escalating anti-Semitic abuse. The United States Congress initially hesitated to authorize Jewish chaplains. Senator Henry Lane Wilson, a founder of the Republican party, was not alone in believing that productive citizens needed to combat the "curbstone Jew broker." General Ulysses S. Grant capped a series of anti-Semitic incidents in the

Union officer corps when he barred "Jews as a class" from the military department of Tennessee in 1862. Several families were driven from their homes before President Lincoln revoked the order.

Suspicion of Jews increased during the late nineteenth century. Senator John T. Morgan called one rival a "Jew dog" in 1878. Although relatively few Americans spoke so bluntly, most Christians continued to believe, as Rev. Morgan Dix of Trinity Church in New York put it, that their "judicial murder" of Jesus was a historical fact. Historical fiction, a thriving genre that included Lew Wallace's novel, *Ben Hur* (1880), treated Judaism as a legalistic faith inferior to Christianity. Many patricians disdained upwardly mobile Jews as the quintessential parvenus of the Gilded Age, and a few joined Henry Adams in fearing their imminent hegemony. Moved by personal dislike as well as snobbery, Henry Hilton barred Jewish financier Joseph Seligman from his hotel in Saratoga Springs, New York, in 1877.

Widespread restrictions against Jews soon followed at other resorts, clubs, and elite preparatory and finishing schools. Poor Jewish and gentile immigrants clashed over jobs, housing, and neighborhood boundaries. Especially during the Depression of the 1890s, conflict went beyond insults and fist fights. For example, New Jersey factory workers rioted to prevent the hiring of Jews, and Mississippi night riders threatened Jewish shopkeepers. Meanwhile, unsympathetic Shylocks whined on stage, grotesque Jews inhabited serious fiction as well as potboilers, hooknosed caricatures filled illustrated magazines, and Jewish pimps and arsonists were favorite subjects for investigative journalists.

The dissemination of unflattering stereotypes and the widespread practice of social discrimination marked a new phase in American anti-Semitism. Yet the late-nineteenth-century shift in mood should not be exaggerated. Hilton's ban on Jews elicited condemnation as well as emulation. Caricatures ranged from calumny to kidding. Some magazines both mocked the immigrants' imperfect adaptation to American ways and condemned anti-Semitic outbreaks abroad. Indeed, while explicitly anti-Semitic movements gained large French and German followings during the 1880s, none arose in the United States. Edouard Drumont's charge that Jewish conspirators controlled the French government helped bring down a prime minister, but an Americanization of this argument, *The Original Mister Jacobs,* published in 1888 by Telemachus Timayenis, a Greek immigrant, attracted slight attention. In short, most Americans continued to hold mixed feelings about Jews. As the *Boston Transcript* mused, "It is strange that a nation [with] so many good traits should be so obnoxious."

Nativism and religious prejudice remained entwined with politics in the decades after the Civil War. Republicans could not resist temptations to ally quietly with foes of "popery." President Rutherford B. Hayes appointed James Wigginton Thompson, an anti-Catholic polemicist, as Secretary of the Navy. Although James G. Blaine, the Republican presidential nominee in 1884, vowed never to criticize the religion of his Catholic mother, a Protestant supporter's denunciation of the Democrats as the party of "Rum, Romanism, and Rebellion" cost Irish-American votes and contributed to Blaine's defeat by Grover Cleveland. Cleveland's victory, repeated in 1892, increased Protestant fears of immigrant voters and Catholic clerics. One Baptist writer surmised that a direct telephone line now linked Cardinal James Gibbons, archbishop of Baltimore, with the White House. The APA dominated Republican politics in several states.

Leaders of the insurgent People's party, founded in 1892, pointedly repudiated the APA, but were less zealous in guarding against anti-Jewish innuendo in their rhetoric. For example, Tom Watson, the Populist floor leader in the House of Representatives, linked the Rothschild banking firm with President Cleveland's disastrous economic policies and charged Democrats with capitulation to "red-eyed Jewish millionaires." Yet Populists in general were no more prone to anti-Semitism than other Americans, and such references comprised a minor part of their vocabulary. William Jennings Bryan, the Democratic-Populist presidential candidate in 1896, shunned anti-Catholic and anti-Semitic appeals in his campaign. Bryan lost to William McKinley, the Republican nominee, who successfully courted both APA members and Catholic Democrats.

* * *

Between 1880 and 1930 the United States accepted roughly twenty-seven million immigrants, most of them Catholics and Jews from Eastern and Southern Europe. Although references to papal conspiracies and Christ's crucifixion persisted in nativist rhetoric, racial and economic motifs became increasingly prominent. The "new immigration" consisted of "beaten men from beaten races," as Francis Walker, president of the Massachusetts Institute of Technology, summarized the emerging orthodoxy in the 1890s. While Josiah Strong worried that Catholics would escape church discipline and rush into radicalism, Terence Powderly, the Catholic president of the Knights of Labor, feared that "foreign serfs" would depress wages. Neither fear was entirely groundless. Employers opposed restrictions on immigration and played ethnic groups against each other. Radical Irish Catholic coal miners took up arms against Welsh Protestant mine owners in Pennsylvania. The patrician organizers of the Immigration Restriction League, less concerned with cheap labor than with the preservation of "Anglo-Saxon" culture, campaigned to bar illiterate immigrants. While Brahmins and biologists sought such legislation, others took direct action in the name of Anglo-Saxon purity. The leader of a New Orleans mob that lynched eleven Italian prisoners in 1891 regarded his victims as "so many reptiles." Yet Italians, often called the Chinese of Europe, fared better than the Chinese themselves. Following decades of West Coast agitation fueled by returning missionaries' denunciations of "heathen" practices, Congress curbed Chinese entry in 1882 and then virtually barred it in 1892.

Although broadly Protestant values remained dominant at the turn of the century, a majority of Americans still belonged to no church. Indeed, a significant minority of Protestants drifted toward casual agnosticism; some immigrant groups, notably the Czechs, strengthened the ranks of free thinkers; and militant agnostics like Robert G. Ingersoll denounced religion as "superstition" before large audiences. Late-nineteenth-century revivals, intended to bolster flagging Protestantism, often opened old wounds and inflicted new ones. For instance, instead of making common cause with Mormons against Ingersoll's "ribald infidelity," Josiah Strong put Mormonism on his list of national "perils." Protestants fought among themselves over Darwinism, biblical criticism, and missionary policy; in some denominations, these controversies resulted in heresy trials. In 1908, some orthodox churchmen pronounced William Howard Taft, a Unitarian who doubted Christ's divinity, unfit for the presidency. Despite their intramural disputes, Protestant theological liberals and conservatives generally shared antipathy to Christian Science, Pentecostalism, the International Bible Students' Association (later known as Jehovah's Witnesses), and other faiths spawned by the spiritual crisis of the late nineteenth century.

The two decades following the critical election of 1896 were marked by stirrings of reform that scholars subsume under the label "progressivism." A few progressives espoused cultural pluralism. By and large, however, reform continued to coexist with and often to reinforce prejudice. Translating old concerns into fashionable terms, some investigative journalists envisioned a conspiracy uniting Mormon leaders and the corporate elite. Similarly, the leading anti-Catholic periodical, the *Menace,* damned the church for thwarting trade unions as well as for plotting to kill "heretics." On the West Coast, progressives applied to Japanese immigrants the degrading images and legal disabilities formerly used against the Chinese. With varying degrees of insensitivity and malice, muckrakers, municipal reformers, and purity crusaders warned against knife-wielding Italians, sullen Slavs, and drunken Irish. And as the most prosperous of the "new immigrants," Jews encountered special suspicion. While philo-Semites noted a "cousinly" affinity between thrifty Yankees and successful Jews, anti-Semites used this stereotype differently and attributed Jewish prosperity to chicanery, clannishness, and crime. In 1908 Police Commissioner Theodore Bingham claimed that half of New York's criminals were "Hebrews." In fact, Jews were generally underrepresented among lawbreakers.

After the turn of the century science buttressed bigotry. Typifying the relatively mild nativism of the 1880s, Josiah Strong had not only believed that most immigrants could be assimilated, but also expected them to help the United States fulfill its divine destiny. By the 1910s, most geneticists, anthropologists, and psychologists maintained that "races" originating in Southern and Eastern Europe were innately inferior to the old Northern European stock and thus were incapable of assimilation. The leading popularizer of this notion, Madison Grant, published *The Passing of the Great Race* in 1916. According to Grant, Sicilians and Polish Jews might steal "Nordic" women, but heredity prevented them from displaying "Nordic" intelligence, courage, or idealism. Ironically, Americans were less tolerant on the eve of World War I, following twenty years of progressivism, than during the 1890s. Tom Watson epitomized this appalling transition. Moving beyond the mild nativism of his Populist phase, Watson assailed the "parasite race" of Jews and the "jackassical" Catholic religion during the 1910s.

Restrictive legislation, job discrimination, and violence resulted from the harsher mood. Presidents Grover Cleveland, William Howard Taft, and Woodrow Wilson vetoed bills imposing a literacy test. But as immigration policy became increasingly rationalized and systematized, entrance requirements were tightened to exclude the "feeble minded," political dissidents, and those unable to pay a head tax (four dollars in 1907, a significant sum for uprooted peasants). Upwardly mobile Jews deemed deficient in character or alien in temperament bore the brunt of discrimination in law, medicine, and other professions. In 1913 Harlan Fiske Stone, dean of Columbia Law School, asserted that "oriental" Jewish minds betrayed a "racial tendency" to memorize instead of thinking creatively. Thinly veiled anti-Semitism marked much of the opposition to Louis Brandeis's confirmation as a justice of the United States Supreme Court in 1916. The most publicized vigilante act committed during the progressive era also involved a Jew, Leo Frank. Convicted in Atlanta of a murder he did not commit, Frank was lynched on 17 August 1915 after his sentence had been commuted. Tom Watson's denunciations of Frank as a "satyr-faced Jew" created an atmosphere congenial to his murderers and to other vigilantes who harassed Jews in Georgia. In November 1915 another Georgian, William J. Simmons, founded the twentieth-century version of the Knights of the Ku Klux Klan.

Nativist brutality must not obscure the continuing complexity of relations among and within religious and ethnic groups. To a greater extent than their antebellum counterparts, post–Civil War immigrants altered the economy, challenged social mores, and ultimately broadened the definition of Americanism. Consequently, it is hardly surprising that spokesmen for the prevailing Protestant culture reacted with alarm. Indeed, many Catholic priests shared Josiah Strong's suspicion of their Italian, Czech, or Polish parishioners. Similarly, the *Hebrew Standard* declared in 1894 that "thoroughly acclimated" American Jews bore no religious, social, or intellectual resemblance to "miserable darkened Hebrews" from Eastern Europe. Representing the mixed feelings of many Americans, successful politicians preached Anglo-Saxon superiority and derided alien influences while soliciting votes from non–Anglo-Saxon immigrants. For instance, President McKinley first accepted APA support and then placed a Catholic on the Supreme Court. Victims of prejudice continued to find their own scapegoats. Denis Kearney, a gifted Catholic agitator, combined eclectic animosities when he accused "foreign Shylocks" of importing Orientals to "debauch" white women. Although racism received scientific sanction and pressure mounted to restrict immigration, most Americans still expected immigrants already landed eventually to assimilate.

World War I ultimately encouraged religious prejudice, nativism, and especially anti-Semitism. The war and its offspring, the Red Scare of 1919–1920, institutionalized federal suppression of dissenters, heightened unfounded belief in conspiracies, legitimated violence against alleged subversives, and increased support for Prohibition and immigration restriction. The Wilson administration prosecuted religious objectors to war in general as well as radical protestors against the Great War in particular. Quakers and Mennonites who refused alternate service went to prison along with leading Jehovah's Witnesses. German-American Lutherans were subject to federal surveillance even though their church supported the war. False rumors, reminiscent of those during the Civil War, accused Jews of evading combat in order to make money, and officials returning from Russia in 1919 repeated the royalist accusation that Communism was "Yiddish." Distrust of German-American brewers eased passage of the Eighteenth Amendment and the Volstead Act. Growing hostility to immigrants facilitated enactment of the literacy test in 1917 over Wilson's second veto. Nonetheless, 600,00 immigrants, one-sixth of whom were Jewish, arrived in 1921 during the postwar depression. In response Congress temporarily limited immigrants from outside the Western Hemisphere to 358,000 annually. Three years later the permanent Johnson-Reed Act cut the figure to roughly 154,000 apportioned according to national origins, a system that blatantly discriminated against Eastern and Southern European Catholics and Jews.

The National Security League, the American Protective League, and other self-designated patriotic societies preached "preparedness" during

1915–1917; persecuted alleged slackers throughout the war, often with Justice Department sanction; moved on to "reds" after the armistice; and persisted in promoting "one hundred percent Americanism" throughout the 1920s. The Ku Klux Klan never enjoyed federal patronage but nonetheless flourished during the postwar recession. At its peak in early 1924 the loosely organized Klan comprised at least two million members and perhaps as many as four million. The Klan included Republicans and Democrats, northerners and southerners, strikers and scabs, farmers and businessmen, con artists and zealots, genteel ladies and sadists. Support was strongest in medium-sized cities where evangelical Protestants encountered sizable but not overwhelming Catholic and Jewish populations. The organization paid less attention to African-Americans than had its Reconstruction ancestor. Rather, as the *Fiery Cross* magazine explained in 1924, the Klan rallied "old stock Americans" against Jews, who "dominate the economic life of the nation," and Catholics, who "dominate the political and religious life." To counteract this twin menace, Klansmen marched, flogged, and occasionally killed.

Anti-Semitism operated in three broad areas during the 1920s. First, discrimination took a new turn with the adoption of explicit quotas limiting Jews at elite universities and professional schools. Columbia and Harvard, for example, cut their Jewish enrollment in half. Similarly, local legal covenants barred the sale of residences to Jews (as well as to blacks and, less often, to Catholics). Such restrictions not only revealed snobbery and religious prejudice but also served, in the famous phrase of journalist Carey McWilliams, as a "mask for privilege" that hindered economic competitors. Second, the tracts popularizing scientific racism focused on Eastern European Jews. Novelist Kenneth Roberts warned that these "human parasites" could not be assimilated in *Why Europe Leaves Home* (1923), a tract against "mongrelization." Third, *The International Jew*, a series of articles first published in Henry Ford's newspaper, the *Dearborn Independent*, placed Jews at the center of a conspiracy theory as farfetched as any in American history.

Like Jedidiah Morse's denunciation of an Illuminati cabal propagated 130 years earlier, this comprehensive conspiracy theory came from abroad. Specifically, it derived from *The Protocols of the Learned Elders of Zion*, ostensibly the records of the Jewish plotters but actually a fabrication concocted by Russian anti-Semites. Elaborating on the *Protocols'* central theme that the elders manipulated both exploitative capitalism and subversive communism to undermine Christian civilization, Ford's staff added characteristic American touches. Jews were accused of spreading religious modernism, fixing the 1919 World Series, and founding farm cooperatives to corrupt the heartland. *The International Jew* won favor among some genteel anti-Semites as well as earthier Klansmen.

The heightened emotions accompanying World War I transformed the major Protestant split into a chasm. Theological conservatives (most of whom were known as fundamentalists after 1920) were victims as well as purveyors of prejudice in the heresy trials, schisms, and polemics of the 1920s. Theological liberals rarely understood the intricacy of fundamentalist theology or the depth of fundamentalist beliefs in original sin, inerrant Scripture, and Jesus' imminent return. When liberals charged them with stupidity, fundamentalists countered with allegations of infidelity and subversion. Fundamentalists were more likely than liberals to hold Jews responsible for Christ's crucifixion and to condemn Catholicism in classic terms as the scarlet whore. Baptist, Methodist, and Disciples of Christ fundamentalists disproportionately joined the Klan.

Even so, not all fundamentalists were bigots, and fundamentalism was not the only source of bigotry. Conservative Protestant clergy occasionally allied with Catholics to censor films or condemn birth control. William Jennings Bryan, the foremost fundamentalist layman, denounced the "libelous" *Protocols*. Whereas many fundamentalists sympathetically interpreted Zionism as the fulfillment of biblical prophecy, social gospelers often derided it as the token of immigrant clannishness. Even the trial of John T. Scopes for teaching evolution cannot be reduced to a simple battle between ignorance and learning. While Bryan volunteered to prosecute Scopes in order to uphold Christianity, Clarence Darrow, a militant agnostic in the fashion of his friend Robert Ingersoll, joined the defense in order to uphold the surrogate religion of science. Looking on, secularists like H. L. Mencken, Sinclair Lewis, and Upton Sinclair portrayed fundamentalism as a conspiracy of yahoos and hypocrites.

Religious and ethnic conflict was central to national politics during the 1920s. Indeed, the Democrats were virtually disabled by divisions over Prohibition, the Ku Klux Klan, and the presidential aspirations of Governor Alfred E. Smith, a "wet" Catholic champion of the "new immigration." Prohibition was not inherently nativist. Some Catholics had allied with the evangelical Anti-Saloon League, the lobby most responsible for the Eighteenth Amendment. Nonetheless, "dry" Protestants, including many League members, had long associated "Romanism" with "besotted ignorance." Furthermore, Catholics disproportionately violated the Volstead Act. In 1924 the Democratic convention rejected Smith and narrowly declined to condemn the Klan by name. After Smith's nomination in 1928, the Klan denounced him as a tool of Pope Pius XI, the "dago on the Tiber." Bob Jones, a prominent fundamentalist minister, claimed to prefer a "nigger" president. Methodist Bishop James Cannon, leader of the increasingly nativist Anti-Saloon League, condemned Smith as the spokesman for "dirty people" from the streets of New York. Nevertheless, prejudice was confined neither to Klansmen nor to the broader community of fundamentalists. In keeping with Republican tradition, presidential candidate Herbert Hoover acquiesced in party cooperation with anti-Catholic militants. The theologically liberal *Christian Century* magazine called Smith the representative of an "alien culture, of a medieval Latin mentality, of an undemocratic hierarchy and a foreign potentate." Smith responded with courage, common sense, and naiveté. He rightly stressed the compatibility of Catholicism and Americanism, but understated the church's participation in politics, diplomacy, and the enforcement of Victorian morality.

Religious and ethnic issues from the 1920s persisted through the Great Depression and World War II. President Franklin D. Roosevelt temporarily healed the Democratic party's cultural wounds and created a religious coalition that included fundamentalists, social gospelers, Catholics, Jews, and former Klansmen. Catholics especially enjoyed unprecedented political power and legitimacy, winning one-quarter of all New Deal judicial appointments. For the first time two Catholics sat in the cabinet. Children of the "new immigration" helped to build the Congress of Industrial Organizations (CIO). Catholic clergy and laymen played a major role in imposing a prim production code on the film industry. Meanwhile, movies portrayed affable singing priests, all-American athletes at Catholic colleges, and fighting Irish regiments. Perhaps the most significant, if perverse, sign of Catholicism's growing acceptance was the career of Charles Coughlin, the "radio priest" who initially supported Roosevelt but later turned against him and became the nation's most powerful activist on the far right.

Numerous far right agitators regarded the New Deal as a bureaucratic threat to American individualism, scorned the CIO as a Communist tool, and ultimately blamed national problems on an international Jewish conspiracy; Coughlin himself began to publish the *Protocols* in 1938. Leaders of the far right varied in background and attitude. Rev. Gerald B. Winrod, a fundamentalist, compared the National Recovery Administration's symbol, the blue eagle, to the Satanic Beast of Revelation, expected Zionist elders to ally with the Antichrist, and traced the Zionist conspiracy back to apostolic times via the Bavarian Illuminati. Rev. Gerald L. K. Smith, theologically more liberal than Winrod and second in notoriety to Coughlin, mixed attacks on "New Deal Communism" with calls to redistribute wealth. Among paramilitary groups the Silver Legion under William Dudley Pelley made the most noise, and the Black Legion committed the most crimes per capita. Like their predecessors, the nativist groups of the 1930s and 1940s attracted solid citizens as well as eccentrics. Moreover, Protestant bigots, now discerning worse threats than the Pope, increasingly cooperated with their Catholic counterparts in assailing Jews, radicals, and New Dealers. Nonetheless, support for far right organizations during the Depression never equaled support for the Klan alone at its peak. The Klan itself faded and finally declared bankruptcy in 1944.

The far right's colorful countersubversion should not obscure less flamboyant bigotry during the Great Depression. On the contrary, the conspiratorial anti-Semitism of Coughlin, Smith, and their fellows converged with mainstream prejudice. According to polls conducted during the late 1930s, at least one-third of the population thought Jews too powerful. In 1937 *Christian Century* complained that Jews who failed to assimilate revealed an "unwillingness to submit . . . to the democratic process." The nation's premier censor, Joseph Breen, a Catholic who headed the motion picture industry's Production Code Administration, regarded Eastern European Jews as the "scum of the scum of the earth." Economic discrimination against Jews reached its zenith during the 1930s. As had been the case since the progressive era, competition between Jews and Catholics, especially the urban Irish, sometimes degenerated into name-calling, street fights, and the desecration of synagogues. The Christian Front, founded in 1938, cited Coughlin's teachings to justify assaults on "Christ killers." The response to these anti-Semitic incidents by Catholic politicians, policemen, and churchmen was less than evenhanded.

Catholic and Protestant leaders also allowed harassment of Jehovah's Witnesses, whose refusal to salute the "graven image" of the American flag and whose denunciations of rival faiths as "rackets" provoked vandalism, beatings, expulsions from schools, and suspensions from relief rolls. During World War II a capricious selective service system imprisoned half of the eight thousand Witnesses seeking exemptions on the grounds of conscience. Despite their growing influence, Catholics themselves were still not fully accepted. Ethnic groups less prosperous than the Irish—Italians, Poles, and Hungarians—encountered more insults and discrimination. Protestant opinion strongly condemned President Roosevelt's appointment of a personal representative to the Vatican in 1940. According to a Gallup poll conducted that same year, 38 percent of the population would not vote for an otherwise qualified Catholic presidential nominee.

The international advance of Nazism and debate over the United States' entry into World War II increased domestic religious tensions. A boycott of German goods begun in 1933 by a minority of Jews with slight gentile support prompted a counter-boycott of Jewish businesses by ethnic rivals. Unlike most Jewish rabbis and Protestant ministers committed to the social gospel, the majority of Catholic priests favored General Francisco Franco's insurrection against the Spanish Republic. The *Catholic World* was not alone in asking why liberals appalled by German anti-Semitism ignored the plight of Spanish Catholics. In general, however, Christian denominations paid scant attention to Nazi persecutions. Only Quakers and Unitarians significantly aided Jewish or gentile refugees, and far right spokesmen such as Coughlin and Winrod lauded Nazism as a bulwark against Communism. Although reputable noninterventionist groups attempted to clear their ranks of bigots, Charles A. Lindbergh, a genteel anti-Semite and amateur race theorist, emerged as the America First Committee's foremost spokesman. Typically exaggerating Jewish power, Lindbergh charged in September 1941 that Jews, along with the British government and the Roosevelt administration, were leading the movement toward war. Ironically, many interventionists at the State Department shared his disdain for Jews.

Throughout the 1930s nativist diplomats denied visas to victims of Nazism, especially Jewish victims. Fewer than thirty-two thousand immigrants arrived in 1935. Roosevelt ordered a more generous interpretation of the Johnson-Reed Act, but left enforcement to the State Department and never sought basic changes in the law. FDR believed that the refugee issue was politically explosive and that increased admission of Jews would further inflame anti-Semitism. He was right on both counts. In 1939 polls revealed that only 8 percent of the population welcomed more refugees. As late as June 1940 Assistant Secretary of State Breckinridge Long, a genteel anti-Semite, instructed subordinates to "put every obstacle" in the path of prospective immigrants. By early 1943 reports of Nazi genocide had reached a skeptical, indifferent public. The Roosevelt administration still made no sustained effort to save European Jews. Indeed, the United States missed opportunities involving little risk: publicizing the atrocities, pressuring Germany through neutrals, and bombing the concentration camps. Certainly the Depression, international realpolitik, military contingencies, and preoccupation with American casualties help to explain the United States' inaction. No doubt remains, however, that American anti-Semitism cost at least several hundred thousand lives.

* * *

During the fifteen years after World War II celebrants of the American way of life could—and did—point to much evidence of subsiding religious prejudice, nativism, and anti-Semitism. Gerald Winrod and Gerald L. K. Smith faded into obscurity; Coughlin, silenced by his bishop in 1942, probably on orders from the Vatican, conducted mass quietly in Michigan. Although Rev. Billy James Hargis, the foremost far right preacher of the next generation, acknowledged Winrod's influence, he neither placed Jews at the center of his own conspiracy theories nor attracted many adherents. George Lincoln Rockwell, who founded the American Nazi party in 1958, established himself as the most notorious admirer of Hitler since Pelley's prime but, despite vigorous self-promotion, led a negligible band.

Many theologically conservative Protestants moved from strident fundamentalism to the stylish evangelism symbolized by Billy Graham. Psychologists, anthropologists, and geneticists now discredited the cult of Anglo-Saxon superiority that their predecessors had framed as science. Men and women tempered by, if not quite melted in, the military pot returned from service more tolerant than before the war. Dwight D. Eisenhower, the latest in a line of presidential believers in belief per se, made religious pluralism rather than "one hundred percent Americanism" synonymous with patriotism. "Our form of government has no sense unless it is founded on a deeply felt religious faith, and I don't care what it is," he allegedly said in 1954.

Eisenhower, more ecumenical than earlier presidents who had routinely proclaimed patriotism as synonymous with Protestantism or Christianity, broadened the American way of life to include the "Judeo-Christian tradition." By the mid-1950s Jews had achieved a level of acceptance accorded to Catholics in the late 1930s. Yet this acceptance had not come easily. During the 1940s anti-Semitic incidents spread to the military, job discrimination persisted, and 55 percent of Americans polled still thought Jews exercised excessive influence. Late in the decade, however, several states outlawed employment discrimination and the U.S. Supreme Court ruled restrictive covenants legally invalid. In 1948 the United States became the first nation to grant de facto recognition to Israel. Films such as *Crossfire* and *Gentleman's Agreement,* both released in 1947, dramatized the dangers of genteel as well as conspiratorial anti-Semitism. Protestant theological conservatives increasingly accepted a philo-Semitic interpretation of Zionism. In *Protestant–Catholic–Jew* (1955) Will Herberg concluded that Protestantism, Catholicism, and Judaism had become equally legitimate variants of the "common culture religion."

Although Herberg alluded to cultural "competition" as well as to "coexistence," he underestimated the diversity, conflict, and prejudice within the "triple melting pot." The decline in anti-Semitism probably owed as much to Jewish activism as to gentile disgust with Nazi atrocities. Genteel anti-Semitism survived sub rosa, and ethnic competition still yielded epithets. In the same year, Congress passed a resolution endorsing Zionism and enacted legislation on the treatment of displaced persons that in practice discriminated against Jews. Some elite colleges retained informal limits on Jewish enrollment until the 1960s. The McCarran-Walter Act of 1952 evidenced continued suspicion of the "new immigration" and retained national origins quotas that favored "more readily assimilable" entrants. Relations between the predominantly liberal National Council of Churches (NCC) and the conservative National Association of Evangelicals (NAE) rarely rose above coolness and often sank lower. Carl McIntire, a maverick Presbyterian and president of the fundamentalist American Council of Christian Churches chided NAE "quislings" for cooperating with the "Marxist" NCC. Moreover, from McIntire's fundamentalist perspective the Catholic church still looked like the scarlet whore of Revelation.

From 1945 to 1960 controversy centering on Catholicism often brought the "triple melting pot" to a boil. Even more than the New Deal, the Cold War legitimated the Catholic church. Unlike many of their Protestant counterparts, few Catholic clergy had flirted with the Popular Front. Yet this aloofness also signaled divergence from the rising currents of cultural liberalism. Similarly, Catholic leaders campaigned against birth control in New England, derided the separation of church and state as a "shibboleth of doctrinaire secularism," and forced the removal of the anticlerical *Nation* magazine from New York City schools. Doctrinaire secularists, liberal Protestants, and a few Jews joined fundamentalists and evangelicals in attacking Catholic influence and insularity. In 1948 militants founded Protestants and Other Americans United for Separation of Church and State (POAU). Spokesmen for the group, led by general counsel Paul Blanshard, mixed fair criticism with cliches, pettiness, and Cold War shibboleths. For example, POAU suspected nuns of "brainwashing" Catholic children, compared Soviet and Vatican "dictatorships," and suggested registering bishops as foreign agents under the Smith Act. In 1951 POAU, along with the NCC and NAE, successfully fought President Harry S Truman's appointment of an ambassador to the Vatican.

Senator John F. Kennedy's 1960 race for the presidency bore superficial resemblance to Smith's race thirty-two years earlier. Both of their candidacies followed a period of controversy concerning Catholicism and politics. Both of these Democratic nominees were opposed by some prominent Protestant theological liberals along with theological conservatives and conspiratorial bigots. W. A. Criswell, a Baptist fundamentalist, feared the "death of a free church and a free state" if Kennedy won in 1960; Norman Vincent Peale, the popular liberal author of *The Power of Positive Thinking* (1952), worried that "our culture is at stake." Yet differences between the campaigns of 1960 and 1928 outweighed the similarities. Open discussion of Senator Kennedy's faith was more decorous, and underhanded anti-Catholic slurs received no encouragement from his opponent, Richard M. Nixon. Shrewder than Smith, Kennedy conceded that some "legitimate questions of public policy" impinged on religion, and he specifically repudiated aid to parochial schools along with diplomatic ties to the Vatican. The Vatican obliquely criticized Kennedy's views, while Cardinal Francis Spellman visibly supported Nixon. Although Kennedy ran well among Catholics, he received a smaller percentage of their votes than Smith in 1928. While his own Catholicism produced a net loss of support, he won by stressing issues unavailable to Smith: the Cold War, an economic recession, and an opponent named Nixon.

During the fifteen years after Kennedy's election celebrants of rapid social change could—and did—discover much evidence that the United States was entering a "post-Protestant," perhaps even a "post-Christian," era. The Immigration and Nationality Act of 1965 abandoned national origins quotas. Even more than his election, John Kennedy's assassination in 1963, followed by the murder of his brother Robert five years later, discredited Catholicism as a reputable national issue. Between 1964 and 1984 five Catholics, including children of Polish and Italian immigrants, were nominated for Vice-president. Even Carl McIntire mellowed sufficiently to praise Senator Barry Goldwater's "Romanist" running mate William Miller in 1964. Pope John XXIII and the Second Vatican Council that he convened further enhanced the respectability of Catholicism. Elsewhere on the religious spectrum, several formerly despised "sects" achieved the standing of "churches," or at least reputable positions within churches. Both Protestants and Catholics welcomed Pentecostals (some of whom preferred to call themselves "charismatics").

Jehovah's Witnesses joined the ranks of socially acceptable conscientious objectors. Mormons, erstwhile symbols of treason and lechery, became unmatched symbols of patriotism and marital fidelity.

Nevertheless, predictions of a tolerant post-Protestant culture proved as unreliable as earlier announcements of pluralist harmony. Movements seeking African-American equality generated anger as well as *agapé*. In contrast to Martin Luther King, Jr., who preached a social gospel against prejudice, Malcolm X declared that the problem most people faced in the world was "how to get freedom from Christians" and asserted that Jews had built Israel with money "taken out of the back of every black brother in the ghetto." Legislation, agitation, and judicial opinions that widened the separation between church and state prompted counterattacks in the name of the sacred; the most controversial Supreme Court decision, *Roe* v. *Wade* (1973), legalized almost all abortions. Many fundamentalists, distressed by cultural changes as well as growing sympathy for liberal theology among evangelicals, quit their devout isolation and turned to televised militancy. Furthermore, cooperation between former religious and ethnic rivals often derived less from generous principles than from mutual enmity toward third parties. Placing white solidarity above all else, the revived Ku Klux Klan even admitted Italian Catholics.

By the late 1970s religious issues had become central to national politics in ways that John F. Kennedy could not have imagined. In 1976, for the first time since 1896, two self-described born-again Christians—Jimmy Carter and Gerald R. Ford—ran against each other for President. Carter defeated Ford in part because he more effectively mobilized evangelicals and fundamentalists. Three years later Jerry Falwell, a Separate Baptist, founded the Moral Majority to combat pornography, abortion, and homosexuality; restore prayer to the public schools; and elect political conservatives. In 1980 groups comprising a "new Christian right" formed part of the coalition that placed Ronald Reagan in the White House. In 1984 Jesse Jackson, a black Baptist minister, sought the Democratic presidential nomination. Following published reports that Jackson had privately called Jews "Hymies," a remark for which he profusely apologized, Republicans labeled Democrats the party of bigotry. Democratic nominee Walter F. Mondale countered that President Reagan would allow

Reverend Falwell to name the next Supreme Court justices. In 1988 Jackson made a second, stronger run for President and Pat Robertson, a Pentecostal preacher with a large television audience, sought the Republican nomination. By the early 1990s, abortion verged on becoming an issue as divisive as Prohibition had been during the 1920s. Now, however, theologically conservative Protestants, Catholics, and Jews coalesced against liberals in their own denominations.

The odyssey of American Jewry highlights the conflicting religious currents since 1960. On the one hand, anti-Semitism declined to the lowest point in more than a century, perhaps to the lowest point ever. During the Kennedy administration two Jews sat in the cabinet for the first time. The Second Vatican Council repudiated belief in collective Jewish guilt for Christ's crucifixion, Catholic orders ceased praying for the conversion of the Jews, and priests taught students about the horrors of the Holocaust. Ebbing economic competition between upwardly mobile Catholics and Jews improved relations on a less abstract level. Anti-Semitism within fundamentalist and evangelical congregations sank to roughly the national average. A move rightward against stereotype by prominent Jews, analogous to the development of a Catholic left, enhanced the image of Jewish Americanness.

On the other hand, Jews still faced greater distrust than any other group associated with the "new immigration." Though plausible estimates vary, as many as twenty thousand Americans belonged to the Aryan Nations, the Order, Posse Comitatus, and comparable neo-Nazi organizations in 1990. These groups, which appealed especially to western farmers hard hit by an agricultural recession, assailed the "Zionist occupation government" in Washington, distributed *The International Jew* along with other classic anti-Semitic tracts, and found their usable past in the activities of George Lincoln Rockwell, Gerald L. K. Smith, and William Dudley Pelley. Many of them promoted a version of "Anglo-Israelite" theology in which Jesus was claimed as an Aryan and white Christians were celebrated as God's chosen people. These sects showed greater enthusiasm for Hitler than had most of their far right antecedents in the 1930s. Their members were also less law abiding. During the 1980s, zealous neo-Nazis counterfeited currency, murdered foes, and provoked fatal shootouts with federal agents.

In the 1970s, 1980s, and early 1990s, as in the 1930s, flamboyant far right agitators obscured less dramatic but ultimately more significant expressions of religious prejudice. Adolescent vandals still defaced synagogues more often than churches. Legitimate disagreements between Jews and non-Jews about mixed marriage, conversion, affirmative action, and Middle East policy sometimes slid into insensitivity or outright bigotry. During the Watergate scandal, President Richard M. Nixon told aides that Jews in particular controled the arts, mobilized the left, and plotted news leaks to destroy his administration. In 1975 General George Brown, Chairman of the Joint Chiefs of Staff, declared that Jews controlled finance and the mass media. Later in the decade polls showed that 8 percent of Americans thought Jews too powerful and 25 percent considered them more loyal to Israel than to the United States. In 1980 Rev. Bailey Smith, president of the Southern Baptist Convention, lamented Jewish estrangement from Jesus and publicly doubted that God heard Jewish prayers, a position he later recanted. According to some fundamentalist critics, the portrayal of an erotic Jesus in the film *The Last Temptation of Christ* (1988) could be explained by Jewish domination of Hollywood. And far right activists shrewd enough to tone down their overt anti-Semitism found a place within the political mainstream. David Duke, a former grand dragon of the Ku Klux Klan who retained neo-Nazi ties, was elected to the Louisiana legislature in 1989; the next year he received 44 percent of the total vote—and a majority of votes cast by whites—as a candidate for the United States Senate.

Like the white majority, the African-American minority had long viewed Jews as "Christ killers" and exaggerated their economic power. Some blacks also envied the Jewish community's achievement of success and solidarity. Starting in the late 1950s, competition between blacks and Jews for white-collar jobs and political influence, reminiscent of earlier rivalry between Irish Catholics and Jews, caused relations to deteriorate. This deterioration was augmented by black Muslim identification with Israel's Arab adversaries. In 1984 Minister Louis Farrakhan, leader of the Nation of Islam, deplored the Jewish "gutter religion." Farrakhan's remark, combined with subsequent embellishments, highlighted disproportionate anti-Semitism among African-Americans. Even many middle class blacks who were not themselves anti-Semites applauded Far-rakhan as a champion of black pride. The popularity of the rap singing group Public Enemy, whose lyrics were intermittently anti-Semitic, revealed similar insensitivity. In short, blacks as well as whites continued to view Jews with a mixture of admiration and jealousy.

* * *

Prevailing interpretations of religious prejudice, nativism, and anti-Semitism in the early 1990s still rely on theories developed during the 1950s and early 1960s. At that time pluralist scholars such as Seymour Martin Lipset, Nathan Glazer, and Richard Hofstad-ter attributed most American countersubversion to "extremists" moved by mental aberration or social "status anxiety." They traced what Hofstadter called a "paranoid style" from Jedidiah Morse to Barry Goldwater via Anti-Masonry, Populism, McCarthyism, and "political fundamentalism." Their work certainly represented an advance be-yond the defenses of bigotry produced by an earlier generation of social scientists. As critics have noted for a generation, however, even sophisticated pluralists underestimated conspiratorial and xe-nophobic attitudes within the cultural mainstream, slighted economic origins of ethnic conflict, too neatly divided villains from victims, and missed continuities between psychological normality and abnormal-ity. Nevertheless, commentators have applied pluralist formulas—albeit with decreasing acuity—to the latest surge in immigration, the rise of various unorthodox religions, and the revival of funda-mentalist controversies dormant since the 1920s.

By the late 1970s the "new immigration" from Eastern and South-ern Europe had become one of several old immigrations. The resid-ual ethnicity of the second and third generations was overshadowed by a large, newer immigration, primarily from Asia and Latin Amer-ica. Scholars and pundits alike mistook the decline of bigotry against Jews and Catholics for the disappearance of nativism per se and exaggerated the hospitality extended to "Hispanics" and "Asian-Americans." Indeed, these broad categories underscore the presump-tion that diverse nationalities should blend into manageable ethnic conglomerates. Like their now-celebrated predecessors, the latest immigrants do change neighborhoods, alter the economy, and modify what it means to be an American. Even when these changes are for the better, as they usually are, some sort of nativist response is all but inevitable.

However, with the partial exception of Moslems from the Middle East, who are routinely portrayed in mass media as irrational and violent "Islamic fundamentalists," contemporary nativists typically stigmatize ethnic groups without stressing their religion. Like successful Jews in the 1910s, Asian-Americans are accused of insularity, aggressiveness, and an overdeveloped work ethic. Poor Hispanics face derision for exhibiting the traits of preindustrial peasants, derision often voiced by the proud grandchildren of preindustrial peasants. Glib criticism of bilingual education, inflated estimates of illegal immigration, and a proposed constitutional amendment declaring English the official national language also mark political discourse. The Immigration Reform and Control Act of 1986, though generous in some respects, nonetheless reflected exaggerated fears that undocumented workers, most of whom entered from Latin America, threatened American culture and prosperity. On the one hand, this legislation offered amnesty to many illegal aliens who came to the United States before 1982; on the other hand, by imposing penalties on employers of illegal immigrants, it made likely increased discrimination against—or at least increased humiliation of—all Hispanic job seekers. Except for occasional violent acts, hostility to legal immigrants in the early 1990s pales beside that of the 1920s. But federal denial of asylum to illegal immigrants from Haiti and Central America—political refugees in fact, if not in name—cost lives. Less restrictive regulations were issued in 1990 but their impact remains unclear.

Contemporary invocations of the "Judeo-Christian tradition," reminiscent of allusions to Christian nationhood 150 years ago, again exclude many believers and unbelievers. In general, these ritual references signal obliviousness rather than animosity. Moslems and Buddhists, for instance, are even less visible now than Jews were during the early national period. Yet many Americans remain eager to ridicule unorthodox faiths. Judges sanction forcible "deprogramming" of adolescent sectarians, media exposés speculate on the neuroses of "Moonies," and erstwhile cultists have supplanted estranged Mormon wives on the lurid lecture circuit. Escaping Brigham Young's fate, Reverend Sun Myung Moon of the Unification Church nonetheless served a prison term for an irregular use of funds that probably would have passed without prosecution, perhaps without notice, in a "mainline" denomination. In short, a plurality of Americans still adhere to a de facto religious establishment, a bland combination of liberal theology and mild reform.

Renewal of the fundamentalist controversy during the past two decades has centered on the new Christian right. Jerry Falwell, the movement's shrewdest spokesman, demonstrated the adaptability of contemporary countersubversives. Unlike members of the old Christian right of the 1930s, Falwell shunned anti-Semitism and—belatedly—approved racial integration. In 1984 he barely protested the appointment of an ambassador to the Vatican. Less typical of the new Christian right, Rev. Jimmy Swaggart, a Pentecostal, doubted the salvation of Catholics who had not been "born again" and pitied anyone who felt enriched "spiritually by kissing the Pope's ring."

While generally pursuing good relations with Jews and Catholics, fundamentalists and evangelicals in the latest far right found new enemies: feminists, homosexuals, and "secular humanists." Ironically, the last label, which would have fit Robert Ingersoll or Clarence Darrow, describes no major figure on the American scene today. Coopted by modernist theology, the community of militant freethinkers has shrunk to insignificance. In fact, the new Christian right's foremost foes are at least pro forma theists. Unfortunately, however, cosmopolitan understanding of fundamentalism has improved little since the Scopes trial. Damning the new Christian right as the latest "paranoid style," most liberals adopt an emotionally satisfying but politically ineffective strategy.

In the early 1990s, the immediate prospects for American religious prejudice are uncertain. Some evidence suggests an ebbing of conflict between religious groups. Although such conflict is not necessarily nativist, it has often provided ideological nourishment for bigots. Despite Pat Robertson's race for the Republican presidential nomination, religion was discussed less during the presidential election of 1988 than in any campaign since 1972. After Robertson's defeat and Jerry Falwell's semiretirement from politics, the new Christian right has lost most of its clout in Washington. Abortion may be the nation's most divisive cultural issue since Prohibition but, unlike Prohibition, it unites conservative Catholics and Protestants instead of dividing them.

Still, the proliferating predictions of religious consensus and comity reminiscent of the 1950s should be viewed with skepticism. Not only does the new Christian right remain powerful on the local level, but fundamentalists are no more likely to disappear than they were in the 1920s. The Catholic Church's staunch opposition to abortion may prompt a cosmopolitan backlash, especially if bishops criticize or excommunicate Catholic officials who take a prochoice position. The recent increase in anti-Semitic incidents, though probably a blip interrupting the long-term trend toward tolerance, may signal something worse. Indeed, the farmers who embraced conspiratorial anti-Semitism during the agricultural recession of the 1980s highlight an important lesson: a national economic crisis would exacerbate religious and ethnic as well as racial tensions.

The labels "religious prejudice," "nativism," and "anti-Semitism" do not describe the same phenomena in the 1990s as in the 1890s, let alone the 1790s or 1690s. Students of these subjects have uncovered, if not fully explained, the grand conspiratorial obsessions that have characterized these phenomena throughout American history. Now we must distinguish more carefully among varieties of bigotry and also between bigotry and other conflicts of interest or opinion. Stereotypes can be flattering as well as derogatory, prejudices run the gamut from transitory misconceptions to implacable loathing, and discrimination ranges from snobbery to genocide. What one American considers religious prejudice, a biased judgment based on insufficient evidence, his neighbor may consider a sacred duty demanded by God. Unless scholars write with greater care, we risk, on the one hand, ignoring prejudices couched in subtle idioms and, on the other hand, misinterpreting legitimate or inevitable conflicts over economic, cultural, and spiritual issues.

2

Henry Ford and
The International Jew

Social scientists and journalists have continued to examine
American anti-Semitism, but discussion among historians has subsided during the past two decades. Throughout the 1950s and 1960s,
however, the subject evoked heated exchanges, with controversy
usually centering on the relationship between nineteenth-century
agrarian radicalism and twentieth-century "extremism." The dili-
gent and sometimes passionate efforts of many scholars produced
little agreement. Indeed, we are tempted to surmise that discussion
of American anti-Semitism passed from fashion among historians
because the leading authorities wore themselves out in controversy.[1]

Returning to the subject today, we enjoy advantages over Oscar
Handlin, John Higham, Norman Pollack, and others who wrote
three decades ago. Scholarship has revealed much about related
topics, including the nation's long tradition of conspiratorial thinking, popular racial theories and practices, and the social psychology
of deviance. This chapter attempts to illuminate anti-Semitism by
focusing on *The International Jew,* a series first published during
the 1920s in Henry Ford's newspaper, the *Dearborn Independent.*
More than any other literary source, these articles spread the notion
that Jews menaced the United States.[2]

When, in mid-1920, writers for the *Independent* attacked a putative Jewish conspiracy, they joined a host of citizens who had perceived alien threats to American virtue. From colonial times through

the Civil War, warnings against sinister plots by monarchists or Jacobins, Catholics or Masons, abolitionists or slaveholders diffused through all classes, sections, and political groups. The social and intellectual turmoil of the late nineteenth century, what historian Robert Wiebe calls the "search for order," nurtured a new wave of countersubversive theories. Populists found the emerging corporate elite more sinister than the slavocracy had been, while centrist politicians like Theodore Roosevelt countered that Populists resembled Marat and Robespierre. Many white Protestants agreed with Rev. Josiah Strong that unassimilated immigrants from Southern and Eastern Europe imperiled "our country."[3]

World War I accentuated both the fear of subversion and efforts to combat it. Americans were encouraged by government agents like George Creel and the Committee on Public Information to believe that Kaiser Wilhelm's domestic allies undermined national security. The nation slid easily from wartime suppression into the Red Scare. Justifying mass arrests and deportations, Attorney General A. Mitchell Palmer warned in 1919 that the "sharp tongue of revolutionary heat" licked church altars, played in school belfries, and crawled "into the sacred corners of the home."[4]

The campaigns against Huns and Bolsheviks obviously encouraged the suspicious dispositions of "one hundred percent Americans." For different reasons, opponents of suppression also doubted surface explanations of social phenomena. Even before the war, reformers had shared with Walter Lippmann the sense that "deception has become organized and strong." Journalists and progressive professors had probed beneath the surface to discover the "real" forces ruling the economy, the Senate, or the Constitutional Convention of 1787. Appalled by the success of wartime indoctrination, Lippmann concluded in 1922 that deceivers of public opinion had increased their power. Similarly, the political scientist Harold Lasswell observed that "more people than ever" were "puzzled, uneasy or vexed by the unknown cunning which seems to have duped or degraded them." Their minds, Lasswell might have added, were thus susceptible to conspiratorial explanations. Indeed, this frame of mind was probably more common after World War I than at any time since before the Civil War.[5]

Nor was it remarkable in an overwhelmingly Christian nation that Jews were placed at the center of one of the most popular conspiracy theories. The connection between Christianity and anti-Semitism is controversial and complex. Among American Christians, mixed feelings about Jews had existed since the Colonial period. Although Protestant creators of holy commonwealths might identify with Old Testament Hebrews, they also inherited a tradition that blamed Jews for Christ's crucifixion and numerous subsequent crimes. By the mid-1800s, evangelists derided Jewish "rebels against God's purpose," politicians sneered at "Judas Iscariot" Benjamin, the Confederate Secretary of State, and the *New York Times* called financier August Belmont an "agent of foreign Jew bankers."[6]

As immigrants poured in from Eastern Europe after the Civil War, actors, clergymen, dime novelists, and serious writers routinely portrayed Jews as libertines, enemies of true religion, and cheats. Some agrarian radicals held foreign Jewish bankers responsible for tight money and depressions. Theologically conservative Protestants said that Jews would return to the Holy Land, possibly in alliance with the Antichrist. On a less abstract level, antagonism ranged from demonstrations against merchants to innuendo in the press about "obnoxious" Jewish traits. Restricted clubs and resorts signaled a deepening concern with the Jewish parvenu, an old image put into modern dress.[7]

Although historians still disagree about the extent of anti-Semitism during the late nineteenth century, tentative conclusions are necessary in order to understand the origin of *The International Jew*. In a nation committed to the "Americanization" of immigrants, the literary caricatures were not, as Oscar Handlin contended, generally devoid of malice. Moreover, the argument, made most forcefully by John Higham, that patricians, radical farmers, and rival immigrant groups were unusually biased probably means that scholars have studied those groups more than others. The dominant attitude among Christian Americans, Leonard Dinnerstein rightly concludes, was an amalgam of "affection, curiosity, suspicion, and rejection." Finally, comparing Americans and Europeans, we can say that anti-Semitism in the United States was relatively less violent, less racist, and less central to the world views of those who accepted it.[8]

The first two decades of the twentieth century witnessed a shift toward greater suspicion and rejection. The lynching of Leo Frank in 1915 was only the most dramatic incident in an era that marked, according to George Fredrickson, a peak of "formalized racism." Less benign than Josiah Strong's *Our Country,* the leading nativist tract of an earlier generation, Madison Grant's book, *The Passing of the Great Race,* rejected the "fatuous" view that Jews could be assimilated. Comparable racial stereotypes were accepted by leading progressives. Indeed, magazines that attacked municipal corruption also worried about the "Jewish invasion." The issues coalesced for the muckraker Burton J. Hendrick, who denounced Jewish theater and liquor "trusts." Though Hendrick, Jacob Riis, and the sociologist Edward A. Ross still mixed sympathy with suspicion, they casually claimed that Jews avoided physical labor; manipulated money without engaging in "basic production"; valued profit more than life itself; destroyed ethical standards in business, law, and medicine; promoted prostitution among gentile women; intimidated the press; and "overwhelmed" Congress with lies during debates on immigration restriction.[9]

After World War I, hostility toward Jews escalated, operating in three overlapping areas. First, "polite" anti-Semites, including President A. Lawrence Lowell of Harvard, restricted admission to clubs, resorts, universities, and the professions. Second, supported by many leading psychologists, such popularizers as Lothrop Stoddard and Kenneth Roberts spread the Anglo-Saxon cult to a wide audience. Third, commentators and members of Congress increasingly associated Jews with radicalism in general and Communism in particular. For example, Dr. George A. Simons, a former missionary in Russia, told a Senate committee that the "so-called Bolshevik movement" was "Yiddish." Simons's allegations, which particularly impressed Senator Knute Nelson, were largely endorsed by other witnesses, including a Northwestern University professor, a Commerce Department agent, two representatives of National City Bank, a YMCA official and vice counsel in Petrograd, and several Russian emigrés.[10]

To Simons, "Yiddish" Bolshevism seemed to "dovetail" with the plot outlined in *The Protocols of the Learned Elders of Zion.* In this notorious forgery created by Russian royalists at the turn of the century, a leader of a secret Jewish world government allegedly explained the plot to destroy Christian civilization. For almost two thousand years, the Elders had been "splitting society by ideas" while manipulating economic and political power. Currently they popularized Darwinism, Marxism, "Nietzsche-ism" and other anti-Christian doctrines, undermined clergy and corrupted governments, and arranged wars that would profit Jews while killing gentiles. Above all, the conspirators controlled both the mechanisms of capitalism and the radical movements pretending to offer alternatives.[11]

Czar Nicholas II and his anti-Semitic protégés, known as the Union of Russian Peoples or Black Hundreds, used the *Protocols* to stir pogroms, but the forgery reached its widest audience after the Romanovs had fallen. During the Russian civil war, White commanders distributed copies to their troops. Almost immediately, emigrés and returning foreigners such as Simons brought the *Protocols* to the outside world. During 1918–1919, as references to "Yiddish" Bolshevism reached the press and congressional hearings, translations were offered to American military and civilian leaders, including President Woodrow Wilson. No one worked harder to disseminate the *Protocols* than Boris Brasol, a Russian lawyer and trade representative who had belonged to the Black Hundreds. After the Revolution Brasol remained in the United States, advised the Military Intelligence Division of the War Department, and in 1920 published an edition of the *Protocols*.[12]

In many respects, this monarchist forgery was an incongruous addition to political discourse in Wilsonian America. But prewar concern about the "great Jewish invasion," wartime wariness of subversion, and continuing fear of deception helped Americans to ignore the *Protocols'* obvious antirepublicanism. Moreover, the *Protocols'* generality left room for interpolations to fit local circumstances. Finally, their basic charges were "Americanized" and disseminated under the imprimatur of a national hero, Henry Ford.

* * *

Along with the nation as a whole, Henry Ford faced a series of crises during 1915–1920. With the introduction of the Model T in 1908, he had begun to achieve his great goal: mass production of a reliable, inexpensive automobile. By the mid-1910s his decision to freeze auto design and expand production instead of paying dividends had alienated subordinates and minority stockholders. Undaunted, he fired employees who disagreed with him, bought out dissatisfied shareholders, and gained full control of the Ford Motor Company in 1920. Thereafter, except for his able son Edsel, he rarely encountered anyone who openly disagreed with him.[13]

On the assembly line, however, employees were attracted to the Industrial Workers of the World. To outflank the Wobblies, in 1915 Ford established the "Five Dollar Day," with the company "Sociological Department" determining which employees merited the high salary. These programs made Ford's national reputation as an industrial statesman, assuring a wide audience for anything he said or did. Increasingly he offered advice on issues unrelated to the Model T. Rev. Samuel S. Marquis, who headed the Sociological Department for five years, believed that Ford's chief ambition was to be "known as a thinker of an original kind." After denouncing the "capitalist" war in Europe, for instance, he chartered *Oscar II,* the famous "peace ship," to transport delegates to a conference of neutrals. In 1916, he condemned American intervention in Mexico. Two years later, drafted by President Wilson, he accepted the Democratic nomination for senator from Michigan.[14]

None of these projects fully succeeded. Inflation eroded the daily five dollars and employees continued to resent oppressive working conditions. Marquis left the Sociological Department in 1920 because Ford's paternalism had degenerated into "brutal" treatment of executives and ordinary workers. Not only was *Oscar II* ridiculed in the press, but the pacifist passengers bickered and Ford abandoned the expedition soon after its arrival in Norway. He lost the Senate race to Truman V. Newberry by 7,500 votes, though he ran remarkably well for a candidate who declined to give a single speech. Indeed, paying more attention to his rival after the election, he financed an investigation of campaign expenditures that prompted Newberry's resignation in 1922. Opposition to the Mexican intervention produced the greatest harm to Ford's reputation. When the *Chicago Tribune* responded by calling him an "ignorant idealist," he sued for one million dollars. He won a judgment of six cents, but *Tribune* lawyers demonstrated that he was ignorant of most matters unrelated to automobiles.[15]

Following his disastrous testimony in the libel suit, Ford became, in the words of biographer Keith Sward, "as inaccessible as the Grand Lama." He remained eager to offer wide-ranging advice, but now usually filtered opinions through Ernest G. Liebold, his secretary since 1911. An ambitious martinet, Liebold expanded his authority by exploiting Ford's quirks, such as his dislike of paperwork and refusal to read most correspondence. The secretary gladly managed public relations, issued statements or answered letters in Ford's name, and exercised power of attorney after 1918. Indeed, he substantially controlled Ford's access to the world outside of Dearborn.[16]

To promote the views that he developed in virtual seclusion, Ford in 1919 purchased a weekly newspaper. The *Dearborn Independent* was designed to disseminate practical "ideas and ideals" without distortion by the "world's channels of information." The Dearborn Publishing Company, moreover, looked like a family enterprise. Henry Ford, his wife Clara, and his son Edsel were respectively president, vice-president, and treasurer. Editorship of the *Independent* was bestowed on E. G. Pipp, a friend of Ford who had edited the *Detroit News.* William J. Cameron, an intelligent but hard-drinking veteran of the *News,* listened to Ford's ruminations and then wrote "Mr. Ford's Page." Both men operated under the watchful eye of Liebold, who detested Pipp and barely tolerated Cameron.[17]

Despite a promise on the masthead to chronicle "neglected truth," the *Independent* at first printed nothing extraordinary. It supported Prohibition, prison reform, the Versailles Treaty, and the League of Nations; yet these serious issues often received less attention than light stories about prominent persons, cities, or colleges. For sixteen months, the newspaper did not mention an alleged Jewish conspiracy. The owner, however, had been contemplating the issue for several years, and had considered raising it during the 1918 senatorial campaign. After the election, Pipp recalled, Ford began to talk about Jews "frequently, almost continuously."[18]

The source of Ford's animus remains obscure. Pipp thought that he wanted anti-Semitic votes in a presidential race. Harry Bennett, who headed the motor company's Service Department, a euphemism for thugs and labor spies, said that failure to secure a loan from Jewish bankers embittered the automaker. Norman Hapgood, author of the "inside story" of *The International Jew,* believed that Ford blamed Rosika Schwimmer, a Jew, for the peace ship's "moonshine errand." Ford himself told Liebold and Fred Black, the *Independent* business manager, that Herman Bernstein, editor of the *Jewish*

Tribune, and other passengers on *Oscar II* had blamed Jewish financiers for the war. Liebold, who said that unspecified behavior by Jewish journalists in Norway "confirmed" Ford's suspicions, obviously shared and encouraged the automaker's bias. Indeed, Ford's secretary suspected Jewish automobile dealers of thwarting company policy and, a generation later, still recalled *The International Jew* as a worthwhile enterprise. Closer to home, Clara Ford may have promoted her husband's bigotry. At least she opposed Jewish membership in their country club and urged Ford to fire an executive whose wife was half Jewish.[19]

Pipp acted briefly as a countervailing influence. Six months after buying the *Independent* in 1919, Ford wanted to run a series on Jewish subversion. The editor held out for almost a year. In April 1920, he quit instead of sanctioning the articles. The imminent anti-Semitic campaign was probably not the only reason for Pipp's departure. Liebold had been undermining his authority and restricting access to Ford. When he resigned, Pipp joined a formidable list of former employees who had refused to be sycophants.[20]

Because the office files of the Dearborn Independent were destroyed in 1963, and because other records for 1920 have disappeared, we must rely on scattered correspondence, self-serving reminiscences, and conjecture to trace the composition of *The International Jew.* Apparently research and writing began toward the end of Pipp's tenure. Investigators directed by Liebold forwarded anti-Semitic information to Dearborn, where, Pipp recalled, Ford swallowed "all . . . that was dished out." Cameron, who succeeded Pipp as editor, did most of the writing. Initially unaware of the *Protocols,* Cameron did little "preliminary work" for the first article. He read "whatever was around," including Werner Sombart's *The Jews and Modern Capitalism.* But Cameron's later protests that he considered the articles "useless" must not be taken at face value. Fred Black recalled that Cameron "walked the floor" for three months before agreeing to write *The International Jew.* Within a year or two, however, he came to believe most of what he wrote. In the meantime, along with other Ford employees, he followed orders.[21]

The first article, "The International Jew: The World's Problem," appeared on 20 May 1920. Liebold had suggested the title and date of publication in order to coincide with an attack on "greedy" Jews by

Leo Franklin, a prominent Detroit rabbi and Ford's former neighbor. Although the *Independent* promised further revelations, the staff seems not to have planned more than a month ahead. Indeed, Black thought that Ford himself did not anticipate a sustained campaign.[22]

Yet several developments kept the series alive until 14 January 1922. Ford, Liebold, and—eventually—Cameron got wrapped up in their project. Ford visited the *Independent* almost every day, concerning himself only with "Mr. Ford's Page" and *The International Jew.* Despite their mutual hostility, Liebold and Cameron consulted often on the series, sometimes poring over articles together until three o'clock in the morning. Critics provided grist for the mill. When former President Taft or columnist Arthur Brisbane attacked *The International Jew,* they were denounced in subsequent articles as "gentile fronts." Moreover, Liebold's agents regularly supplied rumors, clippings, and forged documents.[23]

Liebold and Cameron later denied rumors that they had a large staff of investigators, and surviving evidence, though fragmentary, supports their recollections. Stanley W. Finch, who had become convinced of Jewish immorality while working for the Justice Department, found a place on the payroll. Lars Jacobson tried to show that American relief officials in Europe were covertly sending Jews to the United States; Liebold urged him to consult former Kaiser Wilhelm on the "Jewish situation" in Germany, but there is no record of a contact. From time to time, Ford dealers were obliged to purchase documents or find books about Jews.[24]

The main detective operation, located on Broad Street in New York, was managed by C. C. Daniels, a former lawyer for the Justice Department, whose aides, including several veterans of military intelligence, used secret identification numbers when contacting Dearborn. Norman Hapgood exaggerated only slightly when he said that the group "muckraked everybody who was a Jew or was suspected of being a Jew." It attracted "adventurers, detectives, criminals" and gave credence to their stories. For example, though Daniels's brother Josephus, the Secretary of the Navy, might have told them otherwise, Ford investigators thought that President Wilson took orders from Justice Brandeis over a private telephone line. Daniels's special concerns included Eugene Meyer, Jr., of the Federal Reserve Board, whom he accused of blocking Ford's acquisition of the nitrate plants at Muscle Shoals, Alabama. "As you know," he wrote to Liebold in 1922, "locks and bars make no difference to that portion of God's chosen people seeking to displace the stars and stripes with the Jewish national flag and that calls Lenine [*sic*] the greatest Statesman alive."[25]

Liebold recalled that he needed few European agents because "people came over here and revealed their stories to us." Russian emigrés ultimately provided a translation of the *Protocols*. Here, too, slight surviving evidence obscures the story. Historian Robert Singerman suggests that Boris Brasol, who had written on Bolshevism in the *Independent,* provided a copy. According to Liebold's reminiscences, however, Pacquita de Shishmareff, a Russian emigré married to an American soldier, provided his "first knowledge" of the *Protocols* in mid-June 1920. Liebold told Ford that Shishmareff, who is better known as Mrs. Leslie Fry, possessed "full and thorough knowledge of all Jewish operations in Europe." Whatever the Russian source, on 10 June 1920, W. G. Enyon, a company employee in Delaware, dispatched several copies to Dearborn.[26]

Starting with the 24 July article, the *Protocols* description of an international Jewish conspiracy provided the central thread of *The International Jew.* For the next three years, Liebold expanded his contacts with Russian royalists and their dubious documents. In addition to Brasol and Fry, he consulted several of their friends. A Ford agent in Paris paid 7,000 francs for a report by former Russian judge Nicholas Sokoloff purporting to show that Jewish conspirators had murdered the Romanovs. Liebold was impressed and invited Sokoloff to Dearborn. However, the emigrés soon discovered that they were treated as capriciously as other Ford employees. When Sokoloff fell ill, Liebold "hustled" him out of Michigan, and later refused to support his widow and orphans.[27]

* * *

Although the *Dearborn Independent* was indebted to emigrés for the *Protocols, The International Jew* was not, as historian Norman Cohn contends, "far more a Russo-German than an American product." The alleged manifestations of the "world's foremost problem" coincided with issues that had unsettled the United States since the Civil War. First, the *Independent* complained that both the monopolistic activities of large corporations and the countervailing actions of government had produced a "steady curtailment" of freedom. "Theories of liberty" abounded without halting the "steady tendency toward systematization." At the same time, "Public Health," "Public Safety," and analogous movements produced an "unaccustomed bondage to the State."[28]

Second, joining the search for moral order that intensified after World War I, the *Independent* condemned new styles in dress and music, changing sexual mores, Hollywood "lasciviousness" and the "filthy tide" sweeping over the theater. Sensitive to unraveling family bonds, the newspaper warned that children were drawn from "natural leaders in the home, church, and school to institutionalized 'centers' and scientific 'play spots.'" Third, the *Independent* addressed the issue that had grown in importance since the "endless stream" of immigrants had begun to arrive in the 1880s: what was Americanism? These strangers, especially residents of the "unassimilated province" known as New York, were responsible for the "mad confusion that passes in some quarters as a picture" of the United States.[29]

Fourth, the *Independent* worried about the problem of determining truth in the modern world. Even before the anti-Semitic campaign, the newspaper had shared the prevailing fear of deception by propaganda. People were "born believers" who needed "deeply" to affirm something. But it was hard to know what to believe. *The International Jew* protested that man was ruled "by a whole company of ideas into whose authority he has not inquired at all." Not only did he live by the "say so of others," but "terrific social pressures" on behalf of "broadmindedness" discouraged probes beneath conventional wisdom. Sounding like Walter Lippmann or Harold Lasswell, the newspaper warned that credulity was especially dangerous in the current "era of false labels."[30]

The *Protocols* offered a "clue to the modern maze." Hedging on the question of authenticity, as Liebold did in correspondence, the *Independent* said that the documents themselves were "comparatively unimportant." They gave "meaning to certain previously observed facts." Whether or not an Elder of Zion had actually given these lectures, it was clear that Jews used ideas to "corrupt Collective Opinion," controlled finance, sponsored revolution, and were "everywhere" exercising power.[31]

Ironically, the Jew's ancestral genius had been "spiritual rather . . . than commercial." Mosaic law rendered "plutocracy and pauperism equally impossible" among Israelites, but the tribes had no qualms about exploiting outsiders. Their enslavement of the Canaanites marked the triumph of materialism. During the dispersion, a central office, a modern version of the Sanhedrin, directed the exploitation of gentiles. Over the centuries, Jews created financial institutions to maximize profits and influence: credit, stock exchanges, government loans, holding companies, and renovation of used materials for resale. Simultaneously they used an atheistic "pseudo-Masonry" to spread radical doctrines and, during the French Revolution, came close to total victory.[32]

Bits of information about these machinations passed unseen before gentile eyes. Benjamin Disraeli, "a Jew who gloried in it," dropped a hint in *Conningsby*. Sidonia, a character who personified the "international Jew, full dress," tells a friend that the "world is governed by very different personages from what is imagined by those who are not behind the scenes." Since Disraeli had written his novel, the "hidden hand" had tightened its grip. An unidentified speaker at the sixth Zionist conference predicted the outbreak of World War I, and Jews alone profited from the conflict. Surrounding the major statesmen at Versailles, "princes of the Semitic race" extracted "extraordinary privileges" for their people, including the promise of a homeland in Palestine.[33]

Propaganda about pogroms was part of a "deliberate program" to overthrow the Romanovs. Jacob Schiff financed Japan's war against Russia in 1905 and, at his behest, Tokyo disseminated revolutionary doctrines among prisoners of war. After these tactics installed Bolshevism, the Elders turned to Germany, the "most Jew-controlled" country in the world—with the "possible exception of the United States."[34]

Jews influenced America even before independence. Indeed, Columbus "consorted much" with them. Over the objections of Governor Peter Stuyvesant, they brought slick commercial practices to New Amsterdam in the seventeenth century. Haym Salomon helped to finance the Revolution, but most Jews "were both loyalists and rebels, as the tide turned"; some participated in Benedict Arnold's treachery. The Rothschilds made twenty million dollars by arranging the use of Hessian mercenaries. Fifty years later, the family's first agent arrived—August Belmont, whose "professed Christianity" *The International Jew* did not take seriously.[35]

By the twentieth century, as the Elder of Zion had boasted, Jewry manipulated presidents. Jacob Schiff and his henchmen forced William Howard Taft to abrogate the Russian-American commercial treaty in 1911, thus making the United States a "crowbar to batter down" the czarist regime. Jews formed a "solid ring" around Woodrow Wilson at the start of his administration and more "swarmed" into Washington after the declaration of war. No official held more power than Bernard M. Baruch, chairman of the War Industries Board and "Jewish high governor of the United States."[36]

Following this "historical" survey, *The International Jew* purported to document the current activities of Jewish capitalists, radicals, and propagandists. In the economic sphere, the *Independent* distinguished between Jewish "Finance" and the "creative industry" dominated by gentiles. From the Rothschild family on down, Jews were "essentially money-lenders" who rarely had a "permanent interest" in production. Rather, they seized a commodity "at just the point in its passage from producer to consumer where the heaviest profit can be extracted. . . ." Squeezing the "neck of the bottle" in this way, they dominated the grain, copper, fur, and cotton markets. The rising national debt was another "measure of our enslavement." Furthermore, in 1913, Paul Warburg, a German Jew who had emigrated "for the express purpose of changing our financial system," convinced Congress to pass the Federal Reserve Act. The Federal Reserve Board helped the "banking aristocracy" to contract the money supply and centralize banking.[37]

As the "wonderful" *Protocols* made clear, political power complemented economic control. As early as 1860, August Belmont had chaired the Democratic National Committee. Exaggerating the group's unity, the *Independent* alleged that the Kehillah, a Jewish community council in New York that had begun to disintegrate by 1921, ruled the city through "gentile fronts" and sought to make the United States a "Jewish country." Bernard Baruch's willingness to advise diverse officials typified the Jew's opportunistic disregard for party allegiance. A purported boom for Justice Louis D. Brandeis in

1920 was intended to prepare the public for a Jewish president, "really a short step" from the Jews' current level of influence.[38]

Quoting testimony and statistics from the Senate investigation of Bolshevik activities, the *Independent* went beyond Dr. Simons's denunciation of Yiddish "apostates." It noted that Trotsky belonged to the Jewish "nationality" even though he spurned the religion, said that Communists sacked churches but left synagogues "untouched," and claimed that the soviet (like the New York Kehillah) was an adaptation of the ancient Hebrew kahal. Communism, of course, was a "carefully groomed investment" by Hebrew financiers. Furthermore, the erstwhile "East Sider" Trotsky had left a substantial "endowment" to the United States—a Bolshevik population larger than Russia's. In particular, the Wobblies, International Ladies' Garment Workers' Union, and Amalgamated Clothing Workers inculcated the "Jewish idea" of "getting" without "making," undermined craftsmanship, and threatened the "very cement" that held society together.[39]

Following the *Protocols'* plan to "split society by ideas," Jews or their dupes preached red doctrines in the classroom, wrote treatises to show that depressions were "good," and convinced publishers to keep "certain things out of the public mind and [put] certain things into it." The Jewish "passion for misleading" others, symbolized by their willingness to change their own names, led to the confusing "era of false labels." These machinations paled beside the various forms of moral corruption that the *Independent* examined at length, relating each to supposedly Jewish traits. For example, unlike the "true ring fighter" who took risks, boxer Benny Leonard boasted that he had never been scarred. Leonard and other Jews were "not sportsmen." Rather, they exploited sports for profit, even stooping to fix the 1919 World Series.[40]

The "gigantic Jewish liquor trust" illustrated pushiness and shoddy workmanship. Genteel gentiles had formerly practiced the "science and art" of distilling fine liquor. Ambitious Jews drove them out of business by selling "synthetic poison" under distinguished brand names. The temperance movement did not achieve total victory, the *Independent* said, because Jews were exempted from Prohibition. They were also the foremost bootleggers and their propagandists still promoted the "idea of drink" on stage and screen.[41]

No subject provoked greater anger than "Yiddish" entertainment. Recalling the simple classic, "Listen to the Mocking Bird," the *Independent* lamented, "The only 'birds' the people are encouraged to sing about today are 'flappers.'" In addition to eroticism, jazz and other "moron music" illustrated poor craftsmanship and Jewish responsibility for the "steady tendency toward systematization." Creative individuals had composed the "picturesque, romantic, clean" songs of the late nineteenth century; now "song factories" produced melodies in bulk. Mass acceptance of these "so-called" popular songs merely showed that anything "can be popularized by constant repetition."[42]

Similarly, since 1885, an odd collection of Jews had destroyed the theater's "natural genius." Movies were so "rotten" that no one contested the case against them. The *Independent* added to it, however, by tracing the "psychic poison and visual filth" to the subversive plot sketched in the *Protocols*. Along with "most other useful things," motion pictures had been invented by gentiles. Some Christian directors like D. W. Griffith still filled the screen with "delight and joy." However, as "usurpers" like Carl Laemmle of Universal Studios captured the industry, films joined music and the theater in sensuous decay. They caricatured Christian clergy, mocked rural life, praised Jewish immigrants, welcomed radicalism, and taught murder and safecracking. Hollywood's degradation proved that "oriental" Jews had failed to embrace the "Anglo-Saxon, the American view."[43]

Through four volumes, Jewish vices appeared as the reverse of any "American view." The dichotomies between making and getting, morality and sensuality, fair trade and chicanery, "creative labor" and exploitation, heroism and cowardice were only the beginning. Some of the most important differences impinged on politics. Anglo-Saxons had created the press to prevent secret domination by any minority, but Jews twisted news for their own advantage. Democratic procedures were another Anglo-Saxon inheritance; Jews "instinctively" favored autocracy. One of the "higher traits" of "our race" fostered obliviousness to Hebrew machinations. Eschewing conspiracies themselves, Anglo-Saxons neither expected them among other groups nor followed the available clues "through long and devious and darkened channels."[44]

Above all, gentiles advanced by individual initiative, while Jews took advantage of unprecedented "racial loyalty and solidarity." Because success—a preeminent American and "Fordian" value—could "not be attacked nor condemned [*sic*]", the *Independent* hesitated to criticize Jews for doing "extraordinarily" well. Neither could it concede superiority to another "race." In essence, therefore, the newspaper cried foul. Because Jews took advantage of their position as an "international nation," it was "difficult to measure gentile and Jewish achievement by the same standard." Jews captured the "highest places" only because they began with an unfair advantage.[45]

The *Independent* said that Jewish solidarity required "one rule for the Gentile and one for the Jews." In fact, the newspaper itself not surprisingly held to the double standard. It condemned acts by Jews that, if committed by Christians, would have been considered innocuous, legitimate, or admirable. The wartime ban on the German language and the fundamentalist effort to drive Darwinism from the classroom were acceptable; Jewish objection to *The Merchant of Venice* violated "American principles." George Creel's chairmanship of the Committee on Public Information did not prompt a discussion of Protestant traits; Carl Laemmle's production of *The Beast of Berlin* for the same committee was a "lurid" attempt to profit from war. Jacob Schiff's use of dollar diplomacy on behalf of Russian Jews seemed sinister; efforts by E. H. Harriman to squeeze concession from the Czar passed without comment. Similarly, Irish-American agitation about the Versailles Treaty went unremarked; Jewish concern elicited complaints about the "kosher conference." The immigrant's willingness to change his name was seen as evidence of duplicity, not of a desire to assimilate.[46]

In addition to assuming the worst, the *Independent* singled out Jewish participants in any endeavor and concluded that they were *acting as Jews*. But although Paul Warburg, for example, did play a major role in the passage of the Federal Reserve Act, he acted on behalf of major bankers of all faiths.[47] Although the War Industries Board did create a "system of control such as the United States government never possessed," Chairman Baruch believed that the general welfare was synonymous with capitalism, not Judaism.[48] Jews may have been represented disproportionately in the Soviet hierarchy, but they used their positions to further Marxist ends, including the secularization of Russian Jewry; almost none of the "Yiddish" Bolsheviks spoke Yiddish.[49] Jacob Schiff's objections to the

Russian-American commercial treaty would have meant little if out-rage among grass roots and elite gentiles had not moved three hundred members of the House of Representatives to agree with him.[50]

The disposition to single out Jews and to create a separate standard for them derived from three circumstances. First, as Irving Howe notes, Jewish immigrants from Eastern Europe were "radically different" from the dominant Protestant culture. The *Independent* was incensed by this lack of "conformity" to the nation's "determining ideals and ideas"; the recent arrivals seemed to think that the United States was "not any definite thing yet."[51] Second, as John Higham argues, Jews attracted special attention because they were relatively more successful—and thus more visible—than other groups in the "new immigration."[52]

Third, despite professed indifference to Jewish religious practices, the *Independent* supposed that acceptance of the nation's ideals meant acquiescence in its "predominant Christian character." Jews, however, were determined "to wipe out of public life" every Christian reference. Their "impertinent interferences" included contempt for Sunday blue laws and protests against Christmas celebrations and Bible reading in public schools. Louis Marshall, president of the American Jewish Committee, even said that the United States was "not a Christian country." Such actions by a race that had had "no hand" in building the nation naturally stirred a "whirlwind of resentment."[53]

From this matter-of-fact amalgamation of Christianity and "one hundred percent Americanism," the *Independent* moved on to theology. The transition was easy for Cameron, who had preached occasionally, without benefit of ordination, to a "people's church" in Brooklyn, Michigan. Accepting the mangled history and biblical exegesis of the Anglo-Israelite Federation, Cameron believed that contemporary Anglo-Saxons had descended from the lost tribes of Israel. Hence they were "chosen" to receive the blessings that God had promised to Abraham's progeny. But this divine choice of Israel did not extend to Judea, or to the Jewish offspring of the two southern tribes. On the contrary, Anglo-Israelites were often hostile to contemporary Jews.[54]

Fred Black speculated that Cameron's Anglo-Israelism had prepared him to accept conspiratorial anti-Semitism. Certainly the editor's faith gave a peculiar twist to the discussion of religion in *The International Jew.* Citing the *Protocols'* injunction to undermine the clergy, the *Independent* blamed Jews for biblical criticism and "liberal" Protestantism, a typically mislabeled doctrine that reduced Jesus to a "well-meaning but wholly mistaken Jewish prophet." Discriminating between Israel and the rebellious Judeans, the weekly said that Jesus was not Jewish in the modern sense of the word. Neither was Moses or any disciple—except Judas Iscariot. Fundamentalists also read the Bible through "Jewish spectacles" when they confused modern Hebrews with God's chosen people. Not only did Jews reject Christ, but they abandoned the Old Testament in favor of the Talmud's "rabbinical speculation." Instead of fulfilling the prophetic promise of a return to Jerusalem, as many fundamentalists supposed, Zionism represented the "Bolshevist spirit all over again."[55]

In the broadest sense, then, the *Independent* presented the "Jewish question" as a contest between two peoples, each supposing that God was on its side. There was "no idea deeper in Judaism" than the belief in divine election. But, the newspaper protested, the "Anglo-Saxon Celtic race" was the "Ruling People, chosen throughout the centuries to Master the world." Beneath the bragging, however, there lay a hint of the insecurity that typically fueled nativism in the 1920s. On the one hand, Yankees could beat Jews "any time" in a fair fight. Still, the Kehillah's "extraordinary unity" was impressive. Unpatriotic American "mongrels" and "lick spittle Gentile Fronts who have no tribe . . . would be better off if they had one-thousandth the racial sense which the Jew possesses."[56]

The *Independent* maintained that its pages contained "NO AT-TACK . . . ON THE JEWS AS JEWS" (though it was not always possible to "distinguish the group" deserving censure). Occasionally the weekly made ostentatious efforts to sound fair. It quoted admirable (meaning unobtrusive) Jews, admitted that Paul Warburg's Federal Reserve Act contained "important improvements," and recognized Bernard Baruch's intelligence and energy. On 7 January 1922, a "candid address" to Jews urged them to recover Old Testament morality and practice "social responsibility." If Jews stopped trying "to twist Americanism into something else," they could participate without objection in finance, entertainment, and government.[57]

The newspaper's remedies for the "world's foremost problem" combined faith in expertise, national unity, and publicity. A "scientific study of the Jewish Question" would forestall prejudice by transforming gentile assailants and Jewish defenders "both into investigators." Research by "qualified persons" would yield "society's point of view," which, the *Independent* claimed, was the perspective taken in its pages. In the interim, to combat Jewish adulteration of products, a consumer movement should "educate people in the art of buying." Most important, "clear publicity" must be the "chief weapon" against the Hebrew cabal. Their program would then be "checked the moment it is perceived and identified." Russia, Germany, and England had failed to solve the "Jewish Question," but the United States would succeed—without violence.[58]

While new installments of *The International Jew* continued to unroll in its pages, the *Independent* collected in book form most of the articles that had already appeared; sometimes 200,000 copies were printed in a single edition. The staff sent complimentary volumes to locally influential citizens, especially clergymen, bankers, and stockbrokers.[59]

To supplement *The International Jew,* the *Independent* ran "Jewish World Notes." This regular feature charged that Madame Curie was treated less well in New York than the spurious Jewish scientist Albert Einstein, chided evangelist Billy Sunday for ignorance of the Elders' conspiracy, derided Zionist immigration to Palestine, and feared that President-elect Warren G. Harding, like his predecessors, was falling under Jewish influence. The *Independent* also kept up persistent attacks on alcohol, tobacco, movies, comic books, jazz, Wobblies, Soviets, and immigration. Simultaneously looking to Ford's financial interests, editor Cameron promoted highway construction, opposed federal aid to railroads, and looked greedily toward Muscle Shoals. In 1922, as Ford began to covet the presidency, his newspaper dutifully emphasized the inadequacy of other possible nominees.[60]

Yet the *Independent* had not become merely a compendium of anti-Semitism and other Ford causes. The paper still published travelogues, Western Americana, and portraits of prominent persons. Nor were editorials uniformly intolerant. The weekly applauded women's suffrage, favored the appointment of public defenders, urged federal legislation to halt lynching, asked President Wilson to pardon Eugene V. Debs, and praised Harding for doing so. Occasionally departing from its harsh nativism, the *Independent* said that close relatives of prewar immigrants should be allowed to join them.[61]

When the staff forgot that Jews were supposed to control everything, the *Independent* contained insightful commentary. Thus readers could believe astute analyses of Harding's mediocrity, or they could believe that he was a tool of the "court Jew," advertising executive Albert D. Lasker. The treatment of Harding's predecessor was even more perplexing. *The International Jew* said that "Semitic princes" had manipulated Wilson at Versailles; elsewhere the *Independent* endorsed his diplomacy and denounced "barbaric" Senators who disagreed. When Wilson died in 1924, "Mr. Ford's Page" said that he would "doubtless rank with our greatest presidents."[62]

* * *

If the *Independent* had offered only a perverse mixture of reform, eccentricity, internationalism, and nativism, it would have attracted relatively little attention. But *The International Jew* was extraordinary even during what Higham called the "tribal twenties." Opponents mobilized quickly. The Federal Council of Churches condemned the articles in December 1920. A month later, without specifically mentioning Ford, 119 prominent Christians, including William Howard Taft, Woodrow Wilson, and Cardinal William O'Connell, signed "The Perils of Racial Prejudice," a statement asking gentiles to halt the "vicious propaganda" against Jews. Officials in several cities considered censoring the *Independent* or removed it from public libraries.[63]

At first many Jews wondered, as Louis Marshall asked, if *The International Jew* had Ford's personal "sanction." Returning Ford's annual gift, a new sedan, his former neighbor Rabbi Leo Franklin warned Ford that he was inflicting harm on innocent people. Similarly, Herman Bernstein, a voyager on *Oscar II*, appealed to the automaker's "humanitarian" nature. But even after Jewish spokesmen recognized the depth of Ford's commitment to the anti-Semitic campaign, they disagreed on countermeasures. Following an initial protest, Marshall worked behind the scenes, sponsoring Bernstein's rebuttal, *The History of a Lie,* recruiting signers for "The Peril of Racial Prejudice," and in mid-1921 urging President Harding to intervene. Others preferred more militant tactics. The *American Hebrew* challenged Ford to abide by an impartial investigation, attorneys for the B'nai B'rith Anti-Defamation League advocated laws against the collective libel of groups, Yiddish newspapers rejected advertisements for Ford cars, and individual Jews refused to buy them.[64]

On the other hand, journalist W. J. Abbot expressed "sympathy" with Ford's views and critic John J. Chapman hailed the "lucidity and good temper" of Volume 2. C. Mobray White, an "authority" on revolution for the National Civil Federation, urged supplementary publication of the *Protocols.* According to Liebold, J. P. Morgan, Jr., liked the series. The number of *Independent* readers fluctuated widely over short periods because Ford dealers, who were ordered to sell the paper, showed little enthusiasm for the task. It appears, however, that *The International Jew* temporarily attracted new subscribers.[65]

Liebold responded to protests and praise. Agreeing with the *Independent* that good Jews had "nothing to fear," he urged them to join Ford's crusade against the worldwide peril. But his supercilious tone was hardly reassuring. He accused Marshall of sounding like a "Bolshevik orator," lectured Rabbi Franklin on the importance of principles, and generally praised the newspaper's reliance on "actual facts." Conversely, he thanked friends of *The International Jew* and encouraged their efforts, telling C. Mobray White, for example, that there was "quite a field" for distribution of the *Protocols.* Occasionally he was forced to retreat. "Amazed" by the accusation that he had been Wilson's Jewish "mouthpiece," columnist David Lawrence wrote to Ford, whom he considered a friend. A testy exchange followed with Liebold, the perennial shield, who finally said that the automaker had "no knowledge" of the articles relating to Lawrence.[66]

Indeed, consistently distancing his employer from *The International Jew,* Liebold answered protests in his own name and testified in 1924 that Ford devoted his time to the company's "numerous and complex" operations. The *Independent* promoted the same fiction. Because Cameron explicitly attacked Jews on every page except "Mr. Ford's Page," devoted admirers could believe that Ford was too busy making cars to supervise his own newspaper. The strategy was transparent, but it laid the groundwork for his face-saving retraction in 1927.[67]

Protected by Liebold, Ford may have been unaware of the nationwide protests. Nevertheless, he ordered Cameron in January 1922 to discontinue *The International Jew.* According to Pipp, he realized that the articles hurt both company sales and his amorphous ambition to achieve the presidency. Upton Sinclair said that Ford backed down in order to avoid a counterattack by filmmaker William Fox. Scholars and associates have also attributed decisive influence to Edsel Ford, Thomas Edison, Arthur Brisbane, and President Harding (who dispatched an emissary to Dearborn in mid-1921).[68]

None of the explanations is fully convincing. Subtle pressure by friends, family, and the White House may have moved Ford, but direct threats by Fox—or anyone else—would have made him more stubborn. Unlike his distributors, moreover, Ford ignored the shrinking market for Model Ts, even when the decline had nothing to do with politics. Unfortunately, Ford was no more able than later scholars and journalists to provide an adequate rationale for his action. He offered at least three explanations. In *My Life and Work,* an autobiography composed with Samuel Crowther, he sounded practical. Reports on the "Jewish Question" could cease "for the time" because Americans now knew enough to "grasp the key." Speaking to the journalist Allan Benson, he struck an altruistic note. There was, he said, "too much anti-Semitic feeling." If the series continued, then "something might happen to the Jews. I do not want any harm to come to them." Finally, Ford told Cameron that he needed Jews "on our side" in order to abolish the money standard that they had created. A week after *The International Jew* ceased on 14 January 1922, the *Independent* began an exposé of money and banking.[69]

The pause did not mean that Ford had begun to doubt the existence of a Jewish conspiracy. He still raised the matter in interviews. In addition, Liebold's agents collected fresh material that, Pipp warned, Ford would order into print "whenever the whim may strike him again." Apparently the whim struck within a year. In November 1922, anti-Semitic references resurfaced in the *Independent.*[70]

Scholars pay slight attention to this second wave even though attacks on Jews appeared regularly until 1925. Most themes, including occasional allusions to powerless "worthy" Jews, had appeared before. Instead of an eccentric historical survey, however, the *Independent* now stressed current issues, such as the Dawes Plan (a "subtle scheme" to enrich the Warburgs) and the murder trial of Nathan Leopold and Richard Loeb (proof that judges favored rich Jews). After Ford declined to seek the presidency and endorsed Calvin Coolidge in December 1923, the *Independent* discerned Jewish influence behind Coolidge's rivals, especially Senators Hiram Johnson and Robert LaFollette. Through the winter and spring of 1922–1923, the most vicious articles accused Army Captain Robert Rosenbluth of murdering his gentile superior, Major Alexander Cronkhite. Although the Army ruled that Cronkhite had accidentally shot himself, the *Independent* considered the case, in which Louis Marshall and Felix Warburg aided the defense, an example of Jewish defiance of "Anglo-Saxon law."[71]

The newspaper simultaneously applauded gentiles, including President Lowell of Harvard, who showed signs of discovering the "Jewish Question." The search for kindred spirits even transcended a powerful grudge. When Ford's old adversary, the *Chicago Tribune,* complained of excessive Jewish influence, the *Independent* exulted, "We no longer feel like a lone voice crying in the Wilderness."[72]

Starting in April 1924, the *Independent* focused on "Jewish Exploitation of Farmers' Organizations," and on Aaron Sapiro, the alleged chief exploiter. After serving as counsel to the California marketing bureau, Sapiro began in 1919 to organize farm cooperatives in other states. Within four years, he created the National Council of Farmer's Cooperative Marketing Associations, whose constituent groups represented 700,000 farmers. Presidents Harding and Coolidge, Secretary of Commerce Herbert Hoover, former Governor Frank O. Lowden of Illinois, and Senator Arthur Capper (Republican of Kansas), leader of the congressional farm bloc, encouraged Sapiro and sometimes provided substantial assistance. By 1923, however, many cooperative associations had collapsed and enthusiasm began to ebb among farmers. In 1926 the National Council quietly disbanded.[73]

Despite his organizational ability, legal skill, and personal magnetism, Sapiro's strategy had many weaknesses. He underestimated the complexity of marketing, acted hastily, appointed several inept managers, and ridiculed competing agricultural spokesmen. In the final analysis, moreover, the agricultural depression of the 1920s was beyond his control. Efficient cooperatives provided a means to withhold crops from sale temporarily; they could not permanently raise prices and profits as long as world markets remained glutted. Probably Sapiro's greatest mistake was to promise a panacea when, at best, he offered a palliative.[74]

Believing that Sapiro's Jewish background was "incidental," Fred Black and some other members of the *Independent* staff had wanted to concentrate on defects in his program. Once again it is hard to fix responsibility for the final anti-Semitic emphasis. In 1927, Cameron testified that protest letters from farmers had prompted the series, "Jewish Exploitation." Most of the articles were signed by "Robert Morgan," a pseudonym for Harry H. Dunn. Dunn, who had worked for the *Christian Science Monitor,* the *Boston Post,* and the Hearst chain, wrote frequently for the *Independent.* In this instance, Cameron edited Dunn's articles and apparently wrote some anonymous supplements. Liebold later claimed that he had tried to delete libelous material. If Cameron's recollection is correct, however, Ford had urged him to shun moderation in order to provoke a suit.[75]

In keeping with the *Independent*'s peculiar combination of insight and prejudice, the series mixed sound agricultural economics and absurd allegations of Jewish conspiracy. The weekly chided cooperatives for tending to augment production in an already glutted market, noted Sapiro's occasional mismanagement and exaggerated promises, and claimed in January 1925 that the criticism had "nothing whatever" to do with his religion. But plausible analysis appeared less frequently than assertions that Sapiro rationalized agriculture in order to profit "international Jewry" generally and himself in particular. In the process, he hired "reds" to coerce growers, disrupted the American Farm Bureau Federation, and manipulated "Gentile Fronts" (including Secretary Hoover). He wanted ultimately to unify agriculture in a "Jewish 'holding company.'"[76]

Sapiro was a natural target. Cherishing the myth of the sturdy Christian farmer, the *Independent* and its publisher assumed that Jews entered agriculture only as greedy middlemen. Ford joked that he would pay $1,000 to anyone who brought in a Jewish farmer "dead or alive." Moreover, farm cooperatives fostered the "steady trend toward systematization" deplored in *The International Jew.* And Sapiro's financial backers included two of *The International Jew*'s foremost villains, Bernard Baruch and Eugene Meyer, Jr.[77]

Still the *Independent*'s assault had an ironic aspect because Ford and Sapiro shared more common ground than either realized. Like Ford, Sapiro cherished farming as a virtuous way of life untainted by radicalism or federal planning. Furthermore, he too was a proud man who resented attacks on his character. In January 1925, therefore, Sapiro sent a thirty-one-page letter to Ford and his associates, demanding a retraction of "Jewish Exploitation." When the *Independent* refused to comply, he sued Ford and the Dearborn Publishing Company for $1 million in order to vindicate "myself and my race."[78]

Sapiro's was the third suit provoked by Ford's anti-Semitism. In January 1921, Morris Gest had sought $5 million in damages because the *Independent* accused him of producing lewd plays. Two years later Herman Bernstein had filed a complaint denying that he had told Ford of an international Jewish conspiracy. Neither case came to trial. Nor did they alter the newspaper's course. Yet, as part of a new look that included respectful articles on Sinclair Lewis and Sigmund Freud, after 1925 the *Independent* reduced its anti-Semitism to occasional sniping.[79]

The last extended treatment, "What About the Jewish Question?," appeared in March, 1926. Asserting that contributors had eschewed "sensational" or "arousing" material, the *Independent* denied having been anti-Semitic. On the contrary, by pointing to faults, it had acted as a "rather courageous friend to Jews." The *Independent* affirmed the right of Jews to participate in national life "on equal terms with others" as long as they adopted American ideals. Finally, since wise members of the "race" had come to understand this principle, additional discussion of Jewish power was no longer necessary.[80]

* * *

"What About the Jewish Question?" was an apologia, not an apology. The *Independent* repudiated *The International Jew* only after Sapiro pressed the issue. In March 1927, his suit alleging 141 libels by Ford and the Dearborn Publishing Company began in U.S. District Court in Detroit. Opening for the plaintiff, attorney William Henry Gallagher called the *Independent* Ford's "mouthpiece" and held him responsible for malicious attacks on "Sapiro and his race." The defense, led by Senator James A. Reed, a conservative Democrat from Missouri, responded that the weekly had a "moral duty" to expose Sapiro as a "grafter, faker, fraud, and cheat." The *Independent's* discussion of Jews was irrelevant, Reed added, because the law did not recognize libel of a "race"; Sapiro raised the religious issue merely to "capitalize" on sympathy. Finally, making the familiar distinction between Ford and his newspaper, Reed said that the automaker had not read the series on Sapiro "to this blessed day."[81]

On 18 March, Gallagher called Cameron as his first witness. During six and a half days on the stand, Cameron was determined to protect his employer and save his job even if he had to skate on the edge of perjury. Ford, he conceded, "dropped in from time to time," sometimes discussing public issues "in a general way." Yet he gave wide latitude to the *Independent* staff. Cameron might have "mentioned" the Sapiro series to him. It was more likely, however, that Ford had known nothing until the victim protested. When Cameron tried to explain the articles at that time, Ford waved his hand and gave the "usual formula: You're the editor. Get the facts. Be sure you are right."[82]

Gallagher prodded the witness to say that Ford had initiated the "general series" attacking a supposed Jewish "International ring." Defense counsel rescued Cameron with the persistent objection that "you can't libel a race." Gallagher countered that the *Independent* had "aggravated" the libel of Sapiro by presenting him as an ally of Baruch, Meyer, and others maligned in *The International Jew.* Judge Fred S. Raymond admitted discussion of specific Jews who were Sapiro's alleged henchmen, but overruled evidence relating to the newspaper's broad anti-Semitic campaign. This restriction allowed Cameron to dodge direct answers and preserved the illusion of Ford's aloofness. For example, with the possible exception of "one or two" references to Baruch, the editor recalled no conversation with Ford about "any article on any Jew." He did not add that Ford had spoken often if vaguely about Jews and encouraged him to fill in the details. Nor did he mention that Liebold, not Ford, typically conveyed orders from the front office.[83]

The rival attorneys were skilled and well-matched. Gallagher raised doubts about Cameron's sobriety and Ford's intelligence. On the other hand, defense objections excluded from evidence letters to Ford protesting inaccuracies in "Jewish Exploitation of Farmers' Organizations." Gallagher called James Martin Miller, a former *Independent* employee, to testify that Ford personally had charged Sapiro with manipulating agriculture for a "bunch of Jews." Asking one question to reveal that Miller had sued for back pay, Reed dismissed him: *"That's* all." The two sides persistently clashed over Gallagher's effort to broaden the discussion of anti-Semitism. Poking fun at the defense's "extraordinary sensitiveness" to the word "Jew," Gallagher said that comparable "apprehension" three years earlier would have made the suit unnecessary.[84]

After Gallagher traced his client's rise from an orphanage to eminence, Reed cross-examined Sapiro for two bitter weeks in April. Counsel badgered the witness and deliberately mispronounced his name. Sapiro responded with a mixture of confidence, retaliatory sarcasm, and occasional loss of temper. The two wrangled over Baruch's standing as an economist and Governor Lowden's credentials as a farmer. Moving through a long list of cooperative associations, Reed accused Sapiro of profiteering. In language Ford might have chosen, Sapiro answered that money meant less to him than the farmer's welfare.[85]

Although the press predicted testimony by Baruch, Lowden, and Meyer, none of them was called. The most famous figure in the case also avoided an appearance. At first, Ford planned to take the stand. Then, perhaps recalling his humiliation during the *Chicago Tribune* trial, he changed his mind and walled himself off from process servers. Company officials claimed that a subpoena intended for Ford was mistakenly presented to his brother. After Gallagher threatened to begin contempt proceedings, Ford's lawyers said that he would speak voluntarily. On 31 March, however, he was apparently the victim of a strange accident. A Studebaker sedan forced Ford's car off the road and down a fifteen-foot embankment. The automaker was taken to Henry Ford Hospital, where he was treated and shielded by friendly physicians.[86]

Sapiro suggested that Ford had "faked" the accident, which has never been fully explained, because his "vanity was punctured at the collapse of his case." Indeed, sensing the jury's skepticism, defense lawyers did fear the verdict. On 11 April using reports from some of the fifty Ford Service agents who prowled through the courthouse, they told Judge Raymond that a juror, Mrs. Cora Hoffman, had lied during the voir dire and later was offered a bribe by a Jew who wanted to convict Ford. Because Mrs. Hoffman's vehement denials appeared in the press, Raymond granted a defense motion of mistrial on 21 April. The court scheduled a retrial for 12 September as lawyers continued to spar. Valuing Raymond's restrictions on discussion of the "Jewish Question," Reed blocked Gallagher's attempt to change judges.[87]

Judge Raymond adhered to the legal fiction that the *Independent*'s attack on Jews was largely irrelevant to the suit, but Ford himself knew better. By repudiating *The International Jew,* he could open the way to an out-of-court settlement and avoid testifying. During a meeting on 11 May with Arthur Brisbane, who remained friendly even though the *Independent* had labeled him a "gentile front," Ford mentioned his decision to close the newspaper. At roughly the same time, he told Joseph Palma, head of the United States Secret Service field office in New York, that he had underestimated the impact of the Jewish series; he wanted the "wrong righted." Serving as Ford's emissaries, Palma and Earl J. Davis, a former assistant attorney general, met secretly with Louis Marshall of the American Jewish Committee. On 9 July, Ford announced through Brisbane that "articles reflecting upon the Jews" would "never again" appear in the *Independent.* Liebold, Cameron, and Edsel Ford had known nothing of the negotiations.[88]

The retraction, written by Marshall, allowed Ford to slip through the loophole held open since 1920 by Liebold, Cameron, and a formidable array of lawyers. Ford said that he had failed to "keep informed" about the actions of his newspaper. Thus he was "deeply mortified" to learn that the *Independent* had printed a series based on the "gross forgeries," the *Protocols of Zion.* "Fully aware of the virtues of the Jewish People," he begged their forgiveness, promised to withdraw *The International Jew* from circulation, and pledged "future friendship and good will." Marshall considered the statement "humiliating" and was surprised that Ford accepted it.[89]

Sapiro and Bernstein quickly dropped their suits in return for apologies and reimbursement of legal expenses. On 30 July, the charge that Sapiro had belonged to an international conspiracy was formally "withdrawn" by the *Independent;* the weekly claimed to have accepted Harry Dunn's articles "at face value," only later to learn of their "inaccuracies." Following the usual strategy, the editorial said that Ford had had "no personal knowledge" of the series. Sapiro pronounced himself "entirely satisfied," evidently embraced the illusion that Ford had been "misled," and claimed credit for helping a "great man get right."[90]

* * *

Unfortunately the apologies of 1927, like the remission of 1922, did not mean that Ford had "got right." He closed the *Independent* on 30 December 1927 but—contrary to his lawyers' promise to Marshall—kept Liebold and Cameron, both unrepentant, in his employ. He ordered destruction of thousands of copies of *The International Jew* yet, despite entreaties by Marshall and Bernstein, barely publicized his retraction in Europe. His subordinates intervened to halt circulation abroad only when pressed by Jewish leaders. Furthermore, Ford informed the *Manchester Guardian* in 1940 that "international Jewish bankers" had caused World War II. At roughly the same time, he told the nativist Gerald L. K. Smith that he had allowed Bennett to forge his signature on the retraction, hoped some day to reissue *The International Jew,* and urged Smith to do so if he could not.[91]

Partly due to Ford's laxity, the series continued to circulate among the "rabid Jew baiters" whom the *Independent* had professed to disdain. Historian Norman Cohn estimates that *The International Jew* "probably did more than any other work to make the *Protocols* world-famous." The Nazi youth leader Baldur von Schirach recalled the "great influence" of the books on young Germans of his generation. In *Mein Kampf,* Adolf Hitler applauded Ford's efforts. Within the United States, *The International Jew* provided a usable past for anti-Semites like Smith, who ultimately published an abridged edition. As early as 1922, Norman Hapgood angrily held Ford responsible for setting "loose a malicious force that added fury to similar forces already in existence."[92]

Such anger is justified but insufficient. In addition, analysis of *The International Jew* and its supplements illuminates attitudes toward Jews as well as broader aspects of our culture. First, the text undermines the assumption shared by writers as diverse as Handlin, Higham, and McWilliams that Christian belief and practice hardly influenced anti-Semitism in the United States. *The International Jew* was imbued with Ford's faith that the national "genius" was "Christian in the broadest sense" and destined to remain so. The series portrayed a clash between two "chosen" peoples, and Cameron, the chief compiler, sometimes cast the conflict in terms of Anglo-Israelite theology. Although we cannot infer the attitudes of a complex society from motifs in a single literary source, there is warrant for paying closer attention to the Christian roots of American anti-Semitism.[93]

Second, a reading of *The International Jew* prompts yet another consideration of the much-debated relationship among "populism," "progressivism," and anti-Semitism. Though problematical, the terms "populist" and "progressive" retain utility if used with care. Despite their differing views of settlement houses or strikes, progressives applauded or accepted an economy dominated by corporations and at most wanted to make a hierarchical society more efficient and humane. Two decades earlier, the People's party and its sympathizers had raised more basic questions. They had doubted that the triumph of the "trust" was either inevitable or beneficial. Populism appealed to poor farmers and some urban workers, whereas the various progressive coalitions drew primarily from the middle and upper middle classes. During the 1890s, Populism never achieved respectability. Before World War I, progressivism became the catchword of the day.[94]

Recognizing the limits of these broad categories, we can nonetheless dispute the designation of Ford as a "populist" by Peter F. Drucker, Morton Rosenstock, Allan Nevins, Frank Ernest Hill, Richard Hofstadter, Reynold Wik, and David Lewis. Anne Jardim aptly notes that Ford, the son of a prosperous Republican untainted by agrarian radicalism, worked quietly in Detroit during the embattled 1890s. Moreover, there is no reason to suppose that *Independent* subscribers were aging veterans of the People's party. Most lived in Ohio, Pennsylvania, and Michigan, states where the Populist nominee, General James B. Weaver, had run poorly in 1892.[95]

The newspaper's presidential poll in 1920 is also revealing. Of the six leading candidates—Senator Hiram Johnson, Herbert Hoover,

Leonard Wood, Frank O. Lowden, President Wilson, and Secretary of the Treasury William G. McAdoo—only McAdoo identified in some sense with Populism and several others had specifically condemned the People's party. William Jennings Bryan, an erstwhile Populist nominee, ran a poor third among Democratic prospects; Senator Robert LaFollette, a recently radicalized insurgent, received only scattered support.[96]

While Ford and *Independent* editor Cameron remained aloof from Populism, their weekly explicitly endorsed "sane progressivism." The adjective may seem inappropriate, but the general identification makes sense. Ford contributed $36,000 to Woodrow Wilson's campaign in 1916 and was convinced by the President to run for senator two years later. Throughout the 1920s, he was hailed as the preeminent business statesman whose commitment to efficiency, social service, and paternal labor relations promised industrial peace. Certainly *The International Jew* contained characteristic progressive themes. For example, adapting a growing consumer movement to its anti-Semitic ends, the *Independent* urged a boycott of Jewish merchants. Furthermore, the "Jewish Question" must be subjected to "scientific study" by experts.[97]

The most striking progressive legacy was *The International Jew*'s assertion that "clear publicity" was an American alternative to Jewish disfranchisement or pogroms. Richard Hofstadter observed that progressive intellectuals, scholars and journalists alike, "confirmed, if they did not create a fresh mode of criticism" that purported to uncover "reality." They believed that "reality" was "hidden, neglected, and off stage," something to be dug out from under superficial explanations. Norman Hapgood shrewdly saw that Ford's detectives "muckraked" Jews and suspected Jews. Ford apparently shared the *Independent*'s faith in publicity. In *My Life and Work,* he maintained that the Jewish threat could be "controlled by mere exposure."[98]

Instead of revealing a pernicious Populist legacy, the *Independent*'s anti-Semitic campaigns underscore the diversity within progressivism, a persuasion so diffuse that both Ford and Aaron Sapiro plausibly identified with it. Indeed, for historians who ponder the fate of reform after World War I, their confrontation must be considered something more than a dramatic nativist episode. In addition, the battle between Sapiro and Ford, two nationally known reformers, symbolizes the fragmentation of the progressive "movement" during the 1920s.[99]

From a narrow perspective, the historiographical debate about "populist" anti-Semitism concerned the number of bigots in the People's party and related agrarian protests. Yet such pluralists as Handlin, Hofstadter, and Seymour Martin Lipset were simultaneously making assertions about how ideas, in this case prejudiced ideas, moved within society. At least implicitly, they repudiated Carey McWilliams's contention that anti-Semitism "must be studied from the top down and not from the bottom up." Rather, with varying sophistication, they maintained that hostility to Jews primarily pressed upward from a "populist" mass.[100]

After clearing away jargon about "status anxiety," we should scarcely be surprised that provincials who fear social or cultural change are more likely than their comfortable, cosmopolitan fellows to seek scapegoats and embrace conspiracy theories. While repeating this truism for three decades, however, scholars have slighted the elite contribution to anti-Semitic rhetoric. Many images used by the *Independent* to document alleged Jewish failings were shared by—or borrowed from—Harvard President A. Lawrence Lowell, Professor Edward A. Ross, novelist Kenneth Roberts, and muckraker Burton J. Hendrick. Such urbane progressives and conservatives should not be absolved of responsibility simply because they rejected *The International Jew*'s sweeping conspiracy theory and the Klansman's vulgar agitation. Moreover, because the boundary between "polite" and conspiratorial anti-Semitism has been porous, we must no longer pass over McWilliams's admonition to start investigation at the top.[101]

Third, an interpretation of *The International Jew* helps to sort out "crucial differences in the variety of things called anti-Semitism."[102] The *Independent* distinguished its answers to the "Jewish Question"—consumer protection, scientific study, and publicity—from violent European solutions. Ford himself claimed only to oppose "false ideas," called hatred of individuals "neither American nor Christian," and remained personally fond of several Jews, including the architect Albert Kahn, baseball player Hank Greenberg, and Rabbi Leo Franklin; he was perplexed by Franklin's refusal of a sedan in 1920 to protest *The International Jew*. These actions by Ford and his newspaper, though eccentric or self-serving, nevertheless point to complexities within nativism during the tribal twenties.[103]

A venerable nativist position, presented eloquently in Josiah Strong's 1886 polemic, *Our Country,* held that the "new immigration," including Jews, was *culturally* regressive and therefore must be taught superior Anglo-Saxon ways. The racial theorists who gained prominence after 1900 held that the "new immigration," including those whom Kenneth Roberts called "mongoloid" Jews, was *innately* inferior and therefore incapable of learning Anglo-Saxon ways. Whereas Strong suggested that "our country" might benefit from a blend of "races" under Anglo-Saxon guidance, Madison Grant, the premier "Nordic" ideologue in 1916, insisted that assimilation would backfire, producing a "mongrel" nation. Although the doctrine of inherent racial inferiority never fully superseded the earlier tradition, by the 1920s most nativists mixed the two attitudes in varying proportions. For example, Ford and the *Independent* sometimes ascribed behavior by Eastern European immigrants to "nasty orientalism" or "Tartar" origins. More often, however, they complained that these Jews refused to be like Anglo-Saxons. In the final analysis, *The International Jew,* the major nativist tract of the 1920s, was closer to Strong's assimilationist ethnocentrism than to Grant's biological determinism.[104]

The distinction may provide little comfort to victims of discrimination (though in the long run they gain from it), but it does suggest that the nation's broadly liberal tradition even affects our nativists. Hence, they are more likely than counterparts in Germany or France to judge ethnic targets, in this case Jews, on the basis of individual behavior instead of putative genetic traits. Significantly, the *Independent* did not concur in the basic premise of *Mein Kampf,* that all Jews betrayed "definite racial characteristics." Of course our sweeping generalization about attitudes in several countries requires qualification. Baldur von Schirach probably read *Mein Kampf* and *The International Jew* without noticing major discrepancies. And we still need systematic comparative studies before reaching firm conclusions about bigotry on two—or more—continents. In the interim, however, scholars should be wary of superficial parallels between American nativism and foreign Nazi and Fascist movements.[105]

Fourth, we must ask how thousands, perhaps hundreds of thousands, of readers could believe *The International Jew's* far-fetched thesis that a worldwide Jewish network threatened their way of life. Richard Hofstadter maintained that adherents to such conspiracy theories betray a "paranoid style," a frame of mind qualitatively different from normal thinking. Indeed, the notion that bigots comprise a psychologically abnormal fringe is not only popular among both pluralist scholars and their leftist critics, but also comforting to lay men and women unconcerned with social science method. It is nonetheless misleading. Much as they exaggerate the tolerance of the dominant culture, leading scholars also mistakenly assume that it was imbued with their own version of liberal or radical rationalism. During the 1920s, however, following a government-sponsored war scare and Red Scare, belief in some sort of conspiracy theory may have been the norm instead of an aberration. In this context, *The International Jew's* perverse accomplishment was to combine the inchoate anti-Semitism of the progressive era with the growing postwar fear of hidden forces.[106]

To be sure, belief in a cabal of Zionist elders (as opposed to conspiracies by Huns and Bolsheviks) was not endorsed by the federal government or by a majority of the population. Still we cannot assume that conspiratorial anti-Semites were pathological. In the past three decades some social scientists have rediscovered an old insight from the sociology of knowledge: that much of what we know rests on the authority of others and remains plausible only as long as they confirm it. But these significant "others" need not represent the whole society. In the United States, semiautonomous cultures have often nurtured unconventional world views in the face of sensible objections by outsiders. Among such "cognitive minorities," to use sociologist Peter Berger's term, normality may require belief in *The Book of Mormon, Science and Health,* or *The Protocols of the Learned Elders of Zion.* The compilers of *The International Jew* revealed this phenomenon in microcosm. Working in relative isolation, Ford, Liebold, and Cameron warded off protests and reinforced each other's prejudices.[107]

Finally, what disposed Ford to agree with Liebold that there was a Jewish conspiracy instead of accepting counterarguments by his son Edsel or Arthur Brisbane? Samuel S. Marquis called Ford the "most elusive personality" whom he had ever met. Seventy years later biographers are still trying to capture that personality.[108]

In an astute psychoanalytical interpretation, Anne Jardim relates Ford's behavior to his version of the "universal" ambivalence toward parents. Specifically, he idealized his mother Mary, who died when he was thirteen, but developed an "unconscious fantasy" of abandonment by his father William. To prevent further rejection, he sought "absolute control" in personal and business relations. The aggression toward his father also surfaced as a projection of his own hostility to others. While retaliating against William Ford, he sought to assuage guilt and deny his loss through "restitutive action." In particular, Jardim says, Ford's manufacture of tough vehicles for rural roads, sale of tractors at a loss, and sponsorship of agricultural research were symbolic affirmations that he was "still a farmer's son."[109]

Sometimes Ford channeled aggression into creativity. Although his greatest creation, the reliable, inexpensive automobile, transformed America, the triumph failed to satisfy him. After the Model T conquered the market in the mid-1910s, therefore, he externalized his conflicts in capricious company policy and through the promotion of good, bad, or merely eccentric causes. With varying intensity, he advocated world peace, mass production, funny money, and ballroom dancing, while opposing bankers, liquor, tobacco, Truman Newberry, and the "international Jew."[110]

Jardim does not fully solve what Marquis called the "psychological puzzle" of Ford's life. By building on her insights, however, we can better understand his sponsorship and ultimate retraction of *The International Jew*. As we have seen, Ford's animosity toward Jews grew during the personal crisis after 1915. Seeking to make restitution to the farmer, he was drawn to the convention that Jews were, as Edward Ross wrote, "slovenly" agriculturalists. Moreover, whether or not the process is called projection, Ford attributed to Jews traits that he refused to recognize in himself. For example, in 1920–1921, shortly after Ford had tricked stockholders and exploited his dealers to gain full control of the company, his newspaper accused Jews of violating business ethics. Ford thought that Sapiro inflicted "systematization" on the farmer, but his own machines did more than cooperatives to alter rural mores.[111]

Although anti-Semitism brought into "manageable focus" Ford's hostility to Wobblies, bootleggers, and bankers, Jardim rightly notes that there was "nothing predestined" about his espousal of it. If the United States had not provided copious anti-Semitic imagery, he might have favored a different conspiracy theory. Furthermore, because there were so many targets for his aggression, Ford could almost nonchalantly surrender overt Jew-baiting in 1927. Indeed, after repudiating *The International Jew,* he was increasingly belligerent to unions and drew closer to Harry Bennett, the head of the company labor spies.[112]

In 1923, more than one-third of 260,000 voters polled by *Collier's* favored Ford for president. They overlooked, if they did not endorse, his personal peculiarities, suppression of labor, and sponsorship of anti-Semitism. Ford's reputation thrived partly because it was protected by Liebold and the public relations experts who followed. But they built on a popular craving to esteem an unspoiled country mechanic whose ingenuity and effort had made a contribution to the general welfare as well as a fortune. Marquis reported that many workers on the assembly line denied that Ford knew of their misery. Similarly, Jews initially doubted that he sanctioned the *Independent's* attack; their praise of Ford after his retraction in 1927 moved Louis Marshall to warn against excess. Like their gentile neighbors, Jews wanted to believe in self-made men, benevolent capitalists, and a just system that produced them. In ways that Ford failed to comprehend, these immigrants and their children were embracing American dreams and illusions.[113]

3

Jesus Christ as Business Statesman:
Bruce Barton and the Selling of Corporate Capitalism

Historians rarely sympathize with ad men, advocates of the "gospel of success," or opponents of American entry into World War II. Bruce Barton was all three. Yet he typically appears in only one of these disreputable contexts at a time. Cultural historians remember primarily Barton's authorship of The Man Nobody Knows, a best-seller in 1925–1926 which portrayed Jesus Christ as the "founder of modern business." Students of business record his leadership of the advertising firm Batten, Barton, Durstine, and Osborn (BBDO). And political historians recall President Franklin D. Roosevelt's attack on Representative Barton and two fellow non-interventionists, Representatives Joseph W. Martin and Hamilton Fish; "Great Britain would never have received an ounce of help from us," FDR declared on 28 October 1940, "if the decision had been left to Martin, Barton, and Fish."[1]

Unfortunately, academic specialization and condescension obscure Barton's significance as a combination capitalist, moralist, and isolationist. In The Man Nobody Knows, the pivot of his life, Barton presented a sophisticated gospel of corporate capitalism that he continued to preach as an ad man and then as a congressman. Brought up under the strong influence of liberal Protestantism, Barton legitimized big business, both for himself and for his audience, by finding a precedent in the Christian doctrine of individual responsibility and Jesus' "life of service." In an economy of abundance, Barton explained, corporate leaders must place service above profits, all persons must work and consume vigorously, and advertisements must promote these general values as well as specific goods and services. Since prosperity also depended upon peace abroad, Barton opposed American intervention in foreign wars.

With occasional shifts of emphasis, Bruce Barton for four decades adhered to a consistent world view that he first espoused during the 1920s. Yet this world view increasingly came to embody a number of tensions and ironies. Barton's gospel of optimistic religious beliefs failed to assuage his self-doubts or to bring him peace of mind. His noninterventionist stand brought him into conflict with other members of the eastern corporate elite. Perhaps most disturbing of all, Barton came to fear the public's reflexive applause for America's grandiose global commitments and, by the late 1940s, felt compelled to warn his fellow countrymen against "predigested ideas."[2] Yet few contemporaries had done more than Barton himself to render those whom he called the "masses" vulnerable to advertising puffery and political propaganda. Bruce Barton's popular publications, his business philosophy, and his politics thus need to be reexamined as related aspects of a single complex career.

* * *

Any attempt to evaluate Bruce Barton must take into account decades of his own myth-making. Writers who picture him as a provincial gladhander are victims of his advertising skill. Barton liked to present himself as a "gawky kid from the country," the son of a Congregationalist minister who was not exactly poor but "just didn't have any money." By the time Bruce turned seven, however, his father, the Reverend William E. Barton, held a prominent Boston pulpit with access to the nation's political, economic, and intellectual elite. The Bartons lived comfortably on his ministerial salary, publishing royalties, and perquisites (ranging from ice cream freezers to limousines) sent by admirers. Christianity and capitalism always coexisted in the Barton home; young Bruce was obliged to work in order to build character, not because the family "didn't have any money."[3]

The decisive influence on his son's personality and world view as well as the virtual coauthor of *The Man Nobody Knows*, Reverend

Barton deserves special attention. Bruce Barton could honestly say that he was born in a rural cottage on 5 August 1886, because his father was then temporarily assigned to Robbins, Tennessee, as a circuit-riding preacher. William E. Barton really was a "self-made man" who rose quickly through luck, pluck, labor, and patronage. In 1890, he received a bachelor of divinity degree from Oberlin, and in the next nine years held pulpits at Shawmut Church in Boston and then at the First Church in Oak Park, Illinois, serving there until his retirement in 1924. He lectured widely, taught at several seminaries, and in 1921 was elected moderator of the National Council of Congregational Churches. Friendship with Boston literati prompted a parallel career as a writer of fiction, exhortations to success, and history. His best work, a study of Abraham Lincoln, combined meticulous scholarship, shrewd interviews, and appreciation of his subject's "caution and conservatism." Although Bruce Barton was a prolific journalist by the late 1910s, until publication of *The Man Nobody Knows* he remained in the shadow of his father, the presidential biographer and theologian.[4]

Adapting easily to liberal theology, Rev. Barton deprecated doctrinal controversies and conflated salvation with self-mastery. Like other liberal Protestants he stressed those aspects of the "many-sided" Savior most congenial to his own concerns. William Barton went further than most by playfully composing ersatz "gospels" according to Judas Iscariot and Jesus' brother James. His more conventional explorations of the "inexhaustible Life" included *Day by Day with Jesus,* a guide to Holy Week, and *Jesus of Nazareth,* a pictorial biography. Rev. Barton pointedly denied that Jesus was "weak and puny," and instead envisioned a sturdy Savior using "sanctified muscle" to cleanse the temple at Jerusalem.[5]

According to Rev. Barton, Jesus' "life of service" rendered an "unsocial gospel" a contradiction in terms. Significantly, however, since He never required disciples to surrender all wealth to the poor, modern Christians should not surrender theirs either. Rather, they should strive for wealth and put it to good use. In his most popular books, collections of genial "parables" attributed to a fictional sage, Rev. Barton teased slackers, praised "self-starters," prescribed hard work to cure heartbreak, and urged seekers after success to "Go Out on the Road and Do Business."[6]

An attentive parent, Rev. Barton set especially high standards for his oldest son. Surviving fragments reveal Barton to have been a bright, witty, energetic adolescent who nonetheless doubted his own ability. In high school he debated, managed the glee club, edited the student newspaper, sold syrup on the side, and served as a page at a Republican National Convention. Yet he still questioned his "power to make myself work."[7] After a year at Berea College (where his father had sent him to meet students from poor families) Barton transferred to Amherst. Although he debated again, played football, assisted in history courses, presided over the Christian Association and the honor society, and graduated as valedictorian and the "student most likely to succeed," self-doubt still accompanied his personal striving. Having hoped to follow his father into the ministry, Barton now faced a crisis of faith. He remained loyal to liberal Protestantism, reassured by his father that belief was "more reasonable than unbelief," but decided against entering the clergy. Consciously at least, the decision was less an act of rebellion than an act of submission. He lacked, Barton recalled in 1914, the vigor, patience, and love needed to succeed in "my father's business."[8]

Upon graduation, Barton turned down a history fellowship at the University of Wisconsin and instead worked for six months on a railroad construction crew in Montana, dreaming of representing the state in the Senate.[9] Thereafter he wrote for the *Home-Herald,* a religious monthly in Chicago, and managed the *Housekeeper,* a women's magazine in New York. Both publications failed. Landing on his feet, Barton became assistant sales manager for P. J. Collier and Sons in New York in 1912; his first famous advertisement, on behalf of Collier's Five-Foot Shelf of Harvard Classics, promised the "essentials of a liberal education" in "only fifteen minutes a day."[10]

Throughout the 1910s Barton preached occasionally and wrote regularly for several Protestant magazines. In middle age he liked to recall this work as youthful "muckraking"; these retrospective claims to "radicalism" were exaggerated, but in the early 1910s he was the *Congregationalist and Christian World*'s authority on the "other half of society." He expressed sympathy for prostitutes, favored temperance (though not national prohibition), and condemned black disfranchisement and the "invisible prison" of race prejudice. Focusing on the gulf between capital and labor, he pictured "hollow-cheeked" fathers worn down by struggle, bedraggled mothers torn from suckling infants to toil in the mills, and "willing" workers without jobs. Low wages, stockholder greed, and the "American mania for haste" were responsible for alternating periods of prosperity and depression.[11]

The poor, Barton feared, might embrace the surrogate "religion" of class conflict preached by the Industrial Workers of the World. In these turbulent times, therefore, Christians needed strong leaders. The rural church was "already dead," he warned, and its urban counterpart was threatened by spiritualist cults, apathy, and lack of imagination. Barton hailed ministers like the "pioneer" Washington Gladden, who faced the social crisis by "becoming servants of all." Their institutional churches, offering meeting halls, game rooms, and gymnasiums, simultaneously alleviated poverty and made Christianity more attractive. Barton also praised unconventional ministers: an ex-convict aiding his former cohorts, a skipper attending to sailors at anchor, and an evangelist approaching men and women "in the rush of their business." Preachers should be "salesmen," Barton claimed, who must learn to sell religion seven days a week. Furthermore, along with contemporaries committed to strenuous lives, he favored clergy who were "men's men" with "hard flesh and warm blood."[12]

Still, Barton's version of social Christianity was wider than it was deep. Like his father, he welcomed benevolent capitalists into the ranks of the awakened. He offered no alternative beyond voluntary charity to house the unemployed and, along with many writers associated with the amorphous progressive awakening, slighted structural reform to concentrate on building Christian character. Jesus with $50 million and a large organization, he surmised, "couldn't have done as much as Jesus who was never too busy to love."[13]

What *would* Jesus do? Liberal Protestants in the 1910s reached a near consensus on His robust conviviality, but they divided on whether He was an "industrial comrade" or a "common-sense businessman." Barton stood between these two positions in his first book. *A Young Man's Jesus,* published in 1914, was dedicated to his father, a "young man's preacher." At the outset Barton reclaimed Jesus from "priests and . . . women." Like the author's favorite clergy, Jesus was a "man's man," gifted with strength, hearty laughter, and charm enough to transform any dinner into a "social triumph." Like the best men of the current generation, He was also a "Young Insurgent."[14]

Using muckraker's language, Barton described an ancient world dominated by Roman "degenerates" who exploited the "groaning proletair" in order to finance revelry. Jesus, a "poor peasant," rebelled against the system, drove "grafters" from the temple at Jerusalem, and denounced greed as the "root of all social evil." The "common people" rallied to Him, but "monopolies," "reactionaries," and "vested interests" quickly mobilized in opposition.[15]

Yet the Young Insurgent was no "working class agitator." Rather, much as progressives in the 1910s urged unity across class lines, Jesus refrained from "inordinate" attacks on wealth and recruited followers from "every stratum of society." Indeed, an "infinite" gap separated Him from modern reformers, most of whom misconstrued His greatest legacy, "reverence for human souls." Although Jesus might have led a successful revolt against Rome, He bravely faced crucifixion as a "final protest" against greed. In the last chapter, Barton adapted one of his father's arguments to show that Jesus was "more than a man": His influence through the ages proved that the "Young Man's Jesus is, too, the Young Man's Christ."[16]

A Young Man's Jesus marked the peak of Barton's insurgency. In *Every Week,* a Collier Sunday supplement that he began to edit in 1914, Barton repudiated muckraking and called business the nation's "greatest force for righteousness." Instead of interviewing social gospel ministers, he started in the mid-1910s to publish profiles of corporation presidents, efficiency experts, and deans of business schools. The typical man at the top, he concluded, valued service more than money. To inspire *"divine discontent"* on society's lower rungs, Barton insisted that even "mediocre" men could succeed if they set goals, worked, studied, saved money, and cultivated the "conviction" of triumph. Nor should a man slacken when these practices produced results. Complete "self-satisfaction" signaled inadequate aspirations. (Largely exempt from these recommendations, women were expected to provide tranquil homes and "soothing chatter.")[17]

Acknowledging his forebears among advocates of self-help, Barton in 1921 respectfully interviewed Russell Conwell, the aged author of *Acres of Diamonds.* Reflecting a shift in the gospel of success begun during Conwell's prime, Barton emphasized that the good life required more than money. Greed, he warned, might cost a man's health, reputation, and family life. Even the busiest executive should find time to cultivate a garden with his sons, enjoy good books and music, and retreat from the "world of chatter." Occasional solitude was the "key to contentment."[18]

This softened gospel of success converged with a general cultural trend, but it had more immediate sources in Barton family values. Barton was urging young men to emulate his hard-working yet learned and tolerant father. Certainly Bruce was still trying to live up to that ideal. Like Rev. Barton, he read widely and wrote prolifically, made charitable contributions, and treated his children with warmth. Generous to opponents and curious about ideas, both Bartons cultivated diverse friends. Not every legacy was admirable. While his father wrote for the anti-Semitic *Dearborn Independent,* Bruce noted Ben Franklin's superiority to his employer, a "Jew printer named Keimer," and mocked the "little Jew" who "shined" Americans with Fels soap.[19]

Unfortunately Barton lacked one of his father's enviable traits: peace of mind. Like countless men on the make, he worried that his worldly accomplishments demanded too many sacrifices. Frequently reading Ecclesiastes, he wondered, "What's the purpose of it all?" His purpose, Barton decided, was to do "useful work," raise a "worthy family," and leave the world a "little better." Yet his Job-like question and bland answers about life's purpose, printed incongruously among hymns to "go-getters" in a book called *More Power to You,* suggest that Barton was trying to persuade himself as well as his readers of the value of striving.[20]

Beneath surface optimism, Barton was, according to his brother Fred, a "nervous . . . driving sort" who might have "ended in a sanitarium" (and actually did for a short time in 1928). Since college he had suffered from the "curse" of insomnia; sleep became a minor motif in his writing by 1920 and he attributed "many of the world's ills" to its absence. In addition, sarcasm often pushed through Barton's jovial persona. Answering an earnest inquiry about the way to wealth, for instance, he quipped, "Go down to Wilmington and marry one of the DuPont girls."[21]

Barton's only novel, *The Making of George Groton,* reveals both his growing approval of big business and his reservations about "making it." Young George Groton leaves rural Massachusetts to work for a shady New York stockbroker whose life he has saved. He soon overcomes a sneering rival (complete with mustache and "yellow streak") and enriches himself speculating on Wall Street. He fears, however, that this "best game I ever learned" is nothing more than "gambling." To ease his conscience, George moves to a stately investment firm, but still operates a profitable consulting company, plays the second "great game" of social climbing, and continues to speculate. The hero's lapse from virtue is underlined by his absence from church and his estrangement from Betty Wilson, a childhood sweetheart employed as a New York social worker.

Redemption comes through liberal Protestantism and love. On his deathbed, Betty's father, the town minister, predicts that George will "do great—and good—things." Losing his fortune at virtually the same time, George sees the value of Rev. Wilson's permanent "investment" in humanity. A changed man, he marries Betty and soon returns to business, promoting overseas investments to drain swamps and build railroads. By combining affluence, personal fulfillment, and service, at the end of the novel George has risen to become Barton's ideal businessman.

The Making of George Groton, which contained no hint of Barton's erstwhile muckraking, ultimately endorsed capitalism infused with character. Although George dislikes Wall Street machinations, grumbles about the "great new god, 'Efficiency,'" and condemns speculation, he derides self-styled reformers who play the stock market. The book's most grotesque character, a "new woman," feigns sympathy in order to write profitable stories about the poor. Material success, though morally perilous, is readily available. Unable to understand the working poor, let alone abject deprivation, Barton equated "genteel poverty" with eating "tough steaks" in order to save for the children's education. George Groton never even sinks that low.[22]

While *American Magazine* serialized *The Making of George Groton* in 1917, Barton pursued other work. He mobilized publicity for the YMCA and the United War Work campaign, coining a slogan—perhaps his most famous—for the Salvation Army: "A man may be down but he is never out." An internationalist in 1919, he cheered President Wilson's return from Versailles. And although World War I did not end all wars, it did advance trends that Barton would ride to fame and fortune.[23]

During the early 1900s, many leaders of big business (represented most effectively by the National Civic Federation) had accepted federal regulation, experimented with paternal employee relations, and cooperated with prudent trade unionists. Such compromises were rare among middle-level businesses (represented most effectively by the National Association of Manufacturers [NAM]) and far from universal among large enterprises. Nevertheless, there had been warrant for Barton's prewar assertion that "men at the top" affirmed "service." After the war, executives increasingly claimed to be business statesmen. An enthusiastic participant in this "great new era," Barton celebrated go-getters, chastised malcontents, and hailed a corporate elite free from sloth and dissipation. He especially praised Owen D. Young of General Electric, Theodore N. Vail of American Telephone and Telegraph, and Henry Ford. The economic order was still "far from perfect," but defects were transitional and largely confined to "little business."[24]

To further the trend toward perfection, Barton went into business himself. In January 1919 he joined with Alex Osborn and Roy Durstine to form an advertising agency (a merger nine years later with the George Batten Company provided the famous shorthand identification, BBDO). "The world will be what business makes it," Barton explained in 1920, and advertising, a $500 million industry, would "help business to formulate its ideals." Advertising was essential, Barton believed, because society had "pretty nearly" solved the problem of production. In an economy of abundance, employers who skimped on wages undermined mass purchasing power, the "foundation on which we all have to build." Unfortunately, even affluent citizens might ignore the goods rolling off assembly lines. Advertising, therefore, promoted "new objects of desire." What critics considered a vice, the manufacture of wants, Barton regarded as a virtue. The prospect of acquiring something new spurred individual ambition. Mass consumption also facilitated "big production which in turn makes possible lower prices which in turn makes possible a broader market and still greater demands." Society, like the men who directed it, would thus keep on striving.[25]

Barton's conception of the good society paralleled his definition of the good life. With willed optimism, he insisted that modern society was the "best" ever and getting better. Often confusing progress with bigness, technical innovation, and utility, he noted, for example, that vacuum cleaners and electric refrigerators, subjects of advertising campaigns, had been adopted more quickly than the first sewing machines. These "labor saving" devices were especially valuable because society, like the individual, needed time to cultivate an "appreciation of beauty." When Barton's social optimism faltered, he fell back on a version of the "Law of Compensation"—a call for a broad "historical . . . perspective" and recognition that "good times follow bad."[26]

Throughout the 1920s, Barton recommended further ethical advances in advertising. He believed that internal regulation begun before World War I had removed his profession from "probation." Advertising must nudge the United States toward "better days," and thus must exclude "charlatans." Furthermore, imbued with the spirit of business statesmanship, ad men should avoid "pitched battles" among rival brands, settle for "reasonable" shares of the market and, most important, refrain from promoting defective goods. In sum, any advertising campaign should be an "act of faith."[27]

It was also an act of deception. According to Barton, as well as most of his colleagues who took pride in their high standards, ethical advertising allowed hyperbole and psychological manipulation. As the trade journal *Printer's Ink* observed, "'Puffery' is one thing; lying another." Because modern society produced an "avalanche" of sense impressions, Barton explained, repetitive ads must lodge brand names in a customer's "subconscious mind." At BBDO, he offered prizes for brevity and decorated his office with a huge photograph of Coney Island, a reminder that his audience hardly appreciated subtlety. In demanding positive as well as simple ads, Barton sanctioned farfetched claims. For example, he invoked the name of Lincoln to underscore Marshall Field's "fine service" to public and employees. This affinity for puffery, deceptive though it was, largely saved Barton from the popular tactic of frightening Americans into consumption. Rather, much of his advertising copy was indistinguishable from his optimistic articles and speeches. Whether Barton recognized it or not, such simplicity undermined advertisers' claims to accuracy.[28]

Barton blended his faith in advertising with his liberal Protestantism in his 1925 best-seller, *The Man Nobody Knows*. As early as

June 1921, Barton had mentioned the project to his father, who responded with a "hasty outline," bibliography, copies of his own *Jesus of Nazareth,* and advice to portray a "manly" Savior. Rev. Barton cited Jesus' ability to "pick up" men and build an organization, noted Christianity's triumph through a "worldwide advertising campaign," and recalled "three sets of advertisers" proclaiming the new evangel: shepherds, wise men, and angels.[29]

Barton borrowed much from his father's outline and after publication described *The Man Nobody Knows* as "our" book. The biblical quotation on the flyleaf, "Wist ye not that I must be about my Father's *business?*" had been used elsewhere to stress Jesus' commercial side. Yet to Barton it held a double meaning. He was collaborating with his father on a volume purporting to show that advertising was not, after all, so far from his "father's business."[30]

The Man Nobody Knows began with Barton's synthetic memory of Sunday school, where he had been bored by stories of a "pale," "flabby," "sissified" Jesus. Supposedly he had imagined Samson fighting Jim Jeffries but thought Jesus "something for girls." After entering business, he suddenly realized that the founder of Christianity, the "greatest organization of all," must have been made of sturdier stuff.[31]

The anecdote undoubtedly appealed to readers rejecting "feminized" Protestantism. Yet like many advertisements, it was misleading. Indeed, there was no more likelihood that Bruce had imbibed flabby Christianity in his father's Sunday school than that owners of the Harvard Classics acquired a basic education in fifteen minutes daily. Nor was *The Man Nobody Knows* written to share a sudden insight. Not only had Barton contemplated the project for at least four years, but several themes were repeated from *A Young Man's Jesus.* Once again he minimized theological controversies, slighted miracles, and stressed Jesus' humanity (even declining to capitalize pronoun references).[32]

Everyone had the right to seize the side of Jesus most appealing to himself, Barton said, even if it meant "reading between the lines" of Scripture. Exercising this right a second time, Barton now presented Jesus' life as the "grandest achievement story of all!" He no longer portrayed a rise from peasantry to insurgency, or speculated, as he had in *A Young Man's Jesus,* that a youthful romance was crushed by poverty. In *The Man Nobody Knows,* Jesus comes from a "cheerful and easy-going" middle-class home. Countering the "feminine" emphasis on Mary, Barton envisioned a boy molded also by Joseph's friendliness and vigor.[33]

Although the Son of Man's class origins had changed, his muscles remained "hard as iron." Jesus was an "outdoor man" whose steady nerves signaled strength. Whether or not his healings were miraculous, they showed energy pouring from his body as from a dynamo. Finally, Jesus appealed to women, even worldly women. Paraphrasing from his earlier book, Barton postulated that a true woman, though sometimes willing to mother "thin-lipped, so-called spiritual" lads, was most attracted to "manliness."[34]

Similarly, Jesus remained a "sociable man" whose friendships transcended "social boundaries." Fond of parties, he urged slaughter of a fatted calf to celebrate the prodigal son's return, and turned water into wine at the Cana wedding feast. Unlike Old Testament "thunderers," he was less prophet than companion, the messenger of a "happy God" who wanted humanity "to be happy." It was hardly surprising that Jesus became, as Barton had also said in 1914, the "most popular dinner guest in Jerusalem."[35]

In *The Man Nobody Knows,* however, friendliness no longer furthered insurgency. Rather, Jesus "picked up twelve men from the bottom ranks of business and forged them into an organization that conquered the world." Unlike Moses or John the Baptist, godly men lacking managerial talent, he was a natural "executive." He overlooked petty annoyances, chose capable subordinates, and trained them with "unending patience." Without apology Barton presented Christ as an advertising executive. Indeed, Jesus faced a version of the modern copywriter's problem that "supply always precedes demand." His product, a "great spiritual conception," would help humanity to transcend ritual and thus directly approach God. Yet religions abounded. Men and women, "even more impenetrable" than their twentieth-century descendants who flocked to Coney Island, saw no need for a new one. Therefore, using techniques worthy of emulation by "any sales manager," Jesus created interest.[36]

His attack on the money-changers made "front page news." Nonetheless, he avoided "over-selling," anticipated objections in advance, and shunned "futile" disputes. For instance, willing to render unto

Caesar the coin bearing his likeness, Jesus outwitted the Pharisees and provided "another good laugh for the crowd." The parables also illustrated "all the principles" contained in advertising manuals: brevity, simplicity of expression, repetition, and "deep sincerity."[37]

Jesus was not only a superb ad man, but the "founder of modern business." Sensing that this phrase would draw criticism, Barton followed his own dictum to deflate objections in advance by explaining Jesus' precise meaning. As the founder of modern business, Jesus was an industrial statesman comparable to those whom Barton had praised for more than a decade. He rejected Satan's temptation to mere "material success" and affirmed that anyone seeking greatness "shall be the servant of all." For hundreds of years mankind had considered these remarks "absurd . . . idealistic talk," believing instead that each man must "look after himself" in order to "get ahead." But in the twentieth century, Barton wrote, corporate leaders like Ford, Vail, and George W. Perkins made the "great discovery" that service was more important than dividends.[38]

Conversely, Judas Iscariot prefigured "small bore" businessmen who still "looked out for Number One." Judas was not a "bad fellow at heart." The disciples' treasurer, he worried about their extravagance and lacked the foresight to appreciate Jesus' call for a social order based on service. Rather, Barton wrote, he "could read a balance sheet and he knew that the jig was up. So he made his private little deal with the priests. . . ." Readers could easily imagine Jesus joining George W. Perkins and Samuel Gompers on a strike mediation panel while Judas hired scabs for the NAM.[39]

Judas's figurative descendants ignored health, family, and culture in order to operate an "office treadmill." Wanting personal success above all, they "sacrificed success. Never once forgetting themselves they have forgotten everything else." According to Barton's revised folklore of the invisible hand, individuals must promote the collective good in order to serve their singular interests.[40]

Although business in general and advertising in particular illustrated this "law of service," Barton denied that these activities were uniquely blessed. Jesus affirmed that all work is worship; all useful service prayer. And whoever works wholeheartedly at any worthy calling is a co-worker with the Almighty in the great enterprise that He has initiated but which He can never finish without the help of man.[41]

In *The Man Nobody Knows,* Barton both legitimated advertising, to himself as well as to his readers, and tried to Christianize the social order. The language of corporate responsibility now replaced the rhetoric of insurgency found in *A Young Man's Jesus.* Barton no longer presented Jesus' cleansing of the temple at Jerusalem as a protest against capitalism, but stressed instead his refusal to lead a revolt, despite pressure from His followers. Temporal power would have plunged Him into a "lifetime of bloodshed and intrigue, while his message remained unspoken." No one could question Jesus' right to call some matters "more vital" than money, Barton said, because he had been "handed the wealth of a nation and handed it back."[42]

In both books, however, Jesus personified a new spirit of generosity instead of institutional reform; Barton still adhered to the underlying premise that benevolence by regenerate individuals could transform society. The transformation, he knew, would not be easy. In *The Man Nobody Knows,* as in the author's life, doubt flowed beneath surface optimism. Jesus, like Barton, faced the "perils and crises of success." During crises, the normally gregarious Jesus sought a quiet place to meditate "in communion with his Father." He died almost alone, rejected by his disciples, brothers, and neighbors.[43]

The Man Nobody Knows passed over Jesus' final days "in reverent silence." No paraphrase of the gospels was adequate. "Every man who loves courageous manhood," Barton advised, "ought to read these chapters at least once a year." At the end, the man nobody knew was more than an executive. He was "The Master."[44]

The Man Nobody Knows sold 250,000 copies in eighteen months, remained on the best-seller list for two years, and led nonfiction titles in 1926. In the estimation of James Rorty, an apostate ad man and harsh critic, Barton became a "national figure comparable in influence to Henry Ward Beecher."[45]

Responses to the book were mixed. *Christian Century* credited Barton with a sincere effort to bring Christ to the corporations but chided him for confusing muscles with morality. Most cosmopolitan reviewers rendered harsher judgments. They accused Barton of portraying Jesus as a Babbitt, Rotarian, and "suitcase-carrying drummer." The corporate conversion to service, Gilbert Seldes added in the *New Republic,* had been "a product of competition, not YMCA morality." Presenting the most perceptive critique from the left, Rorty placed *The Man Nobody Knows* in a tradition of religious "salesmanship" reaching back to Benjamin Franklin, and recognized that the author was attempting both to "redeem" Jesus in materialistic times and to exorcise his own doubts about the virtues of advertising. Nevertheless, Rorty savaged Barton for creating a "grotesque ad-man Christ in his own image." Theological and political liberals might have overlooked Jesus' popularity at dinner parties if he had remained the Young Insurgent. To theological conservatives like Rev. Arno C. Gaebelein, Barton's failure to stress Christ's divinity stabbed "at the very heart of Christianity."[46]

On the other hand, Rev. John Haynes Holmes, *New Republic* editor Bruce Bliven, and former presidential candidate John W. Davis praised *The Man Nobody Knows.* Newspapers in Boston, Chicago, and Pittsburgh printed favorable reviews or serialized the book. Some Princeton undergraduates admiringly envisioned Barton's Jesus as captain of their football team. The author received hundreds of letters from grateful readers, including one from a self-described failure who had drawn "courage" from his words.[47]

Although unsurprising in a postwar decade marked both by doubting and defense of Victorian values, the favorable public response was not altogether spontaneous. Businesses distributed thousands of copies of *The Man Nobody Knows.* Appropriately, Alex Osborn promoted his partner's book, urging merchants nationally to make profits and "serve our communities." One gimmick displayed two lighted candles, a Bible, and *The Man Nobody Knows.* This campaign belied the later claim, typical of Barton myth-making, that he had expected to sell only one thousand copies. Furthermore, having created a market, Barton during the next three years published *The Man of Galilee,* which mixed sparse text with copious illustrations of a muscular Jesus, and *The Book Nobody Knows,* a survey of biblical "high spots." The most substantial sequel, *What Can a Man Believe?* appeared in 1927. Barton also wrote titles for the silent film version of *The Man Nobody Knows* and, with his father, advised director Cecil B. DeMille on *The King of Kings.* "Bruce," DeMille said, "they will know Him when you and I are through."[48]

In the three books following *The Man Nobody Knows,* Barton discerned more biblical businessmen, defended scriptural higher criticism, and defined a "minimum creed" for modern times. Religion, he admitted, had caused intolerance, ignorance, and bloodshed. Yet Christianity, the "most optimistic and achieving" faith, had simultaneously brought comfort, civilization, and progress. Belief remained plausible despite recent scientific discoveries. A spontaneously generated universe was "more inconceivable" than the existence of God, and thinking beings must have been created by "Intelligence beyond the universe." Furthermore, "at least as good" as humans, God probably provided an afterlife where earthly injustices were "evened up." Perhaps unconvinced himself by his compound of Emersonian compensation and argument from design, Barton added a plea reminiscent of William James and William E. Barton: "Since faith will do so much, and the lack of it is so destroying, why not believe?"[49]

After establishing the "intelligent man's right to believe," Barton lamented that Protestantism, the more-than-minimum creed with which he identified, still suffered from confusion, declining membership, and inept clergy. Renovated Protestantism required honesty, confidence, and elimination of "absurd" creeds. An ecumenical faith using these "business" methods might someday make religion a "perfectly normal part of life."[50]

Determination of "what can a man believe" was no abstract experiment to Barton, who was increasingly perplexed about the "purpose of it all." He wondered if affluence would destroy "old-fashioned virtues" without bringing "inner peace." Personal difficulties catalyzed these lapses from optimism. Barton's work ethic faltered in the late 1920s when he failed to complete a history of business. Bored by administration, he left daily management of BBDO to Roy Durstine. Plagued by Durstine's incompetence as well as the Depression, firm billings declined for ten years after 1929. By 1928, worsening insomnia took "all the joy" from life, driving Barton to seek relief at a sanatorium. At roughly the same time, despite his hymns to hearth and home, he began a love affair with a woman at BBDO. Rev. Barton, his "best friend," died in 1930, and his daughter Betsey became paralyzed in 1935.[51]

Partly to escape personal problems Barton turned to public matters. "No man ever reached the White House without the help of advertising," he concluded after helping two men get there. As early as 1920, Barton had pushed Calvin Coolidge for vice-president and seconded his nomination at the Republican National Convention. During the 1920s, he drew close to Secretary of Commerce Herbert Hoover, the foremost business statesman in politics. Advising Hoover on his presidential race, Barton stressed his rise from "orphan farm boy," recommended "gracious" references to Alfred E. Smith, and urged brief but "ringing phrases about the obligations of big business." Neither brevity nor graciousness was Hoover's forte, but he incorporated some suggestions into campaign speeches and the inaugural address.[52]

After the Crash, Barton belatedly repudiated "new era" extravagance, urged businessmen to practice the service so often preached, and solicited charity for the unemployed. Interpreting the Depression as an economic and spiritual crisis, in 1932 he produced an inspirational biography of St. Paul, a "failure at forty." This emphasis on voluntary relief, corporate responsibility, and spiritual renewal initially coincided with the Hoover administration program. Although Barton and Hoover remained ideological kin, their respective temperaments ultimately produced different responses to the slump. Unlike the President, who became defensive and insular, Barton fought against his self-admitted "natural conservatism" and advised others to keep their "minds open and . . . souls alert." In late 1931 he urged Hoover to form a "national government" by adding Democrats to the cabinet and edged reluctantly toward endorsement of direct federal relief. It was, he wrote, as "silly" to expect everyone to prosper as to expect everyone to play championship golf. Throughout the world, therefore, government was becoming a kind of "handicap committee," using pensions, taxes, and unemployment aid to achieve "fairer distribution of wealth."[53]

Disappointed by Republican partisanship and inflexibility, Barton nonetheless supported Hoover against Franklin D. Roosevelt, whom he considered "just a name and a crutch." By December 1933, however, he was applauding FDR for reviving national "vitality." The administration had wisely begun direct relief, started public works, sought fair wage levels, and, especially through the National Recovery Administration, prompted constructive "group thinking" among businessmen. Unfortunately, the New Deal also "shackled" business and promised more than it could deliver. Hence Barton in 1934 helped to promote *The Challenge to Liberty,* Hoover's comprehensive critique of the New Deal, and two years later campaigned for Alfred M. Landon.[54]

By the late 1930s Barton considered the New Deal part of a worldwide "revolution" in attitudes. His disdain for the Coney Island multitudes whom he manipulated was reinforced by José Ortega y Gasset's *The Revolt of the Masses,* which Barton considered the most important book published during his lifetime. People now claimed "rights" without fulfilling "duties," Barton concluded in 1938. Because advertising had undermined inner restraint and outward deference to the natural aristocracy of go-getters, he felt ironic complicity in this "revolution." Nevertheless, fighting against his own elitism, Barton responded with a mixture of "good sportsmanship," political realism, and confidence in a benign universe. As beneficiaries of the "new era," businessmen should look on with "serenity" as New Dealers took their turn at bat, remain "sufficiently progressive" to merit future leadership, and "good naturedly" counter criticism.[55]

In 1937, finally fulfilling his boyhood ambition to serve in Congress, Barton was elected to the House of Representatives as a Republican from Manhattan's "silk stocking" district. A good-natured critic himself, he befriended New Dealers and was widely regarded as a liberal Republican. Yet three years in Washington reinforced his "natural conservatism." A 1939 poll of newspaper correspondents listed Barton as one of the ten most capable representatives. Certainly he was one of the most publicized, attracting attention, for example, by introducing a weekly bill to repeal "silly" New Deal legislation. Not only was Barton a professional maker of "news," but, as George Seldes complained, the press catered to an ad man whose accounts ranged from "cheese to steel." By 1940 he was mentioned as a dark horse presidential contender, but he worked enthusiastically for the nomination of Wendell Willkie, whom he considered a far-sighted businessman. At Willkie's insistence, Barton accepted the Republican nomination for senator from New York.[56]

Avoidance of war, the signal issue of 1940, had long concerned Barton. Distressed by American rejection of the League of Nations, he continued during the 1920s to admire Wilsonian "idealism" but retrospectively condemned the intervention of 1917. Indeed, praising Eugene V. Debs for his antiwar stand, he joined with Norman Thomas and other socialists to warn against another conflict. Yet unlike contemporaries who indicted "merchants of death," Barton insisted that "business hates war" and outlined a special role for his own profession. Advertisements must make all peoples "peace-conscious." One of his ads anticipated the joyous day when war, not entombed soldiers, would be "unknown."[57]

During the 1930s, Barton anticipated the demise of the British Empire as well as the "white man's" forced departure from the Far East. In 1934, perhaps blinded by his genteel anti-Semitism, he underestimated Nazi evil; without "in any way" endorsing Nazi attacks on Jews, Barton was "immensely impressed" by Hitler's "courage" and restoration of German "hope." When the European war began in 1939, Barton held views common among noninterventionists. He predicted a quick British defeat, criticized Roosevelt's deceptiveness, favored strong national defense, expected war against fascism abroad to bring comparable dictatorship at home, and urged American neutrality. In October 1939, he voted against lifting the embargo on arms sales to belligerents. The United States, he decided after prayer and "spiritual struggle," should try to stop the war before it "got thoroughly started." Respectful of Britain's "magnificent resistance," he favored limited aid in 1940. Still, his vote on the embargo, combined with FDR's attack on "Martin, Barton, and Fish," indelibly marked him as an intransigent isolationist. Barton believed, probably incorrectly, that Roosevelt's euphonious phrase cost him a Senate seat. Despite a characteristically vigorous campaign, he lost by 800,000 votes to the Democratic incumbent, James M. Mead.[58]

Barton returned to private life with a feeling of relief. Chairman of BBDO until his retirement in 1961, he tried to practice business statesmanship. Bruce, as the 2,000 employees were encouraged to call him, was disorganized, demanding, occasionally lazy, and persistently paternalistic. He required courtesy to office boys, the next generation's corporate leaders, took pride in recruiting youth and promoting "early middle age to the top," and encouraged the staff to buy BBDO stock. The investment program helped the company through hard times, encouraged loyalty, and fostered mobility. By the early 1950s, 250 members of the firm owned shares. "If any organization can count on a continuing future in the advertising business," Barton boasted in 1953, "it should be BBDO."[59]

Until the mid-1950s, Barton commented regularly on public affairs in speeches, articles, and syndicated newspaper columns. His political advice, though sometimes unsolicited, was often astute. He urged Senator Robert A. Taft to emulate an "Old Testament prophet" instead of cultivating false conviviality, recommended new eyeglasses to improve Senator Barry M. Goldwater's image, and in 1961 predicted a comeback by Richard M. Nixon if advisors did not "make [him] talk too often."[60]

Passionate concern regarding foreign policy overcame Barton's wry detachment. By 1947 he concluded that the Truman administration was making an effort, doomed by "history" and "human nature," to "play God around the world." Like many pre-1941 isolationists who later criticized the Cold War, Barton combined ethnocentrism and acuity. On the one hand, he could not take seriously a threat from Russia, a "half-fed, half-clothed, ignorant horde of savages." On the other hand, while Truman exaggerated Communist dangers at home and abroad, Barton opposed universal military training and derided the "outrageous notion" that voters were "too dumb to know the truth." Perhaps influenced by his friend Charles A. Beard, he wanted renovation of American cities to take precedence over foreign aid. Unfortunately, such "realistic" proposals were smothered by internationalists "ten times" less tolerant than prohibitionists had been.[61]

United States intervention in Korea left Barton "sick at heart." It underscored the "folly of our habit of making wholesale 'commitments and guarantees,' without any idea as to how, or to what extent, we can make good." Might he protest, Barton joked sadly to Norman Thomas, by running for Congress "on the Socialist ticket?" Two years of inconclusive combat reinforced his opinion that the "police action" was unconstitutional, unwinnable, and humiliating.[62]

In 1952 BBDO arranged radio and television advertising for the Republican presidential ticket. Barton's belief that political accounts hurt the firm was superseded by his "great affection" for General Dwight D. Eisenhower, his occasional bridge partner. By midsummer he was offering advice and composing campaign slogans. When Richard M. Nixon answered charges of profiting from illegal political contributions, Barton wanted Eisenhower's public response to be "expertly stage managed." Accordingly, after watching the televised speech in the absence of advisors, Eisenhower should wait fifteen minutes and then, "with deep feeling," read a handwritten endorsement of Nixon (composed in advance by Barton). Whether or not he received Barton's memorandum, the General, a master of public relations in his own right, offered no instant endorsement of his running mate. During Eisenhower's presidency, Barton dined at the White House but had scant impact on policy. Indeed, he lamented the administration's refusal to withdraw from Asia and during 1954 became "so worked up by our threatened intervention in Indochina that I can hardly think of anything else."[63]

International crises and personal tragedies tested Barton's strenuous effort to believe in a benign universe. During World War II he absented himself from church because the clergy had snapped to attention when the "bugles began to blow." More importantly, his wife Esther died of cancer in 1951 after three years of suffering. Barton coped by writing a kind of advertisement, an article urging regular physical examinations.[64]

Although Barton's church attendance lapsed again after Esther's death, he not only soon returned to services himself, but also encouraged the national religious revival. He praised Norman Vincent Peale (who responded in kind), contributed money and public relations advice to Billy Graham, and, by the mid-1950s, was promoting faith and work in language reminiscent of *More Power to You.* In 1952 BBDO handled advertising for the Revised Standard Bible ("The Bible Jesus Would Have Loved"; "Biggest Bible News in 346 Years").[65]

Above all, Barton revised *The Man Nobody Knows* and *The Book Nobody Knows* for joint republication in 1956. Much as he had earlier transformed the Young Insurgent into a business statesman, he now recrafted the ahistorical Jesus to fit an era marked by increasingly subtle salesmanship and self-help. Chapter 1 was called "The Leader" instead of "The Executive" (though the latter term survived in the text). Absent, too, were newspaper headlines announcing Jesus' activities. Instead of the businessman's "silent partner," He was, with pronoun capitalization restored, the ideal "companion guide and master" for both genders. These revisions, Barton said, were intended to make the "essential message . . . more immediate." His central theme, virtually unchanged since the 1910s, was that God required service as well as striving. "Wist ye not that I must be about my Father's business?" no longer graced the flyleaf, and, while quoting Luke in the text, Barton acknowledged the Revised Standard alternative, "did you not know that I must be in my Father's house?" In both renditions, however, the "essential remains the same": Jesus "offered his life to men."[66]

In the end Barton's positive thinking could not prevent personal pain. His daughter Betsey drowned in 1962. Bruce, Jr., died a year later. Barton himself paid the cruelest compensation. One of his greatest fears was "that I may some day be old." As a vigorous young man, he had defined old age as a "condition of the soul" and hoped to remain, like his father, perpetually young in spirit. Barton's soul was willing but his body failed. Never fully recovering from a stroke suffered in 1957, he became a garrulous parody of his former self. By the time of his death on 5 July 1967, arteriosclerosis had virtually erased his memory.[67]

* * *

Students of the gospel of success rightly regard Bruce Barton, whose acquaintances ranged from Russell Conwell to Norman Vincent Peale, as an important transitional figure. Historian Warren Susman observes, for example, that he bridged the gap between a "producer ethic," stressing work, independence, and acquisition, and a "consumer ethic: spend, enjoy, use up." More worldly than most positive thinkers, Barton deliberately adapted his version of the "gospel" to meet the changing needs of capitalism. More sensitive than most positive thinkers, he was ambivalent about the changes. Not only did consumption serve in his scheme to sustain the economy, but fresh "objects of desire" compensated for lost autonomy. Because economic consolidation prevented the typical young man from starting his own firm, Barton advised Herbert Hoover in 1928, corporations must provide careers "as satisfying to every side of his nature as he would have had in the days when the field was open." Certainly his acceptance of corporate organization did not extend to docile "organization men." Rather, in his choice of friends, as in his depiction of Jesus, pleasant personality counted for less than character.[68]

Much as Barton redefined success, he modified the cult of true manhood. The two issues intersected. By conceding that most men could no longer own farms or businesses—even as he wanted them somehow to remain independent—Barton loosened the tie between manliness and economic self-sufficiency. Moreover, in place of the stern patriarch who escaped wife and offspring at a male club, he elevated the family man. Jesus again provided the model, welcoming children who "flocked" to his side and women who cherished his company. Equally important, Barton was immune to the convention that war ennobled men. He never portrayed Jesus leading Christian soldiers on to San Juan Hill or Belleau Wood. In the final analysis, *The Man Nobody Knows* simultaneously protested against the "feminization" of religion and contributed to the softening—or "feminization"—of the masculine mystique.[69]

Furthermore, Barton's life illuminates the perennial complex of questions about what happened to progressivism during the 1920s— and 1930s, 1940s, and 1950s. As he may have recognized while embellishing the tale, his abandonment of "radicalism" was commonplace among fellow muckrakers. Indeed, his reclassification of Jesus from a "Young Insurgent" in 1914 to the "founder of modern business" in 1925 paralleled the enthusiastic discovery of industrial statesmen by Ida Tarbell and Burton J. Hendrick. Similarly, Representative Barton's opposition to the New Deal characterized many, if not most, former progressives, some of whom also questioned internationalist foreign policy during World War II and the Cold War. Legitimators of a linear liberal tradition from the Square Deal to the Great Society often attribute such heresies to personal eccentricity. But progressivism spawned many latter-day conservatives because it was largely conservative from the outset.[70]

Although Barton settled to the right of center on our narrow political spectrum, he was neither naive nor unreflective. Thus scholars using him as a symbol for an age must at long last grapple with the complexity of the 1920s. Instead of representing an amorphous "business ethos," Barton signaled divisions between "small bore" entrepreneurs and the corporate elite, and revealed the limits of business statesmanship. At the same time, he stood for millions of Americans who proclaimed the imminent arrival of the good life in order to ease doubts about the "purpose of it all." And condescending historians may finally learn from Barton that they cannot reform or replace corporate capitalism simply by mocking the shrewdest capitalists.

4

The Complexity of American Communism

For most Americans, intellectuals included, few tasks are easier than deriding Communists and few harder than understanding why more than a million Americans, intellectuals included, joined or cooperated with the Communist party during the 1930s and 1940s. Lack of understanding does not stem from lack of energy. Probably more scholars have studied the Communist party than any third party of comparable size. Veterans of old ideological battles, now scattered across the political spectrum, continue to publish memoirs. Their intellectual offspring resume old battles in essays, novels, and films. All sides accuse rivals of misremembering the past and, in this respect at least, all sides are usually correct.

To understand the attraction of American Communism we must first recognize the limits of the New Deal. President Franklin D. Roosevelt neither ended the Great Depression nor initially welcomed the welfare state. Indeed, he was reluctant to push such measures as social security and the National Labor Relations Act, which admirers and detractors alike currently consider synonymous with his administration. Furthermore, critics as diverse as Republican Herbert Hoover and Socialist Norman Thomas complained that New Deal inconsistencies impeded economic recovery. Unemployment, which still stood at 16 percent of the nonfarm work force in 1936, rose by two points after the administration curtailed relief spending. In short, there were good reasons to challenge the New Deal from the left.

Communists seemed an unlikely source of effective protest when the Depression began. The movement's first decade had been marked by intrigue, factionalism, and peculiar interpretations of American life. In 1919, when the Bolshevik Revolution precipitated a split within the American Socialist party, left-wing dissidents organized two offshoots, the Communist party and the Communist Labor party. Accepting an analysis offered by the Third International organized in Moscow—the Comintern—these two parties expected other revolutions to follow soon in Europe and the United States. Instead American Communists faced further splits and the first of this century's Red Scares in 1919–1920. After four thousand suspected members were arrested, both parties went underground in 1920. Inter- and intraparty disputes continued, involving personal rivalries, ethnic conflicts, and differing tactical assessments. Perhaps most important, Communists disagreed among themselves about the merit of organizing legal parties after the Red Scare had ebbed.

Even those who scorned legality rarely burrowed deep enough to evade surveillance. In 1922 Department of Justice agents raided a secret Communist convention at Bridgman, Michigan, scattered the delegates, and seized buried membership lists. The Red Scare almost destroyed American Communism at the outset. By 1922, membership in the Communist parties had dropped from forty thousand to fewer than ten thousand, mostly Eastern Europeans who felt an ethnic bond with the Russian Revolution.

In 1923 the chief contending factions coalesced into a single Communist party and determined to win control of American farmer-labor movements. This strategy, though formulated by the Comintern, looked appealing and plausible. Diverse agrarian rebels, union leaders, and intellectual veterans of the progressive era were actively seeking political alternatives to normalcy. Some leaders of the Farmers Union, the foremost lobby for small farmers, expressed interest in Soviet agricultural experiments. Many trade unionists respected William Z. Foster, a Communist leader who had organized the great steel strike of 1919.

Nonetheless the strategy failed. Communists won control of the Farmer-Labor national convention in 1923 but their victory sparked grass roots defections. Most defectors joined a broad reform coalition supporting Senator Robert LaFollette for president in 1924. Some Communists also wanted to endorse him, expecting this "American Kerensky" inadvertently to open the way for Communist revolution. The Comintern disagreed but the issue became moot when LaFollette rejected Communist aid. Foster, running on the Workers party line, won thirty thousand votes.

During the next four years Communists continued their efforts to "bore within" established labor and farm organizations. Internal party rivalries not only persisted but also intersected with Joseph Stalin's consolidation of power in the Soviet Union. American followers of Leon Trotsky, led by James P. Cannon, were expelled in 1928; those loyal to Nikolai Bukharin, led by Jay Lovestone, were ejected a year later. Although Foster did much of the American dirty work, the post of party secretary eluded him. In 1930 Earl Browder, a bland, self-described "pupil" of Stalin, was chosen instead.

As part of his maneuvers against Bukharin's "right opposition," Stalin ushered world Communism into a "third period." Once again the collapse of capitalism seemed close enough to abandon cooperation with bourgeois parties and unions. Indeed, the signal feature of third period theory was the assertion that liberals and socialists, "social fascists" in disguise, differed little from outright fascists. Proclaiming the slogan "After Hitler, our turn," German Communists scorned a liberal-left alliance against Nazism. In the United States Communists ridiculed the American Federation of Labor and the Farmers Union, groups they had recently tried to bore within, and promoted the Trade Union Unity League and the United Farmers League as revolutionary alternatives.

The Great Depression did not initially alter third period premises. On the contrary, the Crash of 1929 reinforced beliefs that the collapse of capitalism was at hand. The American Communist party, which then contained roughly 7,000 members, continued to scorn liberals, socialists, and independent radicals. According to third period canons, prominent social fascists included philosopher John Dewey, muckraker Upton Sinclair, and Representative Fiorello La-Guardia (Republican of New York). President Franklin D. Roosevelt qualified at best as the latest candidate for American Kerensky; at worst, the New Deal looked like an American version of fascism. Such belligerent dogmatism hurt party recruitment. To think that a version of autocratic Russian Communism could be transplanted here, John Dewey wrote in 1934, was "nothing short of fantastic."

Even during the third period, however, Communist practice was sometimes wiser than Communist theory. The party organized Unemployed Councils in several cities to demand direct relief. Some Communists gave ad hoc assistance to the Farm Holiday Association, an offshoot of the Farmers Union that halted delivery of food to market in order to dramatize the woes of farmers facing default, and the Southern Tenant Farmers Union, which attempted to build an alliance between black and white sharecroppers. Others risked their lives to organize migrant workers in California and assist striking coal miners in Harlan county, Kentucky; Angelo Herndon, a black organizer in Atlanta, Georgia, was sentenced to twenty years at hard labor for organizing an integrated demonstration at city hall. International Labor Defense (ILD), the party's legal arm, moved quickly in 1931 to defend the "Scottsboro boys," nine young blacks convicted of rape by a bigoted Alabama jury egged on by a mob outside the courthouse.

Even during the third period, moreover, Communists enjoyed some advantages over their rivals on the left. For Americans contemplating alternatives to capitalism in crisis, the Soviet "experiment" seemed to prove that planning worked. Especially after Adolf Hitler consolidated power in Germany, Communism and fascism loomed as the only alternatives to collapsing capitalism. In this context, Communist abrasiveness looked like necessary toughness. Communists who organized the poor in the face of billy clubs and shotguns showed bravery if nothing else.

By 1932, some American intellectuals were impressed. Affirming the "Socialism of deeds, not words," 150 of them, including Edmund Wilson, Sherwood Anderson, Malcolm Cowley, John Dos Passos, Langston Hughes, and Sidney Howard supported William Z. Foster and James Ford, the Communist candidates for president and vice-president. This endorsement did not necessarily entail acceptance of all third period presumptions. In a pamphlet called *Culture and the Crisis,* intellectuals for Foster and Ford argued that only the Communists were sufficiently militant to wrest "genuine concessions" from the capitalists. Indeed, by making a fetish of democracy, Socialist candidate Norman Thomas "indirectly" aided the fascist enemy.

Although Foster attracted a longer list of prominent intellectuals, he won roughly 102,000 votes compared to 885,000 for Thomas. With only twenty-three thousand members in 1933, the Communist party remained a sect rather than a mass movement after four years of depression. Moreover, it remained primarily a sect for the foreign born, with Finns and Eastern European Jews contributing particularly large contingents. Most members were unemployed; undoubtedly they were attracted by Communist militancy and immediate demands rather than third period theory. Often the attraction was ephemeral. Thirty-three thousand Communists became ex-Communists between 1930 and early 1934.

Efforts to attract or cooperate with non-Communist radicals proceeded fitfully. In March 1933, worried by Hitler's appointment as chancellor of Germany, the Comintern proposed a "united front from below." Unfortunately, further denunciations of socialists accompanied this grudging offer to ally with them; in February 1934 Communists hurling epithets and chairs turned a Socialist mass meeting at Madison Square Garden into a melee. Even so, Reinhold Niebuhr, Heywood Broun, Roger Baldwin, A. J. Muste, and Adam Clayton Powell, Jr., joined with Communists in campaigns for unemployment relief and racial equality.

In 1935, Communists began attracting supporters with honey as well as vinegar. The Comintern, reflecting Stalin's growing fear of Nazi Germany, proposed a "Popular Front" against fascism. The form of the front and the nature of the allies varied from country to country. Most American Communists, who had been vainly trying to convince Americans that the National Recovery Administration's blue eagle was the New Deal swastika, found the move congenial. Now they repudiated violent revolution, called Communism "twentieth-century Americanism," and sought alliances with liberals, socialists, and independent radicals. Although the Communists nominated Browder for president in 1936, they gave de facto support to Roosevelt. Browder focused his own attack on Republican nominee Alfred M. Landon, a "figurehead" for the "fascist-minded men of Wall Street."

The Popular Front brought increased membership, unprecedented influence, and near respectability. By 1938, the Communist party had grown to sixty thousand members while the Socialists had slipped to eleven thousand. Most new recruits were native-born citizens with white-collar jobs. Browder addressed the National Press Club and was roasted along with other presidential candidates at the Washington correspondents' Gridiron Dinner. Some liberal members of Congress welcomed, though rarely advertised, Communist assistance. Communists in New York operated through the American Labor party to support Mayor Fiorello LaGuardia, ostensibly a Republican. Out west they worked closely with the Farmers Union. By the late 1930s, Communists dominated or significantly influenced such left-liberal umbrella groups as the American Student Union, National Negro Congress, National Lawyers Guild, and American League Against War and Fascism.

Most important, Communists held powerful positions in the Congress of Industrial Organizations (CIO) and several constituent unions. Desperately needing brave, skilled organizers to direct grass roots militancy, CIO President John L. Lewis refused to shake his aides upside down "to see what kind of literature falls from their pockets." Communists Len DeCaux and Lee Pressman served respectively as editor of *CIO News* and CIO general counsel. Union presidents close to the party, if not actual members, included Joseph Curran of the National Maritime Union, Michael Quill of the Transport Workers Union, and Harry Bridges of the International Longshoremen's and Warehousemen's Union.

Relations between the Communist party and the Roosevelt administration reflected mutual opportunism, FDR's penchant for ambiguity, and Communist naiveté. Moved by realpolitik and visions of Russian trade, FDR discounted third period rhetoric and recognized the Soviet Union in 1933. Three years later he ordered the Federal Bureau of Investigation to monitor Communist activities. Also in 1936, FDR repudiated the "support of any advocate of Communism or any other 'ism' which would by fair means or foul change our American democracy." Meanwhile, members of his administration—and Eleanor Roosevelt—addressed Popular Front groups. For their part, most Communists became virtual New Dealers. Thus they could view themselves simultaneously as outsiders, hard-boiled builders of a socialist future, and insiders, allies of the president with friends in high places. The Popular Front, writer Joseph Freeman recalled, was the "sweetest bandwagon in history."

Browder loved riding the bandwagon. In 1938 he claimed that Communists were taking their place within the two-party system, which now consisted of the "New Deal and the anti–New Deal party." Browder had a point, but the Communists' place was less secure than he thought. FDR easily discarded allies when they became liabilities. Indeed, he had already dropped from his coalition both Father Charles Coughlin and Senator Huey Long, whose constituencies exceeded Browder's in size and reputability. Far from convinced that Communism constituted twentieth-century Americanism, nine out of ten Americans polled in 1939 thought party members more loyal to the Soviet Union than to the United States. Congressional conservatives, led by Representative Martin Dies (Democrat of Texas) continued to investigate their allegedly un-American activities.

Viewed from this perspective, Communist participation in the American cultural celebration of the 1930s looks poignant. The party held Lincoln-Lenin Day rallies and hailed Littleberry Browder, an ancestor of its general secretary, who had fought beside George Washington. Communist literary critic Granville Hicks wrote a tract called *I Like America*—and he did. Party organizational secretary Fred Brown urged Communists to act like "regular" fellows—and they did. For example, the *New York Daily Worker* offered excellent coverage of major league baseball and the head of the Young People's Communist League (YPCL) at the University of Wisconsin explained that dialectical materialism coexisted in the club with dates and dances. For thousands of Communists, the party provided a bridge between immigrant enclaves and broader American ways of life.

Yet the Popular Front cannot be reduced to an unambiguous pursuit of respectability. Even though most Communists wanted to like America, they also wanted to change the meaning of Americanism. Their strongest challenge lay in the area of race relations. Recruitment of African-Americans was both helped and hindered by the declaration of the Sixth World Congress of the Comintern in 1928 that blacks in the southern United States comprised a separate nation entitled to "self-determination." Taken literally, this position ran counter to the integrationist aspirations of most African-Americans, including those in the party. Yet the meaning of self-determination was left vague, allowing Communists to infer a mandate to understand, celebrate, and popularize black culture. During the Popular Front, the party reached out to black nationalists and followers of Father Divine, promoted the study of African-American history, and played an important part in efforts to integrate major league baseball. Former vice-presidential nominee James Ford, the party's foremost black, urged his comrades to avoid any "attitude of superiority" toward African-American religion.

The party's approach to race was variously self-serving, inept, and admirable. The Scottsboro case showed Communists at their best and worst. ILD, which publicized the trial while the National Association for the Advancement of Colored People hesitated, ultimately hired Samuel Leibowitz, an able non-Communist attorney, to represent the defendants; Communists also exploited the cause to recruit blacks and almost derailed the defense by trying to bribe jurors. Especially at the local level, as historian Mark Naison has shown, idealism marked the attempt to create an interracial community. Communists chastised bigots in their own ranks, sponsored interracial social events, and calmed angry crowds during incipient urban riots.

Like many of their white counterparts, black leaders made mutually convenient and sometimes mutually admiring alliances with Communists. A cross section of African-Americans initially supported the National Negro Congress, a Popular Front group especially concerned with civil rights, rural poverty, and labor organizing. Augustus Hawkins, Coleman Young, George Crockett, and Adam Clayton Powell, Jr., joined other rising politicians in accepting Communist assistance. Blacks managed these alliances at least as shrewdly as whites. For instance, Communists received more accolades than votes from Harlem residents, who understood that Democrats and Republicans retained the political power in New York. As Powell observed, most African-Americans neither feared Communists nor "fell over backwards" in admiration but judged them "individually" on the basis of their commitment to black equality.

Unexpectedly, Communists enjoyed greater success with white intellectuals than with black voters. Mike Gold, editor of *New Masses* and the writer most loyal to the party, had since the early 1920s scorned prominent authors and urged cultivation of "proletarian literature." Although the term remained ill defined, the basic thrust of Gold's argument was clear. Above all, he desired fiction and poetry by members of the proletariat whom, he thought, would inevitably shun gentility in favor of "vigor and guts." Writers from other classes, even non-Communists, might share this vision; during the 1920s, Gold accepted their contributions to the *New Masses.* Starting in 1929, the Communist party organized the John Reed Clubs to encourage working class writers. Sometimes the clubs succeeded. Notable John Reed Club alumni included Richard Wright and Ralph Ellison.

By and large, poets, playwrights, novelists, and literary critics joined or cooperated with Communists not because they adhered to an ostensibly Marxist aesthetic, but because they, like other Americans, viewed the party as a legitimate means to defeat fascism and promote justice. Often, however, something else was involved. The Great Depression was a cultural as well as an economic crisis. Thus intellectuals who had criticized "traditional" values during the 1920s now saw an opportunity to create or disseminate alternatives. "It gave us a new sense of power," Edmund Wilson recalled, "to find ourselves carrying on while the bankers, for a change, were taking a beating."

Neither recruitment of intellectuals nor transformation of American prose was a Communist priority. Especially during the Popular Front, literary celebrity took precedence over proletarian aesthetics. Relatively few major writers became Communists, but many, including Ernest Hemingway, Archibald MacLeish, and John Chamberlain, either joined the Popular Front's League of American Writers or participated in the American Writers Congresses. Such participation barely affected their prose, let alone their artistic premises, but Communist leaders could have cared less. Literary celebrities could write as they pleased as long as they remained orthodox on one issue, uncritical defense of the Soviet Union.

Nevertheless, the proletarian sensibility did influence American culture. Although some of its products self-destructed from excessive sentiment or crude politics, other works, including Gold's *Jews Without Money* and Wright's *Native Son,* still retain considerable power. Most important, celebration of the worker merged with widespread celebration of "the people," a trend characterizing Hollywood films, Federal Theatre productions, ersatz folk songs, and regionalist murals. Looking back with hyperbole and pride in 1941, Gold regarded the Depression era as a "Second American Renaissance"—a "revolution of taste, morals, aspirations, and social consciousness." These changes came through "no Moscow plot," Gold added, conceding more than he realized about Communist influence. Rather, intellectuals had finally come "to grips with [their] own enormous and wonderful continent."

Notwithstanding Gold's celebration of the American celebration, novelists, poets, playwrights, and screenwriters were less valuable to the Communist party than were intellectuals who interpreted politics for the *Nation, New Republic,* and similar publications. Some commentators—Malcolm Cowley, for example—came from literary backgrounds, but most were journalists or academics. Sometimes skeptical of Moscow's actions, these political intellectuals nonetheless portrayed the Soviet Union as an efficient, planned society moving toward democracy. Whatever their private reservations about Soviet leadership, they considered the Popular Front an essential bulwark against fascism at home and abroad. Popular Front liberals conducted an aggressive defense. Their favorite targets included Trotskyist and Socialist heretics who charged Stalin with betraying socialism, centrist liberals at *Common Sense* who called Nazism and Communism equally "totalitarian," and civil libertarians who favored constitutional rights for native "fascists."

Communist party leaders were even more pugnacious than their liberal allies. At some time between the Crash and Pearl Harbor, they assailed virtually every prominent figure in American political and intellectual life. Even during the Popular Front party strategists mixed deviousness with calls for solidarity on the left. So-called submarines, party members who hid their affiliation, organized Communist "fractions" within farmer, labor, and student organizations. And there were some Soviet spies, though their number, significance, and relationship to American Communism remain a matter of dispute.

Fierce rhetoric, strict discipline, and unswerving public loyalty to the Soviet Union by party leaders obscured divisions within the ranks. Divisions multiplied as membership expanded. Loyalists from the 1920s doubted the fervor of new recruits; young members derided the cultural conservatism of their elders, who, in turn, considered them undisciplined bohemians; and foreign-born Communists looked askance at those born in the United States (a majority by late 1936). Most important, Earl Browder and William Z. Foster, along with their respective supporters, disagreed about the meaning of the Popular Front itself. According to Foster, Browder yielded too much to bourgeois American ways and diminished the party's position as the revolutionary vanguard.

Adherence to Communism or Popular Front liberalism was not necessarily firm or well thought out. Thus, as former *Daily Worker* foreign editor Joseph Starobin recalled three decades later, the party was a "revolving door." Above all, Soviet policy kept the membership door spinning during the late 1930s. Yet American Communism and Popular Front liberalism proved remarkably durable. Both weathered the Moscow purge trials of 1936–1938, in which many old Bolsheviks were convicted of conspiring to overthrow the Soviet system. A commission of inquiry headed by John Dewey correctly judged the trials a "frameup," and rumors circulated on the left that confessing defendants had been tortured.

Most Popular Front liberals nevertheless agreed with the *New Republic* that the purged Soviets were "probably guilty of something." Moreover, the trials coincided with the Spanish Civil War and German assaults on Austria and Czechoslovakia. Afraid to disrupt antifascist unity at a critical time, Communists and Popular Front liberals gave the Soviet regime the benefit of the doubt. At the same time they discounted evidence that Communists had brutally suppressed the Spanish anarchists. As Malcolm Cowley wrote in 1937, Stalin's "personal character" was "relatively unimportant . . . in the face of an international fascist alliance." In mid-August 1939, four hundred notable Americans signed an open letter praising the Soviet Union as a "consistent bulwark" against aggression. Less than two weeks later Moscow agreed to a nonaggression pact with Nazi Germany. Secure on his eastern front, Hitler ordered an invasion of Poland and began World War II in Europe.

The Nazi-Soviet pact cost the Communist party at least 15 percent of its members; in 1940 Browder got only forty-six thousand votes for president, fewer than Prohibition nominee Roger Babson. Departing intellectuals, many of whom had been suppressing doubts about the Soviet Union, were particularly numerous and bitter. Granville Hicks, who left more in sadness than in anger, said that the pact forced him to reconsider "unpleasant facts my faith-bound mind had refused to examine." Journalist Vincent Sheean, a penitent Popular Front liberal, accused the Soviet Union of "blood-thirsty terrorism."

Although temporarily stunned themselves, Browder and other prominent Communists defended the treaty as a diplomatic master stroke and condemned the war as a conflict between competing versions of imperialism. Mike Gold struck back at departing intellectuals, whom he considered naive moralists at best and fascist sympathizers at worst. Even so, Gold's psychological explanation of their defection contained some truth. These "hollow men" had joined the party to ride the bandwagon of history, but now, afraid of being proletarianized, they used the pact as a pretext for jumping off.

Whether or not they believed these arguments, four out of five Communists stuck with the party. For many of them protection of the Soviet Union, the single socialist state, outweighed all other considerations. For many who had been attracted by Communist positions on labor and race relations, foreign policy looked less important than domestic issues—a perspective shared by most Democrats, Republicans, and Socialists. And some Communists feared the consequences of intervention. Along with other noninterventionists they recalled the agonies of World War I. Anyone who had forgotten should visit the "twisted wrecks of humanity" still lingering in veterans hospitals, advised Elizabeth Gurley Flynn, the party's highest-ranking woman.

After France fell and President Roosevelt moved steadily in word and deed to aid Great Britain, the respectability of all noninterventionists was increasingly at risk. Yet Communists bore the added burden of hypocrisy. Unlike Norman Thomas or the leaders of the America First Committee, firm noninterventionists throughout the 1930s, Communists had loudly advocated collective security until the Kremlin shifted tactics. Moreover, while avoiding war with Germany, Soviet armies absorbed three Baltic nations, eastern Poland, and part of Finland. By the spring of 1941, 75 percent of Americans polled by Gallup wanted to outlaw the Communist party. Liberal members of Congress helped to pass the Smith Act, a powerful sedition law, and to extend the mandate of the House Committee on Un-American Activities (HUAC). President Roosevelt called the Soviet Union a dictatorship "as absolute as any in the world," cheered

Browder's imprisonment for lying on a passport application, and toyed with cracking down on the Communist party. Even so, FDR was moved less by visceral anti-Communism than by his mounting fury against all noninterventionists.

Although diminished in size and reputation, American Communism survived the Nazi-Soviet pact. When Germany invaded the Soviet Union in June 1941, the party ended its noninterventionist interlude with a sense of relief, joined in denunciations of conservative noninterventionists as virtual Nazi agents, and rebuilt coalitions with accommodating liberals. Although major literary figures remained aloof, political intellectuals like Freda Kirchwey, editor of the *Nation,* rediscovered Russia's merits and reaffirmed the Popular Front. After the United States and the Soviet Union became uneasy allies in December 1941, American Communists rode the tide of enthusiasm for a co-belligerent. The Russians were "one hell of a people," *Life* magazine concluded in 1943, and a plurality of Americans casually agreed.

Thus the early 1940s, not the Great Depression, marked the peak of Communist influence. The party and YPCL attracted roughly one hundred thousand members; fifteen thousand served in the armed forces. Unlike the Socialists, who remained ambivalent about the war and criticized the policy of "unconditional surrender," Communists wanted total victory and subordinated all other issues to the cause, a popular American as well as Soviet position. Communist labor leaders adhered to the "no strike" pledge despite grumbling by the rank and file. Browder joined other notables in writing a book-length blueprint for the postwar world. Without any sense of contradiction, he urged continued collaboration with the "owning class," preservation of the Soviet-American alliance, and United States supervision of Latin American. In 1944, the party transformed itself into a "political association" and, instead of nominating its own presidential candidate, worked more or less openly for Roosevelt. Though few in number, Communists effectively mobilized voters through unions, the American Labor Party, and the CIO Political Action Committee.

American entry into World War II brought problems as well as opportunities; sometimes these were intertwined. Communists in the military, attracted by opportunities in the wider world, often lost their zeal. On the home front increased visibility meant increased vulnerability. During the 1944 campaign, Republicans, led by presidential nominee Thomas E. Dewey, assailed Communist influence in the CIO and criticized Roosevelt for commuting Browder's prison sentence. When Roosevelt blandly repudiated Communist support, Dewey accurately called his statement a "soft disclaimer." FDR's quiet acceptance of Communist assistance probably gained more votes than it cost. Communist leaders, convinced that they had made a difference, missed a lesson learned by Republicans: anti-Communism remained an effective political issue even when Soviet-American relations were going well.

Within five years the Cold War and complementary Red Scare decimated American Communism. Enthusiasm for the Russians, widespread but shallow, had rested on the assumption that they were, in *Life*'s phrase, "a lot like Americans." Postwar confrontations demonstrated the differences. The Soviets, believing their security at stake, demanded a sphere of influence and sometimes outright control in Eastern Europe. From their tenacious commitment to this position, Washington policy-makers inferred that the Soviets intended to advance across Europe and beyond. Wary cooperation yielded to what historian William Appleman Williams calls the "diplomacy of the vicious circle." President Harry S Truman declared in March 1947 that "nearly every nation must choose between alternate ways of life" and offered aid to those siding with the United States. Stalin responded to the Truman Doctrine by tightening his hold on Eastern Europe. The resulting coups further convinced Washington that Soviet totalitarianism must be contained.

The backwash from these events transformed American Communism. In July 1945 Moscow condemned Browder's Americanist heresy and forced his removal as party leader. Although Eugene Dennis was elected general secretary, William Z. Foster once again emerged as the party's foremost figure. Foster shared Browder's inclination to exaggerate Communist influence but lacked his feel for the wheeling, dealing, and ballyhoo of American politics. The party pressed allies in the labor movement to choose between endorsement of Soviet foreign policy and protection of the immediate interests of the rank and file, most of whom were Truman Democrats; they usually chose the latter. Increasingly convinced that American fascism was at hand, Communist leaders prepared to send two thousand members underground. Once the Cold War began, no pro-Soviet party had a future in American politics, yet extraordinarily inept leadership compounded the problems Communists faced.

The year 1948 produced a critical election for the left. Centrist liberals, whose intellectual mentors included Reinhold Niebuhr and Arthur M. Schlesinger, Jr., endorsed "containment" of the Soviet Union, rejected cooperation with domestic Communists, and favored Truman. Their leading organization, Americans for Democratic Action (ADA), symmetrically repudiated fascists and "Stalinists." Popular Front liberals, whose spokesmen included Norman Mailer and I. F. Stone, rejected containment, endorsed cooperation with domestic Communists, and favored Progressive party candidate Henry A. Wallace. The Communists also favored Wallace—too openly for his own comfort. This latest incarnation of the Popular Front presented an easy target. Partly because he actually feared subversion and partly to outflank Republicans who had used the issue to win control of Congress in 1946, Truman escalated the second Red Scare. Specifically, his administration initiated new loyalty tests for federal employees, issued an Attorney General's list of allegedly subversive groups, and in *United States* v. *Dennis* indicted twelve Communist leaders under the Smith Act. The President made "Henry Wallace and his Communists" a major issue in the 1948 campaign. The charge that Communists dominated the Progressive party became a self-fulfilling prophecy as non-Communists quit to avoid the stigma. Wallace's defeat, with less than 3 percent of the vote, ended Communist political clout. The next year the CIO expelled eleven unions headed by Communists or their close associates.

Allegations of Communist subversion proliferated while party influence ebbed. Recapturing the anti-Communist vanguard from Truman, conservative Republicans charged that liberal Democrats, influenced by those whom Senator Joseph R. McCarthy (Republican of Wisconsin) called the State Department "crimson crowd," had surrendered Eastern Europe at the Yalta conference, lost mainland China in 1949, and settled for stalemate in the Korean War. Few Soviet spies were discovered but many able civil servants were driven from government service. After the Supreme Court affirmed the convictions of the leading Communists in *United States* v. *Dennis* in 1951, federal prosecutors moved on to the party's second echelon. State, municipal, and free-lance countersubversion accompanied the federal Red Scare. Headlines highlighted investigations of noted diplomats, writers, and movie stars, yet most victims of blacklisting and harassment were ordinary citizens. As in the first Red Scare of 1919–1920, they included centrist liberals, socialists, and miscellaneous dissidents as well as Communists and former Communists.

Through it all almost twenty thousand men and women stayed with the party. Some stayed because they still believed in the Soviet Union or envisioned no other life after twenty years of commitment; others stayed despite doubts because they could not abandon their embattled comrades. At least a large minority, led by *Daily Worker* editor John Gates, tried to make the party less autocratic and less dependent on Soviet instructions. Nikita Khrushchev's denunciation of Stalin's atrocities in mid-1956 both shocked and encouraged these reformers. Jessica Mitford, a rank and file activist, thought that Khrushchev's "secret speech" demonstrated Soviet openness to "fundamental change." For the first time, American Communists could and did express "any and all criticism" of the party without fear of expulsion, Mitford remembered. Ultimately the ironic consequences of de-Stalinization in Eastern Europe doomed internal reform. In late 1956 Soviet troops crushed a Hungarian attempt to create an independent Communist regime. During the next two years, three-quarters of American Communists left the party instead of trying to change it.

* * *

The ferment within American Communism during the 1950s was ignored by scholars, not to mention by literary warriors and the country at large. Rather, old cultural battles persisted as the range of acceptable opinion about the party narrowed. To conservative Eugene Lyons, militant anti-Communism inflicted just retribution on perpetrators of "intellectual red terror" in the 1930s. For vital center liberals, McCarthyism and Communism (along with Popular Front liberalism) were comparable "extremist" movements. Postulating a tight Communist "conspiracy," Daniel Bell, Sidney Hook, and Arthur Schlesinger, Jr., were harsher than the Supreme Court majority, which, in sustaining *Dennis,* viewed the party as both an undercover plot and an ordinary political enterprise.

The 1950s were the heyday of extremism studies. Looking at the left "extreme," the Fund for the Republic sponsored a series on "Communism in American Life." Two books in the series, Theodore Draper's *The Roots of American Communism* (1957) and Daniel Aaron's *Writers on the Left* (1961), have not been superseded and most of the volumes reflect thorough scholarship. Yet none of the authors completely escaped Cold War premises or treated committed Communists as normal Americans. On the contrary, scholars and polemicists alike agreed with Bell that Communism had "no real roots in America." Hence, the movement appealed primarily to political innocents and politicized neurotics, many of whom were "masochistic," "immolating," and "castrated" intellectuals searching for a faith. Expulsion from the Communist party, Arthur Schlesinger, Jr., said in *The Vital Center* (1949), devastated Communists "as excommunication would a devout Catholic." Memoirs by former party members who felt immolated or castrated bolstered the interpretation of Communism as a destructive surrogate religion. Converts to Communism underwent a "personal metamorphosis so complete that they were mentally and morally changed into different human beings," Benjamin Gitlow wrote in *The Whole of their Lives* (1948). Thus transformed from "honest idealists" into "knaves," they practiced chicanery, intrigue, and other "black attributes of Satan and his fallen angels."

Starting in the mid-1960s, the vital center faced strong challenges from a renewed intellectual left, which argued that the United States bore at least partial responsibility for the Cold War. In this context, the consensus on the history of American Communism collapsed. Another round of memoirs appeared, this time by men and women who had remained loyal Communist editors, organizers, and defendants well into the 1950s. Unlike Gitlow and his contemporaries, they had left the party without rancor and now stressed the normality of life in the American Communist culture. Furthermore, unlike centrist scholars who had sought to calm the Red Scare by minimizing Communist confluence with the political mainstream, these ex-Communists highlighted party clout. For example, Al Richmond, formerly editor of the *San Francisco People's World,* recalled that Communists and their allies had influenced the "minds of millions" during the Great Depression.

The memoirs by Richmond, Steve Nelson, Peggy Dennis, John Gates, Dorothy Healey, and other former party leaders typically appealed to a specialized audience on the left, but, with the publication in 1977 of books by Vivian Gornick and Jessica Mitford, sympathetic accounts of American Communism reached general readers for the first time in three decades. In *The Romance of American Communism,* Gornick interviewed ex-Communists who were variously prosperous and poor, cynical and proud, radical, liberal, conservative, and apolitical. She showed the complicated "flesh-and-blood reality" behind the "armor-plated word" Stalinism and then rendered a largely favorable verdict. Communists had been "like everybody else, only more so," especially in their concern for social justice. Similarly, Mitford argued in *A Fine Old Conflict* that insularity, self-righteousness, and "dissembling" paled beside party advocacy of civil rights and civil liberties. In her circle, at least, Communists in the 1950s had displayed intelligence, independence, and wit. Indeed, *A Fine Old Conflict* may be the only deliberately funny book about American Communism.

Scholars also began to reexamine the flesh and blood of American Communism. By 1981, serious students of the subject were sufficiently numerous to found an organization, the Historians of American Communism (HOAC). For three decades the field had been dominated by Bell, Draper, Irving Howe, and other veterans of the intellectual wars of the 1930s; now it attracted many former new left activists—and for the same reason. They, too, turned to scholarship to make sense of *their* past politics. Though motives were similar, the social contexts and conclusions were very different. The best new work showed that Communism was indeed rooted in some American communities. All of the revisionists acknowledged the existence of intelligent, honorable, and influential Communists, and some of them explicitly criticized earlier historians for failing to do so. As Maurice Isserman complained, the Fund for the Republic studies made "it hard to understand why anyone with intelligence and integrity would have remained in such a movement for more than the few days or weeks required to discover its gross inadequacies."

By the mid-1980s the academic consensus on American Communism had yielded to a multifaceted debate. On all sides, interpretations of this old radicalism seemed inseparable from evaluations of the new radicalism of the 1960s. Even within the left, younger scholars usually judged Communism more generously than their elders. Whereas Mark Naison credited the party with trying to create an interracial community, Harold Cruse accused it of misunderstanding, even suppressing, African-American culture. Though critical of Communist myopia and authoritarianism, Isserman ultimately praised Browder's attempt to build a distinctly American party. Conversely, Warren Susman complained that the Popular Front had disseminated "an absurd vision of the American past, a peculiar notion of American society in the present, a ludicrous attitude toward American culture in general." Ignoring these differences, critics chided the left in general for romanticizing American Communism. In an atypically intemperate article, Theodore Draper accused "left-wing intellectual Yuppies" of turning their nostalgia into historiography. In *The Heyday of American Communism* (1984), the fullest account of the party in the 1930s, Harvey Klehr stressed that the "decisive formulations" of policy always came from Moscow.

The fiercest academic critics were recent converts from left liberalism or radicalism to conservatism, neoconservatism, or vital center liberalism. Professor Aileen Kraditor, a former party member, updated the argument that Communism was a kind of neurosis. Short-term, rank and file adherents were normal enough, but leaders, especially those who remained after the Nazi-Soviet pact, "needed and wanted authoritarianism." Ronald Radosh, whose old left family had mourned Julius and Ethel Rosenberg as victims of the second Red Scare, decided in 1983 that they had been guilty of espionage. This plausible conclusion served as a springboard for Radosh's leaps rightward. By the late 1980s he was arguing that Americans who had fought for the Spanish Republic were dupes of Stalinism.

Despite these strong feelings, recent debate among academics about American Communism has been relatively thoughtful and decorous. Advocates of conflicting interpretations even serve together on the HOAC "central committee" without denouncing each other as dupes or fascists. Unfortunately, the revisionist approach to American Communism and the Popular Front reached a mass audience through movies and polemics, not monographs and scholarly articles. In particular, Martin Ritt's *The Front* (1976), a comedy about blacklisting, and Lillian Hellman's *Scoundrel Time,* a self-serving rendition of her appearance before HUAC, precipitated an old-fashioned contretemps in 1976. According to Hellman, her refusal to "name names" was simply a matter of "decency." In reply, Diana Trilling contrasted prison terms meted out for contempt of Congress with the greater horror of totalitarianism. An analogous though more tepid controversy followed the appearance of *Guilty by Suspicion,* yet another film about the Hollywood blacklist, in 1991. Resembling the embattled literary warriors of the 1930s and 1940s, participants in these brawls declined to dig beneath their memories to examine the grubby details of politics and diplomacy.

* * *

Among serious historians, who bother with such grubby details as a matter of course, controversy about American Communism centers on three issues: the mental health of party members, their relationship to the Soviet Union, and their impact on American life.

The interpretation of American Communism as a sort of neurosis, presented most articulately by Daniel Bell, Nathan Glazer, Seymour Martin Lipset, and other pluralists in the 1950s, is vulnerable on conceptual and empirical grounds. According to pluralist theory, proper politics consisted of rationally balancing public interests, and any political activity arising from noneconomic personal needs was automatically suspect. These scholars assumed that most Democrats and Republicans had come to practice "pragmatic" politics and praised them for shunning the chiliastic dreams characteristic of extremists. Yet politics without chiliastic dreams evidently bored the foremost pluralists. Leaving Republicans and Democrats to lesser social scientists, Bell, Glazer, and Lipset concentrated on the far left and far right, where they found numerous cases of the personal becoming the political. Probably because they knew more ex-Communists than ex–Ku Klux Klansmen, their treatment of the two "extremes" subtly differed. Whereas far right fundamentalists seemed to suffer from terminal "status anxiety," most rank and file Communists appeared as temporary victims of social circumstances. Even castrated party intellectuals became whole again when they moved to the center. In standard pluralist accounts, men and women joined the party to satisfy inner needs but invariably left it after rationally evaluating the evidence.

This elegant model contained a central flaw: the leading pluralists confused their utopian prescription for American politics—a decorous competition among rational interests led by dispassionate operators—with the actual state of American politics—a passionate mobilization of bigotries and blarney. If they had paid closer attention to Democrats and Republicans, or to Federalists and Whigs beforehand, they would have known better. Earl Browder entered public life to satisfy drives and dreams, but so did Herbert Hoover, Alfred E. Smith, and Abraham Lincoln. Republican foes of free silver in 1896 and Communist foes of Nazism in 1936 insisted with equal fervor that civilization hung in the balance. In the latter case they were right.

Yet they were not always right—or honest or mentally sound. Sharing more conceptual ground with the pluralists than they realized, most revisionist historians of American Communism tended to agree that the personal should be apolitical. In their accounts, enemies of the left show symptoms of status anxiety and paranoid styles while Communists look reflective, altruistic, and amiable. In fact, Americans joined—and quit—the Communist party, as they joined and quit other parties, for a mixture of public and private reasons. Before the 1950s, when attribution of psychological causes became the preferred social science put-down, some Communists acknowledged as much. In his moving autobiography, *Let Me Live* (1937), Angelo Herndon praised the party for providing the education and friendship he craved, used religious language throughout, and explicitly compared his successive conversions to Christ and to Communism.

Although leading pluralists in the 1950s called Communism a religious surrogate, their application of this analogy revealed less about Communism than about prevailing cosmopolitan attitudes toward religion. By and large, intellectuals of that era applauded Protestant neo-orthodoxy, which served a small, cerebral constituency; tolerated liberal Protestantism, which seemed bland or tacky but harmless; feared evangelical Protestantism as a source of the "radical right"; and stereotyped Catholicism as an authoritarian monolith. In this context, the equation of devout Catholics afraid of excommunication with obedient Communists afraid of expulsion was almost automatic.

Ironically, despite its origins as a rhetorical denigration, the comparison with American Catholicism can illuminate the complexity of

American Communism. Both the Communist party of the United States and the Catholic church in the United States were hierarchical institutions belonging to international movements, disseminated alien ideas, suffered persecution, and yielded ultimate authority to foreigners. In both cases, a feeling of embattlement fostered insularity and obedience. Even so, both institutions adapted to American circumstances and encompassed decent men and women as well as scoundrels. Most members felt no divided loyalty and many sought internal reform or tried to circumvent instructions from above or abroad.

Since the 1950s students of religion have documented what should have been obvious, that the behavior of American Catholics cannot be inferred solely from the study of church doctrine, let alone from Vatican pronouncements. For example, Alfred E. Smith in 1928 disagreed with the papacy on the merits of democracy and the separation of church and state; if he had not disagreed, Smith would have been as unfit for the presidency as many Protestants maintained. Fear of excommunication did not prevent millions of Catholics from remarrying after divorce, using artificial means of birth control, or choosing abortion instead of motherhood. Like their Communist counterparts, proponents of church liberalization often grudgingly chose obedience instead of apostasy. During the 1950s, for example, Father John Courtney Murray complied with a Vatican order to cease publishing articles in favor of the separation of church and state. Nor was psychological dissonance absent from the hierarchy itself. Before the Second Vatican Council, Cardinal Richard Cushing presumably prayed for the conversion of the Jews, yet he does not seem to have pressed the matter with his Jewish brother-in-law.

Similarly, revisionist students of the left have documented what should have been obvious, that the behavior of American Communists cannot be inferred solely from party doctrine, let alone from Comintern pronouncements. Rather, there was a complicated, changing culture of American Communism marked by wheeling and dealing, hemming and hawing, skepticism and hope. Those Communists who swallowed their doubts and hoped for reform even during the Cold War were unduly optimistic—Nikita Khrushchev served John Gates less well than Pope John XXIII served Father Murray—but they were not necessarily neurotic, dishonest, or stupid. Some party leaders were shattered by "excommunication" and at least one of them, *Daily Worker* editor Louis Budenz, returned to the Catholic church. Most were not. Certainly James P. Cannon, Jay Lovestone, and Earl Browder survived expulsion with their formidable egos intact. In psychological terms, it was probably easier to break with Moscow than with Rome during the 1930s, 1940s, and 1950s. Unlike the vast majority of American Catholics, relatively few Communists were bound by family ties or childhood memories. Moreover, *their* apostasy was widely applauded and after 1939 they were welcomed by a thriving community of anti-Communist ex-Communists.

Needless to say (though perhaps in essays on this subject otherwise obvious disclaimers are de rigueur), this comparison between American Communism and American Catholicism is intended to explore the dynamics of belief, not to suggest moral equivalence between the Vatican and the Comintern. Joseph Stalin commanded more armed divisions than Pope Pius XII, along with a network of secret police and spies. Those forces killed millions of innocent people and threatened millions more. For half a century vital center liberals have asked, usually rhetorically, how decent men and women could ignore these crimes and remain "Stalinists." In 1984, Harvey Klehr wrote that during the purge trials hundreds of intellectuals "offered their endorsement of Stalin's murder of his Old Bolshevik comrades."

As Vivian Gornick complains, the "armor-plated" epithet "Stalinist" impedes examination of this issue. This label would be misleading even if it carried a smaller emotional charge. The cult of Stalin's personality, a folk religion in the Soviet Union by the late 1930s, had little impact in the United States. Certainly many Communists and Popular Front liberals craved charismatic leadership, but most of them are better described as Rooseveltists than Stalinists. By and large, Stalin was celebrated as leader of the Soviet "experiment," an experiment that seemed to produce prosperity and community.

In fact, Stalin's regime produced famine and terror. It is hardly to their credit that Communists and their allies both failed to see through the facade and slandered those like John Dewey who did so. Nonetheless, this behavior needs to be removed from the realm of demonology and placed in historical context. Most American

Communists did not sanction the "murder" of the Old Bolsheviks because (as Arthur Schlesinger, Jr., recognized in 1960), they considered the purges fair trials leading to just punishment. Certainly some of them told outright lies about the Soviet Union. Yet in 1956 even such stalwarts as Eugene Dennis and Benjamin Davis were shocked by Khrushchev's revelations of mass imprisonments and executions.

Furthermore, Communists were neither the first nor the last Americans to hold firm, fervent, and ultimately mistaken beliefs about governments thousands of miles away conducting affairs in languages they did not understand. Particularly grotesque examples of international misperception marked the 1920s, 1930s, and 1940s. Disillusioned old progressives thought Benito Mussolini an Italian version of Theodore Roosevelt, mass circulation magazines called Hitler a Nazi moderate, and the Roosevelt administration exaggerated Japan's ties to its Axis partners and underestimated its capacity to make war on the United States. Stories of atrocities were especially suspect for a generation that remembered the systematic deception of 1914–1918. Thus, much as conservatives and many liberals discounted reports of Nazi genocide, Communists considered reports of Stalin's crimes the latest form of propaganda.

Although American Communists were extraordinarily loyal to the Soviet Union, they were not without autonomy. Vital center liberals who postulated forty years ago that "Stalinists" could not be independent of Moscow were misled by provincialism as well as by Cold War fears. They paid too much attention to sectarian struggles on the American left during the 1930s, in which many of them had participated, and too little to subsequent developments within world Communism. Judging from recent critiques of the revisionists by Theodore Draper and Nathan Glazer, they still do. Since the late 1940s, however, numerous Stalinists and ex-Stalinists have attempted to create independent Communist regimes or parties. If Josip Broz Tito, Wladyslaw Gomulka, Imre Nagy, and Alexander Dubcek could think and act independently despite the threat of Soviet tanks, would it not be strange for American Communists, threatened with nothing worse than expulsion, always to think and act like pawns of the Kremlin?

Strange but not impossible. To pursue our analogy, American Catholics, outsiders in a predominantly Protestant country, were more obedient to the Vatican than Catholics in Italy or France. Moreover, Joseph Starobin remembered that his Communist comrades often deferred to the Soviets for very American reasons: admiration of apparent success and a "deeply ingrained inferiority complex" that ascribed greater wisdom to Europeans. Yet, as Isserman and others who focus on the rank and file have documented, they did not always defer. Critics of the revisionists discount grass roots dissidence because, as Harvey Klehr argues, Moscow remained the "ultimate source" of party policy. While fitting the party as an institution, Klehr's generalization obscures the mixed feelings of members, even high-ranking members. Lovestone, Cannon, and Browder were expelled precisely because they sought independence from Moscow.

* * *

Although many vital center liberals still think otherwise, acknowledging that most Communists were psychologically normal men and women who aspired to build an American movement is not much of a moral concession. After all, normal Americans can do terrible things. Indeed, if Communists were not neurotic robots, their behavior can be judged even more harshly.

Unlike the intricate controversies over motives, mental health, and party autonomy, there has been surprisingly little analysis of what Communists actually accomplished for good or ill. Orthodox and revisionist historians usually talk past each other instead of meeting their respective arguments. While the former assert that American Communists did great harm by serving Moscow's interests, the latter emphasize domestic good works, especially support for racial equality and industrial unionism. In the movies and memoirs that have appeared since the late 1970s, Communists and Popular Front liberals expect to be loved for the enemies they made: J. Edgar Hoover, Joseph R. McCarthy, and Richard M. Nixon. Curiously, no one systematically compares Communists with their non-Communist contemporaries in order to discover ethical similarities and differences.

The least illuminating aspect of this discussion concerns espionage. Alger Hiss, Julius Rosenberg, and Ethel Rosenberg have become symbols out of all proportion to their importance. In the late

1970s, two books on their legal cases produced well-publicized imbroglios. While criticizing the Rosenbergs' trial and execution, Ronald Radosh and Joyce Milton concluded that they had been spies. Similarly, Allen Weinstein found Hiss guilty of passing documents to the Soviet Union.

The resulting controversies centered on the defendants' guilt or innocence. Participation was not confined to specialists who, whatever their biases, had examined thousands of pages of testimony and evidence. On the contrary, diverse novelists, critics, and editors rendered remarkably confident verdicts. Despite the passion spent, no significant *historical* issues hung in the balance. Whether or not Hiss and the Rosenbergs were guilty, no one can plausibly deny that the Soviet Union spied on the United States. The Soviets themselves no longer deny it. Indeed, in her petition for clemency to President Eisenhower, Ethel Rosenberg denigrated the chief prosecution witness, her brother David Greenglass, on the grounds that he was a spy. Yet espionage has little bearing on evaluations of American Communism. Even after his expulsion, Browder claimed never to have met a spy, and there seem to have been few to meet in party ranks for the obvious reason that left-wing activism was a poor cover for Soviet espionage.

Retrospective discussion of the American Communist role in World War II has been equally confusing. Vital center historians insist that the Communists impeded victory by opposing aid to the Allies and leading strikes in defense plants between September 1939 and June 1940. Thus, as Professor William L. O'Neill writes, "It was no thanks to the Communist party of the United States that freedom survived anywhere in the world." Revisionists respond that the strikes received broad support and barely affected production. Neither side appreciates the pervasiveness and legitimacy of noninterventionist sentiment during 1939–1941. Again talking past each other, both sides fail to compare Communists and their allies with other Americans. If Communists impeded mobilization during 1939–1941, then so did Norman Thomas, who astutely criticized FDR's deception and expansion of presidential power; A. Philip Randolph, who planned a march on Washington to secure equal employment for blacks; and Yale law student Gerald R. Ford, who helped to found the America First Committee.

Like Popular Front liberals and anti-Communist New Dealers, their respective forebears in the 1940s, most revisionist scholars of American Communism and most of their critics share an ironic bond across the ideological abyss. Both sides romanticize World War II as an unambiguously noble cause in which all good citizens constantly sacrificed for victory. Even after Pearl Harbor, however, internal conflict persisted and the United States, alone among major belligerents, never fully mobilized—because most Americans opposed full mobilization. In a sense, then, victory was impeded by senators opposed to a labor draft, industrialists eager to produce consumer goods before VJ Day, striking coal miners whose wages were eroded by inflation, families circumventing rationing via the black market, and soft-hearted socialists who condemned the firebombing of civilians. Viewed in this way, Communist failings may have been the opposite of what O'Neill supposes. After June 1941, no group was more committed to total war and total victory. Party leaders criticized Randolph's planned march on Washington and suppressed wildcat strikes. The *Daily Worker* hailed the airborne incineration of enemy civilians, including those "fascists" who died at Hiroshima and Nagasaki. In this respect, unfortunately, Communism was twentieth-century Americanism.

A more persuasive complaint by vital center liberals is that the Communists degraded American politics with deviousness and calumny. Most revisionist scholars slight this issue, stressing instead the *Gemütlichkeit* within Communist communities, the worthiness of their goals, and the evil of their enemies. Therefore an important question remains largely unexplored—not whether Communists were deceitful and vicious, which they were, but whether they were worse others on the political spectrum.

Bell, Glazer, and Lipset had no doubt that they were. Here too, these first serious students of American Communism were misled by their utopian premise that mainstream politics was an open, fair, and civil competition. This description only partly fits the 1950s and badly distorts the 1920s, 1930s, and 1940s. No Communist front was more disingenuous—or more consequential—than the Committee to Defend America by Aiding the Allies, a Roosevelt front, which, operating with secret funds from the White House, convinced citizens in 1940–1941 that closer military ties with Britain would somehow keep the United States out of war. Nor were deception and calumny confined to extraordinary crises. In 1928 Herbert Hoover acquiesced in a campaign to portray his Democratic opponent, Alfred E. Smith, as a tool of Pope Pius XI; Methodist Bishop James Cannon, the most effective of these campaigners, attended the inauguration as Hoover's guest. Unlike Bishop Cannon, Al Capone never made it to the White House, but he nonetheless aided the Chicago Republican machine; Lucky Luciano served New York Democrats in similar fashion. The disruption of the Socialist rally at Madison Square Garden in 1934 still bulks large in erudite memoirs, yet such harassment, however alien to young intellectuals at the City College of New York, was commonplace across the river in Jersey City, where Mayor Frank Hague, who doubled as vice-chair of the Democratic National Committee, unilaterally defined law and order. Ballots cast on behalf of the dead determined elections in several states; after defeating Lyndon Johnson in 1941, deceased Texans elected him to the U.S. Senate seven years later. And almost everyone indulged the American penchant for what David Riesman calls "big talk"—especially predictions of apocalypse and accusations of subversion.

Yet even amid Depression-era big talk Communist rhetoric was a wonder to behold. Hitler and Mussolini were fascists; John Dewey, Thornton Wilder, and Alfred M. Landon were not. By casually applying the label "fascist" and otherwise abusing opponents, the party helped lower the level of political discourse. Most of the revisionist historians not only miss this point, but also seem surprised that abused liberals and conservatives did not later defend the rights of Communists during the second Red Scare. Such naiveté about mainstream politics, and about ordinary human emotions, characterized many Communists too. Browder was surprised when liberal allies deserted the party after the Nazi-Soviet Pact. A more astute leader would have understood that political parties are not philanthropies and politics is not one of the helping professions.

What nonetheless needs emphasis is that the repudiation of American Communists during the early Cold War involved more cost- benefit analysis than vital center liberals admitted. By and large, they described their stand as a principled response to Stalinist terror and domestic Communist machinations, and highlighted their own purity by also ostracizing other liberals who still cooperated with Communists or refused to denounce them with sufficient vigor. Schlesinger compared this latter group to "doughfaces"—northerners sympathetic to the Confederacy during the Civil War.

If Communists resembled Catholics in their attempt to accommodate American conditions, vital center liberals and Cold War socialists looked like evangelical Protestants struggling to determine the necessary distance from sin. For three decades they scrutinized editorial boards, letterheads, and petitions in order to avoid writing, signing, donating, or marching alongside any Communists or too many doughfaces. Sometimes politically incorrect affection survived in private; Norman Thomas, for example, kept up his friendship with Elizabeth Gurley Flynn. In public, however, they practiced separatist fundamentalism. At the 1956 Democratic National Convention, presidential nominee Adlai Stevenson almost shook hands with his former boss, Henry Wallace, but, deterred by an aide, turned back in the nick of time. Even during the political great awakening of the late 1960s, the strict church of the vital center produced few heretics.

Nevertheless, conservatives have complained since the second Red Scare that vital center liberals were belated anti-Communists. The charge contains some truth if we judge their earlier behavior by their own post–World War II standards. Literary intellectuals aside, no leading Cold War liberal or socialist had belonged to the Communist party and only a few, notably Norman Thomas and Reinhold Niebuhr, had flirted with the Popular Front during the 1930s. Yet most of them had supported a political movement—the New Deal coalition—that encompassed rank and file Communists and fellow travelers. Roosevelt's remarkable coalition also included devout segregationists, corrupt businessmen, authoritarian labor leaders, anti-Semitic Coughlinites, enthusiasts for Mussolini, and some gangsters, as well as millions of ordinary Americans trying to survive the Depression and war. Except for the period of the Nazi-Soviet pact, when he joined the combination Red and Brown Scare, FDR treated Communists and Popular Front liberals like other peripheral, problematic elements in the coalition, privately watching them with a wary eye and publicly overlooking their defects in order to retain their votes and energies on Election Day.

Measured by postwar vital center standards, the Roosevelt coalition looks dangerously latitudinarian. Mixing self-defense and wishful remembrance, Cold War liberals reinterpreted the 1930s and early 1940s to minimize grass roots connections between New Dealers on the one hand and Communists and Popular Front liberals on the other. In addition, they usually deprecated the Communist role in creating the CIO and bolstering the civil rights movement. As Republican red hunters sensed thirty years before leftist historians rehabilitated American Communism, these arguments hid evasions, expediency, and inconsistency. If New Dealers had applied the stringent anti-Communist standards later set by vital center liberals in the 1950s, they would have opposed the CIO until John L. Lewis shook his organizers upside down and fired those whose pockets yielded Communist pamphlets. Indeed, if the electorate in 1944 had applied the stringent anti-Communist standards set by the ADA four years later, they would have voted against Roosevelt. After all, FDR received funds from the CIO, accepted the nomination of the American Labor Party, benefited from the absence of a Communist ticket, and issued only a soft denial (to recall Governor Dewey's phrase) that he wanted such support.

Ex-Communists and Popular Fronters still have trouble imagining that vital center liberals were moved by any principles whatsoever, and vital center liberals usually forget the occasions when conscience and convenience merged. On both sides, intellectuals are more inclined than other veterans of the ideological forty years' war to refight old battles instead of forgetting or reconsidering them. Father John Cronin, a leader of the Association of Catholic Trade Unionists, an anti-Communist group within the CIO, later regretted his red baiting; Sidney Hook and Lillian Hellman went to their graves inveighing, respectively, against Stalinist conspirators and turncoats who named names. When in 1986 colleagues on the House Judiciary Committee praised Colonel Oliver North for invoking the Fifth Amendment, Representative George Crockett (Democrat of Michigan), an attorney for Smith Act defendants during the 1950s, asked why his clients had gone to jail for doing the same thing three decades earlier. The committee simply ignored this wry observation. If Crockett had made his point in a cosmopolitan little magazine, he would have been attacked immediately in other little magazines as a dangerous anti-anti-Communist.

The ideological forty years' war may not end when intellectuals who lived through the Great Depression pass from the scene. Their armory of arguments has been inherited by a second and a third generation, for whom the 1960s brought forth either ecstatic visions or hideous specters from the 1930s. "Without Stalinism," conservative art critic Hilton Kramer claimed—wrongly—in 1976, "there would have been no McCarthyism and no blacklist."

The emphasis on the relationship between intellectuals and Communism is hardly surprising. The party and its fronts appealed disproportionately to intellectuals—not only to novelists, critics, and scholars already famous during the 1930s, but also to obscure young men and women who later achieved prominence, some of whom remain prominent today. Furthermore, though Arthur Schlesinger, Jr., exaggerated when he claimed in 1949 that the Communists attempted to "organize culture itself," they did move further in this direction than Republicans and Democrats (who could take for granted the cultures of the white Protestant small town and the urban ethnic neighborhood). In retrospect many aspects of the Communist cultural mobilization were easy Cold War targets: the theory of social fascism, the notion of an independent black belt in the South, the crudest experiments in proletarian literature, and the wackiest Popular Front celebrations. And then, of course, there were insults remembered and scores to settle.

Even so, concentration on intellectuals and Communism distorts our understanding of the movement. Intellectuals comprised only a small fraction of the membership. They exerted little influence at party headquarters in New York, let alone in Moscow. The organization of culture concerned American Communist leaders much less than the organization of industrial workers and sharecroppers. Nor did Stalin approve the Nazi-Soviet pact because Lillian Hellman and I. F. Stone had recently signed a petition endorsing his regime. In short, the main events of the 1930s and 1940s did not occur in the CCNY cafeteria.

In 1973 revisionist historian Norman Markowitz wrote with insightful hyperbole that there was no secondary literature on American Communism. The subject was so wrapped up in ideology and emotion that even ostensibly dispassionate histories actually qualified as primary sources. This problem persists, though the range of interpretation has widened. Yet the study of American Communism may be approaching a major shift. Inevitably it will be affected by the democratization of Eastern Europe and the collapse of Communist rule in the Soviet Union itself, events that have ended the Cold War era. Perhaps these great changes will merely refuel old fires, as orthodox scholars cite the attempt by hardliners to overthrow Mikhail Gorbachev in 1991 as proof of Commun*ism*'s innate depravity, while revisionists cite the conversion to democracy by Gorbachev and Boris Yeltsin as proof that Commun*ists* can reform their system. With luck, however, we may finally be able to discuss American Communism as an ordinarily difficult historical issue.

5

It Can't Happen Here: Novel, Federal Theatre Production, and (Almost) Movie

The publication in 1935 of Sinclair Lewis's *It Can't Happen Here,* a tale of triumphant American fascism, added a catch phrase to our language. For fifty-seven years, the rhetorical question implicit in the title has been used to warn allegedly oblivious citizens that tyranny, variously defined, could conquer our country unless they were eternally vigilant. In 1973, for example, Lewis's son Michael recorded portions of the novel, which, the record jacket declared, showed how "home-grown hypocrisy leads to a nice brand of home-grown authoritarianism, as American as My Lai and Watergate." In 1988 *It Did Happen Here* served as the title of a collection of memoirs by victims of censorship, deportation, blacklisting, and vigilante violence.[1]

Although the phrase, "It can't happen here," is evidently timeless, Lewis's book itself remains decidedly an artifact of the 1930s. The aborted effort to transform the novel into a Hollywood movie and the successful stage version sponsored by the Federal Theatre Project illuminate the cultural, political, and economic life of the Depression era.

By the time Lewis wrote *It Can't Happen Here,* he had already added several catch-phrases to the American language. Indeed, he had been a leading satirist of the cultural conflicts of the 1920s. *Main Street,* which appeared in 1920, told of the effort by Carol Kennicott, a slightly liberated and slightly silly woman, to rebel against her restricted life in a small town, Gopher Prairie,

Minnesota. In 1922, Lewis made *Babbitt* synonymous with conformity among provincial businessmen. *Elmer Gantry,* published in
1927, provided an agnostic's tour of America's ordeal of faith, as the
author followed Gantry's climb from rustic fundamentalism through
New Thought to vapid Methodist eminence.[2]

According to his friend, journalist Vincent Sheean, Lewis was a
"loudly avowed socialist" who probably voted for Norman Thomas in
1928. Yet he neither translated his vows into action nor defined his
position with precision. Ironically, though he dealt in an almost
systematic way with religion and feminism, Lewis never wrote the
"labor novel" that he had planned for years. His marriage in 1928 to
Dorothy Thompson, the foremost woman foreign correspondent, did
not initially alter Lewis's views. He does not seem to have shared her
interest in the Soviet Union, nor did he accompany Thompson there
during their courtship. During the 1932 presidential campaign, he
grumbled that both Herbert Hoover and Franklin D. Roosevelt said
"absurd things."[3]

Within a half decade, however, the Depression and Thompson
combined to deepen, if not to refine, Lewis's political interests. After
returning briefly to his unfinished labor novel, he settled in Vermont
to write *It Can't Happen Here* during the summer of 1935.[4]

* * *

Fascism, regarded by Americans as an interesting but distant issue during the 1920s, became by the early 1930s a matter of
intense concern. Among a growing band of leftist intellectuals convinced of capitalism's doom, Italy under Benito Mussolini served as
a frightening reminder that socialism and the welfare state were not
the only alternatives. Adolf Hitler, whom most commentators considered a kind of German Mussolini, was even more frightening than
Hitler. "So long as Italy was the chief fascist country, fascism to
many people merely meant castor oil," Raymond Gram Swing wrote
in 1935. "Then Germany increased the vocabulary of repression to
include concentration camps, steel whips, and anti-semitism."[5]

Liberals and radicals were eager to denounce European fascism
but were almost at a loss to explain it. During the "third period," the
Communist party formulated an influential, if misleading, interpretation. Ignoring sophisticated analysts in their own ranks, party

leaders insisted that Mussolini had been a capitalist agent all along. Moreover, fascists, "social fascists," and liberals differed only in the tactics they used to serve capitalists. This theory, expanded to include the new chancellor of Germany, received classic expression at the Comintern plenary session in December 1933. Fascism, said George Dimitrov, was the "open terrorist dictatorship of the most reactionary, most chauvinist and imperialist elements of finance capital." Anti-Communist liberals offered an alternate but not completely antithetical theory. As Alfred Bingham argued in *Insurgent America*, fascism was "essentially" a revolt by frightened members of the middle class; they joined Hitler and Mussolini in order to avert class war, to protect their property, and to experience a sense of "social solidarity."[6]

The explanation of fascism was more than an academic concern because commentators feared that this horrible system might develop in the United States. Journalist George Seldes, who had been expelled from Italy by Mussolini a decade earlier, warned in 1935 that American fascism was already "formidable." It needed "only a Duce, a Fuehrer, an organizer and a loosening of purse strings of those who gain materially by its victory, to become the most powerful force threatening the Republic." "The usual complacent assumption that we cannot become fascist, simply because America is 'different' or too large," Raymond Gram Swing agreed, "does not bear analysis."[7]

By 1935, the search for precursors and forerunners was well underway. Predictably, liberals and radicals detected incipient fascism among their traditional foes. According to the *Nation*, urban bosses like Mayor Frank Hague of Jersey City represented the "most characteristic form of fascism," the Roman Catholic hierarchy nurtured "potential fascism," and corporations illustrated "our native Führerprinzip." Benjamin Stolberg, an independent Marxist, pointed to vigilantes who served the privileged class. Swing wrote that antilabor violence, legislative curbs on political dissent, and escalating nationalism among Elks and American Legionnaires fitted into a "pattern of fascist action." For Anna Wallace of the *New Republic*, faculty dismissals, censorship, and the psychological conditioning of teachers were "unmistakable symptoms" of fascism on campus. Hamilton Basso warned that "frightened fundamentalists" were vulnerable to "fascist tending" demagogues.[8]

The lists were eclectic but not indiscriminate. Extant or potential fascists usually fell into four sometimes overlapping categories. The first consisted of German nationals and untrustworthy German-Americans. Second, commentators quickly applied the label "fascist" to such far-right agitators as William Dudley Pelley of the Silver Shirts, Gerald B. Winrod of the Defenders of the Christian Faith, and Elizabeth Dilling, author of *The Red Network,* as well as to more complicated figures like Senator Huey P. Long (Democrat of Louisiana) and Father Charles E. Coughlin. Third, fascism meant increased government power, exhibited in both Mussolini's corporate state and the New Deal National Recovery Administration. Communists played a fourth variation on this theme. Applying the canons of the third period, they said that President Roosevelt, the far right, and "social fascists" under Norman Thomas all participated in the common drift toward fascism. After proclaiming the Popular Front in 1935, the Communist party continued to assert that fascism was the terrorist dictatorship of reactionary capital, but it detached New Dealers, compliant socialists, and some enlightened capitalists from the enemy ranks.[9]

These related theories of American fascism, like the two major models purporting to explain Italian and German developments, rarely appeared in pure form. For example, less inclined to systematic analysis than the *Nation* or the *New Republic,* writers for *Harper's* or the *Saturday Evening Post* mixed references to sinister German-Americans, native far-right anti-Semites, opportunistic agitators, and mysterious financiers who supposedly backed the movement. Dorothy Thompson not only assailed Coughlin, Pelley, and Winrod but also discerned the "very soul of Fascism" in FDR's "mystical compact" with the masses. By 1935, Stuart Chase complained, he could "hardly go out to dinner, open a newspaper, [or] turn on the radio" without encountering the term "fascist."[10]

In order to write *It Can't Happen Here,* Sinclair Lewis had to find his way through this conceptual maze. As he had done with *Arrowsmith* and *Elmer Gantry,* Lewis consulted experts. In this instance, they included independent Marxist Benjamin Stolberg and George Seldes, Lewis's neighbor in Vermont. Neither was so influential as Dorothy Thompson. By the mid-1930s, she was determined to use her influence as a syndicated columnist with eight to ten million readers to rally opposition to both German Nazism and Hitler's American friends. *It Can't Happen Here,* Vincent Sheean said, was the most enduring legacy of their stormy marriage.[11]

* * *

The novel, published in late 1935, opens in the spring of 1936, when it "seemed impossible . . . to know anything surely." Senator Berzelius (Buzz) Windrip, a presidential contender reminiscent of Huey Long, clowns, bullies state legislators, invokes Jesus' name and promises (in an autobiography called *Zero Hour—Over the Top*) to make everyone a "king and ruler." He goes beyond the Kingfish by creating a private militia called Minute Men by the members, Minnie Mouses by their foes. In 1936, Windrip defeats Franklin Roosevelt for the Democratic presidential nomination and then overwhelms both FDR and Republican Senator Walt Trowbridge in the November election.[12]

Presenting Windrip's associates, Lewis indulged his penchant for grotesque names and sarcastic descriptions. Dr. Hector Macgoblin, a "cultured doctor and burly boxing fan," heads the Department of Education and Public Relations. Colonel Dewey Haik, a veteran of fifteen minutes in combat, commands the Minute Men. The "intellectual dressmaker" Lee Sarason is Windrip's brain trust. Mrs. Adelaide Tarr Gimmitch, a plump foe of women's suffrage who sounds like Elizabeth Dilling, writes Windrip's campaign song. Bishop Peter Paul Prang, a Methodist Episcopal version of Father Coughlin, catechizes a League of Forgotten Men over the airwaves.[13]

Assisted by this retinue, President Windrip proclaims martial law on the day after his inauguration, arrests one hundred members of Congress, and confines Supreme Court justices to their homes. These measures are necessary, he explains, to defend the nation against a "combination of Wall Street and Soviet Russia." During the next two years, he eliminates former allies (including Bishop Prang and the American Legion), consolidates the states into eight provinces, disbands all political parties except his own American Corporate State and Patriotic Party, burns books by Mark Twain and Woodrow Wilson, and transforms the educational system. Independent colleges are combined into eight "central Corpo universities" that emphasize advertising, sports, military training, business correspondence, and the "cultivation of will power."[14]

At first most Americans support the new order; they are encouraged to do so by newspapers with "large red headlines and many comic strips." The Minute Men are even more convincing. Nevertheless, by mid-1937, the New Underground, headed by Walt Trowbridge, is functioning in Canada, and copies of Trowbridge's weekly, *A Lance for Democracy,* reach the United States. This opposition provokes an escalation of terror. In October 1937, Windrip imprisons thousands of persons who had been influential under the old order. Concentration camps—formerly college campuses—now house Raymond Moley, Heywood Broun, George Seldes, and other writers who differ "grotesquely except in their common dislike" of the Corpo regime. By the end of 1937, the population at large feels "fear, nameless and omnipresent."[15]

Fort Beulah, Vermont, reveals the development of dictatorship in microcosm. The novel's main character, Doremus Jessup, the middle-aged editor of the *Fort Beulah Informer,* is a self-described "indolent and somewhat sentimental Liberal." Before the 1936 election, he tells neighbors that Windrip will establish a "real fascist dictatorship." Francis Tasbrough, a boyhood friend, replies, "That couldn't happen here, not possible." Doremus grumbles, "The hell it can't." Very soon, Tasbrough helps it to happen as Windrip's commissioner for northern Vermont. Throughout the novel, Doremus's friends and family divide for and against the Corpo state. Even his wife Emma continues to like Windrip because he speaks "beautifully about pure language, church attendance, low taxation, and the American flag."[16]

After attacking the "pirate gang" in Washington, Doremus is arrested and deprived of his newspaper. His son-in-law, Fowler Greenhill, is summarily executed for protesting the arrest. Doremus, his lover Lorinda Pike, and his younger daughter Sissy form the nucleus of the Fort Beulah Underground; his widowed older daughter Mary Greenhill dies assassinating a Corpo official. When their conspiracy is discovered, Doremus is rearrested on 4 July 1938, beaten, and sentenced to seventeen years in a concentration camp. District Commissioner Tasbrough observes that he always was a "smart aleck." Vermont's concentration camp contains a typically incongruous mix, including the local Jewish tailor, who had preached "100 percent

Americanism," denounced "Kikes," and voted for Windrip. Ultimately Linda bribes a guard to permit Doremus's escape to Canada.[17]

While Doremus languishes, the Corpo regime is transformed for the worse. Windrip's vice-president departs to join the New Underground. Canada and Latin America decline to join Windrip's "inevitable empire." A rebellion breaks out in Minnesota and the Dakotas. The crestfallen dictator becomes "as unbouncing and unbuzzing as Buzz might be." In 1938, he is overthrown and exiled by Lee Sarason. Outraged by Sarason's homosexual orgies in the White House, Dewey Haik, the chief Minute Man, soon seizes power. He provokes war with Mexico and turns the United States into a "well-run plantation, on which the slaves were better fed than formerly, less often cheated by their overseers, and kept so busy that they had time only for work and for sleep, and thus fell rarely into the debilitating vices of laughter, song, . . . complaint or thinking." But the Mexican war turns to stalemate. The western rebels take up arms against Haik and they are joined by part of the regular army.[18]

At the close of *It Can't Happen Here* the fate of the United States remains uncertain. Neither the Corpos nor the rebels know "enough to formulate a clear, sure theory of self-government, or irresistibly resolve to engage in the labor of fitting themselves for freedom. . . ." During more than two years of despotism, most citizens have learned little "except that it was unpleasant to be arrested too often." To teach that more than comfort is at stake, Doremus Jessup returns from Canada as a New Underground agent.[19]

Throughout the novel, Lewis concurred in the widespread view that fascism would conquer the United States under an assumed name. During the 1936 campaign, Windrip denounces "all 'Fascism' and 'Nazism' so that most of the Republicans who were afraid of Democratic Fascism, and all of the Democrats who were afraid of Republican Fascism, were ready to vote for him." The candidate and his manager shrewdly manipulate American symbols. Rejecting red, brown, and black shirts as signs of European tyranny, they dress their militia in nineteenth-century cavalry uniforms. Windrip's showmanship reminds Doremus of P. T. Barnum and Florenz Ziegfeld. Sarason resembles the "acknowledged masters" of press agentry, Theodore Roosevelt and Edward Bernays. Americans could be duped into fascism, Lewis implied, because they had been duped by others for so long. Nor was credulity the only reason to fear that it could happen here. Recalling the Red Scare of 1919–1920, the charge that Al Smith stood in the shadow of the Pope, and the legislative bans on evolution, Doremus says that no country "can get more hysterical—yes, or more obsequious—than America!"[20]

Except for such trappings as a corporate structure, which was imported "more or less" from Europe, the fascist regime is built of American stuff. For instance, Dr. Macgoblin, the regime's racial theorist, reads Lothrop Stoddard as well as Houston Stewart Chamberlain. The anti-Semitic practices are also distinctive. Macgoblin considers *The Protocols of the Learned Elders of Zion* "bunk but awful handy in propaganda." He personally beats an old rabbi to death; Corpo troopers harass poor Jews. But affluent Jews may vacation anywhere as long as they pay double rates. They must also give extra graft to local officials and "sound their ecstasy in having found in America a sanctuary after their deplorable experiences among prejudices in Europe." Observing Windrip's activities, the Nazi *Völkischer Beobachter* laments the racial "compromise" that signals continued, if partial, allegiance to the "liberal tradition."[21]

Although Lewis shared the prevailing ambiguity of his contemporaries, he ultimately decided that a uniquely American fascism would differ from European versions in style rather than substance. In 1936–1937, even Doremus believes that "humor and pioneer independence" will make dictatorship here "absolutely different from anything in Europe." The "earthy" demeanor that distinguishes Windrip from "fervent Hitlers" elsewhere only deceives Americans again. Victims, including Doremus, discover that "whips and handcuffs hurt just as sorely in the clear American air as in the miasmatic fogs of Prussia." The "biology of dictatorships," he concludes, requires a uniform evolution.[22]

Lewis's portrait of American fascism fitted no single theory but borrowed from all of them. At various levels, it consisted of imperialism, militarism, and rule by a small group of con men. Big business gains when Windrip forgets his pledge to slay the "ancient dragon" of monopoly. Still, Lewis had less in common with neo-Marxist interpreters like Seldes and Stolberg than with liberal theorists like Alfred Bingham who considered fascism primarily a middle-class rebellion. Doremus's hired hand, Shad Ledue, joins the Minute Men to avenge the scorn heaped on him by Fort Beulah. As an officer, he would be respected by "substantial men of affairs, even dry-goods jobbers." Perhaps Sissy Jessup would finally kiss him.[23]

Certainly Lewis did not intend to write a fictional version of Bingham's *Insurgent America*. Rather, he was merely continuing to criticize the stock figures he had ridiculed before the Crash. In Washington and Fort Beulah, prudes, prohibitionists, and hypocrites throng to Windrip's banner. Buzz is the "Professional Common Man," who shares "every prejudice and aspiration of every American Common Man."[24]

Reviewing *It Can't Happen Here,* Max Lerner said that Lewis had rewritten *Main Street,* only now "he has put Caliban in." It is probably more accurate to say that Lewis expected American fascism to be babbittry writ large. Occasionally he made the connection explicit. Appearing before the national convention of Booster Clubs, Dr. Macgoblin uses "good, old time Elks Club humor" to joke about the government. The audience was delighted that the "Big Boys . . . even kidded themselves." Reading an account of the festivities, Doremus drives home the point: "This is revolution in terms of Rotary."[25]

Doremus's personal life encapsulates the enduring conflict among skeptics, boosters, and timid souls who cling to respectability. Emma Jessup, a "solid, kindly [and] worried" woman who resembles Mrs. George Babbitt, hopes that the Corpos will allow Doremus to return from exile if he apologizes. In other ways, however, *It Can't Happen Here* lacks the tentative faith in the younger generation that marked the end of *Babbitt*. When George Babbitt's son breaks with convention to marry his sweetheart, he wistfully wishes them well. Doremus's son Philip, a devout conformist who aspires to a Corpo judgeship, lauds Windrip's "real sure-enough statesmanship." Doremus puts a "paternal curse" on him, "not so much because you are a traitor as because you have become a stuffed shirt." For solace and support, the editor must turn to his younger daughter Sissy, a less naive version of Carol Kennicott, who combines personal liberation with spying, and to his lover Lorinda Pike, the "village crank" who suggests Carol in spunky middle age.[26]

The difference between Carol's petty crusades in *Main Street* and Sissy's espionage in *It Can't Happen Here* illustrates Lewis's move, shared with many intellectuals, from wry criticism in the 1920s to commitment in the 1930s. Nevertheless, along with most writers who made this transition, Lewis lacked a coherent political or ideological analysis. Doremus works with brave Communists, including Fort Beulah's own Karl Pascal. At the same time, he laughs when Pascal and the village socialist "quite happily" continue to split Marxist hairs in the concentration camp. Concluding that Communism is as "theocratic" as fundamentalism, Doremus declines to jump from Windrip's "frying pan" into Stalin's "fire." On the national level, Walt Trowbridge is the undisputed hero; Lewis refers often to his integrity but says nothing about his politics. Appropriately, at the novel's end, the insurgents cannot formulate a plan to restore America. Neither could Lewis.[27]

Instead of offering a political program, Lewis joined in the American cultural celebration that characterized the Depression era. Corpo persecution brings out character and integrity, often in odd places. Minnesota, the home state Lewis satirized in *Main Street,* now becomes the center of democratic rebellion. The priest and pastor who join the Fort Beulah Underground are as far from Elmer Gantry as Lewis's clergymen can be. Walt Trowbridge possesses traces of Will Rogers, Senator George Norris, and—above all—"a touch of Lincoln."[28]

References to the Civil War appear often in *It Can't Happen Here.* Escapees to Canada use hiding places created by the underground railroad. Doremus, grandson of a Union veteran, begins to understand that the abolitionists "had to be violent" in order to stir their slothful fellow citizens. Like the Civil War, Corpo tyranny is a judgment on the "respectable, lazy-minded" Americans who acquiesced in Windrip's victory much as their ancestors had ignored slavery. But Doremus's awakening implies that the nation can also wake up. In Lewis's last passage, Doremus rides

> out, saluted by the meadow larks, and onward all day, to a hidden cabin in the Northern Woods where quiet men awaited news of freedom.
>
> And still Doremus goes on in the red sunrise, for a Doremus Jessup can never die.[29]

* * *

Few critics found literary merit in *It Can't Happen Here,* but most applauded the effort on Lewis's terms, as a "propaganda book."

The novel also struck a popular nerve and quickly sold 320,000 copies. Yet Lewis wanted a still wider audience. Even before publication, he asked Sidney Howard, who had earlier adapted *Dodsworth* for the stage, to do the same for *It Can't Happen Here*. Unimpressed by the novel and bored with such adaptations, Howard declined. Yet the two writers soon found themselves collaborating in a more lucrative medium, the movies. In October 1935, Metro-Goldwyn-Mayer (MGM) paid Lewis $40,000 for screen rights to the novel and offered Howard $22,000 to write the script. The studio was "rooting for a big picture," MGM story editor Samuel Marx told Howard.[30]

Perhaps so, but MGM, the largest, most prestigious, and most conservative Hollywood studio, approached *It Can't Happen Here* warily. Louis B. Mayer, vice-president in charge of the studio at Culver City, California, had represented the state on the Republican National Committee, helped to derail Upton Sinclair's EPIC campaign for governor in 1934, and visited President Herbert Hoover at the White House. Irving Thalberg, the able head of production until early 1933, was equally conservative politically though less afraid of controversy. Under their leadership, MGM, unlike Warner Brothers, had shied away from socially relevant—let alone socially critical—films. The notable exception, *Gabriel Over the White House* (1933), had yielded internal division and external controversy. In *Gabriel,* a corrupt president given a mysterious reprieve from death becomes a hero by using authoritarian means (including raids by art deco tanks) to crush domestic crime and enforce international peace. Mayer, who regarded the film as a veiled critique of Hoover and an endorsement of President-elect Roosevelt, grudgingly approved release in early 1933. The controversy over *Gabriel* reinforced Mayer's disposition to shun political films. Before acquiring the rights to Lewis's novel, he had worried that a film version would offend the Roosevelt administration and his doubts may have lingered despite assurances from MGM subordinates that it would not.[31]

With some modification, Lewis's novel could be brought to the screen not as an overtly political film but as one of the proliferating cinematic celebrations in which "the people" ultimately prevail against earthquakes, fires, and their own darker sides. In other words, a movie version of *It Can't Happen Here* might have less in common with *Gabriel Over the White House* than with *San Francisco,* also scheduled for release by MGM in 1936, or with *In Old Chicago* (1938) and *Northwest Passage* (1940), which followed later in the decade. But the adaptation would not be easy. Politics aside, Lewis's story contained more sex and violence than film censors here and abroad were likely to permit. Evidently Mayer did not want to risk the studio's best talent on the project. Lucien Hubbard, assigned to produce, specialized in quickly created grade B movies. Director J. Walter Ruben had made an excellent gangster film, *Public Hero No. 1* (1935), and a solid family drama, *Riffraff* (1935), but remained relatively unknown.[32]

Any script for *It Can't Happen Here* would have to survive the scrutiny of William Harrison (Will) Hays, president of the Motion Picture Producers and Distributors Association (MPPDA), and his aide, Joseph I. Breen, chairman of the Production Code Administration (PCA). Since 1922, Hays had tried to improve Hollywood's image and preserve foreign markets by prodding studios to curb depictions of sex, violence, and controversy. For example, the Production Code adopted in 1930 warned that audience sympathy must "never be thrown to the side of crime, wrong-doing, evil or sin." Enforcement was lax until 1934, when Hays, pressed by an effective Roman Catholic lobby, established the PCA. Administrator Breen, a Catholic journalist turned Hollywood bureaucrat, concerned himself primarily with lust and larceny, yet he also guarded against radicalism and questionable representations of the "history, institutions, prominent people and citizenry of all nations."[33]

Typically the PCA made suggestions and negotiated with studios during production instead of forbidding films outright. In these "code wars," as two historians call the negotiations, directors surrendered some scenes to save others and script writers wrote blatantly unacceptable dialogue as a distraction from borderline prose. Breen enjoyed the game and thought of himself as something better than a censor. Although decisions were generally said to emanate from the "Hays office," Hollywood's foremost watchdogs did not always agree. Breen concentrated on sex, violence, and foul language; Hays, who dealt directly with Hollywood's financial backers, was more likely to find incipient radicalism. In 1935, for example, Hays disliked but Breen defended *Black Fury,* a powerful Warner Brothers melodrama about striking miners.[34]

In these difficult circumstances Sidney Howard seemed ideal to adapt Lewis's bulky, opinionated book. An experienced screenwriter as well as a noted playwright, he knew that Hollywood demanded simplification and circumspection. He got along with Lewis, no easy task, and had won an academy award for the film version of *Arrowsmith* (1931). A liberal whose political commitments had been deepened by the Depression, Howard was familiar with the issues raised in *It Can't Happen Here*. He had even considered writing his own exposé of native fascism for the *Nation*.[35]

Yet Howard brought liabilities as well as assets to the project. The more he pored over Lewis's novel, the less he liked this "stinking, synthetic, phony piece of tripe." He also disliked southern California, the studio system in which writers counted little, and director Ruben, whom he described as a "loud-mouthed long-winded Jewish product of Hollywood." Nor was this lapse into genteel anti-Semitism, incongruous in someone writing a cinematic tract against bigotry, the sum of his ideological confusions. Like Lewis and many other intellectuals in the 1930s, Howard felt that he should move leftward and become politically more active but had trouble deciding how. In 1932, he had endorsed Communist presidential candidate William Z. Foster. A liberal like himself was a "feeble article," he mused, something akin to a "man who admits he's sick but refuses to see a doctor." After submitting several "treatments" sketching the screenplay, he arrived at the MGM studios on 26 October 1936. The script was far from finished when he came back East a month later. So, grumbling all the way, he returned to Hollywood shortly before Christmas. "Christ, how I loathe this job and what a flop it is going to be too," Howard wrote his wife.[36]

Loathing did not prevent Howard from understanding the aesthetic and political problems he faced. He needed to make Fort Beulah a microcosm for the whole country while removing some major characters and breathing life into others. Doremus looked like a New England version of *Emporia Gazette* publisher William Allen White but Howard felt "completely stumped" by Lewis's attitude toward Buzz Windrip. Ultimately he portrayed Windrip as an "infectious dolt," the kind of candidate George Babbitt would have supported. Louis B. Mayer's conservatism and the Production Code raised other problems. Howard feared that the studio would twist *It*

Can't Happen Here into a polemic against President Roosevelt. He wondered whether MGM and the Hays office would permit explicit treatment of anti-Semitism and enough violence to show the horror of dictatorship. In the last instance, fortunately, a "little torture goes a long way on screen."[37]

Howard's professionalism ultimately overcame his disgust and homesickness. He developed respect for Ruben, who solicited his advice on casting. Lionel Barrymore, chosen to play Doremus, would perform "superbly," Howard concluded. Trying to remain faithful to a novel he disliked, Howard was in regular contact with Lewis, seeking advice on cuts and explaining Hollywood's restrictions. Explicit references to anti-Semitism were forbidden, he wrote, but the actors playing generic persecuted foreigners would look Jewish. The "unsexing" of the relationship between Doremus and Lorinda was partly a consequence of casting. Few old actors could play love scenes "without being revolting" and Lionel Barrymore was not one of them. For his part, Lewis remained atypically cooperative.[38]

Ultimately Howard retained most of the story line as well as Lewis's tone. Buzz comes to life as an infectious dolt until he dies, the victim of Haik's bullets and plot condensation. Once again Philip embraces the Corpo regime, Mary sacrifices herself fighting it, Emma bumbles along, Lorinda exudes spunk, and Doremus represents everyman, whose "timid soul" and "drowsy mind" allowed dictators to triumph. More effectively than Lewis, Howard tied national events to developments in Fort Beulah. Consistent with Hollywood expectations, the romance between Sissy and Julian (James Stewart) bulks larger in the script than in the book. As in many other films of the 1930s, love interest coexisted with satire and amorphous liberal politics. While Miss America designs a new Corpo flag for Windrip, bankers and opportunists enrich themselves at the expense of "the people" and Republicans help Communists battle Minute Men in the streets.[39]

Most important, American fascism looked at least as brutal as in Lewis's novel. Doremus is whipped and machine guns from the White House shoot into a defenseless crowd. When Corpos execute Mary's husband Fowler, the camera turns "to the muzzles in close up and they are fired almost in our faces."[40]

The script was nearly finished by the third week of January 1936, but Howard and Ruben, like Lewis before them, had trouble settling on an ending. Howard rejected Lewis's suggestion of "wedding bells" for Doremus and Lorinda, a finale also likely to appeal to Mayer. Wanting to portray the victory of democracy as probable but not yet certain, the director and screenwriter decided essentially to follow the novel. Doremus, disguised as a patent medicine salesman, rides off into the sun with a load of ammunition for the New Underground; Lorinda sits beside him and the music swells to the strains of "John Brown's Body." The choice of vehicle presented a last problem. Howard's initial preference, a horse and buggy, had become something of a Republican party symbol. Lewis suggested a "terribly rattle trap old Ford." On 27 January, Howard and Ruben agreed on a battered automobile devoid of company designation. "Everybody happy," Howard wrote in his diary.[41]

On the contrary, the script's odyssey had barely begun. MGM attorneys urged deletion of references to famous institutions and individuals ranging from Johns Hopkins University to Upton Sinclair, and insisted on "localizing" fictional characters in order to avoid lawsuits by outraged Windrips, Sarasons, Haiks, and Ledues. Moreover, parts of the script, such as the American emulation of the Nazi salute, were "most offensive." Studio executives hoped that Hubbard could solve these problems with "slight changes." An MGM agent overseas raised a more basic issue. If the film reflected on dictatorships, "prevalent" European countries, important markets for MGM, would heavily censor or ban it.[42]

Most important, PCA Administrator Joseph I. Breen met with Hubbard on 30 January and the next day sent Mayer a seven-page evaluation of the script. Breen also wanted to remove references to actual products, institutions, and social movements, including Communism and Italian Fascism. With an eye to European markets, he warned against any Corpo salute "even suggestive" of the Nazi version. In keeping with usual PCA practice, he asked deletion of references to God. Perhaps out of habit, he detected erotic dangers even though Doremus and Lorinda had been "unsexed." When Emma bathed Doremus's battered body after his escape from the concentration camp, she must not be shown looking down into the tub. Above all, Breen complained about "excessive" brutality, violence, and public disorder. Beatings should be kept to a minimum, murders had to take place off screen, and Minute Men must not fire into defenseless crowds.[43]

The story was so inherently "inflammatory," Breen concluded, that *"only the greatest possible care"* could save it from widespread rejection. Moreover, as Breen had told Hubbard, even a careful production would probably be banned in most countries and shown here only after "considerable negotiation" with local censorship boards. In short, though Breen did not (and strictly speaking could not) forbid production of *It Can't Happen Here,* he predicted low financial returns and "enormous" difficulties.[44]

Even before Breen met with Hubbard on 30 January, rumors circulated that MGM, under pressure from the Hays office, would stop production. Ruben and Howard, led to think otherwise, continued to work on the film. Discounting the rumors, Howard was "amazed" by MGM's determination to produce *It Can't Happen Here.* Mayer's only instructions were "not to pull my punches," he wrote Roger Baldwin of the American Civil Liberties Union (ACLU) on 11 February. Of course there had been loud and ridiculous "squawks" from the Hays office, but these could be deflected or dealt with in a revised script. Howard's revisions, which required some punch pulling to mollify Breen, nonetheless left a powerful story intact. For example, while excising some violence and deleting calls for a "new American revolution," Howard showed that an American fascism would be as cruel as its European counterparts. In this instance, at least, his liberalism was not a feeble article.[45]

On 13 February, the day after Howard finished script revisions, MGM canceled production of *It Can't Happen Here.* Too upset "to make any sense of it all," he said nothing publicly but told Lewis that Will Hays had considered the project offensive to Republicans. Lewis's agent added the rumor that Hays feared offending Hitler and Mussolini, who might, in turn, lead a boycott of American films. Accordingly, while Howard sulked, Lewis responded with a characteristic mixture of arrogance and insight. The novelist called Hays the "dictator of the motion picture industry," accused the MPPDA of "cowardice," and questioned its right to bar films about social problems. *It Can't Happen Here* had become the nation's most popular novel by exploring issues "very much on the public mind." Hardly a partisan tract, the story contained a Republican hero, Walt Trowbridge, and appealed to many Republicans, including Senator William E. Borah. The world was full of fascist propaganda, Lewis noted, but the Hays office did not ban Italian or German films. His own book was "propaganda for only one thing: American democracy." "I wrote *It* Can't *Happen Here*," Lewis quipped, "but I begin to think that it certainly *can*."[46]

The next week brought contradictory responses from MGM, a grudging statement by Hays, and comment from Rome and Berlin. The production had been suspended "because it would cost too much," Mayer announced, adding disingenuously that the Hays office had "not said a thing one way or another." Without any sense of contradiction, however, he also noted Hays's fear that the film would involve motion pictures in domestic politics while simultaneously annoying Hitler and Mussolini. Hays called the whole controversy "phony." He denied concern for Republican sensibilities, and cited MGM's *A Tale of Two Cities* (1935) and *Les Miserables* (1935) as two recent films with "political backgrounds." Viewing events from afar, an unspecified Italian official praised the American film industry for refusing to spread the "nonsense" in Lewis's book; a spokesman for the German Film Chamber called Lewis a "full-blooded Communist" (prompting him to laugh, "I'm glad they don't make me an anemic one").[47]

Starting to make sense of it all, Howard on 23 February publicly attacked both MGM and Will Hays's "Presbyterian and Republican caution." Contrary to Hays's assertion that finances doomed *It Can't Happen Here*, Howard said that the film's $642,000 budget was comparable to that of *Arrowsmith*, which had been produced by Samuel Goldwyn in 1931. Rather, Hays and Breen had "talked the producers out of making it." To prove the point, Howard quoted from Breen's letter to Mayer and recalled his more candid remarks in conversation, "Things like freedom of speech and freedom of the press are all right to talk about, but do they belong on the screen?"[48]

The accusations by Lewis and Howard came closer to the truth than the denials by Hays and Mayer. As Breen's letter shows, the Hays office pressed MGM hard to drop the project. Whether or not Hays preferred films compatible with Republican platforms, he certainly concerned himself with the preservation of foreign markets. In 1936, moreover, Hays was particularly worried about cinematic relations with Italy. Indeed, nine months after the controversy over

It Can't Happen Here, he personally convinced Mussolini—for whom he felt much respect—to modify restrictions on imports from Hollywood.[49]

Mayer had special reasons to fear domestic politics and international complications. Not only had *Gabriel Over the White House* elicited complaints in 1933, but in 1935 foreign censors had cut scenes from *A Tale of Two Cities.* Moreover, the controversy over filming Lewis's novel coincided with two similar imbroglios. Catholic spokesmen opposed production of *Forever,* which treated adultery, and Turkey threatened a boycott if MGM filmed *The Forty Days of Musa Dagh,* Franz Werfel's novel about the Turkish massacre of Armenians. *New York Times* Hollywood correspondent Douglas W. Churchill estimated that MGM would lose $600,000 on *It Can't Happen Here* because bans were likely in Japan, France, and Great Britain as well as Germany and Italy. Nevertheless, the decision to drop the film faced internal opposition. Irving Thalberg protested, "We've lost our guts, and when that happens to a studio, you can kiss it goodbye."[50]

Outside Hollywood, cancellation of *It Can't Happen Here* prompted widespread and usually critical reaction. The *Christian Science Monitor, Baltimore Sun,* and *New York Post* editorially attacked MGM and the Hays office. "There have apparently been no memoranda of protest from the Hays Office concerning recent films glorifying vigilantism and painting labor unions as rackets," the *Post* said. The Author's League of America charged the film industry with cowardice and demanded Hays's removal. An ad hoc group, the Legion of Freedom, organized a postcard campaign to Mayer, with participants vowing to boycott MGM films until Lewis's novel reached the screen. The ACLU tried to stir a Senate investigation of Hays, asked Secretary of State Cordell Hull whether foreign governments had protested the production, and demanded from Mayer an "honest" explanation of the film's demise.[51]

A coalition including the ACLU, Pen Club, Newspaper Guild, American League Against War and Fascism, National Council Against Censorship, and New Theatre League planned a mass demonstration against all censorship. The program was to include speeches by Sidney Howard, Elmer Rice, and Lillian Hellman, as well as scenes from such banned or bowdlerized works as Erskine

Caldwell's Tobacco Road, Hellman's *The Children's Hour,* and *Ethiopia,* an aborted Federal Theatre production. Meanwhile, Doubleday, Doran, and Company advertisements highlighted the controversy and sales of *It Can't Happen Here* doubled to 5,000 copies per week.[52]

Hays and Mayer rode out the storm, perhaps sensing that their critics would soon turn to other causes. MGM answered what studio executives considered a "great number" of protest postcards with a form letter; any "adequate" production would entail "enormous" expenses unlikely to be recouped at the box office, but a simplified script might be possible in the future. A Senate investigation was impossible, Gardner Jackson informed the ACLU, because opinions diverged on the facts of the case. The State Department pronounced "without foundation" rumors that foreign governments had denounced the MGM production. The anticensorship demonstration fizzled, plagued by difficulty in securing a theater, postponements, and springtime; with the arrival of "warm weather and everything," Mark Marvin of the New Theatre League concluded at the end of March, interest was "definitely worn out." Neither Lewis nor Howard wanted to participate in any such rally, which the novelist called "a Roman—or Moscow—holiday with us as the goats." By October, his anger at MGM diminished, Howard started writing the script for a less ambiguous contribution to the American celebration, *Gone With the Wind.*[53]

Will Hays, appointed in early March to a fifteenth year as president of the MPPDA, called for "common sense" in distinguishing between "pictures with a message and self-serving propaganda." "The question of public order, of public good, of avoiding the inflammatory, the prejudicial or the subversive is a problem of social responsibility everlastingly imposed" on producers and distributors. The industry had demonstrated its ability to treat the "vital subjects of the day," Hays added, with an oblique reference to *It Can't Happen Here,* "notwithstanding such artificial controversies as may be raised to the contrary." Nineteen years later, Hays's autobiography cited Lewis's novel as evidence of American freedom but never mentioned the aborted screen adaptation.[54]

* * *

Eight months after MGM abandoned production, *It Can't Happen Here* reached a national audience under the auspices of the Federal Theatre Project (FTP). Sinclair Lewis had chosen this route, he told the press, because he wanted to warn Americans about fascism, because he doubted the commercial theater's willingness to deliver this message, because the Federal Theatre would offer a "non-partisan" production, and because FTP Director Hallie Flanagan was a "great lady." As was often the case, Lewis spoke hyperbolically, forgetting that he had been concerned with money as well as messages.[55]

At a 22 July meeting of FTP officials, Francis Bosworth of the Play Bureau suggested producing *It Can't Happen Here*. Encouraged by Flanagan, he traveled to Vermont to secure Lewis's cooperation. The novelist, who was on the verge of signing with a commercial producer, hesitated. Bosworth convinced him that concurrent performances in several cities (a scheme proposed by FTP Deputy Administrator William Farnsworth) would provide substantial exposure and, at the rate of $50 per week per theater, adequate royalties. From the perspective of Flanagan and her staff, simultaneous openings in diverse locations promised to bring favorable publicity and help build local constituencies. The Federal Theatre "emphasized material from our own age and country," Flanagan later recalled, and *It Can't Happen Here* was a story by "one of the most distinguished American writers, based on a living belief in American democracy."[56]

The Federal Theatre, created as part of the Works Projects Administration (WPA) in mid-1935, was still shaky politically, administratively, and aesthetically. WPA Administrator Harry Hopkins wanted to create a "free, adult, uncensored" national theater, yet even many of his subordinates regarded the FTP as just another relief program. Congressional conservatives disliked all New Deal cultural experiments and looked askance at Hallie Flanagan, who urged FTP units to respond to an "age of expanding social consciousness." Only 10 percent of the productions ultimately fitted that description; as with many New Deal agencies, local officials were often less liberal than the national office.[57]

Yet Federal Theatre personnel also included avid New Dealers, Popular Front liberals, and Communists, and their activities caused controversy from the outset. In early 1936, controversy over *Ethiopia,* an FTP "living newspaper" condemning the Italian invasion, had reached the White House. Wary of offending the Italian government, FDR had banned the portrayal of any foreign leader without State Department approval, which was denied in the case of Benito Mussolini. Instead of modifying the script, as Flanagan wished, the New York project canceled *Ethiopia.* However, actors appeared as sitting Supreme Court justices, Secretary of Agriculture Henry A. Wallace, and Communist leader Earl Browder in *Triple A Plowed Under,* a living newspaper about rural poverty, and *Injunction Granted,* a sympathetic treatment of organized labor.[58]

After the rights to *It Can't Happen Here* were secured on 21 August the Federal Theatre staff immediately began planning for the national opening in late October. Twenty-eight FTP units expressed serious interest in the play. The rise of an American dictatorship, Flanagan recognized, could be "handled in many ways." The nonpartisan Federal Theatre approach would encourage regional artistic autonomy. Thus, instead of showing economic causes of—or antidotes to—dictatorship, Flanagan advised FTP directors, the basic script would stress tyranny's capacity to conquer in a "harmless and attractive guise." Each unit was free to move the "locale" from Vermont and design scenery and costumes "to fit its own region."[59]

Unfortunately, a stagestruck Sinclair Lewis sought—and received—a primary role in transforming *It Can't Happen Here* into a play; he wrote the basic script and helped produce the play at the Adelphi Theatre in New York. Equally unfortunate was the choice of a collaborator, John C. Moffitt, film critic for the *Kansas City Star* and sometime screenwriter. Moffitt joined Lewis in Vermont during late August; the two worked rapidly if not well. On 9 September, believing that the script was undergoing "final revisions," Flanagan advised local theatre units to hire casts and start rehearsals.[60]

By all accounts, the first script was awful. Even Lewis was dissatisfied. Vincent Sherman, selected to direct the play at the Adelphi, urged a long postponement of the opening in order to prepare a new script. Flanagan, New York FTP Director Philip Barber, and WPA Administrator Hopkins, concerned with the Federal Theatre's political vulnerability, said that postponement was impossible. Consequently, Lewis and Moffitt came to New York, where, with copious advice from Sherman and Bosworth, they struggled to revise the script. As Sherman remembered, the group rehearsed all day and then tried to patch and repair at night. Lewis, sometimes drunk and sometimes sober, enjoyed acting out various parts, particularly that of effete Effingham Swan. From time to time, Dorothy Thompson rendered judgment on her husband's prose: "Sinclair, it stinks." Since Lewis and Moffitt had ceased speaking to each other, Bosworth, Sherman, and other neutrals conveyed messages between their respective suites at the Essex House hotel. Lewis almost quit, *Variety* reported, when a stenographer accidentally mixed Moffitt's revisions with his own.[61]

A bad first script was not the only problem facing local Federal Theatre units. Often they were burdened by cramped quarters, miserable acoustics, low budgets, and inept actors. Nonetheless, they displayed considerable imagination. The Yiddish *It Can't Happen Here* in New York sought a lively, voluble mood. In Birmingham, Alabama, the atmosphere surrounding Windrip's rise was that of a gaudy political rally. In Seattle, where the cast was black except for those portraying Windrip and Sarason, the play was modified to stress the impact of race prejudice. Similarly, the Spanish-language production in Tampa, Florida, emphasized the threat of nativist demagoguery to Cuban-Americans.[62]

Sets, stars, and costumes also reflected local option. The realistic Fort Beulah constructed on the Adelphi stage contrasted with the strikingly modern look at the Columbia Theatre in San Francisco. The Suitcase Theatre, designed to visit schools, small towns, and Civilian Conservation Corps sites, used an ingenious system of sliding panels to change scenes. The impressionist set at the Yiddish production, Hallie Flanagan said, left an "effect of light and shade almost Rembrandt in quality." Lorinda Pike looked frumpy on most stages, but in Detroit and Seattle she was pretty, even sexy. Actors playing Doremus Jessup typically exuded craggy endurance; Seth Arnold, cast in the role at the Adelphi, might have modeled for Grant Wood. At Boston's Repertory Theatre and at the Adelphi, Corpos resembled nineteenth-century American cavalry (as they had in the novel). Elsewhere they looked like bellhops (Los Angeles), a high school band (Seattle), or the Royal Canadian Mounted Police (San Francisco). Most often, however, Windrip's bullies called to mind the tailored troops of Mussolini or the Kaiser instead of Black Jack Pershing's doughboys or Phil Sheridan's horsemen. Undoubtedly budgetary constraints affected the selection of uniforms. But the dominant European look also suggests an underlying faith that it couldn't happen here.[63]

As with the New Deal generally, we can see the limits of the Federal Theatre's experimentation. Local producers wanted to enliven the play with references to living Americans and world leaders, a strategy Lewis had used in the novel and the FTP permitted in the living newspapers. Here Flanagan opposed all such allusions, not only in scripts but also in publicity material. She had no desire further to inflame congressional conservatives who were pressing to curtail or terminate FTP activities. As she well understood, too, her superiors were even more afraid of political complications.[64]

Day-to-day enforcement of in-house censorship fell to E. E. McCleish, who was placed in charge of a "central information bureau" on 4 September. The "general rule" in publicizing *It Can't Happen Here* was to "avoid all controversial issues." Specifically forbidden were references to (or graphics suggestive of) foreign powers. So was the term "fascism." Posters must be simple and bold but they could not picture firing squads, burning buildings, mobs assaulting police, or "helmets of classical design." There must be no mention of MGM's canceled film. Also proscribed was the theme used by Doubleday to sell Lewis's novel: "What Will Happen When America Has a Dictator!" *It Can't Happen Here* "isn't anti-anything as it comes into the Federal Theatre," McCleish advised, "It is simply pro-American." Any questions—and all promotional copy—had to be cleared with the national office.[65]

Clearance was not easy. During October, the Cleveland FTP was forced to redesign posters mentioning an American dictatorship and warned against sending speakers to a rally sponsored by the American League Against War and Fascism. The San Francisco unit had to scrap a poster showing a blot—labeled "Fascism"—oozing across a map of the United States. Flanagan "absolutely" forbade Indianapolis's reference to Topeka and San Simeon, the home towns respectively of Alfred M. Landon and William Randolph Hearst. When rehearsals showed that the play ran in excess of three hours, FTP officials decided to cut controversial scenes showing Windrip in the

White House and Doremus in a prison camp. Less than candid, Flanagan told local units that Lewis wanted to "concentrate the action within a small American community."[66]

McCleish tried to limit publicity on *It Can't Happen Here* until roughly two weeks before the opening. Yet the press—and enemies of the Federal Theatre—focused on the issue of a government agency dramatizing a book considered too controversial for Hollywood. The conservative polemicist Harold Lord Varney thought the production "PROPAGANDA—naked and unconcealed." Even *Variety* expected *It Can't Happen Here* to aid President Roosevelt's reelection effort. By late October, a Federal Theatre survey later concluded, newspapers had devoted 78,000 lines to the play—and it had not yet opened.[67]

On 1 October, Bosworth, acting head of the Play Bureau, informed all directors that a "strengthened" script by Lewis would be available "in a few days," and suggested that they use it at their discretion. Nonetheless, difficulties continued until opening night. Logistical problems combined with political prudence to force cancellation of the play in New Orleans, stomping grounds of the late Huey Long. The always touchy New York FTP unsuccessfully requested a special dispensation to open later than all others.[68]

Hallie Flanagan, who spent the last week in New York, insisted that *It Can't Happen Here* would "open on time in every theatre even if the actors have to walk around the stage reading their parts off a script in their hands and wearing signs to identify themselves." At 7:00 A.M. on 25 October, Lewis telephoned Flanagan to protest that construction of sets at the Adelphi had been botched; though nearly hysterical, he was right, and she ordered a quick rearrangement. The St. Louis unit, long near collapse, had managed to put together a version of *It Can't Happen Here;* facing unyielding opposition from Missouri state officials, Flanagan on 26 October dropped the local production. The Federal Theatre had planned to distribute copies of Windrip's platform and the New Underground newspaper during intermission, but, within hours of the opening, complaints from WPA Assistant Administrator David Niles caused this gimmick to be scrubbed.[69]

On the evening of 27 October 1936, *It Can't Happen Here* was performed at twenty-one theatres in seventeen states. In Newark, where mechanical snags caused delays and omission of two scenes, the audience nonetheless responded with "volleys of patriotic applause." Indiana Governor Paul McNutt and Representative Louis Ludlow attended the Indianapolis show. The New York Yiddish version included the powerful concentration camp scene. Flanagan visited this performance as well as that at the Adelphi, where Lewis answered curtain calls and demands for a speech by declaring, "I have been making a speech since seven minutes to nine." At a party afterwards, Lewis announced plans to collaborate with Vincent Sherman on a play about anti-Semitism, and pronounced the Adelphi rendition of *It Can't Happen Here* a "great show."[70]

On the contrary, the play was much weaker than the novel, which Lewis himself had denigrated as a "bad book." Its flaws are usually attributed to Lewis's ineptitude as a dramatist, his poor relations with Moffitt, and logistical problems afflicting the Federal Theatre. Indeed, *It Can't Happen Here* was a play written by a committee and produced by embattled subcommittees. Not surprisingly, then, the action moved slowly, characters lacked depth, and the plot must have remained obscure to many viewers unfamiliar with the novel. Yet flaws also resulted from the decision to "avoid all controversial issues." For instance, Doremus looked like a "pitiable dodderer" (as *Time* noted) partly because his adulterous affair with Lorinda was turned into a middle-age flirtation. Sissy Jessup, the novel's rebel girl, was absent from the play.[71]

Furthermore, although the book integrated suppression in Vermont with developments nationwide, the Federal Theatre avoided naming senators or Supreme Court justices by restricting most scenes to Fort Beulah. Windrip, whose continuous presence would have enhanced the play's vigor and forced the development of some political voice, disappears after the first act. In the final scene, Mary Greenhill holds Swan and other Corpos at gunpoint while her son David, Lorinda, and Doremus flee to Canada. Flanagan said that she had never seen an audience "more attentive and more moved" than the men and women watching this sequence at the Adelphi. Yet, in a political play virtually devoid of a political stance, Mary might just as well have been a brave widow holding off desperados in a grade B western. Looking back in 1974, director Vincent Sherman aptly concluded that *It Can't Happen Here* was "rather tame and mild compared to what could be done."[72]

The multiple openings elicited diverse reactions. Predictably, some critics condemned *It Can't Happen Here* as New Deal propaganda. The *Montclair (New Jersey) Times* considered the "bad play, poorly acted" at the Mosque Theatre in Newark worth seeing because a "Fascist government" already ruled nearby Jersey City under FDR's "first lieutenant," Frank Hague. *Motion Picture Daily* chided an incompetent "leftist frolic at the taxpayer's expense." Perhaps seeking to vindicate the decision by MGM to drop *It Can't Happen Here,* this Hollywood house organ somehow discerned in the Federal Theatre production a "rousing cheer for the class war."[73]

Most New York reviewers, while agreeing that the script was weak, took pains to observe that poor prose served the good cause of preserving democracy. Perhaps moved by his brother George's friendship with Lewis, Gilbert Seldes told radio listeners that the Adelphi housed a "tremendously moving, exciting and genuinely inspiring piece of work." With greater accuracy, Brooks Atkinson of the *New York Times* doubted that this sluggish play could alarm anyone about the threat of dictatorship. Many critics agreed with Douglas Gilbert of the *New York World-Telegram* that the triumph of a clown like Windrip was "preposterous." Lewis retorted, "What about Huey Long? . . . To a certain extent it has happened here. What about the crazy war fever of 1916?"[74]

Critics outside New York expressed greater enthusiasm. Often aware of the script's defects, they nonetheless cheered not only the play's contributions to the contemporary American celebration but also the creativity of local producers, directors, and actors, as well as the very existence of a Federal Theatre with regional affiliates. According to FTP surveys, most members of the audiences shared these sentiments. Many of them rarely attended plays. Some were offended by the mild profanity in *It Can't Happen Here.* Overwhelmingly, however, they welcomed a federally sponsored theater providing socially relevant entertainment.[75]

For Federal Theatre officials, *It Can't Happen Here* was a success, albeit a flawed success. A fresh target for congressional snipers, the production nevertheless made a splash, inspired regional creativity, and, as Flanagan noted, "taught us our weaknesses as well as our strengths." Several companies enjoyed extended runs or successful tours of towns and campuses. Within four months of the opening, *It*

Can't Happen Here was seen by 270,000 people at an average cost of thirty cents.[76]

* * *

In retrospect, the odyssey of *It Can't Happen Here* from Lewis's typewriter through MGM studios to Federal Theatre stages illuminates the culture, economics, and politics of the 1930s. Lewis was a representative intellectual in making a transition from satirical commentary in the 1920s to political commitment in the 1930s. He also revealed the shallowness and confusion that often characterized such commitment. During the two years after *It Can't Happen Here* opened, he starred in a new version of the play (in which Lewis, as Doremus, holds off the Corpos at the end), took pride in Nazi Germany's ban on the novel, and refused to certify his "Aryan" origins to Germans seeking to produce *Dodsworth*. At the same time, however, his amorphous political commitment began to ebb. In 1938, he helped to dilute the phrase, "It can't happen here," by arguing that "it" had already happened with the victory of "intellectual softness." Lewis's proposed play about anti-Semitism, like his labor novel, remained unfinished. In 1941, he flirted with the America First Committee (AFC), a reputable and frequently astute noninterventionist group, but his flirtation owed less to antiwar sentiments than to his estrangement from Dorothy Thompson, a fervent interventionist. Finally, *Gideon Planish,* a roman à clef published in 1943, ridiculed uplifters ranging from AFC leader Robert Wood to George Seldes, from German-American propagandist George Sylvester Viereck to Dorothy Thompson.[77]

Second, the fate of *It Can't Happen Here* in Hollywood draws our attention from films as cultural artifacts to film making as a business. In 1941, noninterventionist senators complained that recent movies encouraged American entry into World War II. These attacks, which sometimes veiled anti-Semitism, prefigured the Cold War Red Scare in Hollywood. Even so, such films as *Confessions of a Nazi Spy* (1939) and *Sergeant York* (1941) did contribute to the interventionist mood before Pearl Harbor. By and large, these films appeared after Hollywood had lost most European markets. The cancellation of *It Can't Happen Here* in 1936 shows that Hollywood moguls believed that they could do business with Hitler. Like their counterparts in the automobile and chemical industries, moreover, they made concessions to keep doing business.[78]

Third, production of *It Can't Happen Here* fell short of the ideals WPA Administrator Hopkins had enunciated in July 1935. Instead of being "free, adult, uncensored," the Federal Theatre in this instance was cautious, ambivalent, and self-censored. In other words it was a New Deal agency—more experimental than most though nonetheless marked by shortcomings typical of the Roosevelt administration. After a decade of conservative retrenchment we may be tempted in the 1990s to rally 'round the welfare state and uncritically celebrate Franklin Roosevelt as its founder. But the limitations of the New Deal must not be forgotten.

6

Is Poland a Soviet Satellite?
Gerald Ford, the Sonnenfeldt
Doctrine, and the Election of 1976

On 6 October 1976, twenty minutes into the second debate of
the presidential campaign, panelist Max Frankel of the *New York
Times* decided to "explore a little more deeply our relationship with
the Russians." Was it possible, Frankel asked President Gerald R.
Ford, that the Soviets were getting the "better of us"? Not only were
France and Italy "flirting with Communism," but the United States
had recognized the German Democratic Republic and, by signing the
Helsinki accords, Ford had virtually conceded Soviet "dominance in
Eastern Europe." In a convoluted response, Ford tried to show that
he had negotiated with the Soviets "from a position of strength." Grain
sales had benefited American farmers and strategic arms limitation
talks with General Secretary Leonid Brezhnev were going well. Moreover, it "just isn't true" that the Helsinki accords, accepted by thirty-five
national leaders, including Pope Paul VI, had "turned over to the
Warsaw Pact nations the domination of Eastern Europe." On the contrary, Ford concluded, "There is no Soviet domination of Eastern Europe, and there never will be under a Ford administration."[1]

During the next several minutes, a bemused Max Frankel probed
further, a defensive Gerald Ford alternately held and shifted his
ground, and a delighted Jimmy Carter went for Ford's jugular. Did "I
understand you correctly, sir," Frankel asked, with a slight smile
and a condescending tone, that the "Russians are not using Eastern
Europe as their own sphere of influence?" Ford offered a threefold

reply: that Yugoslavians, Romanians, and Poles did not "consider themselves" dominated by the Soviet Union; that Yugoslavia, Romania, and Poland were in fact "independent, autonomous nations"; and that the United States did not "concede" that these nations were under Soviet domination. All three points were to some extent true, but Democratic nominee Jimmy Carter was in no mood to discuss nuances. After grinning broadly and dissociating himself from any criticism of the Pope, Carter looked earnest and repeated some of his favorite campaign themes: Ford sanctioned secret diplomacy, failed to stand up to the Soviets, and yielded to pressure from those even less firm than himself. The Helsinki accords "may have been a good agreement at the beginning," he admitted, but under Ford's weak leadership "we have failed to enforce" the provisions protecting human rights. Now in debate, Ford "apparently" endorsed the "so-called Sonnenfeldt Doctrine . . . that there is an organic linkage between the Eastern European countries and the Soviet Union." Then, seeking to placate northern Catholics suspicious of a southern evangelical Protestant, Carter declared, "And I would like to see Mr. Ford convince the Polish-Americans and the Czech-Americans and the Hungarian-Americans that those countries don't live under the domination and supervision of the Soviet Union behind the Iron Curtain."[2]

* * *

Ford's denial of "Soviet domination" stands out as one of the great presidential gaffes of the past century. In the retrospective judgment of Carter's running mate, Walter F. Mondale, the remark cost Ford the election. Yet Ford's answers to Frankel's questions and his subsequent attempts to explain those answers revealed more than a slip of the tongue compounded by tactical errors. From another perspective, the controversy over the "Soviet domination" of Eastern Europe looks like a Cold War ritual in which candidates, journalists, and ethnic spokesmen played familiar roles. If President Ford was confused about our Eastern European policy, his confusion was shared, if not so graphically demonstrated, by predecessors in the White House.[3]

At least since Josip Tito of Yugoslavia had broken with Stalin, thoughtful Cold Warriors had to consider the possibility that Eastern European Communists were not all alike. Some, even while remaining authoritarian, might lead their nations out of Moscow's orbit. Thus, even as the Truman and Eisenhower administrations spoke in apocalyptic terms of containment or liberation, they experimented with other means of influencing events in Eastern Europe. In 1950, the United States offered aid and encouraged trade with Yugoslavia. Until the mid-1950s, only Tito's regime was deemed sufficiently independent to merit special treatment. Indeed, starting with the Export Control Act of 1949, legislative restrictions virtually ended economic ties to the rest of Eastern Europe. In 1956, however, the Eisenhower administration decided that the new Polish Communist regime of Wladyslaw Gomulka deserved credits and agricultural assistance. Whether or not Gomulka was independent of Moscow was a "pretty close decision," Secretary of State John Foster Dulles explained, but increased connections with the United States would nurture whatever independence there was. In 1960, Poland received most favored nation status.[4]

Policy-makers pursued this strategy of soft liberation with mixed feelings, often inadvertently undermined their own efforts, and faced charges of inconsistency from less compromising Cold Warriors and spokesmen for Eastern European ethnic organizations. The Republican promise of full-scale liberation, a linchpin of the 1952 campaign, affected foreign policy long after Eisenhower had adopted a de facto strategy of containment. For example, emigrés encouraged by Dulles's rhetoric founded the Assembly of European Captive Nations, which, aided by Eastern European ethnic lobbies, secured from Congress in 1959 a denunciation of the Eastern bloc as a "dire threat to the United States." Members of Congress typically exaggerated both the power and the anti-Communist fervor of these lobbies. Many were letterhead organizations. Others were as concerned with domestic discrimination and patronage as with foreign affairs. Moreover, even avidly anti-Communist Polish-, Czechoslovakian-, or Hungarian-Americans, moved by pride or family ties, sometimes favored negotiations with Communist governments in order to help the population.[5]

The strategy of soft liberation and the difficulties of implementation continued into the 1960s and then took a decisive turn with the election of Richard M. Nixon. President John F. Kennedy openly acknowledged Communist polycentrism—at least in Eastern Europe—and threaded legislative loopholes to preserve Poland's most favored nation status. Addressing a largely Polish-American audience in 1962, Kennedy noted "varying shades, even within the Communist world," and defended his policy as a way "to seize the initiative when the opportunity arises, in Poland in particular and in the other countries . . . behind the Iron Curtain." Lyndon B. Johnson used executive orders and exhortation to "build bridges across the gulf" dividing the United States from Eastern Europe. By the mid-1960s, trade was sufficiently visible to provoke boycotts, led by Eastern European ethnic organizations, of Polish meat and Yugoslavian tobacco. Yet Johnson's bridge building showed signs of success, as Romania moved away from the Soviet Union, Hungary loosened economic controls, and Czechoslovakia attempted to create socialism with a human face. Perhaps it was "not necessary to think of liberation as the product of some cataclysmic clash of nations," Secretary of State Dean Rusk optimistically suggested. Then, in August 1968, the Soviet Union and four Warsaw Pact allies invaded Czechoslovakia. According to General Secretary Brezhnev, such "fraternal" military action was sometimes necessary to save socialism from its enemies. This assertion, a justification of the invasion and a veiled threat to other Eastern bloc countries, came to be known in the West as the Brezhnev Doctrine.[6]

President Nixon's Eastern European policy, though never a high priority, fitted into his grand scheme of detente. Addressing the issue in 1970, Nixon conceded that Soviet fears of disorder in or invasion through Eastern Europe were neither novel nor "purely the product of Communist dogma." Accordingly, he denied seeking to undermine Soviet "legitimate security interests." At the same time, he viewed the Eastern European countries "as sovereign, not as part of a monolith," and accepted "no doctrine" abridging their right to improve relations with the United States. Convinced that nationalistic Communists could be drawn toward the West, Nixon worked to lift all restrictions on nonmilitary trade. The first president to visit Eastern Europe, he showed unseemly enthusiasm for Tito, Nicolae Ceausescu of Romania, and Edward Gierek, who had succeeded Gomulka as the Polish Communist party leader in 1970. Nixon and his chief foreign policy advisor, Henry A. Kissinger, cared less about maximizing freedom in Eastern Europe than about minimizing Soviet influence.[7]

Although cultivating Communist diversity made more sense than broadcasting empty promises of liberation, the effects of bridge building should not be exaggerated. From the early Cold War to detente, American policy was primarily a response to changes in Eastern Europe rather than their cause. Moreover, not only were Hungary, Czechoslovakia, and Poland subject to the ultimate sanction of Soviet intervention, but they also remained commercially and culturally closer to Western Europe than to the United States. Nevertheless, as Washington's interest in Eastern Europe grew, so did suspicion among Soviet leaders, who wanted American trade to bolster Eastern European economies without undermining Communist leadership or strong ties to Moscow. As with much of detente, American and Soviet goals differed, and neither side would be fully satisfied.[8]

At least since World War II, both sides had considered Poland the most important Eastern European country. From Moscow's perspective, Poland was not only the largest satellite but, aside from the Soviet Union itself, also the leading contributor to the Warsaw Pact. On the other hand, many Americans viewed Poland as the preeminent symbol of Soviet aggression and betrayal of World War II agreements. Indeed, avid Cold Warriors concurred in former Ambassador Arthur Bliss Lane's charge that Poland had been betrayed by Roosevelt and Truman. In the early 1960s, President Kennedy cited Poland as proof of polycentrism. Finally, Poles comprised the third largest ethnic group of the "new immigration" from the turn of the century, and by the 1950s the Polish-American Congress (PAC) was the most influential Eastern European ethnic lobby. Since 1948, most PAC leaders had favored Republican presidential candidates, whom they expected to take a harder line toward the Soviet Union, yet rank and file Polish-Americans voted disproportionately Democratic.[9]

* * *

Gerald Ford inherited detente, the strategy of building bridges to Eastern Europe, and Henry Kissinger (in the dual roles of Secretary of State and National Security Advisor) along with the presidency in August 1974. He kept all three. Among his first diplomatic duties was receiving Edward Gierek in October. Kissinger advised that Gierek wanted signs of United States "interest in Poland as an independent political entity and respected trading partner." The Polish Communist leader received honors usually accorded a head of state and returned home with promises of increased economic cooperation. Polish-Americans disagreed among themselves about the visit. Aloysius Mazewski, president of the PAC since 1968, declined to attend the White House dinner for Gierek. On advice from the National Security Council, a meeting between Ford and Mazewski along with other skeptical Polish-Americans was scheduled after Gierek's departure.[10]

The year 1974 was not a propitious time to pursue either detente with the Soviet Union or closer connections with Eastern Europe. Following a characteristic Cold War pattern, the Soviet and American governments accused each other of reneging on ambiguous agreements and took retaliatory actions that added to the acrimony. For example, convinced that the United States was meddling in emigration policy and generally encouraging dissent, Soviet leaders cracked down on dissidents at home and in Eastern Europe. In December 1974, Congress passed the Jackson-Vanik amendment, which denied most favored nation status to nonmarket states with restrictive emigration policies. Moscow in turn abrogated the Soviet-American Trade Agreement of 1972 and pressed Warsaw Pact allies to act similarly.[11]

The Conference on Security and Cooperation in Europe (CSCE) was an especially controversial product of detente. The Soviets, in keeping with their well-known subordination of realpolitik to legalism and moralism, had long desired such a conference to legitimate post–World War II boundaries. Nixon and Kissinger agreed to the CSCE in exchange for the opening of talks on the reduction of armed forces in Europe. They saw nothing to lose, since the boundaries were already guaranteed by military might and bilateral agreements, but expected little gain. For almost three years, first in Helsinki and then in Geneva, junior American diplomats dealt in obscurity with counterparts from thirty-four nations. The proceedings seemed too "abstruse" and "pedantic" to merit Kissinger's attention. Europeans took the conference seriously. In particular, astute Western Europeans, joined by some Americans, pushed for "Basket

Three" provisions guaranteeing religious liberty, freedom to travel, and other human rights.[12]

Ford also took the conference seriously. By May 1975, Kissinger was involved if unenthusiastic, arranging a compromise on Basket Three with Soviet Foreign Minister Andrei Gromyko. The President planned to sign the Final Act in Helsinki on 1 August and to visit Poland, Romania, and Yugoslavia on the same trip. Republicans more conservative than Ford were outraged. His presence in Helsinki, Senator James Buckley (Republican/Conservative of New York) warned, would have the effect of "sanctifying and consolidating the Soviet sphere of influence." Protests from Eastern European and Baltic ethnic organizations poured into the office of Myron Kuropas, who had been appointed Ford's special assistant for ethnic affairs in January 1975. Some compared Helsinki to Yalta, an emblem of Eastern Europe's betrayal. Others held out slight hope that Basket Three would bring greater freedom yet sought assurances that the United States had not abandoned the struggle.[13]

As CSCE negotiations drew to a close in mid-1975, exiled Soviet dissident Aleksandr Solzhenitsyn toured the United States denouncing detente as the product of Western weakness and ignorance. He too considered the Helsinki accords a "betrayal of Eastern Europe." Nevertheless, Senator Jesse Helms (Republican of North Carolina) and other conservative Republicans urged Ford to invite Solzhenitsyn to the White House. Kissinger and Brent Scowcroft, who had become National Security Advisor in November 1975, warned that such a meeting, though politically popular among conservatives, would lend weight to Solzhenitsyn's reactionary views, offend the Kremlin, and perhaps jeopardize strategic arms limitation talks. The President himself privately called Solzhenitsyn a "god damn horse's ass." The White House politely announced that Ford was too busy to see him before leaving for Helsinki, but the real reasons leaked to the press and enraged Republican conservatives. Brezhnev now held "veto power" over the President's appointment calendar, columnist George Will charged. Ford belatedly agreed to see Solzhenitsyn (who then claimed to be unavailable) and admitted that the issue had been poorly handled. On the contrary, James Burnham wrote, Ford's failure to honor Solzhenitsyn, like his approval of the Helsinki accords, represented the perverse "logic of detente."[14]

Before departing for Helsinki, at the signing session, and during his Eastern European sojourn, Ford repeatedly explained his position and tried to counter conservative criticism. The Helsinki accords did not endorse Soviet control of Eastern Europe. American negotiators had surrendered nothing more than the theoretical right to change borders by force, a right we would never exercise. In return, the Soviets agreed to abide by the human rights provisions in Basket Three. The United States would carefully monitor progress. In short, the accords, like the policy of dealing with Poland, Romania, and Yugoslavia, fostered freedom instead of sanctioning oppression. Ford knew but did not emphasize that Brezhnev read the Final Act differently. Nonetheless, he considered the CSCE an American triumph.[15]

In the six months following the signing in Helsinki, the administration was encouraged by both the effect of the accords in Europe and the domestic response. Ford publicly pronounced "mixed" the Communist record of compliance on Basket Three. In house, National Security Advisor Scowcroft reported that the Soviets, "surprised and stung" by criticism of their human rights policies, had been put on the "political defensive." The National Security Council (NSC) was also pleased that press coverage had taken a favorable turn and the flood of protests from Eastern European ethnic spokesmen had subsided.[16]

The flow had subsided but not stopped. As before the Helsinki signing, some letters contained strident denunciations of appeasement from paper organizations; others were pained expressions of concern by emigrés and influential ethnics. For example, Professor Nicholas Nyaradi of Bradley University, a former Hungarian minister of finance, feared that the accords would legitimate de facto Soviet control over Eastern Europe. Understanding that the United States could not "go to war in order to 'liberate' Eastern Europe," he nonetheless urged persistent, peaceful efforts to reestablish self-determination as well as a "solemn declaration" that this goal had not changed. Moreover, speaking as a Republican activist and Ford acquaintance, Nyaradi reported hearing rueful references to a "Ford-Brezhnev Doctrine."[17]

White House advisors remained concerned enough to urge frequent statements, often to ethnic groups, reiterating Ford's interpretation of the Helsinki accords. The President sent a "Dear Nick" letter to Professor Nyaradi with the expectation that it would receive wide circulation. In February 1976, Ford accepted the post of honorary patron of the Estonian Salute to America's Bicentennial. In preparing presidential statements for such occasions, NSC staff members, wary of international ramifications, sometimes clashed with political advisors, who sought maximum benefits from Cold War rhetoric. The latter group usually lost. For instance, although Ford reaffirmed nonrecognition of the Soviet Baltic conquests, he avoided the term "self-determination." Similarly, against the advice of Kuropas and William Baroody, the administration declined to support a bill creating a joint executive-legislative commission to monitor the Helsinki accords. The object was worthy, Scowcroft believed, but the mechanism was "another congressional intrusion" on presidential authority; ultimately Scowcroft acquiesced in a "low key" signing ceremony when the bill passed. To be sure, the NSC staff was not unaware of domestic politics. Rather, some members understood the electorate better than the political professionals. As A. Denis Clift warned, "bellicose" rhetoric both obscured the "long, painstaking process" needed to advance human rights in Eastern Europe and undermined Ford's "responsible 'Presidential'" image.[18]

* * *

The issue of Ford's Eastern European policy simmered but did not catch fire until 22 March 1976, when syndicated columnists Roland Evans and Robert Novak reported with typical foreboding an internal administration debate over what they called the "Sonnenfeldt doctrine." According to Evans and Novak, Helmut Sonnenfeldt, counsellor to the State Department and Secretary Kissinger's "faithful mirror," advocated American acceptance of a Soviet sphere in Eastern Europe. Specifically, speaking to American diplomats at a London conference in December 1975, Sonnenfeldt had favored a "permanent 'organic' union" between the Soviet Union and Eastern Europe. The columnists quoted passages from a "transcript" of Sonnenfeldt's remarks, which, they said, sanctioned Soviet domination.[19]

Sonnenfeldt, along with Kissinger, had indeed addressed a meeting of twenty-eight American ambassadors in London over the weekend of 13–14 December. Asked by the chair, Assistant Secretary of

State Arthur Hartman, to discuss Eastern European policy, Sonnenfeldt spoke briefly and without notes. A two-hour discussion followed. According to Sonnenfeldt's recollections, he used in this "brainstorming" session basic concepts and some of the same language he had been using since 1968. Sonnenfeldt said that he had endorsed a more "organic" relationship between Eastern Europe and the Soviet Union, by which he had meant a more "natural" relationship. Clarifying the meaning of "organic" in a colloquy with Ambassador Elliot Richardson, Sonnenfeldt had explained that this natural state entailed an end to Soviet cultural imperialism and military force. Explaining the issue differently, Sonnenfeldt had looked forward to the "Finlandization" of Eastern Europe. Hungary was already going in this direction, he had said, praising Communist leader Janos Kadar for shrewdly moving his country toward greater economic freedom despite the presence of Soviet tanks. In short, Sonnenfeldt was explaining a long-standing if complex American position, not propounding a new policy, let alone a doctrine.[20]

Although no transcript or official minutes were kept of the London meeting, some of the twenty-eight ambassadors took notes. So did Hartman's aide Warren Zimmerman, who subsequently wove the discussion into a single text. Sonnenfeldt remembers regarding this summary as a "fair rendition" of the session despite reservations about some of Zimmerman's "elegant formulations." Moreover, such a report for the record hardly seemed significant. Sonnenfeldt's office sent it forward to Kissinger, and in February 1976 an official State Department summary based on Zimmerman's compilation was cabled to participants.[21]

Perhaps if Sonnenfeldt had anticipated public disclosure of this summary he would have treated the matter less casually. Judging from the excerpts later printed in the *New York Times,* the most complete text currently available, the telegram was susceptible to misunderstanding and vulnerable to willful misinterpretation. On the one hand, to anyone not present in London, the text looked in form like an address by one speaker—Sonnenfeldt—rather than a compilation of loosely connected thoughts discussed in a seminar. On the other hand, because the telegram was in fact a brief summary of a long brainstorming session, important topics were skipped, insufficiently developed, or treated without adequate context. According to Sonnenfeldt, for example, his hope for the "Finlandization" of Eastern Europe, a phrase that clarified his meaning, was absent from the summary because the American ambassador to Finland objected to the term.[22]

Though problematical, the published official text supports Sonnenfeldt's recollection that he had said nothing new. The central theme was that nothing could prevent the Soviet Union's emergence as an imperial "superpower." Rather, the American task consisted of "managing or domesticating" this power. Fortunately, the Soviets were beset by internal problems and remained "inept" imperialists, lacking "genuine friends" in Eastern Europe other than the Bulgarians. Soviet ineptitude gave the United States time to develop its management plans. Americans needed a "coherent trade strategy" to "maximize leverage" on the Soviets and "break down" internal autarky. Overall, the text showed Sonnenfeldt recommending a familiar version of containment.[23]

Yet, as avid Cold Warriors had complained for a generation, containment fell short of liberation. Along with other strategists of containment, Sonnenfeldt expressed willingness to "live in a world with" the Soviet Union. More prudent than some, he predicted neither internal collapse nor imminent liberalization of the Soviet system. The official State Department text outlined a parallel strategy for Eastern Europe. It was in the "long-term interest" of the United States to foster greater autonomy there. Yet an "excess of zeal on our part" might backfire, prompting the Soviets to tighten control over their satellites. Accordingly, the United States "must strive for an evolution that makes the relationship between the Eastern Europeans and the Soviet Union an organic one." Indeed, the current "inorganic, unnatural relationship" was more likely than the general conflict between East and West to ignite World War III.[24]

A fair reading of the official State Department text revealed that Sonnenfeldt favored increased Eastern European freedom and independence from Soviet control. Nonetheless, a fair reading also revealed his belief that Moscow would inevitably exercise great influence within this Soviet "area of national interest." The United States sought to affect the "emergence of Soviet imperial power by making the base more natural and organic so that it will not remain founded on sheer power alone. But there is no alternative open to us other than that of influencing the way Soviet power is used." Sonnenfeldt did not lack sympathy for the Eastern Europeans but, speaking privately with American diplomats, he had used the language of realpolitik unadorned by the politically necessary rhetoric of liberation.[25]

The absence of such rhetoric made the official State Department summary useful to critics of Ford and Kissinger's policy of detente. Some of these avid Cold Warriors acquired copies of the text, which they circulated among Washington journalists during February and March. The source of this leak remains unknown. Sonnenfeldt himself recalls rumors that it sprung from the Department of Defense. He told inquiring reporters at the time that he had enunciated no new policy, and most apparently believed him. Evans and Novak either thought otherwise or could not resist an opportunity to embarrass the administration. Nor did they stop with the observation that high-ranking officials no longer thought in terms of liberation. Indeed, they misconstrued and poorly paraphrased the State Department summary. As Sonnenfeldt recalls with rancor, nowhere did he or the official text refer to an "organic union" between the Soviet Union and Eastern Europe, let alone a "permanent" union.[26]

Until 6 April, when the *New York Times* published the official text, which Sonnenfeldt called a "reasonable though very compressed" version of his remarks, public information about his putative doctrine was virtually nonexistent. Nonetheless, relying on Evans and Novak's column, Eastern European ethnic leaders expressed concern and Republicans more conservative than Ford assailed the administration. On 24 March, the White House Office on Ethnic Liaison reported protests in progress by Czechoslovakian-, Hungarian-, Latvian-, and Lithuanian-Americans. Highlighting the obvious, Baroody warned that the putative doctrine undermined Ford's efforts to "assuage" Eastern European ethnic leaders in the wake of Helsinki, and Kuropas anticipated a "very negative impact" on the forthcoming Wisconsin primary. The benefits were not lost on Ronald Reagan, who denounced both Sonnenfeldt and the Helsinki accords, which, he said, "put the American seal of approval on the Red Army's World War II conquests."[27]

Initially the White House, along with Sonnenfeldt himself, underestimated the significance of this controversy. When it persisted, the administration responded with a mixture of denial, clarification, internecine bickering, and increased ethnic assuagement. Aside from regretting the adjective "organic" and accusing Evans and Novak of distorting his views, Sonnenfeldt kept a low profile, leaving most of the rebuttal to Kissinger. Kissinger reaffirmed his faith in Sonnenfeldt, deplored leaks to the press, asserted that the United States "in no sense" recognized Soviet "dominion" over Eastern Europe, and pledged to encourage independence there "as responsibly as possible." Testifying before the House Foreign Affairs Committee on 29 March he offered the orthodox interpretation of Sonnenfeldt's "unfortunate word . . . 'organic.'" "What he meant was a more historic relationship, a relationship in which the Soviet Union was not so predominant." White House replies to protest letters, cleared through the National Security Council, denied the existence of a Sonnenfeldt Doctrine.[28]

* * *

The imbroglio over the Sonnenfeldt Doctrine merged with two larger controversies. Diverse critics maintained that Ford was not smart enough to handle the presidency, and thus Kissinger would gain even greater control over foreign policy than he had had under Nixon.

Denigration of Ford's intelligence was a popular sport among Washington insiders. Lyndon Johnson had joked in the cleanest of his insults that Ford had played football too often without a helmet. Ford's selection as Vice-President during the Watergate scandal was widely interpreted by the news media as Nixon's "impeachment insurance" because Congress would hesitate to elevate such a dullard to the presidency. The condescending tone that marked Max Frankel's follow-up question in the debate was typical. Interviewing Ford soon after Nixon resigned, Harry Reasoner of ABC stressed fears that "you have not got the magnitude of the grasp of the presidency." "You are aware there is a world out there?" Reasoner added (a remark prudently omitted from the broadcast).[29]

The President had played football—with a helmet—at the University of Michigan, but he had also graduated in the upper third of a distinguished Yale Law School class. Indeed, deciding to pardon Nixon in 1974, he had recalled the lesson of his Yale professors, leading proponents of "legal realism," that wise policy sometimes took precedence over the letter of the law. Though no intellectual, Ford had acquired during twenty-five years in Congress a solid, if conservative, understanding of domestic and foreign policy. Yet his faithful defense of Republican orthodoxy while House minority leader had made him seem anything but imaginative.[30]

Significant and trivial incidents combined to reinforce the President's reputation for ineptitude. Well-publicized divisions wracked the White House staff, a potpourri of Nixon holdovers, former congressional aides, and new appointees. Ford himself gave confused or inaccurate descriptions of some major administration policies, including the terms for renegotiating a new Panama Canal treaty. Ultimately, literal rather than metaphorical stumbles did the most damage. Photographers recorded Ford bumping his head while entering his Marine helicopter, tumbling on a ski slope, and tripping down the stairs of *Air Force One* in Austria. His apparent clumsiness provided material for several comedians. Trying to deflect the satire, Press Secretary Ron Nessen appeared on *Saturday Night Live,* where a stumbling Chevy Chase impersonated Ford each week before twelve million television viewers. Newscasters also highlighted Ford's slips because, as Robert Pierpoint of CBS argued, they were "almost symbolic" of administration failures.[31]

Ford was smart enough to curb Henry Kissinger's independence and aggressive self-promotion. Indeed, his replacement of Kissinger by Scowcroft as National Security Advisor was intended to send just such a message. Nonetheless, complaints about the Secretary of State's "lone ranger" diplomacy persisted. There was no consensus, however, on where the lone ranger was riding. According to Ronald Reagan, who was challenging Ford for the Republican presidential nomination, Kissinger had allowed the Soviets to exploit detente; according to Jimmy Carter, already emerging as the likely Democratic nominee, Kissinger's secretive balance of power politics failed to reflect the "essential decency and generosity and honesty of the American people."[32]

In the context of these growing political problems, Ford addressed the issue of Eastern Europe on 3 April 1976. Speaking to representatives of Milwaukee area ethnic organizations, he stressed that American policy "in no sense" accepted Soviet "dominion of Eastern Europe or any kind of organic union." Rather, his administration tried "as responsibly as possible" to encourage Eastern European autonomy. He had stated this position "categorically" before leaving for Helsinki and had made it clear to Yugoslavians, Romanians, and Poles while visiting their countries. It was "very difficult" for Eastern European governments "to adopt a total independence from the Soviet Union," but the Helsinki accords helped in this and other respects. The agreement not only "forced" the Soviets and other Communist governments to "give more humane treatment," but also represented the "greatest political liability, propaganda loss to the Soviet Union, period."[33]

Still, the Republican right and many representatives of Eastern European ethnic groups remained skeptical about Ford's position on Eastern Europe and his ability to direct his own administration's foreign policy. The Coordinating Committee of Hungarian Organizations urged Sonnenfeldt's dismissal. The National Lithuanian Society of America demanded that Kissinger conform to Ford's express position on the Baltic states. Equally dissatisfied with Kissinger's "short denial," Aloysius Mazewski of PAC called the Sonnenfeldt Doctrine a "greater infamy than the Yalta Pact."[34]

Although the President and Secretary of State had used almost exactly the same language, Senator James Buckley accused them of holding "wholly inconsistent" positions, with Kissinger far less willing to press for Eastern European autonomy. As long as Kissinger held office, Buckley declared, Ford could "not claim to be fully in charge of foreign policy." Furthermore, Buckley may have been the Capitol Hill conservative who leaked the summary of Sonnenfeldt's remarks to the *New York Times* one day before the Wisconsin primary. Secretary of Defense Melvin Laird, perhaps Kissinger's foremost rival within the administration, openly predicted that Ford would appoint a new Secretary of State after the election. Amid the rumors and maneuvering, Kissinger quipped that he felt an affinity for Deng Xiao-ping, the Chinese vice-premier then in eclipse, because "I am in the wall poster stage myself." Ultimately Ford stuck by Kissinger, whom he called "one of the greatest" secretaries of state.[35]

* * *

By the time Ford had narrowly defeated Reagan for the Republican nomination in mid-August, the Eastern European issue was only one of several problems that apparently doomed his candidacy. As White House pollster Robert Teeter observed, Reagan had further enhanced the President's unwanted image as an error-prone "loser." Now Ford trailed Carter by twenty points in most polls. No presidential candidate had ever overcome such a gap in seventy-three days. Yet Ford believed that he could meet what Teeter euphemistically called a "unique challenge."[36]

Whereas the President and his advisors had underestimated Reagan and overestimated the power of incumbency, they entered the fall campaign with an appreciation of Ford's weaknesses and Carter's strengths. The Democratic candidate was intelligent, disciplined, and able to "send political signals with a light touch," Teeter summarized. Carter courted diverse constituencies by presenting himself as a fiscally conservative advocate of full employment, a defender of "traditional" family values who nonetheless supported the Equal Rights Amendment, and a foe of military intervention who would stand up to the Soviets. Though often effective, these contradictory signals also raised suspicions that Carter was an arrogant, unprincipled opportunist. Conversely, most Americans liked Ford even if they doubted his competence. Thus he needed both to mobilize that good will and to personify strong leadership.[37]

Ford also needed votes from Democrats to win. Fortunately, there existed what Teeter called "targets of opportunity." They included Catholics whose ancestors had emigrated from Eastern Europe. Republicans had been shooting at this target intermittently for at least a generation. In 1951, while promising to liberate Eastern Europe from godless Communists, the party had established an Ethnic Origins Division under former Ambassador Arthur Bliss Lane. Twenty years later, promising to pursue detente with chastened Communists, Richard Nixon had tried to bring blue-collar Catholics into an emerging Republican majority. In 1972, Nixon became the first Republican presidential nominee to win a majority from Catholic voters, many of whom regarded him as a culturally conservative alternative to the supposedly subversive Democrat, George McGovern.[38]

Ford, facing a culturally conservative Democrat, expected fewer defections in 1976, yet he nonetheless believed that his campaign "must" cultivate ethnic Catholics. As the Republicans knew, Jimmy Carter had little understanding of this traditionally Democratic constituency—and vice versa. Attempting to court them, Carter in April had endorsed neighborhood "ethnic purity" but the remark had backfired and almost cost him critical African-American support. Ford's advisors also struggled to find an effective strategy. The most sophisticated among them, including Teeter, David Gergen, Stuart Spencer, Michael Raoul-Duval, and Richard Cheney, understood that Catholics were increasingly cosmopolitan and prosperous. By and large, these aides urged Ford to affirm family values, skirt the volatile issue of abortion, and minimize appeals to parochial interests in foreign or domestic policy. On the other hand, Baroody and Kuropas exaggerated the influence of ethnic lobbies, the political impact of Eastern European policy, and the unpopularity of the Helsinki accords.[39]

Ultimately Ford's tactics combined routine ethnic puffery, endorsement of solid households in sound neighborhoods, and promises of special consideration. According to the campaign pamphlet promoting his administration "from an ethnic perspective," Ford not only had signed the Ethnic Studies Heritage Act but also had appointed "more ethnic Americans" than any other president; these included two Polish-Americans, Myron Kuropas, the first White House assistant for ethnic affairs, and Mitchell Kobelinski, director of the Small Business Administration. Sometimes subordinates briefed ethnic spokesmen on the Helsinki accords so that the President could concentrate on less onerous matters. For example, meeting with Aloysius Mazewski and other Polish-Americans on 7 September, he proclaimed Pulaski Day, introduced Kuropas and Kobelinski, and deplored Polish jokes. Yet Ford was forced to deny, "for the tenth time," as he put it, that a Sonnenfeldt Doctrine existed. Even so, his prospects among Poles and other Democrats descended from the old new immigration looked promising. Many Catholics felt little affinity for Carter's evangelical Protestant style. In late September, a Republican poll showed Ford receiving 53 percent of the Catholic vote.[40]

Seeking to eradicate his image as an inept "loser," Ford challenged Carter to a series of debates. After emissaries negotiated about lighting, lecterns, and the degree of deference due a president, the candidates agreed to three debates under the auspices of the League of Women Voters. By the time the first took place on 23 September, Carter's lead in the polls had diminished. Earlier that month, prominent Catholic bishops had obliquely criticized his position on abortion. Then Carter's attempt to explain Christian morality to *Playboy* in earthy language reinforced what his aide, Hamilton Jordan, called the "weirdo factor." Even so, pundits and polls agreed that Carter would probably beat the President in debate. Expectations were so low, journalist Richard Reeves wrote, that "If Ford doesn't trip, he wins."[41]

Carter felt sufficiently confident to prepare relatively little for the first debate. Meanwhile, Ford watched films of the Kennedy-Nixon debates as well as Carter's debates with opponents in the 1970 Georgia gubernatorial race, studied his adversary's personality and positions, met with a "Debate Group" to plan strategy, pored over briefing books, and answered tough questions from advisors in a mock debate setting. When the rivals met on 23 September to debate domestic issues, Carter at first seemed hesitant to confront the President of the United States. By the time he had hit his stride, a technical glitch disrupted the proceedings for twenty-seven minutes. Ford, in the face of prevailing low expectations, demonstrated a solid knowledge of government. Most commentators and viewers polled believed that Ford had won the debate. Carter's lead in the Gallup poll dropped from eighteen to ten points.[42]

When they met again, on 6 October, to debate foreign policy, Ford felt under siege. A special prosecutor was investigating his congressional finances, rumors persisted that he had arranged a deal to pardon Nixon, and Secretary of Agriculture Earl Butz made a well-publicized racial slur and then clung to office for five days before resigning on 4 October. Moreover, Ford was worried about a meeting with Reagan on 8 October. Preoccupied and perhaps overconfident, he prepared less carefully the second time around.[43]

Once again, however, Ford studied briefing books, underlined pertinent passages with a felt-tip pen, and scrawled brief notes. He planned to contrast Carter's "reckless, ignorant" statements with his own experience and prudence. Rejecting a resumption of the Cold War, he would continue to reduce tensions with the Soviet Union by negotiating "from strength." Annoyed by charges that Kissinger controlled foreign policy, Ford considered a rebuttal via historical analogy, comparing their relationship to that between Eisenhower and Dulles. Along with most pundits, he expected a question on Eastern Europe, where Polish industrial workers, students, and younger Catholic clergy had recently demonstrated against the government's economic policy. Carter had played a "delicate game," the NSC briefing book warned, "flailing" the administration for the Sonnenfeldt Doctrine while "carefully avoiding any intention to roll back the Iron Curtain." Ford expected to repeat his opposition to spheres of influence and to cite his Eastern European tour as a responsible way to encourage freedom. "Borders not to be changed by force. Who wants to change by force?" he noted.[44]

In short, Ford was ready to respond—for the eleventh time, so to speak—that there was no Sonnenfeldt Doctrine. Unfortunately this was not Max Frankel's question. Hearing Ford's answers to Frankel, Carter aide Stuart Eizenstadt exclaimed, "That is the dumbest thing I've ever heard," and pollster Patrick Caddell went even further: "Jesus, he's lost his mind." Afterward, Mondale joked that he was looking for a Polish bar because drinks would be free for Democrats.[45]

White House Chief of Staff Richard Cheney believed that Carter had improved his debating style but thought that Ford, stronger on substance, had won again. Yet questions at the postdebate press conference given by Cheney, Scowcroft, and Stuart Spencer centered on Ford's responses to Frankel. Scowcroft pronounced Ford's meaning "clear," and Spencer professed to see no political problem. Cheney wanted to issue an immediate clarification but Ford, considering his "slip" minor, rejected the idea. Preliminary survey data, including a computer hookup allowing fifty-two residents of Washington state to rate the debaters second by second, were encouraging. By the next morning, however, protests from Eastern European ethnic groups had begun to reach the White House, media coverage highlighted Ford's exchange with Frankel, and Teeter's latest polls were signaling overwhelming defeat. Reluctantly and without admitting error, Ford told a California college audience that the United States "had never conceded—and never will concede" Soviet domination over Eastern Europe. Indeed, during the debate he had shown "firm support" for Poles, Romanians, and Yugoslavians who struggled to be "less dependent" on Moscow.[46]

This cogent statement of a position Ford had enunciated dozens of times failed to end the controversy. In part, he was a victim of the journalistic inclination to present an infelicitous phrase as evidence of deep moral or intellectual failing. Carter had suffered similarly after defending "ethnic purity" and revealing the lust in his heart to *Playboy.* Ironically, rising expectations about Ford's ability worked against him; having "won" the first debate, he was now expected to get his syntax straight. As *Newsday* observed, Ford had "stumbled badly despite all the advantages of incumbency." Most important, Ford had violated a Cold War taboo, openly acknowledging the limits of American influence in Eastern Europe, as well as the complexity of politics there, without simultaneously expressing prescribed levels of outrage. Therefore he faced ritual condemnation from editors and politicians who knew no better plan for liberating Eastern Europe but who did not have to admit it at the moment.[47]

According to the *Los Angeles Times,* Ford's answers to Frankel constituted "either a momentary lapse of reason or evidence of a profound misunderstanding of one of the most important world security problems." Primarily on the basis of those answers, Haynes Johnson of the *Washington Post* presented Ford as a "plodding and faltering" debater. Lesser reporters interviewed ethnic spokesmen or prowled Polish-American neighborhoods to record the anticipated rancor. Lev Dobriansky, president of the Congress of Ukrainians in the United States, switched his support from Ford to Carter, and Aloysius Mazewski, a loyal Republican, phoned the White House for an explanation. Few commentators viewed this Cold War political ritual from the outside. Historian Waldo Heinrichs perceived a tactical conflict between two Cold Warriors, columnist James Reston accused the two parties of "playing games with each other," and former Democratic National Committee chairman Robert Strauss took an almost anthropological delight in the spectacle. Carter need not "do much" to profit from Ford's gaffe, Strauss noted. "Let nature take its course.... The more they try to explain it, the more glue you get on you," he predicted on 7 October.[48]

If Strauss expected Carter to stand mute, he misunderstood his party's nominee. Certainly Carter understood Ford's intention, the complicated situation in Eastern Europe, and the long-standing policy of cultivating Communist governments there. As Sonnenfeldt ruefully remembers, the Democratic candidate had received an official State Department briefing on the absence of any new policy or doctrine. If doubts remained, Carter could have consulted his chief foreign policy advisor, Zbigniew Brzezinski, who in the mid-1960s had urged "weaning away" nationalist Communist regimes from the Soviet Union and had written one of President Johnson's speeches on the subject. Indeed, while attacking Ford's answer to Max Frankel, Carter had given himself an escape route via one of his favorite rhetorical devices, the stringing together of words or concepts with subtly different meanings. He had sarcastically asked Ford to convince Eastern Europeans that they were free from Soviet "domination or supervision." If, however, the President's statement did convince viewers that there was no Soviet "domination," then Carter could fall back on the softer term, "supervision." Doug Bailey, an advertising executive in the Ford campaign, considered the Democratic candidate's "ingenious use" of language an effective way of "waffling" on issues. At a deeper level, Carter's tendency to shade meanings reflected his innate appreciation of complexity, a character trait he necessarily suppressed in an aggressive pursuit of the presidency.[49]

Conveniently for Carter, three decades of Cold War had made most voters believe that monolithic Communist regimes dominated Eastern Europe. Accordingly, he was able to abandon careful locutions and escalate his attack. In a playful mood, he reported the demise of Polish-Americans for Ford. Turning serious, he said that Ford had "disgraced" the United States. The "ridiculous" denial of Soviet domination reflected "confusion about our people, about the aspirations of human beings, about human rights, about liberty, about simple justice." Perhaps Ford had been "brainwashed" in Poland. Walter Mondale also saw signs of ineptitude and lax morality. Ford's answers, which, Mondale said, would have disqualified him for promotion to the third grade, also called to mind his "disgraceful" refusal to meet Solzhenitsyn. Similar messages characterized Democratic advertisements in the Eastern European ethnic press.[50]

Media coverage made Ford's slip, initially unnoticed by most television viewers, a major issue. A majority of the sample Teeter had surveyed by telephone immediately after the debate called Ford the winner; no one mentioned his convoluted answers on Eastern Europe.

The next evening, a similar sample judged Carter the winner by a margin of 61 to 19 percent, and many respondents volunteered that Ford seemed "mixed up." Although journalists sought quaint responses from working-class ethnics, the President apparently lost most support among college-educated voters.[51]

As Robert Strauss had predicted, the verbal slip stuck to Ford like glue. Subsequent explanations only made him stickier. Reluctantly yielding to entreaties from advisors, he tried twice on 8 October to lay the matter to rest. First, addressing the San Fernando Valley Business and Professional Association, he joked to sympathetic laughter, "It has been alleged by some that I was not as precise as I should have been the other day." With another vulnerable phrase, he set out to "explain what I really meant." He had met the strong Polish people and knew that they did not consider themselves "forever dominated—if they were—by the Soviet Union." When Cheney and Spencer predicted—accurately, as it turned out—that the press would use the phrase, "if they were," as evidence of Ford's befuddlement, he tried again. Speaking from a Glendale, California, parking lot, Ford acknowledged the imprecision of his debate answers, stressed his long-standing support of Captive Nations Week, and lamented the "tragic" presence of Soviet troops in Poland. Even so, he continued to speak as a thoughtful Cold Warrior, noting the Polish "desire for liberty" and denying Romanian and Yugoslavian subordination to the Soviet Union.[52]

Ford wanted his parking lot press conference to end the "misunderstanding." On the contrary, professing increased perplexity, reporters besieged Press Secretary Ron Nessen, White House Chief of Staff Richard Cheney, and other presidential assistants for further clarification. On 9 October the *Washington Post* compared Ford to a juggler who lost sight of one Indian club and then found the others falling to his feet. The White House press corps privately joked that the second debate had moved Edward Gierek to exult: "Free at last, free at last." Senior advisors urged Ford to make his position absolutely clear. As he recalled, they thought Americans worried less about Eastern European policy than about a confused president. Lower in the White House hierarchy, Baroody and Kuropas urged many meetings to pacify Eastern European ethnics, and A. James Reichley proposed a stern counterattack, blaming Presidents Roosevelt and Truman for surrendering Eastern Europe at Teheran, Yalta, and Potsdam.[53]

Ford's hesitancy to explain his debate answers further may have reflected stubbornness, as he later wrote, yet it was understandable stubbornness. Admission of any "slip" would reinforce his public image as the president who couldn't walk, ski, or talk straight. Furthermore, if he concurred in the judgment that Eastern Europe consisted of simple Soviet satellites, then he denigrated his own diplomacy. As Senator Buckley had discerned, the President's Eastern European policy was not entirely congruent with Kissinger's. Unlike his Secretary of State, Ford cared deeply about the inhabitants of Eastern Europe and believed that his efforts had improved their lives.[54]

Ultimately, Ford's stubbornness yielded to Cold War political reality. Addressing leaders of Eastern European ethnic lobbies on 12 October, he "bluntly" admitted making a "mistake," and then declared that the "countries of Eastern Europe are, of course, dominated by the Soviet Union." This time, he made no attempt to distinguish between Poland and Yugoslavia or, for that matter, between Poland and Bulgaria. Absent too was any reference to his diplomatic efforts to foster independence in Eastern Europe. This tougher line also characterized subsequent White House responses to protest letters. Debating Walter Mondale on 15 October, Ford's running mate, Senator Robert Dole, accused two Democratic presidents of accepting the "enslavement" of Eastern Europe at Yalta and Potsdam. The Cold War ritual had run its course. On 20 October, Cheney assured Ford that his campaign was "back on track."[55]

Although the track led to defeat two weeks later, the President never stopped believing that his basic position was correct. In 1989, after Poland had appointed a non-Communist prime minister, Ford wrote in the *Washington Post* that he had "come out pretty well as a prophet." Moreover, the growing movement in Eastern Europe toward democracy and away from Soviet control was partly the product of a patient exercise of American influence as exemplified by his own administrations. Thus Ford was "prouder than ever to have signed the Helsinki accords." In short, the strategy of soft liberation had been vindicated. [56]

* * *

The related controversies over Sonnenfeldt's putative doctrine and Ford's alleged misunderstanding of Eastern Europe during the campaign barely affected Soviet-American relations. According to Sonnenfeldt, though the Soviets knew better, they cited his own remarks as evidence that the administration was taking a harder line. The President's belated affirmation of Cold War shibboleths in late October 1976 might have annoyed Soviet leaders. Already perplexed by Carter, however, they probably would have overlooked this rhetorical ritual if it had kept Ford in office. During both controversies the news media exhibited routine irresponsibility. Evans and Novak distorted Sonnenfeldt's remarks and exaggerated their significance. Perhaps such behavior should be expected from columnists, especially columnists known for their partisanship. Media coverage of Ford's convoluted statements on Eastern Europe is more disturbing. Where they should have seen a slip of the tongue and stubbornness, most reporters, in search of a lively story, claimed to find evidence of ignorance or immorality.[57]

Undoubtedly Ford's response to Max Frankel in the second debate will live in legend as one of the great errors of presidential campaigning, comparable to James G. Blaine's failure in 1884 to repudiate Rev. Samuel Burchard's denigration of Democrats as the party of "rum, Romanism, and rebellion," and Charles Evans Hughes's failure in 1916 to call on Governor Hiram Johnson of California. All three candidates lost close elections and two of them, Blaine and Ford, apparently lost support among ethnic groups (Irish and Eastern Europeans, respectively) whom they had successfully cultivated in the past. Yet the differences are greater than the similarities. Blaine, who probably never heard the remarks he was supposed to repudiate, and Hughes, who did not know that he and Johnson occupied the same hotel, erred by omission. Ford, an incumbent president, seemed unable to understand American policy toward Eastern Europe. In fact, he did understand this largely inherited, anomalous policy very well but had trouble explaining it in politically acceptable terms.

In a postmortem, Ford's pollsters concluded that the imbroglio over Eastern Europe had "stalled the President's momentum." This metaphor, like "organic," requires explication. Certainly the controversy cost Ford time and energy. Whether it also cost many votes is harder to determine. After the debate, Ford's support among Catholics dropped from 53 to 48 percent while remaining constant among Protestants. Ultimately Ford received 41 percent of the Catholic vote, a showing weaker than Nixon's in 1972 (52 percent) but stronger than Nixon's in 1968 (33 percent) and 1960 (24 percent). On the basis of a small sample, Patrick Caddell concluded that Carter had beaten Ford among Polish-Americans, 59 to 41 percent. A postelection study of Cleveland voters, also based on a small sample, suggests that Ford's remarks on Eastern Europe had little impact, but that Carter's endorsement of "ethnic purity" helped him. The President might have attracted a few more ethnic Cold Warriors if he had not bogged down in Eastern Europe, yet these votes would not have swung the election. Ford's gaffe was significant, not because it alienated a narrow ethnic constituency, but because it seemed to prove the point stressed by Reagan and Carter, that Ford lacked the intelligence to govern.[58]

Joking about the demise of Polish-Americans for Ford in 1976, Jimmy Carter enjoyed the latest but not necessarily the last laugh. As president, Carter also traveled to Eastern Europe, acknowledged that governments there enjoyed varying amounts of autonomy, and worked to maximize their independence. Much as Ford changed from a reflexive to a reflective Cold Warrior, Carter initially urged Americans to forsake an "inordinate fear of Communism." Perhaps Carter's chuckling in 1976 had obscured the central meaning of Ford's gaffe: during the Cold War virtually anyone could be charged with softness toward the Soviets and, especially if evidence included an infelicitous phrase, somebody would believe it. In due course he too would learn.[59]

7

God and Jimmy Carter

After the shouting and voting ended, *Church and State* magazine correctly concluded that the election of 1976 had raised "more religious and church-state related issues than any since 1960," when John F. Kennedy was elected the first Roman Catholic president. The impact of these issues should not have been surprising. The election occurred amid a religious awakening and followed a decade of war, racial conflict, cultural questioning, and economic crisis. Furthermore, the Republican and Democratic presidential candidates, incumbent Gerald R. Ford and former Governor of Georgia Jimmy Carter, were the most devout pair of major party nominees since William McKinley defeated William Jennings Bryan in 1896.[1]

Discussion of religion and the presidency concentrated on Carter, a self-described "born again" Christian. He did not intend—and probably did not expect—his relationship with God to be a major campaign issue. Earlier in his career, he had hesitated to answer questions about his religion but, since these arose often in Georgia, finally decided to reply "very frankly." Still, he remained reticent about volunteering information; honesty and eagerness to witness for his faith conflicted with a desire for privacy. In his campaign autobiography, *Why Not the Best?*, Carter described himself as a "Christian," and during the primaries affirmed "traditional" values of hard work, honesty, and family that many voters associated with religion. Yet Baptist churchman was only one of the roles he played, and one he advertised less than his experiences as a governor, businessman, farmer, submariner, and nuclear engineer. Admiral Hyman Rickover, who had reinforced Carter's perfectionist tendencies, bulked larger in *Why Not the Best?* than theologian Reinhold Niebuhr, who was merely quoted on the frontispiece along with Dylan Thomas and Bob Dylan. Carter's spiritual rebirth a decade earlier went unmentioned. Carter probably sensed that a presidential candidate's conversion narrative would disturb some readers, but, perhaps because prayer and Baptist piety meshed easily with his own daily routine and Georgia politics, he underestimated how many other Americans would consider them extraordinary, dangerous, or bizarre.[2]

After Carter's victory in the New Hampshire primary raised him from the status of dark horse to front runner, commentators tried to make sense of his personality and world view. Typically stressing individual quirks and ignoring social class, they explained neither very well, and Carter emerged as a populistic, technocratic, Wilsonian enigma. Nothing looked quirkier than the candidate's religion, especially after his sister, Ruth Carter Stapleton, described her brother's conversion in the *Washington Post* on 12 March. Carter corroborated her story except for minor details; according to his account, for example, no tears had been shed. The conversion had involved no mysticism, "no wave of revelation . . . no blinding flash of light or voice of God." The "quiet" reassurance he had felt, Carter told reporter Jules Witcover, was a "typical experience among Christians."[3]

Indeed it was. According to a Gallup poll conducted later in 1976, 48 percent of American Protestants and 18 percent of American Catholics had been born again. Apparently few of them reported for the national media, which continued to treat Carter's religion as anything but typical. In late March, so many reporters descended on the Plains, Georgia, Baptist Church, where Carter taught a men's Sunday School class, that they had to be restricted to a pool of four. Ruth Carter Stapleton received much publicity in her own right. A born again Christian whose books and newsletters offered a mixture of soft theology, softer psychology, positive thinking, and compassion, Stapleton was persistently misidentified (to her consternation) as a "faith healer."[4]

Throughout the campaign, Carter continued to answer questions about his religion and, especially when they were intelligently posed, gave informative answers. Unfortunately, except for Bill Moyers, who interviewed Carter on network television in May, no one posing intelligent questions commanded a large audience. Nonetheless, Carter's statements in 1976 revealed a thoughtful Southern Baptist layman who favored a sturdy wall of separation between church and state.[5]

Carter explained that his whole life had been "shaped in the [Baptist] church." His adult conversion had marked an important transition instead of a final point of certainty. Thereafter, his "personal relationship" with Jesus grew stronger, he prayed without "special effort," and felt "at peace with the world." He tried to emulate Christ's example, seeking especially to control "self-pride and self-satisfaction." Similarly, recognizing that his religious world view retained inconsistencies and anomalies, he constantly looked for better answers; he liked to quote Paul Tillich's observation that religion was a "search for truth." Carter not only acknowledged American religious diversity but explicitly identified with early Baptists like Roger Williams and John Leland who had championed freedom of conscience. Accordingly, resisting church pressure, he had voted in the Georgia Senate to permit eighteen-year-olds to drink alcohol, and later ended regular religious services in the governor's mansion. He also rejected proposals to restore compulsory prayer to public schools. Nor would he use the White House as a "pulpit" to spread his own religious views. Rather, along with other recent presidents, he would support the general "principles of the Judeo-Christian ethic."[6]

Although Carter's stands on foreign policy and domestic economics were shrewdly imprecise, he displayed a clear, consistent position on religion. Why then did the issue continue to haunt him during the campaign? First, as in 1928 and, to a lesser extent, 1960, religion was part of a broader cultural conflict. Evangelical and fundamentalist Protestants on the one hand, and Roman Catholics, Jews, and cosmopolitan intellectuals on the other, had through generations of conflict developed stereotypes about each other that were difficult to forget. Second, as in 1928 and 1960, questions relating to church-state relations were very much on the national agenda. For example, many theologically conservative Protestants now coalesced with Catholics in urging federal aid to parochial schools as well as required prayer in public schools, and some Orthodox Jews joined them in denouncing *Roe* v. *Wade,* the Supreme Court decision that had legalized most abortions in 1973. Third, although Carter and Ford denied seeking votes on the basis of religion, the temptation was hard to resist and their respective parties were even less fastidious. Moreover, Carter made important tactical errors in mobilizing these issues. Fourth, citing Jesus' teachings, Carter often declared that "all of us are sinful" without prudently adding that Americans in the aggregate were less sinful than others. This neo-Calvinist judgment had some appeal after Watergate and the Vietnam War, but, in the final analysis, it contradicted the venerable belief that God was on our side. Indeed, even secularized doubts about American mission would have been controversial.[7]

Carter tried to break down stereotypes about born again Baptists. He was least conciliatory toward—and least successful with —cosmopolitan intellectuals. For instance, Arthur M. Schlesinger, Jr., accused him of misunderstanding Niebuhr. Carter was more effective with Jews, many of whom recalled the long-standing affinity between theologically conservative Protestantism and anti-Semitism. According to a disgruntled speech writer, Carter had derisively said in May 1976 that his primary opponent, Senator Henry Jackson, "had all the Jews." The Carter campaign quickly denied the charge. Furthermore, the candidate himself noted the many Jews on his staff; recalled a fellow Baptist, President Harry S Truman, who had recognized Israel in 1948; and, in an uncharacteristic reference to Bible prophecy, called Israel's creation a "fulfillment" of Scripture.[8]

Catholics were more numerous than Jews and proved to be more skeptical of Carter. Though comprising less than one-quarter of the population, they typically provided one-third of the Democratic vote. Although few Catholics belonged to Carter's inner circle, he recognized their influence within the Democratic coalition. At the national convention, he was placed in nomination by Representative Peter Rodino, an Italian Catholic from Newark, New Jersey. Yet such symbolic gestures did not solve what the *Washington Post* called Carter's "Catholic problem." Not only did he seem culturally alien to—and personally ill at ease with—northern working-class audiences, most of them disproportionately Catholic, but also his opposition to a constitutional amendment banning abortion troubled many priests and parishoners. Six of eight "right to life" amendments considered by the ninety-third Congress had been introduced by Catholic legislators, and several members of the church hierarchy had testified in favor of these bills. In addition, roughly half the members of the most powerful antiabortion lobby, the National Right to Life Committee, were Catholics.[9]

Carter's religion enhanced his appeal to white fundamentalist and evangelical Protestants as well as to most blacks. At minimum, it highlighted his commitment to morality in government and deflected charges of callous opportunism. Furthermore, though leading evangelicals, including the editors of *Christianity Today,* remained prudently noncommittal, rank and file born again whites, eager for national acceptance, paid scant attention to Carter's theology and overlooked political differences to embrace him as one of their own.[10]

For African-Americans, Carter's conversion to Christ was less significant than his conversion to the cause of racial equality, but religion nonetheless enhanced his appeal. There were strong theological and cultural affinities, though relatively few institutional ties, between born again whites and most black evangelicals. Addressing a convention of the African Methodist Episcopal Church, Carter stressed this "mutual faith." Sixty percent of southern blacks were Baptists, and the Southern Baptist Convention (SBC) contained almost four hundred African-American congregations. Even northern blacks were used to the amalgamation of religion and politics. Thus, as William Lee Miller observed, Carter was the only recent presidential nominee who actually looked comfortable at a black church service.[11]

For many cultural conservatives, the pious Carter family offered an attractive alternative to Betty Ford's candid feminism. The President's wife considered *Roe* v. *Wade* a "great, great decision," and acknowledged that adolescents, including her own daughter, might have love affairs. Carter avoided criticizing Mrs. Ford, yet his campaign in conservative constituencies benefited from the controversies she ignited. Democratic appeals to born again whites included an advertisement in *Christianity Today,* asking, "Does a Dedicated

Evangelical Belong in the White House?" And African-Americans were unlikely to miss Martin Luther King, Sr.'s, benediction at the national convention: "Surely the Lord sent Jimmy Carter to come on out and bring America back where she belongs."[12]

Privately, Ford felt "discomfited" by Carter's open discussion of his faith; publicly, the President declared without naming names that no candidate should "deliberately exploit religion for his or her political advantage." The heated campaign obscured both Ford's willingness to exploit religious symbolism and his religious affinities with Carter. He became the first president to address the SBC, wooed prominent Catholic clergy, and won covert support from evangelist Billy Graham.[13]

Ford's religious references, like Carter's, came naturally. He had been raised in the Episcopal church and had attended services since his youth. Starting in his late forties, he had grown more devout, partly through the influence of Billy Zeoli, an evangelist from his home state of Michigan. Accordingly, Ford had attended congressional prayer breakfasts regularly, read the Bible daily, and sometimes quoted Scripture in interviews (though with less facility than Carter). He prayed for guidance during crises; his decision to pardon former President Richard M. Nixon followed services and communion at St. John's Episcopal Church. Ford's religious commitment deepened further when his oldest son Michael entered Gordon-Conwell Theological Seminary. At the same time, he felt a "strong ecumenical feeling" and endorsed a "wall of separation" between church and state. For example, he ended the practice, begun by Nixon, of holding Sunday services at the White House.[14]

The President and Carter differed in two important ways. An easygoing optimist, as opposed to Carter, who trained himself to think positively, Ford had few doubts that God blessed America. At the level of federal policy, he wanted more doors through or tunnels under the wall between church and state. Specifically, he favored tax credits for parents whose children attended parochial schools, had favored a constitutional amendment providing prayer in public schools (though he hedged on this issue in 1976), and seemed less willing than Carter to tax church-owned property.[15]

Both candidates personally opposed abortion and wished that the issue would go away. As president, Ford had accepted but did not push the so-called Hyde amendment to bar use of Medicaid funds for abortions. During the campaign, he endorsed a "'people's' amendment" to the Constitution allowing voters to ban abortion in their respective states (a position his wife said would "not do you a damn bit of good" politically). Despite Catholic pressure, Carter rejected legislation in favor of moral suasion and contraception, which, he said, would render abortions unnecessary. Any local option amendment discriminated against the poor by allowing rich women to "fly from one state to another and have abortions in an unrestricted way." Although Carter promised to abide by *Roe* v. *Wade,* he found this position personally distasteful. Against the advice of his staff, he often took pains to call abortions "wrong" and condemned Medicaid payments for them.[16]

A controversy over abortion during August and September highlighted Carter's "Catholic problem." First, Archbishop Joseph Bernardin, president of the National Conference of Catholic Bishops (NCCB), contrasted the "timely and important" Republican repudiation of abortion with Carter's "deeply disturbing" acceptance of the prochoice plank in the Democratic platform. After joining other leaders of the hierarchy in meetings with the candidates, Bernardin said that he felt "encouraged" by Ford but "disappointed" by Carter. Then, apparently pressed by bishops who either favored Carter or opposed any lapse from public neutrality, Bernardin retreated. He noted that a right to life amendment was only one of their social concerns, which also included the elimination of poverty, arms control, and international human rights—issues where the NCCB stood closer to Carter than to Ford. For his part, Carter reiterated his position that the federal government should never "do anything to encourage" abortion.[17]

Despite Bernardin's retreat, the controversy left the impression that the Catholic hierarchy was tilting toward Ford. Whether Catholic voters would move in the same direction remained uncertain. Patrick Caddell, the most influential Catholic in Carter's inner circle, expected their long-standing Democratic loyalty to prevail because, according to his polls, most Catholics viewed abortion as an issue largely outside the President's control. As late as the weekend before the election, however, other polls revealed a slim lead by Ford among Catholic voters.[18]

The most peculiar manifestation of the religious issue in 1976 was the reaction to Carter's interview in *Playboy.* He was not the first prominent Baptist to duel with this worldly monthly; six years earlier the Christian Life Commission of the SBC had sponsored a forum on the *"Playboy* philosophy." Although Carter probably believed, as he suggested in retrospect, that his appearance in the magazine constituted "part of Christ's commission" to spread the gospel, more mundane reasons played their part. Carter sought not only to impress worldly voters, but also to test himself against cosmopolitan antagonists who considered him, as he told interviewer Robert Scheer, an "ignorant peanut farmer."[19]

Prodded by Scheer, Carter tried once again to explain his views on religion, sexual morality, and the separation of church and state. He sounded variously candid, irritable, and eager to show that he was "not a packaged article you can put in a little box." After the conversation moved on to less personal issues, Carter made a last effort to convince *Playboy* readers of his complexity. He returned to a favorite theme, Jesus' warning against "pride, that one person should never think he was better than anybody else. . . ."

> I try not to commit a deliberate sin. I recognize that I'm going to do it anyhow, because I'm human and I'm tempted. And Christ set almost impossible standards for us. Christ said, 'I tell you that anyone who looks on a woman with lust in his heart has already committed adultery.'
>
> I've looked on a lot of women with lust. I've committed adultery in my heart many times. This is something that God recognizes that I will do—and I have done it—and God forgives me for it. But that doesn't mean that I condemn someone who not only looks on a woman with lust but who leaves his wife and shacks up with somebody out of wedlock.
>
> Christ says, Don't consider yourself better than someone else because one guy screws a whole bunch of women while the other guy is loyal to his wife. The guy who is loyal to his wife ought not to be condescending or proud because of the relative degrees of sinfulness.

The *Playboy* interview did not end with lust in the heart. Rather, Carter resumed his discussion of governmental ethics. Religion, he implied, would prevent him from taking "on the same frame of mind that Nixon or Johnson did—lying, cheating and distorting the truth."[20]

Nevertheless, the headlines, commentaries, and jokes centered on lust. Prominent theological conservatives wondered why Carter had spoken to *Playboy;* most agreed with Rev. Bailey Smith that "screw" was not a "good Baptist word." On the other hand, Joseph Duffey, a Democratic campaign manager and former professor at Hartford Theological Seminary, said that early versions of the Bible had been written in analogous "street Greek." Rev. Bruce Edwards, Carter's friend and pastor at the Plains, Georgia, Baptist Church, also defended his applied theology. Martin Luther King, Sr., quipped, "They can't kill you for lookin'." Outside evangelical and fundamentalist circles, the *Playboy* interview, which became public in late September, reinvigorated what Hamilton Jordan called the "weirdo factor," the suspicion that Carter was too strange to be president.[21]

In the final analysis, Carter's religion helped him to win the election. A Gallup poll in October showed 10 percent of voters unimpressed by Carter's faith, 20 percent impressed, and 70 percent reporting no effect. According to exit polls on Election Day, he ultimately received roughly 68 percent of the Jewish vote and 55 percent of the Catholic vote (in the latter case, 6 percent less than the Democratic average between 1952 and 1972). Ford had effectively courted affluent Catholics, but the abortion issue does not seem to have made much difference. Only one-quarter of voters polled favored a constitutional amendment restricting abortion, and a majority of them supported Carter. He received 46 percent of the Protestant vote. A majority of evangelicals voted Republican, as was usually the case, but Carter won by cutting the margin from 7.2 million in 1968 to 3.2 million. And he was the first Democrat to carry the Southern Baptist constituency since Truman in 1948.[22]

* * *

James Earl Carter, Jr., had indeed lived his whole life in the church. During childhood and adolescence, it had been the Plains, Georgia, Baptist Church. Carter was born in Plains on 1 October 1924, the first child of James, Sr., a matter-of-fact Baptist, and Lillian Gordy Carter, a free-thinking and free-speaking Methodist. At age eleven, Jimmy came forward and was baptized at the Plains Church by Rev. Royall Callaway. Callaway, a dispensational premillennialist whose wife had been secretary to Rev. Bob Jones, Sr., anticipated

God's imminent judgment and Jesus' quick return. In 1977, Carter recalled that "the subject of Callaway's sermon was quite often 'by God's word, you're going to hell. Because of your sin, you deserve death.'" Yet his boyhood congregation may not have been devoid of theological liberalism. Rev. Jesse Eugene Hall, who held the pulpit from 1923 to 1927 and from 1931 to 1941, preached that the "day" mentioned in Genesis did not necessarily mean twenty-four hours.[23]

Whatever theology Carter absorbed as a boy, there is no doubt that he acquired from his demanding parents a prodigious work ethic and strong sense of discipline; his prayers asked God to help him do his best. These traits were reinforced at the United States Naval Academy and subsequently in the submarine service under Admiral Hyman G. Rickover. At Annapolis, Carter seems to have thought more than usual about life's purpose. From the perspective of 1976, these reflections looked to Carter like the product of sophomoric bull sessions. Certainly he experienced no crisis of faith. Immediately after graduating in 1946, Carter married a local woman, Rosalynn Smith, in the Plains Methodist Church, fathered three children in quick succession, and began climbing upward in the Navy. At Annapolis and on submarines, he taught informal Bible classes.[24]

Carter resigned his commission and returned to Georgia after the death of his father in 1953. Explaining this decision, Carter always emphasized the family's financial needs and the sense of community he felt in Plains, but he also may have been influenced by the slow pace of advancement in the Navy. His father had been a prominent figure in Sumter County, and Carter soon followed in his footsteps. He joined—and often led—fraternal, civic, and charitable organizations. As a matter of course, Carter rejoined the Plains Baptist Church, immediately began to teach Sunday school classes, and was chosen a deacon in 1962. That same year he won a seat in the state senate. Carter and the Plains Baptist minister, Rev. Robert Harris, disagreed about prohibition and civil rights. Carter opposed the former and, though still less than an integrationist, voted against the church's explicit ban on "Negroes and civil rights agitators." Despite their disagreements, Rev. Harris urged fellow Baptist clergy to elect Carter governor in 1966.[25]

Defeat in the Democratic primary precipitated Carter's spiritual rebirth. Apparently he had felt for some time that affluence and local fame did not bring a sense of satisfaction. Failure to win the nomination prompted a reassessment of his life. At roughly the same time, he began to doubt that he was actually a "great Christian." When Rev. Harris asked in a sermon, "If you were arrested for being a Christian, would there be enough evidence to convict you?" Carter concluded that evidence was insufficient in his case. Rather, he resembled the Pharisee in Luke 18:10–13, who thanked God for his superiority. Sometime during this reassessment, either during late 1966 or early 1967, Carter took the famous walk with his sister Ruth and asked, "What is it that you have that I haven't got?" She said that "everything I am" belonged to Jesus. Carter then opened his heart and (as he later told two psychobiographers) felt "release and assurance" as well as a "genuine interest in other people I hadn't experienced before."[26]

Although the chronology and morphology of Carter's conversion remain unclear, we can say with some certainty how it affected him. He increased his witnessing for Christ, organizing a Billy Graham film crusade in Georgia and spending several weeks as a Baptist missionary in Pennsylvania and Massachusetts; from all accounts, he developed great admiration for the men and women less successful than himself who spread or accepted the gospel. What Carter considered his enhanced interest in other people also may have influenced his endorsement of racial equality after winning the Georgia governorship in 1970. Yet his basic personality stayed intact. He remained ambitious, retained his passion for detail (taking copious notes on the missionary trail), and still placed heavy demands on his subordinates, family, and—most of all—himself. Indeed, now determined to walk in Jesus' steps, he was harder on himself than ever.[27]

An astute friend, Judge William Gunter, observed that religion gave Carter a "modicum of humility." It was not achieved easily. He worked hard to be humble. *Playboy* was only the most notorious place in which Carter reminded himself and others that warnings against pride were central to Christ's message. Often he cited his own arrogance or aloofness to illustrate this "number one sin." Perhaps, he suggested at least once, Southern Baptists should adopt the Primitive Baptist practice of washing each other's feet as an antidote to self-importance.[28]

224

Constantly probing his conscience, seeking a "deeper relation-ship with Christ," Carter was probably the most introspective president since Abraham Lincoln. Curiously, he paid much less attention to the intellectual side of religion. For instance, Norman Mailer found him unwilling or unable to discuss Søren Kierke-gaard, whom he quoted occasionally, and Garry Wills noted his slim knowledge of biblical higher criticism. Carter admitted in 1977 that he "wasn't a very good historian of the Bible." These lapses are revealing, since Carter customarily tried to become expert in every field he encountered. Perhaps unconsciously he chose to keep religious faith—a realm of release, reassurance, and warmth—relatively unscathed by the technical complexities that afflicted other parts of his life.[29]

To be sure, Carter read the Bible daily (often in Spanish to practice that language), quoted it readily, and came to terms with the ques-tion of inerrancy. Belonging to a loose denomination that ranged from premillennialists to covert "Christian realists," he explicitly reserved the "right to make my own interpretation." Carter did not consider everything in the Bible "literally true," he told *Time* in 1976, adding that portions were "obviously written in allegories." He showed virtually no interest in the most popular figurative scheme, premillennial dispensationalism; his reference to Israel as the fulfill-ment of divine prophecy was atypical.[30]

Apparently no reporter asked Carter whether he—along with Jer-ry Falwell, Pat Robertson, and Hal Lindsey—expected Jesus to return in his lifetime. His reading of Revelation sounded post-millennial: "Jesus stands at the door and knocks . . . but he can't break down the door. He doesn't want to. It must be opened by our understanding." On the other hand, he hesitated to surrender the supernatural. In a convoluted denial before the 1976 election, Carter "saw no reason to disbelieve" the Genesis account of Eve's creation from Adam's rib. Probably he was worrying less about inerrancy than about the ballots of theological conservatives. In 1977, however, he took a similar position on Lazarus's return from the dead. This story, "hard to believe on a scientifically analyzed basis," nonetheless embodied the great Christian promise of eternal life.[31]

In addition to Scripture, Carter studied the writings of Reinhold Niebuhr, a "theologian for whom I really cared." When William

Gunter introduced him to Niebuhr's writings on politics in the late 1960s, Carter allegedly called them the "most amazin' thing I've ever read." Arthur Schlesinger's skepticism notwithstanding, his enthusiasm was hardly surprising. Many younger Southern Baptists were drifting toward neoorthodoxy. Furthermore, Niebuhr and Carter shared a concern for complexity in general and paradox in particular. Both understood, in Carter's paraphrase, that "love and kindness meant a great deal in one-to-one relationships but not in dealing with structures of corporate groups." Indeed, at the level of personality, Carter, who charmed small groups but left mass audiences cold, almost personified this Niebuhrian premise.[32]

Although Carter never presented a full exposition of his religious beliefs, we can piece together his theology as well as his position on church polity, the social gospel, and religious liberty. Carter's religious world view reflected his Baptist heritage, personal discipline, study of Niebuhr, and near obsession with pride. Christianity was "simple" enough for a child to understand. Carter liked to quote the first Bible verse he learned, at age four: "God is love." This loving God knew, however, that men and women were sinners who deserved damnation. Sins could not be ignored but they could be forgiven. Jesus Christ, crucified on the cross, bore humanity's punishment and thus opened the way to forgiveness. Anyone believing in Him received eternal life. Christianity possessed something "absolutely unique" among religions, Carter said, a "personal relationship to a living God in Christ."[33]

Carter unswervingly preached salvation by grace. God never ranked sinners according to their relative sinlessness, and no one did anything to merit salvation. "Taking our status in life as an indication of God's approval . . . is a profound mistake." Sinners needed to swallow their pride before they were able to accept the grace freely given. Salvation eased some worries; no Christian needed to fear death. Moreover, the Holy Spirit, an "extension of God's redemptive presence on earth," served as counselor and comforter.[34]

While bringing comfort, spiritual rebirth did not end God's "stringent" demands. On the contrary, He expected Christians to measure themselves against Christ's "perfect example [at] every moment of our existence." Jesus Himself had urged, "Be perfect. . . ." The command was impossible to fulfill. Men and women could never totally avoid sin; they merely substituted one sin for another. Persistently attempting the impossible might seem especially daunting to anyone who believed with Carter that success and good works served as no evidence of God's favor. Yet Carter himself, citing Niebuhr, hailed what he called the "creativity of anxiety." Anxiety, a synonym for the awareness of sin, energized the struggle "always to improve one's self, to pray, to learn, and then attain a worthy objective."[35]

According to Carter, the earthly church existed to preserve and teach sound doctrine. Yet the church's very existence raised two problems. Institutional religion—"you might say instant religion"—encouraged pride, smugness, and ease. Paradoxically, though Christ preached humility, it was "almost impossible" for Christians gathered together to avoid a sense of superiority. Furthermore, churches had always tended to complicate Christianity's simple, sound doctrine. Carter's account of the Gnostic heresy highlights his disdain for those who intellectualized religion. The well-educated, snobbish Gnostics who condescended to their humbler brethren reached the wrong conclusions about Jesus' divinity.[36]

In Carter's view, the Baptist church's virtues included doctrinal and organizational simplicity. Yet Baptists were no less vulnerable to pride than other men and women. Furthermore, partly because they feared corruption by the state, many Baptists chose to "turn inwardly and to stay that way." Preaching love in isolation was meaningless, Carter insisted. Baptists—and all other Christians—must translate love into "simple justice" by "partnerships with Christ to improve the lives of others." Such partnerships helped those who gave as well as those who received. While seeking justice for others, Carter said, perhaps recalling his personal battle against pride, that "we can forget about ourselves. We can even forget about getting credit for that accomplishment."[37]

Countries were at least as susceptible to pride as individuals. Acknowledging a debt to Niebuhr, Carter speculated that individuals were less likely to admit national flaws than personal shortcomings. At its worst, national pride resembled idolatry, the substitution of a "flag or a way of life or a government for God." Yet even milder cases of jingoism prevented countries from correcting their errors.[38]

Applying these Niebuhrian premises to the United States in the 1970s, Carter inferred that God might not always be on the American side. Even after the Watergate scandal and Vietnam War, the United States remained a "good country, the greatest on earth." Its strengths included the capacity "to be humble and not blatant and arrogant." Americans needed to ask difficult questions and remedy mistakes. During the 1976 campaign, Carter sensed a grass roots eagerness for excellence and higher ethical standards. Leaders had failed, but now the United States would have a government "as good as our people are."[39]

With the possible exception of Richard Nixon, Carter was the most psychologically complicated president of this century, and his complicated religious sensibility was an important part of that complexity. Cosmopolitan commentators called him an enigma because he failed to fit their stereotype of the noisy, bible-thumping fundamentalist or evangelical. Not only was Carter intelligent and thoughtful, but also his manner of self-presentation lacked the flamboyance associated with evangelical Christians at least since the 1920s. Rev. James Wall, who managed Carter's Illinois primary campaign, said that he resembled a Southern Baptist Sunday school teacher rather than an evangelical preacher, and, according to Wall, Carter liked this characterization. Clearly Carter's cultivation of a plain style reflected his private battle against pride. At the same time it served, sometimes deliberately and sometimes inadvertently, to make him in 1976 a symbol of the pervasive public mood of mild repentance. After Watergate and Vietnam, a presidential candidate who shunned ceremony, swallowed his best applause lines, and prayed on his knees looked like an appealing contrast to the arrogance of Lyndon Johnson and Richard Nixon. On 20 January 1977, Carter's decision to leave his limousine and walk in his own inaugural parade found favor even among those who had voted for Ford. It was by no means clear, however, how long Americans would prefer to live in a humble country under a president who strived to exude humility.[40]

* * *

From the outset Carter's religion affected the image of his presidency and his prospects for reelection more than his substantive policies. His continuing activities as a Baptist layman often stirred controversy. Shortly before the election, despite the best efforts of Carter and Rev. Bruce Edwards, the deacons of the Plains

Baptist Church had reaffirmed a ban on African-American membership. After much maneuvering, acrimony, and publicity, the congregation approved integration in early 1977 but forced Edwards's resignation and drove a liberal contingent, including the President's mother, to form the separate Maranatha Baptist Church. While in Plains, Carter attended both churches. In Washington, he worshipped and taught Sunday school at the First Baptist Church, where attendance, contributions, and media attention immediately increased.[41]

In April 1977, Carter discussed a favorite theme, the sin of pride, with his Sunday school class and used Caiaphus, the high priest who presided over the trial of Jesus, to illustrate an "attitude that is part of all of us," the tendency to "worship ourselves." According to an Associated Press reporter, Carter also called the trial "illegal" and said that Caiaphus and the other priests had "decided to kill" Jesus because he had challenged their power. Others present at the Sunday school lesson remembered no such remarks. But if the wire service report was accurate, as many Jews feared, then the President had come close to holding them collectively responsible for the murder of Jesus. Some complained to the White House and to Jewish defense organizations, recalling that such allegations of "deicide" had long been anti-Semitic staples.[42]

Among those concerned, Rabbi Marc Tanenbaum, director of national interreligious affairs for the American Jewish Committee, suggested to Robert Lipshutz, the President's counsel, a strategy "that might help make a major plus out of this event." With White House approval, Tanenbaum prepared a statement on the crucifixion that the President accepted virtually unchanged as his public response to the controversy. In a letter to Rev. John Steinbruck, a Lutheran minister, Carter explained that although Jesus' "foreordained" death had required "human instruments," Jews bore no "collective responsibility."[43]

The well-publicized letter to Rev. Steinbruck should have ended the controversy, but in this case, as in several others, Carter's lapses into linguistic imprecision kept it alive. According to press reports in December 1977, Carter told another Sunday school class that Jewish leaders had "arranged" Jesus' crucifixion. The White House responded to another round of protests by citing the President's denunciation of the myth of deicide. At the same time, Lipshutz and Stuart Eizenstat, head of the domestic policy staff, urged Carter to express himself with greater care.[44]

A proposal by Carter to expand Southern Baptist missionary efforts provoked both enthusiasm and distress. He met with church leaders at the White House and, via videotape, urged the SBC to create an International Missionary Corps. Basking in the glow of a Southern Baptist president, the SBC voted to do so. An acquaintance from the First Baptist Church in Washington even reported that Carter planned a postpresidential missionary career, a report Carter turned aside with strained humor. An old friend, Jack U. Harwell, editor of the *Georgia Christian Index,* complained that Carter had undermined the Baptist commitment to the separation of church and state when he used the White House to "plot denominational strategy." Carter denied any impropriety, noting that the meeting had occurred during his lunch hour, but promised "to be careful" in the future. Presidential Counsel Lipshutz, concerned about the weirdo factor as well as the First Amendment, also discouraged deep involvement in denominational affairs. Carter remained in touch with SBC leaders and often urged fellow Baptists to work in the world but, after 1977, offered no detailed advice.[45]

Along with other contemporary presidents, Carter celebrated American religious pluralism in speeches to Protestant, Catholic, and Jewish groups. His contributions to this familiar genre were unusually thoughtful, ecumenical, and personal. He cited Niebuhr to Southern Baptists, quoted a Yiddish proverb to Mormons, and claimed "brotherhood" with Moslem Anwar Sadat at the National Religious Broadcasters convention. He confessed his own pettiness, ethnocentrism, and pride. Resurrecting a theme from *Why Not the Best?* he worried in 1978 that he still worked harder for himself than for God.[46]

Along with other contemporary presidents, Carter routinely proclaimed National Prayer Day and International Clergy Week. If legally possible, he would have left the signing of all such boilerplate proclamations to Vice-President Walter Mondale. Perhaps because he was so pious, Carter felt little need for official declarations of piety. One religious ceremony that deeply moved him was welcoming Pope John Paul II to the United States. He helped to plan the event down to small details, including the choice of Leontyne Price to sing the Lord's Prayer, and he looked back on the papal visit as "one of the best days of my life."[47]

Issues with a religious dimension remained on the national agenda during Carter's term. Some, such as the underrepresentation of Catholics and Jews in the ranks of military chaplains, never reached the President's desk. Others yielded ephemeral disputes. Following precedents set by Nixon, Ford, and Franklin D. Roosevelt, Carter appointed a personal representative to the Vatican, a decision criticized by Protestant theological conservatives and militant atheists; his choices were both Catholics: David Walters, a supporter from Florida, and former Mayor Robert F. Wagner, Jr., of New York. Despite pressure from many Catholics and evangelical Protestants, as well as a minority of Orthodox Jews, Carter continued to regard as unconstitutional tax credits for parents whose children attended parochial schools.[48]

Carter tried to keep his distance from the increasingly volatile question of tax exemptions for the private schools themselves. Yet in the long run, federal court decisions, the administration's commitment to racial equality, and congressional support for the rapidly growing number of fundamentalist and evangelical academies made presidential involvement unavoidable. By the mid-1970s, roughly one million students attended five thousand of these academies. Although many of them had been founded as segregated alternatives to racially mixed public schools, others represented devout attempts to escape secularization, not integration. Even so, African-Americans were generally underrepresented. In 1971 the Internal Revenue Service (IRS) ruled that racially discriminatory private schools were not entitled to tax exemptions. Still, the issue lay in abeyance because the schools were required only to declare that they did not discriminate. After federal courts ruled that several of them did discriminate despite their declarations to the contrary, the IRS began to tighten screening procedures.[49]

Regulations published for public consideration in 1977 demanded remedial action from schools judged discriminatory by the courts and established a second category of "reviewable" schools that had enrolled few minority students. Representatives of evangelical, fundamentalist, and some Hebrew academies protested that the proposed rules subjected them to review on the basis of statistics alone even though they did not discriminate. Accordingly, in early 1978 the IRS offered more flexible regulations that did not require specific remedies for all schools enrolling few blacks. Carter told irate parents that the legal issues, as well as evaluations of individual schools, were best left to the IRS. He wanted both to shield that agency from political pressure and to separate himself from a dangerous political issue.[50]

Ignoring the IRS's responsiveness to representatives from the Christian academies and sensing Carter's political vulnerability, congressional conservatives pressed the issue. The IRS must "get off the backs" of Christian schools, declared Senator Jesse Helms (Republican of North Carolina). In late 1979, Congress passed Helms's amendment to the Treasury Department appropriation, which virtually barred the IRS from enforcing the regulations. Since the appropriation was essential and the amendment applied for only one year, Carter signed the bill. Possible loss of the tax exemption in the future still worried many evangelicals and fundamentalists. According to Rev. Jerry Falwell, a recently politicized Separate Baptist, the IRS "threat made us realize that we had to fight for our lives."[51]

Abortion remained the most powerful issue related to religion. Spokesmen for right to life and prochoice groups began lobbying with Carter's aides even before the inauguration, and extensive mail campaigns continued throughout his term. The Supreme Court ruled in June 1977 that federal assistance for abortions was not a constitutional right. Carter agreed. The ruling was unfair to poor women, he conceded at a press conference on 12 July, but "many things" in life were unfair. Government could not make "opportunities exactly equal, particularly when there is a moral factor involved." Consistent with this position, Carter approved legislation restricting Medicaid funding for abortions and demanded strict compliance by the Department of Health, Education and Welfare.[52]

The question of government funding for abortions divided the administration almost as much as it divided the country. Secretary of Health, Education and Welfare Joseph A. Califano believed that federal funds should be available only when, in a physician's opinion, the pregnant woman's life was at stake, and in cases of rape or incest that had been reported promptly to the authorities. On the other hand, many members of the White House staff were staunchly prochoice. Margaret (Midge) Costanza, head of the Office of Public Liaison, complained on their behalf to Carter after his press conference of 12 July. He later met with the dissident staff members but remained unmoved. News reports of this internal dispute embarrassed the President, and Costanza, whose influence had been slight from the outset, slipped further in his regard and was eased out of office a year later.[53]

Connections between Carter's religious beliefs and foreign policy are harder to isolate. At a very general level, his doubts about the uniqueness of American virtue fostered his temporary repudiation of the "inordinate fear of Communism" and his permanent openness to the Third World. Carter was often perceived as a Wilsonian, and he certainly was one in the sense that all presidents since Woodrow Wilson have been Wilsonians. Like all presidents since Wilson, Carter believed that American ideals and interests went hand in hand. Like most of them, he exaggerated the "commonality of the aspirations of human beings throughout the world." In 1978, for instance, he declared that Christians, Jews, Moslems, and Hindus worshipped the "same God." Nonetheless, unlike Wilson and most subsequent presidents, Carter preached a version of internationalism containing little condescension toward weak, poor, or nonwhite nations.[54]

Although the cause had had congressional champions before Carter's presidency, he quickly came to personify concern for human rights abroad. Carter traced the "modern concept of human rights" back to the "laws of the prophets of the Judeo-Christian tradition." His most important actions in this area saved lives, notably in Argentina, Brazil, and Chile. Yet Carter also considered religious liberty a human right. Publicly, he prodded the Soviet Union to lift restrictions on Jewish immigration. Privately, he urged the People's Republic of China to permit the circulation of Bibles and return of Christian missionaries.[55]

No region seemed more closely connected to religious concerns than the Middle East. Carter apparently believed that most of the peoples in the region were descended from Abraham, and accepted the Book of Exodus as valid history. Nor did the President repudiate his statement that Israel fulfilled divine prophecy. To be sure, his Middle East policy derived not from theology, but from geopolitics and personal affinities. During grueling negotiations that produced the Camp David accords in September 1978, Carter developed a close friendship with Egyptian President Anwar Sadat and a deep dislike for Israeli Prime Minister Menachem Begin. In Carter's mind if not in actuality, a common interest in religion served at least as a diplomatic lubricant among the three. In this case, as in most others, Carter felt closer to Sadat, who enjoyed discussions of comparative religion, than to Begin, who cited the Bible to support Israeli land claims.[56]

Media coverage of the relationship between God and the Carter family improved little after the 1976 election. The *New York Times* marveled that Carter addressed fellow Baptists as "brothers and sisters in Christ." The President's piety moved John Osborne of the *New Republic* to recall the intolerant Baptists he knew as a youth. Though more sympathetic, William Greider of the *Washington Post* speculated that Christianity made Carter too earnest, humble, and strange to govern effectively. The major news weeklies continued their bemused coverage of Ruth Carter Stapleton, enjoying especially her role in the (temporary) conversion of pornographer Larry Flynt.[57]

* * *

As a neo-Calvinist aware of human limitations, Carter should have been prepared for the trials of the presidency. His favorite quotation from Niebuhr, displayed on the frontispiece of *Why Not the Best?,* sounded a warning: "The sad duty of politics is to establish justice in a sinful world." Nonetheless, Carter underestimated how much effort would be needed to maintain stability, let alone to move toward justice. By mid-1979, his coalition was collapsing, and religious issues, especially those issues that shaded into ethnic politics, contributed to the collapse.

Among major ethnic groups, the President paid closest attention to American Jews. Carter and his inner circle were aware of Jewish influence on the national scene, Hamilton Jordan told the President early in 1977, but, coming from "our Georgia southern political experience," they did not yet understand how that influence was exercised. Still, prospects for good relations seemed bright. As Carter had said in 1976, several of his closest advisors were Jewish; two of them, Stuart Eizenstat and Robert Lipshutz, had long been active in Jewish affairs. In addition, Mark Siegel, the son of a rabbi and former executive director of the Democratic National Committee, joined the White House staff as a liaison with Jewish groups. Furthermore, the administration emphasis on international human rights encompassed Jews persecuted in the Soviet Union. Finally, though Carter's born again background seemed strange to many Jews and dangerous to some of them, he worked hard to understand all religions and admired persons who suffered for their faith. Specifically, he proclaimed days of remembrance for victims of Nazi genocide and charged a presidential Commission on the Holocaust, headed by Elie Wiesel, with creating a lasting memorial to their memory. Political benefits aside, Carter's speeches on these occasions revealed a Christian appalled by anti-Semitism.[58]

Nevertheless, except for a brief period following the Camp David accords, relations between the administration and American Jews steadily deteriorated. The intractable nature of two international problems, the plight of Soviet Jewry and the Arab-Israeli conflict, made some tension inevitable, but careless actions and remarks by subordinates, relatives, and Carter himself increased the strains.

From the outset Carter had protested Soviet harassment of dissidents and restrictions on Jewish immigration. Whereas the Soviets accused Carter of meddling in their internal affairs, avid Cold Warriors and some Jewish leaders thought the administration insufficiently zealous, even though Jewish emigration reached a peak of 51,320 in 1979. By mid-1977, according to Eizenstat, unfounded rumors circulated that National Security Advisor Zbigniew Brzezinski was anti-Semitic.[59]

Carter worked hard to sustain an evenhanded approach to the Arab-Israeli conflict. In mid-1977 he criticized Prime Minister Begin for permitting new settlements on the disputed West Bank of the Jordan River; even the locutions of diplomacy could not hide their mutual enmity. At roughly the same time he signed legislation to counteract Arab boycotts of American companies trading with Israel. The political luster eroded over the next eight months, however, as businessmen, Jewish groups, and the White House staff struggled to formulate effective regulations. In March 1978, Carter's plan to sell sophisticated fighter planes to Saudi Arabia as part of a Mideast aid package that also included Israel prompted Mark Siegel's resignation. Not only did Siegel disagree with the Saudi arms deal and Carter's criticism of West Bank settlements, but he also felt excluded from policy decisions and suspected the National Security Council of lying to him.[60]

Meanwhile, as rumors persisted that Carter blamed Jews for Jesus' crucifixion, his sister Ruth agreed in May 1978 to address B'nai Yeshua, an organization of "Hebrew Christians." During the ensuing controversy, Rabbi Marc Tanenbaum of the American Jewish Committee charged B'nai Yeshua with deceiving "ignorant young" Jews to promote conversions. Worried White House aides urged Stapleton to cancel her speech. Ultimately she did so, concluding that an appearance at a Jews for Jesus convention might seem to "negate" Judaism.[61]

Although Carter's standing among Jews improved substantially after he mediated the Camp David accords in September 1978, the resurgence proved ephemeral. The next diplomatic step, negotiation of a peace treaty between Egypt and Israel, took longer and elicited more acrimony than the President had anticipated. By the time he secured an agreement the following March, his achievement was almost overshadowed by a controversy involving his brother. In early 1979, Billy Carter, whose national reputation had declined from rustic sage to red neck buffoon, played host to visiting Libyan officials. Billy blamed the "Jewish media" for criticizing his association with the Libyans and observed, regarding United States Mideast policy, that there were a "hell of a lot" more Arabs than Jews. As criticism grew, he turned earthy, declaring on 14 February that Jews "can kiss my ass as far as I am concerned now."[62]

According to Edward Sanders, Siegel's successor as Jewish liaison at the White House, Jewish leaders thought Carter slow in distancing himself from Billy. They had a point. Initially administration spokesmen said merely that the President neither controlled his brother nor shared any of Billy's views that "could be interpreted" as anti-Semitic. At a press conference on 27 February Carter bravely reaffirmed his love for his brother. Instead of stopping there, however, he yielded to his penchant for hyperbole and declared despite mounting evidence to the contrary that Billy had "never made a serious critical remark against Jews or other people in our country."

Leon Charney, an unofficial advisor on Mideast policy, later recalled that many Jews began to suspect Jimmy Carter of believing in private what Billy Carter said in public.[63]

Certainly the President was no anti-Semite. Unfortunately, another case of sloppy speaking increased Jewish suspicion in July. As with the controversial Sunday school lessons, Carter's exact words remain in dispute. At a White House dinner for prominent journalists, one of several arranged to coax kinder treatment from the news media, Carter apparently compared the zeal of the Palestine Liberation Organization (PLO) with the emotional intensity of the civil rights movement. When Leonard Silk, a columnist for the *New York Times*, reported these remarks, prominent Jews denounced the President for acknowledging any similarity between a group conducting guerilla warfare and a nonviolent protest esteemed by most Americans. White House spokesmen vainly explained that Carter's comparison dealt only with the degree of fervor, not with the relative merits of the causes. Even Silk was surprised by the uproar, which he said verged on "paranoia," and privately apologized to Carter for writing the column.[64]

Less than two weeks later Andrew Young, the American Ambassador to the United Nations, conferred on procedural matters with a representative of the PLO. Not only did such contacts violate American policy, but Young also misled the State Department by claiming that the meeting had been accidental. Carter sadly accepted Young's resignation on 15 August. Although Secretary of State Cyrus Vance, incensed because Young had misled him, was most responsible for the ambassador's de facto firing, the news media stressed protests by Israeli officials and American Jews. Several prominent African-Americans complained that Young had been treated unfairly and some of them believed that he had been victimized by Jews. The President responded with pleas for pluralism and denunciations of anti-Semitism. Whereas African-Americans had few appealing political alternatives and remained overwhelmingly loyal to Carter, Jews now saw another reason to quit his coalition.[65]

Roman Catholics, too, had played a small part in Carter's "Georgia southern" political experience; only 10 percent of American Catholics lived in the South. Although a majority of Catholics voted for Carter in 1976, many of them, dissatisfied with his compromise on abortion or perplexed by his evangelical demeanor, did so without enthusiasm. In January 1977 a minor incident highlighted continued Catholic wariness. An irreverent young aide, appointments secretary Greg Schneiders, said that Carter called him his "Catholic advisor"; Schneiders advised that Catholicism was a "farce" and inferred from personal experience that the church did a "better job of screwing people up than any other institution." Although cosmopolitan *Commonweal* magazine made light of these remarks, Bishop James J. Rausch, general secretary of the United States Catholic Conference, spoke for other Catholics who considered them "insulting" and worried about Schneiders's influence on Carter.[66]

A more serious political problem was the belief that the President appointed few Catholics. Looking back in 1980, historian David J. O'Brien accused Carter of "unusual neglect" and insensitivity. Such complaints owed as much to Catholic insecurities as to Carter's inept handling of ethnic politics. In fact, some high officials, including Secretary of Health, Education and Welfare Joseph Califano, Attorney General Benjamin Civiletti, and perhaps Secretary of State Edmund Muskie had been appointed at least partly because they were Catholics. Yet the most influential Catholics, Zbigniew Brzezinski and (technically outside the administration) pollster Patrick Caddell, had been chosen without regard to religion. With the possible exception of Joseph Califano, who as Lyndon Johnson's assistant had helped to plan the Great Society, Brzezinski and Caddell enjoyed greater influence than any Catholic in the previous three administrations. Neither they nor the President advertised their religious backgrounds, however, and touchy Catholics lamented the lack of advertisement instead of rejoicing that Catholics now held high office as a matter of course.

Unlike his tumultuous relations with Jews, Carter's lingering Catholic problem involved no dramatic confrontations or, aside from abortion, no issue with a large theological dimension. Despite disagreement over a right-to-life amendment, the President remained on good terms with leading Catholic clergy, including Pope John Paul II, whom he visited at the Vatican in 1980. At home Carter's position on abortion probably alienated fewer working-class Catholics than his relative economic conservatism. From the outset, his emphasis on government efficiency rather than expansion of the welfare state placed him to the right of most Democrats in Congress and the labor movement. Several of his harshest critics were Catholics, including Senator Edward Kennedy (Democrat of Massachusetts) and George Meany, president of the AFL-CIO, and their opposition legitimated latent hostility among blue-collar Catholics.[67]

Carter's growing Protestant problem was a matter of shattered expectations rather than persisting suspicion. Evangelicals and fundamentalists who had felt kinship with Carter during the excitement of 1976 soon discovered that he was theologically and politically less conservative than they had supposed. After Bert Lance resigned as director of the Office of Management and Budget in September 1977, no born again Christian held cabinet rank. Nor did Carter try to recruit them. Conversely, his administration included well-known cultural liberals. Sarah Weddington, who had argued the case for abortion in *Roe* v. *Wade,* succeeded Costanza in 1978 as head of the office of public liaison. Similarly, the White House Conference on Families provided a forum for feminists and gay rights activists as well as traditionalists. The sense of betrayal felt by many fundamentalists and evangelicals was channeled into political action by a new Christian right that began to organize almost as soon as Carter was elected. In mid-1979 Rev. Jerry Falwell joined with conservative political professionals to form the most important of these groups, the Moral Majority.[68]

On one level, the new Christian right represented a response to judicial decisions since the late 1940s that challenged Protestant primacy, to the sexual upheaval of the late 1960s, and to the long-term secularization of everyday life. The attacks on Betty Ford in 1976 suggest that some such insurgency would have developed in the 1970s even if Carter had lost in 1976. Yet his candidacy, which politicized previously apathetic theological conservatives, raised their expectations, and highlighted questions of personal behavior, inadvertently increased the size of the movement.

Although issues with a religious dimension contributed to Carter's political embattlement, his worst problems were essentially secular: an ideologically divided Democratic party; rising prices of primary products, especially petroleum; economic "stagflation" that no one knew how to cure; the inexorable dialectic of Cold War animosity; and old Bolsheviks in the Kremlin who died too slowly. These problems were largely beyond the President's control. Nonetheless, Carter compounded his difficulties by yielding to what critics called arrogance—what he called pride. At home, he disliked courting or compromising with Congress. Abroad, eager to outshine Ford, he abandoned a nearly finished strategic arms limitation treaty in favor of a "comprehensive" plan that elicited Soviet suspicion and raised Cold War tensions. If Carter is a tragic figure, it is because he recognized his fatal flaw—pride—but, despite good will and high intelligence, could not master it.

* * *

Carter's ability to motivate Americans decreased during his term. He had won the presidency by promising a government as good as the people. To Arthur Schlesinger, Jr., such populism represented sentimentality unworthy of a Niebuhrian. Yet it was consistent with the "early" Niebuhr, the critic from the 1930s who understood the importance of myths and symbols to any social movement. Carter understood their power too, as he had demonstrated during the campaign, but he felt uneasy using them. Emotional appeals conflicted with his neo-Calvinist plain style and promise never to lie to the electorate.

Even so, in July 1979, as motorists fumed in gasoline lines and Carter's energy legislation stalled in Congress, he made a special effort to inspire the nation. Exactly three years after buoyantly accepting the Democratic nomination, he delivered a televised speech on the American "crisis of confidence." He began with a favorite theme, that isolated officials had failed an inherently decent, strong, and wise citizenry. As Carter proceeded, however, he came close to saying that the people were no better than their floundering government. There was "growing disrespect" for social institutions. Too many citizens tended "to worship self-indulgence and consumption." Americans needed to restore faith in each other, in democracy, and in the nation's future. The speech, which was largely drafted by Caddell, a Catholic, nonetheless fitted the President's evangelical style. Indeed, it came as close to a call for a day of fasting and humiliation as any other modern presidential speech. Initially, this jeremiad boosted Carter's standing in the polls; within a week, however, Carter mismanaged a reorganization of his cabinet, and his popularity declined steadily thereafter.[69]

As part of the staff reorganization, Carter named Rev. Robert M. Maddox to the new post of special assistant for religious liaison. Maddox, a Baptist minister from Calhoun, Georgia, had offered to fill such a position in 1977 but was politely rebuffed. He had continued to offer unofficial advice, warning especially of disaffection among evangelical Protestants. Finally appointed a speech writer in May 1979, he had urged Carter not to admit failure in the "crisis of confidence" address. The new religious liaison quickly concluded that the administration, trying to avoid the taint of sanctimony, had inadvertently annoyed diverse denominations. Maddox immediately began an ecumenical campaign to mend fences. He met, promised to consult, and sometimes prayed with evangelicals, charismatics, social gospelers, Hasidic Jews, Catholic bishops, and followers of Hare Krishna.[70]

Maddox tried to involve Carter in the religious fence mending. The President addressed the National Council of Catholic Charities, United Jewish Appeal, and National Religious Broadcasters; in November 1979, he held his first meeting with Billy Graham at the White House. Yet neither Carter nor his senior staff shared Maddox's enthusiasm for cultivating religious leaders. Soon after his appointment, Maddox stressed the growing political power of evangelicals, fundamentalists, and charismatics in general as well as the influence of television preachers in particular. Many of them would help Carter or at least soften their criticism if the President paid more attention to them, Maddox believed. After five months of trying, he arranged a meeting in January 1980 between Carter and a contingent of television evangelists, including Jerry Falwell, Jim Bakker, Rex Humbard, and Oral Roberts. Few fences were mended.[71]

* * *

Issues related to religion affected the election of 1980 even more than the election of 1976. In May, Pope John Paul II forbade Representative Robert Drinan (Democrat of Massachusetts), a Jesuit priest, to seek reelection, and rumors circulated that the decision turned on Drinan's prochoice voting record. Shortly before the Massachusetts Democratic primary, Cardinal Humberto Medeiros of Boston issued a pastoral letter urging Catholics to vote against prochoice candidates. President Carter faced a "credibility problem" among Jews, as Stuart Eizenstat put it, and the problem steadily worsened as Congress investigated Billy Carter's financial ties to Libya and the United States voted at the United Nations to condemn Israeli control of East Jerusalem. And though initially ignored by politicians and journalists alike, the new Christian right steadily built a political infrastructure.[72]

Two Roman Catholics, California Democratic Governor Jerry Brown and Senator Edward Kennedy, challenged Carter's renomination, but only Kennedy made a serious race. The cultural differences between Kennedy and Carter seemed stark, especially in the President's mind. Superficially their rivalry looked like the latest skirmish in the venerable conflict between northern Catholic Democrats and southern Protestant Democrats. Yet Kennedy, the most famous Catholic in America, ran only slightly better among Catholics than among other voters in the primaries. Indeed, while losing New York, New Jersey, and California, Carter received a higher percentage of votes from Catholics than from Democrats as a whole. This support did not mean that his Catholic problem was solved. Rather, it showed that Catholics too had doubts about Kennedy's character and tended to rally behind a president during an international crisis.[73]

Jewish disaffection may have cost Carter dearly. After several defeats, Kennedy seems to have been on the verge of quitting the race if he lost in New York. Less than a month before the primary, Donald McHenry, who had succeeded Andrew Young at the United Nations, backed a resolution condemning Israeli settlements in the West Bank and East Jerusalem. As Carter subsequently explained, he had authorized McHenry's vote believing that references to Jerusalem had been deleted. Many Jews remained unconvinced by this confession of confusion. According to Mayor Edward I. Koch of New York, the United Nations vote revealed not only Carter's insensitivity to Israeli interests, but also the pro-Arab bias of McHenry, Brzezinski, and Vance. Kennedy, too, questioned Carter's commitment to Israel. On 25 March, he easily beat Carter in New York, receiving more than three-quarters of the Jewish vote, and stayed in the race. According to an estimate by the *Washington Post,* Jews gave Kennedy 80 percent of their votes in all of the primaries.[74]

Two self-described born again Protestants ran against Carter in the general election. Independent candidate John Anderson, a member of the Free Evangelical Church, had been converted as a youth. Republican Ronald Reagan was a religious eclectic. The offspring of a Protestant-Catholic mixed marriage and Hollywood's flexible mores, he sometimes claimed membership in the Disciples of Christ, his mother's church, and occasionally attended Presbyterian services in southern California. From time to time he sought advice or discussed questions of faith with evangelical clergy, including Billy Graham. He had always asked God's help, Reagan said in 1976, but at some unspecified point he had felt a "new relationship" that "could be described as 'born again.'" Though much less knowledgeable than Ford or Carter, Reagan showed greater interest in religion than Presidents Eisenhower or Kennedy. His eclectic curiosity encompassed dispensationalist Bible prophecy, the charismatic revival, the Shroud of Turin, and astrological predictions.[75]

Reagan welcomed the new Christian right as a junior partner in his coalition. In August Jerry Falwell, Pat Robertson, and other prominent theological conservatives sponsored a "national affairs briefing" in Dallas for eighteen thousand of their fellow ministers. The chief national affairs under consideration were ebbing American power abroad and threats to faith and family at home. Although Carter and Anderson were invited too, only Reagan attended. The "nonpartisan" gathering could not endorse him, Reagan said coyly, but he endorsed "what you are doing."[76]

Precisely what Reagan endorsed and how closely he expected to cooperate with the new Christian right remained deliberately vague throughout his campaign. Certainly he favored a right to life amendment and his party platform promised the appointment of judges who would "honor the sanctity of innocent human life." By and large, however, he eschewed even rudimentary analysis of church-state relations in favor of pious quips. A favorite one-liner simultaneously highlighted his hostility to federal authority and his support of prayer in public schools. Education was deteriorating because God had been "expelled from the classroom" and bureaucrats had moved in.[77]

In the wake of Reagan's appearance at the national affairs briefing, news media belatedly discovered the new Christian right. Their reporting was even worse than the coverage of Carter's religion during the previous four years. After puzzling over dispensational premillennialism, accepting the claims of immense audiences made by television preachers, and expressing ahistorical amazement that so many devout Protestants had become politically active, commentators usually borrowed an explanatory framework from pluralist social science. Specifically, they interpreted the new Christian right as the latest "extremist" movement, which, by definition, differed qualitatively in tactics, ideology, and perhaps mental health from mainstream groups. This time, however, the extremists, in alliance with Reagan Republicans, threatened to take over. To syndicated columnist Anthony Lewis, scenes from the national affairs briefing were the "scariest" thing he had ever seen on television.[78]

The new Christian right represented a potential liability to Reagan as well as an asset. Their militancy might frighten Catholic and Jewish voters; even some Protestant theological conservatives viewed the movement skeptically. Moreover, prominent new Christian rightists had not yet mastered the discourse and demeanor necessary to avoid embarrassment in national politics. For example, Charles Darwin seemed at least as menacing as Leonid Brezhnev to the ministers gathered at Dallas, and they urged the teaching of Genesis in public schools along with the theory of evolution. Worse yet, Bailey Smith, president of the SBC, declared that "God Almighty does not hear the prayer of a Jew, for how in the world can God hear the prayer of a man who says that Jesus Christ is not the true Messiah." After initial waffling Jerry Falwell issued a joint statement with Rabbi Marc Tanenbaum of the American Jewish Committee affirming that God did indeed hear the "heart cry of any sincere person who calls on him."[79]

The central motif of Carter's campaign stigmatized Reagan himself as an extremist. To prove the point, the Democrats stressed his hostility to the welfare state and his hawkish foreign policy; Reagan's connection to the new Christian right was usually left to second-rank campaigners, such as Robert Maddox and Patricia Roberts Harris, Secretary of Health and Human Services. Evidently Democratic professionals understood better than did strict secularists in the media that a former movie star with a skimpy record of church attendance could not be painted as a Christian zealot.[80]

In religion as in economics and foreign affairs, Reagan deflected criticism by presenting himself as an amiable moderate. For instance, he admitted having "a great many questions" about the validity of evolutionary theory, asserted without evidence that scientists increasingly shared these doubts, and made equal time for the "biblical story" sound like elementary fairness. Nor did he doubt that God heard prayers from Jews. While Reagan deflected criticism, Republicans in general and the new Christian right in particular portrayed Carter as much more liberal—politically and theologically—than he was. According to Falwell, Carter had admitted appointing homosexuals to the White House staff because he was president of all Americans, homosexuals included. The conversation Falwell cited had never taken place.[81]

Some of Carter's advisors hoped that fear of right-wing Protestants in Republican ranks would neutralize Jewish distrust of the administration. Alfred Moses, who in 1980 succeeded Edward Sanders as White House liaison to Jewish groups, wanted to emphasize Reagan's ties to a "blatantly anti-Semitic" Christian right. An effort to do so backfired late in the campaign. According to a radio spot sponsored by the Carter-Mondale Re-Election Committee, Jerry Falwell, who denied that God heard prayers from Jews, would join Reagan in the White House and then "they'll purify the land as someone else did some years ago." Angered by this veiled comparison to Adolf Hitler, Falwell filed suit and forced withdrawal of the ad. Less flamboyant aspects of the Democratic "outreach" to Jews praised Carter for preventing PLO membership in the International Monetary Fund, arranging increased emigration from the Soviet Union, and negotiating the Israeli-Egyptian peace agreement. Republicans countered that Carter's already excessive pressure on Israel would increase in a second term. In public the President opposed a Palestinian state, columnist William Safire wrote, but privately he was moving toward acceptance.[82]

Although infuriated by their attacks, Carter preferred to ignore the new Christian right and, when questioned by the press, responded with restraint. He believed that the news media had exaggerated the influence of new right preachers on evangelical Protestants, who were no more monolithic than other social groups. Falwell's opposition in 1980 was hardly surprising, Carter noted, since the founder of the Moral Majority had also "castigated" him in 1976. Conservative clergy had the right to express their views "even from the pulpit." However, in his own daily Bible reading, Carter told chuckling reporters, he found no passages specifying "whether or not we should have a Department of Education . . . or whether you should have a B-1 bomber or the air-launched cruise missile." Finally, Carter said that he never felt "any incompatibility" between his Christianity and his presidential duties, and he thought that most Americans shared his opposition to religious tests for public office.[83]

Nor did criticism from the new Christian right change Carter's position on issues relating to religion. He repudiated the plank in the Democratic platform that endorsed federal funding for abortions but still opposed a right to life amendment. He answered *Science* magazine's inquiry about the teaching of evolution as a Christian and a scientist. There was "convincing" scientific evidence that the earth was 4½ billion years old. His "personal faith" led Carter to believe that God controlled the "on going processes of evolution." Public school curricula should be decided by state and local boards of education operating with due regard for the "constitutional mandate" to separate church and state."[84]

Robert Maddox offered elaborate plans for appealing specifically to religious voters but, with the exception of Rosalynn Carter, no one in the President's inner circle favored this strategy. Carter met occasionally with ministers, priests, and rabbis, made the usual rounds of ethnic groups, and personally bestowed the Medal of Freedom on Elie Wiesel. He retained the support of some prominent theological conservatives, including Oral Roberts, Jimmy Allen, and Jim Bakker, for whom cultural affinity was more important than political ideology or theology; at the end of the campaign, Carter knelt in prayer with Bakker on *Air Force One*. Yet his piety was much less in evidence in 1980 than in 1976. Indeed, as public displays of religiosity became politically advantageous, Carter, moved by pride in the best sense, made them less often.[85]

A religious issue dominated the 1980 presidential election, but not a "Judeo-Christian" issue. In November 1979, Iranian militants seized the United States embassy in Teheran. Most of the staff remained hostages for the next fourteen months. Clearly, though Christians and

Moslems might worship the same God, they did not necessarily worship Him in the same way or with the same political consequences. Carter, accustomed to pluralist competition in the American triple melting pot, was no more able than secular officials to see that the Islamic revolution was other than madness. Reagan presented the hostage crisis as an emblem of national decline under Carter. Two of Reagan's favorite quotations highlighted his belief that the decline could be reversed. The United States remained, in John Winthrop's phrase, a "city upon a hill," and her citizens still held the power, as Tom Paine had said, "to begin the world over again."[86]

After Reagan's victory, Jimmy and Rosalynn Carter took the defeat hard. They returned to Plains, joined the Maranatha Baptist Church, and threw themselves into work and reflection. In 1984 they joined Habitat for Humanity, a charity whose members repaired slum housing with their own hands. Reporters marveled that a former president rode on a chartered bus, slept in a dormitory, and hammered nails for other people. Of course this charitable endeavor was consistent with Carter's long-standing battle against personal pride as well as his commitment to simple justice achieved through individual effort. He still considered religion an ongoing search for truth and showed continued respect for faiths different from his own moderate evangelical Protestantism. Deliberately seeking out diverse religious services, he felt moved by fundamentalist singing in rural Georgia and Buddhist chants in the Himalayas.[87]

Emotionally renewed by 1987, Jimmy and Rosalynn Carter wrote *Everything to Gain,* a self-help book for others who faced great disappointment in middle age. Whether trekking through Asia or monitoring elections in Panama, the former president continued to set high standards for himself and others. Yet, as he wrote in *Everything to Gain,* Carter came to appreciate the "beneficial effects of backing off for a while." Backing off for a while certainly benefited his postpresidential prose. *Keeping Faith,* the memoir published in 1982, was turgid and defensive. *An Outdoor Journal,* published in 1988, was marked by eloquent language, self-deprecating humor, and an almost pantheistic appreciation of nature as "God's miraculous creation."[88]

In the darkest moments after the 1980 election, Rosalynn Carter wondered if God had wanted her husband to lose. With characteristic emphasis on individual responsibility, Carter replied that people were not "robots" controlled from heaven. Supernatural intervention aside, religious factors contributed to Reagan's victory. Carter received only 40 percent of the Catholic vote compared to 50 percent for Reagan and 7 percent for Anderson; no Democratic nominee had done so poorly since John W. Davis in 1924. For the first time in a half-century, a Democrat fell short of a majority among Jews. Carter won 45 percent of their votes, Reagan 39 percent, and Anderson 14 percent. Evangelicals swung back heavily to the Republicans, though Carter's born again style may have prevented a worse debacle. He received 31 percent of votes cast by all white Protestants.[89]

For many voters Carter's apparent arrogance—what he called pride—had obscured his accomplishments. The same trait also led him to underestimate Reagan. Viewing religious pluralism as the norm, he was unprepared for an Islamic revolution in Iran. Furthermore, Carter's religious style diverged from the muscular Christianity that had dominated both Protestantism and Catholicism since the progressive era. In 1976, as voters searched their souls following the Vietnam War and the Watergate scandal, Carter had struck a chord when he defined national greatness partly as the capacity to be "humble and not blatant and arrogant." Four years later, as voters watched Iranians humiliate American hostages on the nightly news, Carter's forbearance looked like weakness. Indeed, it may have reminded many men of the "feminized" faith they had been taught to shun. According to columnist George Will, for example, Carter was not a "muscular politician" able to lead a "muscular nation." Ultimately voters preferred a muscular Protestant who had first achieved fame playing a Catholic football star in the movies, a football star whose nickname, the Gipper, he then appropriated as his own. Ronald Reagan never doubted that God was on the American side, and with no sense of contradiction he quoted the puritan John Winthrop and the infidel Tom Paine to prove the point.[90]

Notes

Introduction. The Complexity of American Religious Prejudice

1. Gene Wise, *American Historical Explanations: A Strategy for Grounded Inquiry* (Homewood, Ill.: Dorsey Press, 1973), ix.

2. John Higham, *History: Professional Scholarship in America* (New York: Harper Torchbooks, 1973), 132. Peter Novick, *That Noble Dream: The "Objectivity Question" and the American Historical Profession* (New York: Cambridge University Press, 1988), 324. Richard Hofstadter, *The Progressive Historians: Turner, Beard, Parrington* (New York: Vintage, 1970), 442.

3. Ibid., xv, 173, 318, 226.

4. William James quoted in John E. Smith, *The Spirit of American Philosophy* (New York: Oxford University Press, 1963), 49. Charles A. Beard, "Written History as an Act of Faith," reprinted in Robert Allen Skotheim, ed., *The Historian and the Climate of Opinion* (Reading, Mass.: Addison-Wesley, 1969), 11–20.

5. Ibid., 11, 13, 19. Carl Becker, *Everyman His Own Historian: Essays on History and Politics* ([1935], reprint Chicago: Quadrangle, 1966), 234, 249, 254.

6. Hofstadter, *Progressive Historians,* 439.

7. On the confident mood among historians during the 1950s and early 1960s, see Higham, *History,* 132–144, and Novick, *Noble Dream,* chapter 12.

8. Samuel Eliot Morison, "History as a Literary Art," in Oscar Handlin, Arthur Meier Schlesinger, Samuel Eliot Morison, Arthur Meier Schlesinger, Jr., and Paul Herman Buck, eds., *The Harvard Guide to American History* (Cambridge, Mass.: Harvard University Press, 1954), 44–45.

9. Irwin Ungar, "The 'New Left' and American History," reprinted in Skotheim, *Climate of Opinion,* 135–163. Hofstadter, *Progressive Historians,* 465–466. Novick, *Noble Dream,* 417.

10. Hofstadter, *Progressive Historians,* 465–466.

11. Jesse Lemisch, *On Active Service in War and Peace: Politics and Ideology in the American Historical Profession* (Toronto: New Hogtown Press, 1975), 46.

12. Howard Zinn, *The Politics of History* (Boston: Beacon Press, 1970), 24, 297. Martin Duberman, *The Uncompleted Past* (New York: Random House, 1969), 335. Warren Susman, *Culture as History* (New York: Pantheon, 1984), xii. William Appleman Williams, *Some Presidents: Wilson to Nixon* (New York: Vintage, 1982), and *Empire as a Way of Life: An Essay on the Causes and Character of America's Present Predicament Along with a Few Thoughts About an Alternative* (New York: Oxford University Press, 1980).

13. Hofstadter, *Progressive Historians*, 459.

14. Zinn, *Politics of History*, 40, 24. Lemisch, *On Active Service*, 117.

15. Henry Abelove, Betsy Blackmar, Peter Dimock, and Jonathan Schneer, eds., *Visions of History* (New York: Pantheon, 1984), 81, 174, 203. Lawrence W. Levine, "The Unpredictable Past: Reflections on Recent American Historiography," *American Historical Review* 94 (June 1989), 679.

16. E. P. Thompson, *The Making of the English Working Class* (New York: Pantheon, 1964), 12.

17. For a fair review of recent historiographical trends, which both documents and celebrates the rise of the kind of social history described here, see Eric Foner, ed., *The New American History* (Philadelphia: Temple University Press, 1990).

18. T. J. Jackson Lears, "The Concept of Cultural Hegemony: Problems and Possibilities," *American Historical Review* 90 (June 1985), 567–593.

19. Derrida quoted in Novick, *Noble Dream*, 543. Sacvan Bercovitch, ed., *Reconstructing American Literary History* (Cambridge, Mass.: Harvard University Press, 1986), viii.

20. Jonathan M. Wiener, "Radical Historians and the Crisis in American History, 1959–1980," Christopher Lasch, "Consensus: An Academic Question," Carl N. Degler, "What Crisis, Jon?" *Journal of American History* 76 (September 1989), 428, 458, 470. Russell Jacoby, *The Last Intellectuals: American Culture in the Age of Academe* (New York: Basic Books, 1988). Roger Kimball, *Tenured Radicals: How Politics Corrupted Higher Education* (New York: Harper & Row, 1990).

21. Gertrude Himmelfarb, *The New History and the Old* (Cambridge, Mass.: Harvard University Press, 1987), 21, 25.

22. Beard, "Written History," 18. Michael Kammen, ed., *"What Is the Good of History?" Selected Letters of Carl L. Becker, 1900–1945* (Ithaca: Cornell University Press, 1973), 156–157.

23. Significantly, the left largely ignored Martin Sklar's book, *The Corporate Reconstruction of American Capitalism, 1890–1916: The Market, the Law, and Politics* (New York: Cambridge University Press, 1988), an important study of corporate-government relations during the Progressive era.

24. Joan Wallach Scott, "History in Crisis? The Other Side of the Story," *American Historical Review* 94 (June 1989), 680–692. George Lipsitz, "Lis-

tening to Learn and Learning to Listen: Popular Culture, Cultural Theory, and American Studies," *American Quarterly* 42 (December 1990), 621.

25. John E. Toews, "Intellectual History After the Linguistic Turn: The Autonomy of Meaning and the Irreducibility of Experience," *American Historical Review* 92 (October 1987), 906. Richard Gid Powers, "Anticommunist Lives," *American Quarterly* 41 (December 1989), 723, suggested that I had begun to deconstruct McCarthyism. Professor Powers, a leading authority on the Red Scare of the 1950s, tells me that he intended this reference as a compliment, for which I thank him.

26. David Harlan, "Intellectual History and the Return of Literature," David A. Hollinger, "The Return of the Prodigal: The Persistence of Historical Knowing," and Harlan, "Reply to David Hollinger," *American Historical Review* 94 (June 1989), 581–626. Robert Berkhofer, "A New Context for American Studies," *American Quarterly* 41 (December 1989), 588–613. Wise, *Historical Explanations,* 34.

27. Becker, *Everyman,* 242, 245.

28. Diane Ravitch and Chester E. Finn, Jr., *What Do Our 17-Year-Olds Know? A Report on the First National Assessment of History and Literature,* "Foreword" by Lynne V. Cheney (New York: Harper & Row, 1987).

29. David Lowenthal, "The Timeless Past: Some Anglo-American Historical Preconceptions," *Journal of American History* 75 (March 1989), 1275–1276, 1279.

30. Jerome S. Bruner, *The Process of Education* (Cambridge, Mass.: Harvard University Press, 1962), 32. Becker, *Everyman,* 245.

31. Beard, "Written History," 14.

Chapter 2. Henry Ford and *The International Jew*

1. John Higham's *Strangers in the Land* was reviewed critically by Oscar Handlin, *Political Science Quarterly* 71 (1956), 453–454, and Nathan Glazer, "Closing the Gates," *Commentary* 21 (June 1956), 587–588. Norman Pollack, "Handlin on Anti-Semitism: A Critique of 'American Views of the Jew,'" *Journal of American History* 51 (December 1964), 391–403, prompted a reply by Handlin in the same volume, p. 807. See also Pollack, "Fear of Man: Populism, Authoritarianism, and the Historian" [with comments by Handlin and Irwin Ungar], *Agricultural History* 39 (1968), 59–85, The major book by historians in recent years is David A. Gerber, ed., *Anti-Semitism in American History* (Urbana: University of Illinois Press, 1986).

2. This series was reprinted in four volumes. In this chapter, it is cited from these books using the short title *International Jew* (*IJ*). The full titles are: *The International Jew: The World's Foremost Problem,* Vol. 1 (Dearborn: 1920); *Jewish Activities in the United States,* Vol. 2 (Dearborn: n.d.); *Jewish Influences in American Life,* Vol. 3 (Dearborn: n.d.); *Aspects of Jewish Power in the United States,* Vol. 4 (Dearborn: n.d.).

3. Bernard Bailyn, *The Ideological Origins of the American Revolution* (Cambridge, Mass.: Harvard University Press, 1967), especially pp. 144–159. David Brion Davis, ed., *The Fear of Conspiracy: Images of Un-American Subversion from the Revolution to the Present* (Ithaca, N.Y.: Cornell University Press, 1971), 34, 141. Davis, *The Slave Power Conspiracy and the Paranoid Style* (Baton Rouge, La.: Louisiana State University Press, 1969). Robert M. Wiebe, *The Search for Order 1877–1920* (New York: Hill & Wang, 1968). John Higham, *Strangers in the Land: Patterns of American Nativism 1860–1925* (New York: Atheneum, 1966), chapters 1–3. Josiah Strong, *Our Country* (Cambridge, Mass.: Harvard University Press, 1963), chapters 9 and 10.

4. George Creel, *How We Advertised America: The First Telling of the Amazing Story of the Committee on Public Information that Carried the Gospel of Americanism to Every Corner of the Globe* (New York: Harper & Brothers, 1920).

5. Walter Lippmann, *A Preface to Politics* (Ann Arbor: University of Michigan Press, 1969). Lippmann, *Public Opinion* (New York: Macmillan, 1961), 29. Harold Lasswell, *Propaganda Technique in World War I* (Cambridge, Mass.: Harvard University Press, 1971), 2–3.

6. Leonard Dinnerstein, *The Leo Frank Case* (New York: Columbia University Press, 1968), 66–67. John Higham, "Social Discrimination Against Jews in America, 1830–1930," reprinted in Abraham J. Karp, ed., *The Jewish Experience in America: Selected Studies from the Publications of the American Jewish Historical Society* (New York: KATV Publishing, 1969), 5:351–355. Louis Harap, *The Image of the Jew in American Literature: From Early Republic to Mass Immigration* (Philadelphia: Jewish Publication Society of America, 1974), chapter 2. Irving Katz, *August Belmont: A Political Biography* (New York: Columbia University Press, 1968), 39, 82, 144.

7. Moses Rischin, *The Promised City: New York's Jews, 1870–1914* (New York: Harper Torchbooks, 1970), 259. Oscar Handlin, *Adventure in Freedom: Three Hundred Years of Jewish Life in America* (Port Washington, N.Y.: Kennikat Press, 1971), 170–184. Richard Hofstadter, *The Age of Reform: From Bryan to FDR* (New York: Vintage, 1955), 77–81. Jonathan D. Sarna, "The Mythical Jew and the 'Jew Next Door'" and David A. Gerber, "Cutting Out Shylock: Elite Anti-Semitism and the Quest for Moral Order in the Mid-Nineteenth Century American Marketplace," in Gerber, *Anti-Semitism*, 57–78, 201–32.

8. Dinnerstein, *Leo Frank*, 65. Higham, "Anti-Semitism in the Gilded Age," *Mississippi Valley Historical Review* 43 (March 1957) 559–578. Oscar Handlin, "American Views of the Jew at the Opening of the Twentieth Century," in Karp, *Jewish Experience*, 5:1–22. Robert A. Rockaway, "Anti-Semitism in an American City: Detroit, 1850–1914," *American Jewish Historical Quarterly* 64 (September 1974), 42–54. William F. Holmes, "White Capping: Anti-Semitism in the Populist Era," *American Jewish Historical Quarterly* 63 (March 1974), 244–261. Norman Pollack, "The Myth of Popu-

list Anti-Semitism," *American Historical Review* 68 (October 1962), 76–80. Walter T. K. Nugent, *The Tolerant Populists: Kansas Populism and Nativism* (Chicago: University of Chicago Press, 1963), 109–115.

9. Dinnerstein, *Leo Frank,* chapters 5–8. George M. Fredrickson, *The Black Image in the White Mind: The Debate on Afro-American Character and Destiny, 1817–1914* (New York: Harper Torchbooks, 1971), xiii. Higham, *Strangers,* 271, 155–157. Thomas F. Gossett, *Race: The History of an Idea in America* (Dallas: Southern Methodist University Press, 1963), chapters 12– 15. Robert Singerman, "The Jew as Racial Alien: The Genetic Component of American Anti-Semitism," in Gerber, *Anti-Semitism,* 103–128. Madison Grant, *The Passing of the Great Race* (1916, reprint, New York: Arno Press, 1970), 167, 12, 16, 91, 77. Jacob Riis, *How the Other Half Lives: Studies Among the Tenements of New York* (New York: Sagamore Press, 1957), 78–79. Burton J. Hendrick, "The Jewish Invasion of America," *McClure's Magazine* 40 (March 1913), 140, 147, 150, 154–157, 163. Hendrick, "The Great Jewish Invasion," *McClure's Magazine* 28 (January 1907), 307–321. Edward Alsworth Ross, *The Old World in the New* (New York: Century Company, 1914).

10. Higham, "Social Discrimination," 369; Higham, *Strangers,* 276. Carey McWilliams, *A Mask for Privilege: Anti-Semitism in America* (Boston: Little, Brown, 1948), 232. Theodore Lothrop Stoddard, *The Rising Tide of Color: Against White World Supremacy* (New York: Charles Scribner's Sons, 1920), 163. Kenneth Roberts, *Why Europe Leaves Home* (Brooklyn, N.Y.: Bobbs-Merrill, 1922), 118, 115, 114. Robert D. Schulzinger, *The Making of the Diplomatic Mind: The Training, Outlook, and Style of United States Foreign Service Officers, 1908–1931* (Middletown, Conn.: Wesleyan University Press, 1975), 131. United States Congress, Senate, 65th Congress, 3d session, *Hearings Before a Subcommittee on the Judiciary. Bolshevik Propaganda,* 11 February–10 March 1919. The phrase "polite anti-Semitism" is from Edward H. Flannery, *The Anguish of the Jews: Twenty-three Centuries of Anti-Semitism* (New York: Macmillan, 1965), 248.

11. On the origin and spread of the *Protocols,* see Norman Cohn, *Warrant for Genocide: The Myth of the World-Conspiracy and the Protocols of the Elders of Zion* (New York: Harper Torchbooks, 1969), chapters 1–4. In this chapter we have used a "standard" edition of the forgery, Victor E. Marsden, trans., *The Protocols of the Learned Elders of Zion* (Los Angeles: Christian Nationalist Crusade, n.d.).

12. Cohn, *Warrant,* 156–157. Robert Singerman, "The American Career of the *Protocols of the Elders of Zion," American Jewish History* 71 (September 1981), 49–70.

13. Allan Nevins with Frank Ernest Hill, *Ford: The Times, the Man, the Company* (New York: Charles Scribner's Sons, 1954), chapters 12–22. Nevins with Hill, *Ford: Expansion and Challenge 1915–1933* (New York: Charles Scribner's Sons, 1957). Keith Sward, *The Legend of Henry Ford* (New York: Atheneum, 1968), chapters 2–5.

14. Samuel S. Marquis, *Henry Ford: An Interpretation* (Boston: Little, Brown, 1923), 8. For the peace expedition the standard historical account is Barbara S. Kraft, *The Peace Ship: Henry Ford's Pacifist Adventure in the First World War* (New York: Macmillan, 1978).

15. Allan L. Benson, *The New Henry Ford* (New York: Funk & Wagnalls, 1923), 299. Spencer Ervin, *Henry Ford vs. Truman Newberry: The Famous Senate Election Contest* (New York: Arno Press, 1974).

16. Ernest G. Liebold, "Reminiscences," Ford Archives, Henry Ford Museum, 1–21.

17. David L. Lewis, *The Public Image of Henry Ford: An American Folk Hero and His Company* (Detroit: Wayne State University Press, 1976), 135–138. Liebold, "Reminiscences," 432. "It Is Your Paper," *Dearborn Independent* (*DI*), 20 February 1920, 4.

18. E. G. Pipp, *Henry Ford: Both Sides of Him* (Detroit: Pipp's Magazine, 1926), 66–69.

19. Harry Bennett, *We Never Called Him Henry* (New York: Gold Medal Books, 1951), 46. Norman Hapgood, "The Inside Story of Henry Ford's Jew-Mania," Part 2, *Hearst's International* 42 (July 1922), 14. Liebold, "Reminiscences," 409–410, 1161. Henry Neller to Ford, 22 January 1924, Liebold to C. M. Alexander, 26 January 1924, L. G. McClanahan, Report on Jones Motor Company, Box 199, Fair Lane Papers, Accession 1, Ford Archives. Anne Jardim, *The First Henry Ford: A Study in Personality and Business Leadership* (Cambridge, Mass.: MIT Press, 1970), 159. William J. Cameron, "Reminiscences," Ford Archives, 208.

20. Lewis, *Public Image,* 139. Pipp, *Both Sides,* 68–69. Garet Garrett, *The Wild Wheel* (New York: Pantheon, 1952), 147. Liebold, "Reminiscences," 9, 423. Fred L. Black, "Reminiscences," 24, 132, 138.

21. Hapgood, "Inside Story," Part 1, *Hearst's International* 41 (June 1922), 16, 18; Part 5, *Hearst's International* 42 (October 1922), 110. Pipp, *Both Sides,* 68–69. Cameron, "Reminiscences," 15–16. Interview with Fred L. Black et al. (28 May 1951), Ford Archives, 40.

22. Liebold, "Reminiscences," 459–460. Black, Interview, 36.

23. Liebold, "Reminiscences," 451, 456, 442. Black, Interview, 27.

24. Liebold, "Reminiscences," 48, 481. Lars Jacobson to Liebold, 24 February 1921, *Dearborn Independent* file, Box 2, Accession 272 Ford Archives. Liebold to Jacobson, 2 February 1921, Lars Jacobson file, Box 13, Accession 285, Ford Archives.

25. Hapgood, "Inside Story," Part 1 (June 1922), 15, 18, 128; Part 2, 15; Part 4, *Hearst's International* 41 (September 1922), 47–48, 133–134. C. C. Daniels to Liebold, 5 January, 4, 14 February, 21 June 1922. "Eugene Meyer, Jr.," "Circulation of the *Independent*," in Daniels file, Box 51, Accession 285; Liebold to Jacobson, 18 June 1920; Daniels to Liebold, 6 July 1920, Box 199, Accession 1, Ford Archives.

26. Liebold, "Reminiscences," 438, 465. Liebold to Ford, 4 August 1920, File 1117–1119, Box 100, Accession 662, Ford Archives. W. G. Enyon tele-

gram to Liebold, 10 June 1920, *Dearborn Independent* file, Box 2, Accession 572, Ford Archives. Singerman, "American Career," 71–74.

27. Russel Monro to Liebold, 23 October 1923, March 1924; Boris Brasol to Liebold, 3 November 1923, 3 February 1924; Brasol to Ford, 25 November 1924; G. A. Zahnow to Brasol, 4 December 1924, File 4, Box 2, Accession 572, Ford Archives. Liebold, "Reminiscences," 466.

28. Cohn, *Warrant,* 161. *IJ,* 1:135.

29. Ibid., 2:94, 119, 152; 1:135.

30. Ibid., 1:145–146; 4:116–117. For the *Independent's* extensive concern with propaganda, the "art of insinuating one idea under cover of another," see "What is Propaganda?" *DI,* 5 May 1923, 4; "Propaganda or Facts?" *DI,* 17 March 1923, 15; "Mr. Ford's Page," *DI,* 20 March 1920, 3; "Mr. Ford's Page," *DI,* 3 April 1920, 3; "Propaganda," *DI,* 4 June 1921, 4; "Propaganda," *DI,* 13 August 1921, 4; Lewis Harper, "Propagandists Impose on the American People," *DI,* 21 June 1922, 8, 10.

31. *IJ,* 1:116, 95, 143, 20–21, 14, 85; 3:239.

32. Ibid., 1:2, 14, 105–108, 1–16, 19–20, 35, 172; 4:187.

33. Ibid., 2:192, 195, 208, 87, 89, 232–243, 187; 1:133.

34. Ibid., 3:192–193; 4:181; 2:48.

35. Ibid., 1:33–36; 4:72, 67–108.

36. Ibid., 2:200, 197–209, 67; 1:9, 57–65.

37. Ibid., 1:53, 33–34, 178; 2:77–78; 3:222, 245, 250.

38. Ibid., 2:165, 143; 3:144, 255; 1:112.

39. Ibid., 1:102, 215, 167–174, 227; 3:106, 110–112; 4:44.

40. Ibid., 1:123, 194–200; 4:47–49; 2:217, 212; 3:39–45.

41. Ibid., 4:18, 7, 20, 14, 8; 1:140.

42. Ibid., 3:70, 73, 75–76, 83.

43. Ibid., 2:108, 140, 125–126, 120–121, 134, 116–118.

44. Ibid., 1:50, 189–190, 103, 71, 184; 4:236.

45. Ibid., 1:12, 147, 53, 85. See the essay "Success," in Henry Ford, *My Philosophy of Industry* (New York: Coward McCann, 1929), 55–80.

46. *IJ,* 1:16; 2:181, 240; 4:181.

47. Gabriel Kolko, *The Triumph of Conservatism: A Reinterpretation of American History, 1900–1916* (Chicago: Quadrangle, 1967), chapter 9.

48. *IJ,* 2:57–65. James Weinstein, *The Corporate Ideal in the Liberal State, 1910–1918* (Boston: Beacon Press, 1969), 221–226.

49. Solomon M. Schwartz, *The Jews in the Soviet Union* (Syracuse: Syracuse University Press, 1951). Harry G. Schaffer, *The Soviet Treatment of Jews* (New York: Praeger, 1974), 5–9.

50. Thomas A. Bailey, *America Faces Russia: Russian-American Relations from Early Times to Our Day* (Ithaca, N.Y.: Cornell University Press 1950), 216–223. William Appleman Williams, *American-Russian Relations, 1981–1947* (New York: Rinehart, 1952), 77–78. Max H. Laserson, *The American Impact on Russia: Diplomatic and Ideological, 1784–1917* (New York: Macmillan, 1950), 353–371. Morton Rosenstock, *Louis Marshall, Defender*

of Jewish Rights (Detroit: Wayne State University Press, 1965), 71–79. Naomi W. Cohen, "The Abrogation of the Russo-American Treaty of 1832," *Jewish Social Studies* 25 (January 1963), 3–41.

51. *IJ,* 2:151–153. Irving Howe, *World of Our Fathers* (New York: Simon & Schuster, 1976), 40.

52. Higham, "Social Discrimination," 350–351, 362.

53. *IJ,* 2:169; 4:134, 186, 183.

54. Charles Samuel Braden, *These Also Believe: A Study of Modern American Cults and Minority Religious Movements* (New York: Macmillan, 1950), chapter 11. Cameron, "Reminiscences," 58.

55. Black, Interview, 4. *IJ,* 4:46–47, 227, 238–239. "Was Jesus a Jew?" *DI,* 6 October 1923, 6, 15. For other examples of Anglo-Israelism, see Paul Tyner, "Where Are the Lost Tribes of Israel?" *DI,* 23 May 1925, 14–15, 27; Mark John Levy, "Why the Anglo-Saxons Are the Descendants of the Lost Ten Tribes of Israel," *DI,* 19 February 1927, 22–24.

56. *IJ,* 1:102, 152, 210; 3:195, 252, 178; 4:50–52.

57. Ibid., 2:252–253, 36; 1:47; 4:233.

58. Ibid., 1:82–83, 116, 61; 4:239, 241; 2:243; 3:95.

59. Sward, *Legend,* 259. For a surviving sample of persons receiving complimentary copies of *The International Jew,* see *Dearborn Independent* file, Box 200, Accession 1, Ford Archives.

60. "Jewish World Notes," *DI,* 21 May 1921, 9; "Jewish World Notes," *DI,* 25 April 1921, 9; "'He Won't Go'—Jews Won't go to Palestine," *DI,* 12 June 1920, 4; "Jewish World Notes," *DI,* 4 December 1920, 9; Lewis Harper, "'Beer and Wine' Are Not American Tipples," *DI,* 11 November 1922, 2; H. O. Bishop, "Will They Send Princess Nicotine to Join John Barleycorn?" *DI,* 28 February 1920, 15; "Baring the Heart of Hollywood: The Truth About the Motion Pictures," *DI,* 29 October 1921, 11, 15; Richard Harvey, "Perpetuating Ideals of Idiocy and Depravity," *DI,* 14 January 1922, 8, 10; Edward Jerome Dies, "The Syndicalist at Work in America," *DI,* 24 September 1921, 2–3; "Avoid This Poison Gas," *DI,* 22 January 1921, 4; "The Danger at Our Door," *DI,* 26 Febuary 1921, 4; "Immigration and Arithmetic," *DI,* 12 March 1921, 4; "Dawn of a New Industrial and Economic Era Believed Near in the Great Muscle Shoals Power and Nitrate Project," *DI,* 10 September 1921, 12–13; "The Nation's Roads," *DI,* 22 December 1923, 8; "Mr. Ford's Page," *DI,* 24 January 1920, 3; "A Year of Harding: 'Show Me,' Still the Rule," *DI,* 11 March 1922, 10. For the Ford presidential boom, see Nevins, *Expansion and Challenge,* 300–305, and Sward, *Legend,* 123–131.

61. "Women and the Ballot," *DI,* 21 April 1926, 11–12; John B. Wallace, "The Public Defender—A New Bulwark," *DI,* 14 May 1921, 2; E. E. Miller, "Must We Have a Federal Anti-Lynching Law?" *DI,* 30 July 1921, 12; "As to 'Political Prisoners,'" *DI,* 21 August 1920, 4; "A Good Neighbor," *DI,* 14 January 1922, 4; "Is There No Help for These?" *DI,* 7 Febuary 1920, 4.

62. "Will the Bigger Harding Emerge?" *DI,* 28 October 1922, 4; "Mr. Lasker Reveals Himself," *DI,* 4 November 1922, 4; "Lasker Again," *DI,* 7

April 1923, 4; "No Secret Diplomacy," *DI,* 27 August 1920, 4; "To Congress—Don't," *DI,* 6 March 1920, 4; "The President's Stand," *DI,* 27 March 1920, 4; William Atherton DuPuy, "Is League of Nations a Failure? Here's Answer," *DI,* 10 March 1923, 8; Huston Thompson, "Woodrow Wilson, Master of Dreams," *DI,* 8 May 1926, 12–13; "Mr. Ford's Page," *DI,* 16 Febuary 1924, 7.

63. Rosenstock, *Louis Marshall,* 147–152. Lewis, *Public Image,* 140.

64. "An Open Letter to Henry Ford," *Jewish Criterion,* 25 June 1920, 1. Charles H. Joseph [*Criterion* editor] to Ford, 26 June 1920, J. articles—Comments Against file, Box 100, Accession 662, Ford Archives. Rosenstock, *Louis Marshall,* 157–177. *New York Times,* 29 July 1927. Franklin to Ford, 14 June 1920, *Dearborn Independent* file, Box 2, Accession 572, Ford Archives. Lewis, *Public Image,* 14. Herman Bernstein, *The History of a Lie: "The Protocols of the Wise Men of Zion"* (New York: J. S. Olgivie, 1921).

65. Charles S. Bryan to Ford, general file, Letters and Telegrams, 3827–3831, Box 4, Accession 23; C. Mobray White to Ford, 30 August 1920; Liebold to White, 1, 23 September 1920; White to Liebold, 14, 25 September 1920, J. Articles—Comments for file, Box 100, Accession 662; W. J. Abbot to Cameron, n.d., *Dearborn Independent—The International Jew,* 1919–20, file; Chapman to Cameron, 11 July 1921, *Dearborn Independent—The International Jew,* January-June 1921 file, Box 200, Accession 1, Ford Archives. Liebold, "Reminiscences," 497, gives Morgan's opinion. For the *Independent's* circulation, which fluctuated from 148,000 to 640,000, depending on the pressure put on Ford dealers to sell the paper, see Lewis, *Public Image,* 140, 510, n. 22.

66. Rosenstock, *Louis Marshall,* 159. Liebold to Franklin, 23 June, Franklin to Liebold, 24 June 1920, *Dearborn Independent* file, Accession 572; Liebold to Abe Manheimer, 8 September 1920, to Charles H. Joseph, 30 June 1920, to Frank J. Kunstler, 10 August 1920, to Irene Levine, 1 December 1920; Lawrence to Ford, 27 December 1920, Liebold to Lawrence, 3, 19 January, Lawrence to Liebold, 6 January 1921, J. Articles—Comments Against file, Accession 662; Liebold to White, 1 September 1920, J. Article—Comments for file, Box 100, Accession 662, Ford Archives.

67. Liebold to George Henry Payne, 15 January 1921, Article file, Box 100, Accession 662; Liebold deposition, 13 December 1924, Herman Bernstein case file, Box 199, Accession 1, Ford Archives. Occasionally "Mr. Ford's Page" made an oblique reference to a "dark stream of power whose objective for centuries has been the destruction of a civilization that is slowly becoming Christian." See *DI,* 28 October 1922, 5.

68. Jardim, *First Henry Ford,* 145–146; Pipp, *The Real Henry Ford* (Detroit: Pipp's Weekly, 1922), 21–26. Upton Sinclair, *The Fliver King: A Story of Ford America* (Pasadena: n.p., 1927), 26. Nevins, *Expansion and Challenge,* 322; Lewis, *Public Image,* 145; Rosenstock, *Louis Marshall,* 175–178; Dealer's Comments file, Box 100, Accession 662, Ford Archives.

69. Ford, with Samuel Crowther, *My Life and Work* (Garden City, N.Y.: Garden City, 1922), 252. Benson, *New Henry Ford,* 357–358. Nevins,

Expansion and Challenge, 316. "What Do You Know About Money as Money?" *DI,* 21 January 1922, 2, began the new series on finance.

70. Benson, *New Henry Ford,* 358–359. "If I Were President: An Authorized Interview," by Charles W. Wood, *Collier's,* 4 August 1923, 6. Pipp, *Both Sides,* 71.

71. "Pro-Jewish Propaganda, *DI,* 8 December 1923, 8; Westin Estes, "Soviet Gold—Does It Go to Wall St.—Or Not?" *DI,* 9 June 1923, 10, 14; Paul Tyner, "World in Pawn to Single Family," *DI,* 25 August 1923, 9; "Immigration," *DI,* 12 May 1923, 4; Albert Sidney Gregg, "Cleveland Jews Fight the Interest Sharks," *DI,* 19 May 1923, 7; Charles Albert Collman, "Commercializing the Gangsters of the Ghetto," *DI,* 17 November 1923, 10; Llewelyn Smith, "Negroes of Harlem Exploited by Jews," *DI,* 29 December 1923, 9; "They Got Their Letter," *DI,* 24 April 1926, 10; C. C. Daniels, "What's in a Name—Sweetening the Rose," *DI,* 13 September 1924, 2; Hamilton York, "Cabal May Govern World's Gold," *DI,* 8 November 1924, 2; "What About the German Loan?" *DI,* 8 November 1924, 8; "New York Court Procedure," *DI,* 15 September 1923, 4; "To Hang at 19," *DI,* 27 September 1924, 8; "Mr. Johnson," *DI,* 1 December 1923, 8; "Politics," *DI,* 6 September 1924, 8; "Senator LaFollette," *DI,* 4 October 1924, 8; "Double Jointed," *DI,* 30 April 1921, 4; Charles Albert Collman, "The Mysterious Killing of Major Cronkhite and Amazing Actions of Captain Rosenbluth," *DI,* 30 December 1922, 3, 11; "Truth Crushed to Earth," *DI,* 6 January 1923, 13; "Trying a Case in the Newspapers," *DI,* 13 January 1923, 7; Collman, "The American Jewish Committee Would Substitute Itself for Country's Laws," *DI,* 27 January, 1923, 8, 14; "Senator," *DI,* 3 March 1923, 4; Collman, "Federal Law Flouted in Cronkhite Case," *DI,* 7 April 1923, 6, 11; Collman, "His Son Was Probably Murdered—Pershing," *DI,* 21 April 1923, 6–8; Collman, "Cabinet Dragged Into Cronkhite Case Through Intrigues of Racial Clique," *DI,* 28 April 1923, 12–13; Collman, "Shall Rosenbluth Be 'an American Dreyfus?'" *DI,* 26 May 1923, 10. For a brief review of the Rosenbluth case, see Rosenstock, *Louis Marshall,* 179–181.

72. Walter M. Wolff, "Anti-Semites in Germany!—Where and Why?" *DI,* 17 January 1925, 2; "Chats with Office Callers," *DI,* 27 February 1926, 12; "To the President of Harvard," *DI,* 3 February 1923, 4; "News from Russia," *DI,* 2 October 1926, 11.

73. Grace H. Larsen and Henry E. Erdman, "Aaron Sapiro: Genius of Farm Cooperative Promotion," *Mississippi Valley Historical Review* 49 (September 1962), 242–259, 262–265. James H. Shideler, *Farm Crisis: 1919–1923* (Westport, Conn.: Greenwood Press, 1976), 99–103, 111–113, 117, 249. William T. Hutchinson, *Lowden of Illinois: The Life of Frank O. Lowden* (Chicago: University of Chicago Press, 1957), 2:513–527.

74. Shideler, *Farm Crisis,* 102–103, 117, 253–254. Larsen, "Aaron Sapiro," 260, 266–267.

75. Black, "Interview," 41. *New York Times,* 22, 23 March 1927. Liebold, "Reminiscences," 483.

76. "Why Sapiro's Cooperatives Had Trouble," *DI,* 20 Febuary 1926, 14–15; "Bingham, Sapiro vs. Co-operation," *DI,* 17 January 1925, 8; Robert Morgan, "Jewish Exploitation of Farmers' Organizations," *DI,* 12 April 1924, 4; "A Word to Congress," *DI,* 23 January 1926, 10; Morgan, "Sapiro Trust in the Northwestern Hay Crop," *DI,* 23 August 1924, 10, 14; Morgan, "More Destructive than the Boll Weevil, " *DI,* 13 September 1924, 10–11, 14; "Aaron Spouts Again," *DI,* 31 January 1925, 8; Morgan, "World Cotton Control by Sapiro Plan," *DI,* 11 April 1925, 4, 14; Morgan, "Sapiro's Peach and Fig Growers," *DI,* 2 May 1925, 18; Morgan, "Potato Growers Beat Sapiro at His Own Game," *DI,* 26 July 1924, 6, 14; Morgan, "To Save an Industry from Sapiro Hands," *DI,* 2 August 1924, 6, 14; Morgan, "Sapiro Burr in Oregon's Golden Fleece," *DI,* 9 August 1924, 6, 14; Morgan, "Sapiro Invades the Tobacco Field," *DI,* 16 August 1924, 5, 14; Morgan, "Sapiro and Raisin-Growers," *DI,* 20 September 1924, 10, 14; Morgan, "Sapiro's Dream—An International Wheat Pool," *DI,* 30 August 1924, 6, 14; Morgan, "Wheat Farmers Drop Two Millions a Year," *DI,* 19 July 1924, 6; Morgan, "When Co-operation Has No Strings to It," *DI,* 13 December 1924, 4, 14.

77. Liebold, "Reminiscences," 475. Hutchinson, *Lowden,* 2: 520–521, 524. Shideler, *Farm Crisis,* 115, 258–260. Morgan, "Jewish Exploitation of Farmers' Organizations II: The Story of the Sapiro Boys," *DI,* 19 April 1924, 5. On Ford's ties to rural America and vice versa, see Reynold M. Wik, *Henry Ford and Grass-roots America* (Ann Arbor: University of Michogan Press, 1973), especially chapter 7, on cooperatives and the Sapiro case.

78. Larsen, "Aaron Sapiro," 252, 128. Shideler, *Farm Crisis,* 101. Hutchinson, *Lowden,* 2:547. *New York Times,* 29, 14 March 1927. Sapiro, "Demand for Retraction," 6 January 1925, Aaron Sapiro case, 1925–1927, file, Box 199, Accession 1, Ford Archives.

79. Rosenstock, *Louis Marshall,* 168–170. *New York Times,* 2, 3 February 1921. Bernstein to Ford, 5 July 1923, Box 199, Accession 1, Ford Archives. "Dr. Joseph Collens Tells What He Thinks of Sigmund Freud—The Man and His Methods," *DI,* 2 January 1926, 4; William L. Stidger, "Honestly—Who is Babbitt?" *DI,* 6 March 1926, 2, 26. The continued sniping usually appeared in unsigned columns called "I Read in the Papers that—" and "Chats With Office Callers."

80. "What About the Jewish Question?" *DI,* 13 March 1926, 6–7.

81. Nevins, *Expansion and Challenge,* 318–319. The files relating to the Bernstein and Sapiro suits have been removed from the Ford Archives by the Ford Motor Company.

82. *New York Times,* 26, 19, 23 March 1927.

83. Ibid., 26, 23, 25, 22, 24 March 1927.

84. Ibid., 22, 23, 26, 28, 29, 25 March 1927.

85. Ibid., 6, 5, 13, 7, 8, 15, 12 April, 18 March, 24 July 1927.

86. Ibid., 13, 14, 15, 16 March, 1 April 1927. Nevins, *Expansion and Challenge,* 318–320. Bennett, *Never Called Him Henry,* 49–53.

87. *New York Times,* 28 May, 25, 28 March, 12, 20, 2, 22 April, 2 July 1927.

88. Ibid., 8, 9, 11, 12 July 1927. Cameron, "Reminiscences," 32–33. A. F. H. Creech to Liebold, 12 May 1927, with enclosures on Eugene Meyer, Jr., file 254, Box 603, Accession 285, Ford Archives. Bennett, *Never Called Him Henry,* 55–56. Rosenstock, *Louis Marshall,* 187–193. Nevins, *Expansion and Challenge,* 320–321. Lewis, *Public Image,* 145–157.

89. Jardim, *First Henry Ford,* 151–153. Rosenstock, *Louis Marshall,* 192.

90. *New York Times,* 17, 18, 19, 21, 25, 26, 27 July 1927. "Sapiro Case Settled," *DI,* 30 July 1927, 11. Rosenstock, *Louis Marshall,* 195.

91. Lewis, *Public Image,* 147–154. Rosenstock, *Louis Marshall,* 197–199. Bennett, *Never Called Him Henry,* 49, 56. Elna M. Smith and Charles F. Robertson, eds., *Besieged Patriot: Autobiographical Episodes Exposing Communism, Traitorism, and Zionism From the Life of Gerald L. K. Smith* (Eureka Springs, Ark.: Smith Foundation, 1978), 161–162. Smith, interview with author, August 1969. Bernstein to Frank Campsall, 8 December 1927, Campsall to Bernstein, 11 August 1928, Marshall to Ford, 12 May 1928, 3 April 1928, Samuel Untermeyer to C. B. Longley, 25 November 1927, Jewish Material, 1928, file, Box 199, Accession 1; Marshall to Ford, 23 December 1927, Marshall to Campsall, 17 January 1928, Campsall to Marshall, 5, 17 January 1928, Aaron Sapiro case, 1925–27 file, Box 199, Accession 1, Ford Archives. Boxes 199–200 in Accession 1 also contain much randomly filed material on attempts overseas to suppress *The International Jew.*

92. *IJ,* 4:245. Cohn, *Warrant,* 159. Lewis, *Public Image,* 143. Hitler, *Mein Kampf* (Boston: Houghton Mifflin, 1943), 639. Hapgood, "Inside Story," Part 3, *Hearst's International* 42 (August 1922), 47.

93. McWilliams, *Mask for Privilege,* 48. Handlin, *Adventure,* 174. Higham, "American Anti-Semitism Historically Reconsidered," in Charles Herbert Stember, Marshall Sklare, and George Salomon, eds., *Jews in the Mind of America* (New York: Basic Books, 1966), 247. Ford, *My Life,* 251.

94. Peter G. Filene, "An Obituary for 'The Progressive Movement,'" *American Quarterly,* 22 (Spring 1970), 20–34. Lawrence Goodwyn, *Democratic Promise: The Populist Movement in America* (New York: Oxford University Press, 1976), especially chapters 13–15. Kolko, *Triumph of Conservatism.* Christopher Lasch, *The Agony of the American Left* (New York: Knopf, 1969), chapter 1.

95. Peter F. Drucker, "Henry Ford: Success and Failure," *Harper's Magazine* (July 1947), 3–8. Hofstadter, *Age of Reform,* 81. Rosenstock, *Louis Marshall,* 137–148. Nevins, *Expansion and Challenge,* 618. Sward, *Legend,* 143. Wik, *Ford and Grass-roots,* 10–11; Lewis, *Public Image,* 81. Jardim, *First Henry Ford,* 105. *New York Times,* 26 March 1927.

96. "*Independent's* National Poll on League and Presidency," *DI,* 5 June 1920, 1, 3: Johnson, 20,130; Hoover, 15,693; Wood, 10,818; Lowden, 8,145; Harding, 1,820; Wilson, 7,095; McAdoo, 5,049; Bryan, 3,902; LaFollette (write-in), 1,809.

97. *DI,* 22 November 1924, 8. Pipp, *Both Sides,* 37–38. Lewis, *Public Image,* chapters 10, 13. Cameron, "Reminiscences," 8, 225.

98. Hofstadter, *Age of Reform,* 198, 201. Hapgood, "Inside Story," Part 1, 15. Ford, *My Life,* 251.

99. Spencer C. Olin, Jr., *California's Prodigal Sons: Hiram Johnson and the Progressives, 1911–1912* (Berkeley and Los Angeles: University of California Press, 1968), 181.

100. McWilliams, *Mask for Privilege,* 124. Seymour Martin Lipset and Earl Raab, *The Politics of Unreason: Right-Wing Extremism in America, 1790–1970* (New York: Harper & Row, 1970).

101. Daniel Bell, ed., *The Radical Right: The New American Right Expanded and Updated* (Garden City, N.Y.: Doubleday, 1963).

102. Charles Glock and Rodney Stark, *Anti-Semitism and Christian Beliefs* (New York: Harper & Row, 1966), 103.

103. Garrett, *Wild Wheel,* 147. Ford, *My Life,* 251. Sward, *Legend,* 147, 453.

104. Ford, *My Life,* 250. "Are the Jews 'God's Chosen People?'" *DI,* 22 September 1923, 2. Strong, *Our Country,* 211. Roberts, *Why Europe Leaves Home,* 49. Grant, *Passing of the Great Race,* 17, 90–92.

105. Hitler, *Mein Kampf,* 306.

106. Richard Hofstadter, *The Paranoid Style in American Politics and Other Essays* (New York: Vintage, 1967), chapter 1.

107. Peter Berger and Thomas Luckmann, *The Social Construction of Reality: A Treatise in the Sociology of Knowledge* (Garden City, N.Y.: Anchor, 1967), chapter 3. Berger, *A Rumor of Angels: Modern Society and the Rediscovery of the Supernatural* (Garden City, N.Y.: Anchor, 1970), 6.

108. Marquis, *Henry Ford,* 168.

109. Jardim, *First Henry Ford,* 162, 169, 171, 65, 119, 156, 118, 184–185, 182.

110. Ibid., 69, 180, 140.

111. Marquis, *Henry Ford,* 3. Ross, *Old World,* 160.

112. Jardim, *First Henry Ford,* 158, 141, 153. Nevins, *Expansion and Challenge,* 211n, 519, 515, 592.

113. Sward, *Legend,* 126. Marquis, *Henry Ford,* 172. *New York Times,* 14, 16 July 1927. Rosenstock, *Louis Marshall,* 197. Lewis, *Public Image,* chapter 30.

Chapter 3. Jesus Christ as Business Statesman

1. Standard accounts of Barton's career are Richard Stephen Shapiro, "The Big Sell—Attitudes of Advertising Writers About Their Craft in the 1920s and 1930s" (Ph.D. Dissertation, University of Wisconsin, 1969), chapter 6; John Frank Cook, "Messiah of Business: A Study of Bruce Barton" (masters thesis, University of Wisconsin, 1962); James A. Neuchterlein, "Bruce Barton and the Business Ethos of the 1920s," *South Atlantic Quarterly* 76 (Summer 1977), 293–308; Richard M. Huber, *The American Dream of Success* (New York: McGraw-Hill, 1971), chapter 14; Lawrence Chenoweth, *The American Dream of Success: The Search for the Self in the Twentieth*

Century (North Scituate, Mass.: Duxbury Press, 1974), 47–50; and John G. Cawelti, *Apostles of the Self-Made Man* (Chicago: University of Chicago Press, 1965), 197–199. The most astute treatments are lamentably brief: Donald Meyer, *The Positive Thinkers: A Study of the American Quest for Health, Wealth and Personal Power from Mary Baker Eddy to Norman Vincent Peale* (Garden City, N.Y.: Anchor, 1966), 159–162; Otis Pease, "Barton, Bruce," in John A. Garraty, ed., *Encyclopedia of American History* (New York: Harper & Row, 1974), 62–63; Warren Susman, "Piety, Profits, and Play: The 1920s," in Howard H. Quint and Milton Cantor, eds., *Men, Women, and Issues in American History* (Homewood, Ill.: Dorsey Press, 1975), 2:192–200; Stephen Fox, *The Mirror Makers: A History of American Advertising and Its Creators* (New York: Morrow, 1984), 101–112; and T. J. Jackson Lears, "From Salvation to Self-Realization," in Richard Wightman Fox and T. J. Jackson Lears, eds., *The Culture of Consumption: Critical Essays in American History, 1880–1980* (New York: Pantheon, 1983), 29–37.

2. Bruce Barton (hereafter BB), "Behind Our Own Iron Curtain," 20 May 1949 speech in the Bruce Barton Collection, State Historical Society of Wisconsin (hereafter BC), 6, 13, Box 138.

3. The myth of the "self-made" man characterized most of Barton's obituaries: *New York Times,* 6 July 1967; "Advertising: Word Man," *Newsweek,* 70 (13 July 1967), 78–79; "The Classic Optimist," *Time,* 90 (14 July 1967), 18. See also BB, *On the Up and Up* (Indianapolis: Bobbs-Merrill, 1929), 72; William E. Barton (hereafter WEB), *The Autobiography of William E. Barton* (Indianapolis: Bobbs-Merrill, 1932), 267–270; Fred B. Barton, "Bruce Barton as a Brother," BC, Box 4; BB to Clarke, 25 December 1902, BC, Box 3.

4. WEB, *Autobiography,* 83–84, 120, 143–196, 218–228, 268. WEB, *Esther T. Barton: A Biographical Sketch* (n.p.: Foxboro Press, 1926), 15–27. WEB, *The Life of Abraham Lincoln* (Indianapolis: Bobbs-Merrill, 1925), 1:297.

5. WEB, *Autobiography,* 46, 97. WEB, *Jesus of Nazareth: The Story of His Life and Scenes of His Ministry* (Boston: Pilgrim Press, 1903), 155, 295–345, 375–376, preface. WEB, *Four Hitherto Unpublished Gospels* (New York: George H. Doran, 1920), chapters 3–4. WEB, *Day By Day with Jesus: A Book for Holy Week* (Oak Park, Ill.: Puritan Press, 1913), 59–60.

6. WEB, *Jesus of Nazareth,* 279, 347. WEB, *The Wit and Wisdom of Safed the Sage* (Boston: Pilgrim Press, 1919), 16. WEB, *More Parables of Safed the Sage* (Boston: Pilgrim Press, 1923), 79–82, 89–92.

7. BB, "My Father's Business," *Outlook,* 107 (27 June 1914), 494. BB, "The Great Discovery," *Reader's Digest* 60 (June 1952), 121. "Bruce Barton: Everything ad men should be, he is," *Printer's Ink* 274 (10 February 1961), 54–55. Robert L. Bishop, "Bruce Barton—Presidential Stage Manager," *Journalism Quarterly* 43 (Spring 1966), 86. BB to Clarke, 25 December 1902, BC, Box 3. BB, "My Thirty-Two Years at School," *American Magazine* 87 (April 1919), 34.

8. "Everything ad men should be," 54. Fred Barton, "Brother." BB, "My Father's Business," 494–497. WEB, *Autobiography,* xv–xvi.

9. Barton at first intended to study and then teach history, and so he accepted a fellowship at the University of Wisconsin. He never enrolled, however. The reasons for this change of heart remain obscure.

10. "Everything ad men should be," 55. BB, "Thirty-Two Years," 68, 70. BB, "When I Run for Congress," *Woman's Home Companion* 60 (November 1924), 12. BB to John Foster Dulles, 19 May 1944, BC, Box 18. Julian Lewis Watkins, *The 100 Greatest Advertisements* (New York: Dover, 1959), 28-29.

11. BB, "Thirty-Two Years," 70. BB, "Panaceas and Sudden Ruin," 15 February 1947 speech, BC, Box 138. BB, "Special Attractions for 1913," *Congregationalist and Christian World* 97 (December 1912), n.p. BB, "Where the Path Turns Down," *Congregationalist and Christian World* 98 (15 May 1913), 650. BB, "Ten Years of Dying: Life in a Back Seat," *Continent* 45 (20 August 1914), 1159, 1162. *New York Telegram,* 17 August 1928. BB, "The Negro and the Nation," *Congregationalist and Christian World* 98 (2 June 1913), 5. BB, "The Church that Saved a City," *Congregationalist and Christian World* 99 (5 November 1914), 587–588. BB, "A Certain Ethiopian," *Congregationalist and Christian World* 98 (30 January 1913), 152. BB, "Those Who 'Carry the Banner,'" *Continent* 46 (11 February 1915), 173–174. BB, "With the IWW in New Bedford," *Congregationalist and Christian World* 97 (1 August 1912), 141–142. BB, "My Father's Business," 496.

12. BB, "The Country Church I: What is Happening to It?" *Congregationalist and Christian World* 99 (4 August 1914), 16, 869. BB, "Trying to Get Warm at Other Altars," *Continent* 42 (21 November 1912), 1650–1651. BB, "The Tyranny of the Text," *Outlook* 108 (30 December 1914), 1014, 1016. BB, "Good Fruit from Stony Ground," *Continent* 44 (24 July 1913), 1022–1023. BB, "Ahoy, Captain Benn," *Continent* 45 (15 October 1914), 1417–1418. BB, "Go Tell John," *Continent* 45 (16 July 1914), 993. BB, "Four Who Answered," *Congregationalist and Christian World* 99 (28 May 1914), 721, 711.

13. BB, "Four Who Answered," 711. BB, "Church that Saved a City," 587–588. BB, "The Star: A Christmas Mystery," *Congregationalist and Christian World* 97 (19 December 1912), 909–910. BB, "A Prophet of Good Health," *Congregationalist and Christian World* 101 (1 June 1916), 723. BB, "A Day with Decker," *Congregationalist and Christian World* 99 (15 January 1914), 85.

14. Bouck White, *The Call of the Carpenter* (Garden City, N.Y.: Doubleday, Page, 1911), 301. William T. Doherty, "The Impact of Business on Protestantism, 1900–1929," *Business History Review* 28 (June 1954), 144–150. BB, *A Young Man's Jesus* (New York: Pilgrim Press, 1914), 32–33, 58, 45, 1, 92.

15. BB, *Young Man's Jesus,* 77–172.

16. Ibid., 60, 61, 91–114, 216, 233.

17. "Everything ad men should be," 55. BB, *More Power to You: Fifty Editorials from "Every Week"* (New York: Century, 1917), 57–60, 92–117, 47.

BB, *On the Up and Up,* 62, 87, 115, 178. BB, *Better Days* (New York: Century, 1924), 41. BB, "Moses Could Have Used This Man," *American Magazine* 81 (January 1916), 52–53. BB, "You Don't Altogether Like Your Job?" *American Magazine* 91 (May 1921), 34, 117. BB, "A Big Human Fellow Named Cutter," *American Magazine* 100 (August 1925), 16–17, 112. BB, "The Most Accurate Man in the World," *American Magazine* 90 (August 1920), 206. BB, "What to Do If You Want to Sit at the Boss's Desk," *American Magazine* 93 (February 1922), 28–29.

18. BB, *More Power,* 15–28, 47–49, 54–56, 121–125. BB and Russell Conwell, "Conversation Between a Young Man and an Old Man," *American Magazine* 92 (July 1921), 13–15, 108–110, 112.

19. BB to Dulles, 19 May 1944, BC. BB, *More Power,* 88. BB, *Better Days,* 50–51, 129, 131, 146. BB to Jackson Martindell, 28 March 1960, BC, Box 3. BB to William Lyon Phelps, 12 December 1930, BC, Box 143. BB, "Thirty-Two Years," 34, 68, 70. BB, *The Story of Business* (c. 1928, unpublished), chapter 12 [2], BC, Box 134. BB, "Houston's Tax Reformer," *Congregationalist and Christian World* 100 (21 October 1915), 570. *New York Times,* July 6, 1967.

20. BB, *More Power,* 61, 94–97, 122. BB, "Thirty-Two Years," 34, 72. BB, "My Father's Business," 496.

21. Fred Barton, "Brother." Ben Duffy, "What Is He Like at Work?" *Youth's Companion* (4 February 1926), 5. BB to Merle Thorpe, 2 June 1929, BC, Box 28. BB, *More Power,* 126–127. Charlie Brower, *Me, and Other Advertising Geniuses* (Garden City, N.Y.: Doubleday, 1974), 17, 27.

22. BB, *The Making of George Groton* (Garden City, N.Y.: Doubleday, Page, 1918).

23. WEB, *Esther T. Barton,* 30. Fred Barton, "Brother." *New York Times,* 6 July 1967. BB to Dulles, 19 May 1944, BC.

24. James Weinstein, *The Corporate Ideal in the Liberal State: 1900–1918* (Boston: Beacon Press, 1968). BB, *Better Days,* 79–111, 37–38. BB, *"Maybe* It is a Wild Idea," *National Electric Light Association Bulletin* 13 (June 1926), 387. BB, "Who Are The Friends Of The People?" *National Petroleum News* (7 January 1925), 70. BB, "Modern Distribution," *Chain Store Age* (November 1929), 64. BB, "The Creed of an Advertising Man," reprint from *Printer's Ink* 141 (3 November 1927), 2. BB, "The New Business World," 30 November 1929 speech, BC, 18, Box 135. David Potter, *People of Plenty: Economic Abundance and the American Character* (Chicago: University of Chicago Press, 1969), 169.

25. Brower, *Advertising Geniuses,* 71–78. BB, "The New Business World," 15, 12. BB, *"Maybe* It is a Wild Idea," 387.

26. BB, *Better Days,* 146, 75. BB, "Creed of an Advertising Man," 2. BB, untitled speech, 26 June 1934, BC, 2, Box 136. BB, "Modern Distribution," 64.

27. BB, untitled speech to National Association of Manufacturers, 14 September 1928, BC, 11, Box 135. BB, "Creed of an Advertising Man," 2. BB, "Who Are The Friends?" 72, 71. BB, "Is Advertising an Economic Waste?" 17

January 1924 speech, BC, Box 135. Bernard Lichtenberg in collaboration with BB, *Advertising Campaigns* (New York: Alexander Hamilton Institute, 1926), 334, 116–117, 331.

28. BB, "I See by the Papers," *Data Book* (May 1924), 196. Lichtenberg and BB, *Advertising Campaigns,* 330. Brower, *Advertising Geniuses,* 110. BB, "A Man Who Waited on Mrs. Lincoln—and a Boy Who Started Work Yesterday," BC, Box 77. BB to Ed [Streeter], 5 January 1928, BC, Box 75. Daniel Pope, *The Making of Modern Advertising* (New York: Basic Books, 1983), 219. For advertising strategies, see Potter, *People of Plenty,* chapter 8; Stuart Ewen, *Captains of Consciousness: Advertising and the Social Roots of Consumer Culture* (New York: McGraw-Hill, 1976), 69–76, 53–54, 98–99; Martin Mayer, *Madison Avenue, USA* (New York: Harper and Brothers, 1958); and Otis Pease, *The Responsibilities of American Advertising: Private Control and Public Influence* (New Haven: Yale University Press, 1958), chapters 1–4. The best treatment of the sociology and ethos of the advertising industry during Barton's heyday is Roland Marchand, *Advertising and the American Dream: Making Way for Modernity* (Berkeley: University of California Press, 1985), especially chapters 1–3.

29. BB, *The Man Nobody Knows: A Discovery of the Real Jesus* (Indianapolis: Bobbs-Merrill, 1925). I have used a reprint with the same pagination (New York: Triangle Books, 1940). WEB to BB, 28 June 1921, BC, Box 143. WEB, "Advertising to Fill a Church," in W. B. Ashley, ed., *Church Advertising: Its Why and How* (Philadelphia: J. B. Lippincott, 1917), 157–163.

30. BB to WEB, Sunday, n.d., BC, Box 143. WEB to BB, 28 June 1921, BC, Box 143. Luke 2:49 (King James), italics added by BB.

31. BB, *Man Nobody Knows,* preface, n.p.

32. Ibid., 8, 46, 185, 15, 157, 124, 41, 42.

33. Ibid., 42, 9, 10, 40, 41, 162. *Young Man's Jesus,* 79.

34. *Man Nobody Knows,* 28–52. *Young Man's Jesus,* 28–29.

35. *Man Nobody Knows,* 37, 131, 65–75, [iv]. *Young Man's Jesus,* 61, 171.

36. *Man Nobody Knows,* [iv], 29–30, 7, 23, 27, 128, 9, 92–106. WEB to BB, 28 June 1921, BC.

37. *Man Nobody Knows,* 127, 99, 112, 117–118, 143, 153.

38. *Man Nobody Knows,* 159, 163, 16, 173, 164–170.

39. Ibid., 178, 177, 81–82.

40. Ibid., 191.

41. Ibid., 180.

42. *Young Man's Jesus,* 111–114, 226. *Man Nobody Knows,* 84, 12, 210, 37, 85, 56.

43. *Man Nobody Knows,* 81, 84, 12.

44. Ibid., 213, 193.

45. James Rorty, *Our Master's Voice* (New York: John Day, 1934), 315. Alice Payne Hackett, *Sixty Years of Best Sellers: Advertising, 1895–1955* (New York: R. R. Bowker, 1956), 139, 141.

46. "Booming Religion as a Business Proposition," *Christian Century* 412 (21 May 1925), 458–459. "Jesus as Efficiency Expert," *Christian Century* 42 (2 July 1925), 851–852. Charles Francis Potter, "Present Day Portraits of Jesus," *Bookman* 61 (25 July 1925), 590–591. C. Everett Wagner, "Religion Rings the Cash Register," *Plain Talk* 2 (April 1928), 455–459. Hubert C. Herring, "The Rotarian Nobody Knows," *World Tomorrow* 8 (December 1925), 382. James L. Dwyer, "Books," *Commonweal* 2 (1 July 1925), 214. Gilbert Seldes, "The Living Christ," *New Republic* 43 (24 June 1925), 127, and "Service," *New Republic* 43 (15 July 1925), 207. Rorty, *Our Master's Voice,* 284, 319, 320–321, 329. Amos H. Gottschall, *The Book Entitled: "The Man Nobody Knows" Under The Dissecting Knife* (Harrisburg: Amos H. Gottschall, [1925?]), 1, 4.

47. John W. Davis to B. L. Chambers, 13 April 1926, BC. Bruce Bliven to BB, 2 May 1925, BC. Elliott S. Norton to Margaret Sanger, 31 August 1925, BC. Unsigned letter to BB, 25 May 1925, BC. "Comments on *The Man Nobody Knows* by Bruce Barton," BC, Box 107. *Pittsburgh Press,* 3 July 1926. *Boston Herald,* 2 January 1926. See generally "Reviews and Best-Seller Lists," BC, Box 107 and BC, Boxes 108–110, letters to Barton down through the 1950s. Shapiro, "Big Sell," 266.

48. BB, *What Can A Man Believe?* (Indianapolis: Bobbs-Merrill, 1927), 210. Rorty, *Our Master's Voice,* 323. Alex Osborn, "Will Dealers Follow the Lead?" *Advertising and Selling Fortnightly* 5 (10 March 1926), 40, 70. BB to William S. Skin, 18 July 1960, BC, Box 110. Dean Cornwell and BB, *The Man of Galilee: Twelve Scenes from the Life of Christ* (New York: Cosmopolitan Book Corporation, 1928). BB, *The Book Nobody Knows* (Indianapolis: Bobbs-Merrill, 1926). WEB, "Chaplain-in-Ordinary to a Film," *Dearborn Independent,* 9 April 1927.

49. BB, *Book Nobody Knows,* 29, 271–290. *What Can A Man Believe?* 28, 136, 73–88, 249.

50. BB, *What Can A Man Believe?* 231, 184, 205–208, 213, 221.

51. Ibid., 140–201. Cornwell, *Man of Galilee,* 137. Brower, *Advertising Geniuses,* 73, 82. BB to Herbert Hoover, 2 June 1928, BC, Box 28. BB to Merle Thorpe, 2 June 1929, BC. BB to Don Davis, 26 November 1931, BC, Box 76. BB, sworn statement, April 1946, BC, Box 144. "Word Man," 78–79. Cook, "Messiah of Business," 89–91. Fox, *Mirror Makers,* 111–112.

52. BB, "The New Business World," BC, 12. BB, "A Governor Who Stays on the Job," *Outlook* (28 April 1920), 756–757. Cook, "Messiah of Business," 66–68, 71–74. *New York Times,* 23 September 1926. Hoover to BB, 16, 25 June 1928, BC, Box 125. BB to Hoover, 10 September 1928, BC, Box 28. BB to George Akerson, 22 October 1929, BC, Box 29. Joan Hoff-Wilson, *Herbert Hoover: Forgotten Progressive* (Boston: Little, Brown, 1975), 123. Bishop, "Presidential Stage Manager," 85–86.

53. BB, untitled speech to Minneapolis Civic and Commerce Association, February 1935, BC, 4, 6, Box 136. BB, untitled radio talk for New York Unemployment Committee, 14 November 1932, BC, 3, Box 135. BB, untitled

speech to Minneapolis Community Chest Unemployment Campaign, 2 November 1931, BC, Box 135. BB, *He Upset the World* (Indianapolis: Bobbs-Merrill, 1932), 51, 170. BB, untitled speech to Boston Emergency Campaign, 19 December 1934, BC, 2, 3, Box 136. BB, untitled speech to Amherst student body, 17 October 1932, BC, Box 134. BB to Hoover, 28 September, 22 December 1931, 14 July 1932, BC, Box 29. Hoover to BB, 12 July 1932, BC, Box 29. BB, "Handicaps," *Redbook* 58 (November 1931), 11.

54. BB to Larry [Richey], 22 January 1932, BC, Box 29. BB, "History and the New Deal," *Southwestern Banker* 3 (December 1933), 7–10, 17–18. BB, "The Deflation of Ballyhoo," 24 November 1933 speech, BC, 5, 7, Box 135. BB, "The Good and the Bad in Mr. Roosevelt," 1936 speech, BC, Box 151. BB to Herbert Hoover, 7, 19, 23 June, 13, 27 July, 7 August 1934, BC, Box 29. Hoover to BB, 7, 23 June, 22 August 1934, BC, Box 29.

55. BB, "Let Us Take the Middle Road!" *Hearst's International–Cosmopolitan* 104 (June 1938), 30–31, 92. BB to Eugene C. Pulliam, 23 September 1943, BC, Box 42. BB to Herbert Hoover, 6 June 1932, BC, Box 29. BB to Minneapolis Civic and Commerce Association, BC, 7, 9–10, 15. BB, "The Public," *Vital Speeches of the Day* 2 (16 December 1935), 176.

56. BB, "The American Republic Ended in 1940," 15 November 1949, BC, Box 138. "Bruce Barton of New York is a Salesman of a Liberal GOP," *Life* 9 (21 October 1940), 100–101. "A One Man Platform" and "What I Intend to Do If Elected," Congressional campaign file, 1936–1937, BC. "Washington Correspondents Name Ablest Congressmen in *Life* Poll," *Life* 6 (20 March 1939), 15, 17. George Seldes, "Barton, Barton, Barton and Barton," *New Republic* 96 (26 October 1938), 328. "Mr. Barton is Drafted," *Time* 36 (7 October 1940), 16. BB, "Inside Willkie's Head," *Collier's* 116 (21 September 1940), 15, 67–70. Cook, "Messiah of Business," 91–98. Donald Bruce Johnson, *The Republican Party and Wendell Willkie* (Urbana: University of Illinois Press, 1960), 36, 79, 90.

57. BB, "Virile Young Men Can Win the Peace—Tired Old Men Lost It Before," speech, c. 1944, BC, Box 138. BB to Dulles, 19 May 1944, BC. *New York World-Telegram,* 17 August 1928. BB to Kirby Paige, 6, 15 May 1931, BC, Box 104. BB, "Creed of an Advertising Man," 6. BB, untitled speech to unspecified newspaper association, 1931, BC, Box 135. "Unknown," undated advertisement from *Good Housekeeping,* BC, 1, Box 126.

58. BB to Dulles, 19 May 1944, BC. BB, untitled speech to Twenty-Third Annual Conference of Hammerhill Agents, 21–22 August 1934, BC 14, Box 136. BB to Alfred M. Landon, 6 January, 17 February 1941, BC, Box 37. BB to Franklin D. Roosevelt, 8 May 1941, BC, Box 50. BB to John F. Kennedy, 17 January 1956, BC, Box 35. Cook, "Messiah of Business," 102–105.

59. BB to Landon, 6 January 1941, BC. *New York Times,* 6 July 1967. Brower, *Advertising Geniuses,* 83, 16. Duffy, "What Is He Like at Work?" 5. Mayer, *Madison Avenue,* 102. BB to Ben Duffy et al., 8 April 1953, BC, Box 76.

60. "With Hustle and Hope," *Time* 54 (20 October 1949), 82. BB to James S. Milloy, 30 January 1952, BC, Box 67. BB to Barry M. Goldwater, 26 August 1960, BC, Box 23. BB to Richard M. Nixon, 20 March 1961, BC, Box 50.

61. BB to Eugene C. Pulliam, 23 September, 1 October 1947, BC, Box 42. BB to Robert A. Taft, 27 June 1947, BC, Box 67. BB to Thomas E. Dewey, 2 July 1948, BC, Box 17. BB to Mary Beard, 26 December 1944, BB to Charles Beard, 24 June 1946, Charles Beard to BB, 6 March 1945, 19 June 1946, 24 April 1948, BC, Box 7. BB to Arthur H. Vandenberg, 22 October 1947, BC, Box 42. BB, "Are We Biting Off More Than We Can Chew?" *Reader's Digest* 53 (December 1948), 45–48. BB, "Behind Our Own Iron Curtain," 13. Justus D. Doenecke, *Not to the Swift: The Old Isolationists in the Cold War* (Lewisburg, Pa.: Bucknell University Press, 1979).

62. BB to Norman Thomas, 13, 10 July 1950, BC, Boxes 6–7. BB, "Ugly Facts About Korea" (King Features Syndicate), BC, Box 6.

63. BB to Stuart Alsop, 9 July 1958, BC, Box 1. BB, "Memo re: General Eisenhower," 14 July 1952, BB to B. C. Duffy, 23 September 1952, BC, Box 19. Stanley Kelley, Jr., *Professional Public Relations and Political Power* (Baltimore: Johns Hopkins University Press, 1969), 150, 163–179. Bishop, "Presidential Stage Manager," 85. BB to Goldwater, 27 April 1954, BC, Box 23.

64. BB to Harry Emerson Fosdick, 24 September 1956, BC, Box 21. BB to Beard, 27 October 1943, BC. BB, "After a Long Illness," *Reader's Digest* 60 (April 1952), 1–3.

65. BB to Fosdick, 24 September 1956, BC. Norman Vincent Peale to BB, 5 January 1942, BB to Peale, 21 December 1944, BC, Box 51. BB to George Champion, 2 October 1956, BB to Bob Foreman, 31 January 1955, BC, Box 23. "Word Man," 78–79. Mayer, *Madison Avenue*, 42.

66. BB, *The Man Nobody Knows and The Book Nobody Knows* (Indianapolis: Bobbs-Merrill, 1956), preface, 1, 115, 54, 82, 71, 12, 101–102.

67. "Word Man," 78–79. BB, "Thirty-Two Years," 73. Brower, *Advertising Geniuses,* 15–20. *New York Times,* 6 July 1967. Louise MacLeod to Ray Henle, 14 August 1964, BC, Box 29.

68. Susman, "Piety, Profits, and Play," 192. BB to William C. Donovan, 10 October 1928, BC.

69. BB, *Man Nobody Knows,* 82. Peter Gabriel Filene, *Him / Herself: Sex Roles in Modern America* (New York: Mentor, 1975), 96–106.

70. Louis Filler, *The Muckrakers* (University Park: Pennsylvania State University Press, 1976), 375–378. Otis L. Graham, Jr., *An Encore of Reform: The Old Progressives and the New Deal* (New York: Oxford University Press, 1967), 24–91, 156.

Chapter 5. *It Can't Happen Here*

1. Sinclair Lewis, *It Can't Happen Here* (Garden City, N.Y.: Doubleday, Doran, 1935). Herbert Mitgang, "Babbitt in the White House," on *It Can't Happen Here* (New York: Caedmon Records, 1973). Bud Schultz and Ruth Schultz, *It Did Happen Here: Recollections of Political Repression in America* (Berkeley and Los Angeles: University of California Press, 1988).

2. *Main Street* (1920, reprint, New York: New American Library, 1970). *Babbitt* (1922, reprint, New York: New American Library, 1965). *Elmer Gantry* (1927, reprint, New York: New American Library, 1970). Mark Schorer, *Sinclair Lewis: An American Life* (New York: McGraw-Hill, 1961), 473–474.

3. Vincent Sheean, *Dorothy and Red* (Boston: Houghton Mifflin, 1963), 132, 56–57. Marion K. Sanders, *Dorothy Thompson: A Legend in Her Time* (Boston: Houghton Mifflin, 1973), 135–136.

4. Schorer, *Sinclair Lewis,* 608.

5. Raymond Gram Swing, *Forerunners of American Fascism* (New York: Messner, 1935), 13.

6. John M. Cammett, "Communist Theories of Fascism, 1920–35," *Science and Society* 31 (Spring 1967), 149–163. Alfred M. Bingham, *Insurgent America: Revolt of the Middle Classes* (New York: Harper and Brothers, 1935), 105, 125–126, 138, 145, 171.

7. George Seldes, *Sawdust Caesar: The Untold Story of Mussolini and Fascism* (New York: Harper and Brothers, 1935), xiii. Swing, *Forerunners,* 168.

8. "Tinder for the Fascist Fires," *Nation* 146 (4 June 1938), 633. Benjamin Stolberg, "Vigilantism, 1937," *Nation* 145 (14 August 1937), 166. Amy Schecter, "Fascism in Pennsylvania," *Nation* 140 (19 June 1935), 409–411. Anna Wallace, "Fascism Comes to Campus," *New Republic* 81 (9 January 1935), 239. Hamilton Basso, "The Little Hitlers of Asheville," *New Republic* 88 (2 September 1936), 101.

9. Leo P. Ribuffo, *The Old Christian Right: The Protestant Far Right from the Great Depression to the Cold War* (Philadelphia: Temple University Press, 1983), 21–22.

10. Ibid. Peter Kurth, *American Cassandra: The Life of Dorothy Thompson* (Boston: Little, Brown, 1990), 224. Stuart Chase, *The Tyranny of Words* (New York: Harcourt, Brace, 1938), 136.

11. Schorer, *Sinclair Lewis,* 608–609. Sheean, *Dorothy and Red,* 262, 260, 270–271. Sanders, *Dorothy Thompson,* 211. Kurth, *American Cassandra,* 199–209, 218, 232.

12. *It Can't Happen Here,* 127, 120, 102–103.

13. Ibid., 100, 157, 80, 20, 39, 2.

14. Ibid., 169, 360, 173, 265, 249–252.

15. Ibid., 343, 260–263.

16. Ibid., 57, 25, 354.

17. Ibid., 208, 236, 341, 270, 169, 12–13.

18. Ibid., 410–411, 418, 427.

19. Ibid., 450, 458.

20. Ibid., 93, 68, 12.

21. Ibid., 204, 412, 190, 318.

22. Ibid., 344.

23. Ibid., 9, 189, 107.

24. Ibid., 87.

25. Ibid., 100. Max Lerner, *Ideas Are Weapons: The History and Uses of Ideas* (New York: Viking, 1939), 280.

26. *It Can't Happen Here,* 13, 287, 291, 82, 333, 7.

27. Ibid., 299, 133, 49.

28. Ibid., 33, 323, 244.

29. Ibid., 458.

30. "Statement by Mr. Sinclair Lewis, 15 February 1936," Folder 104, Lewis Collection, Yale University. Sidney Howard White, *Sidney Coe Howard* (Boston: Twayne, 1977), 31. Lewis to Howard, 21 July 1935, Lewis folder; Howard to Ann [Watkins], 18 October 1935, Outgoing correspondence; Sam Marx to Howard, 21 October 1935, MGM folder, Howard Collection, University of California, Berkeley. J. Robert Rubin to Louis B. Mayer, 4 October 1935, *It Can't Happen Here* file; Charles K. Stern to Robert E. Kopp, Sidney Coe Howard file, Metro-Goldwyn-Mayer archives (hereafter MGM), Culver City, California.

31. Thomas Schatz, *The Genius of the System: Hollywood Filmmaking in the Studio Era* (New York: Pantheon, 1988), 29–47, 98–124, 159–175. Bosley Crowther, *Hollywood Rajah: The Life and Times of Louis B. Mayer* (New York: Holt, Rinehart, and Winston, 1960), 136, 147, 178–181. Andrew Bergman, *We're in the Money: Depression America and Its Films* (New York: Harper & Row, 1972), 115–118. Louis B. Mayer to J. Robert Rubin, 19 September 1935, *It Can't Happen Here* file, MGM.

32. Schatz, *Genius of the System,* 170–171. John Douglas Eames, *The MGM Story: The Complete History of Fifty-Seven Roaring Years* (New York: Crown, 1987), 112, 115, 125, 149.

33. Stephen Vaughn, "Morality and Entertainment: The Origins of the Motion Picture Code," *Journal of American History* 77 (June 1990), 39–65. Leonard J. Leff and Jerrold L. Simmons, *The Dame in the Kimono: Hollywood, Censorship, and the Production Code from the 1920s to the 1960s* (New York: Grove Weidenfeld, 1990), 14–54.

34. Leff and Simmons, *Dame in the Kimono,* xiv, 65, 68–69.

35. Charles E. Scott, "Sidney Howard: American Playwright" (Ph.D. dissertation, Yale School of Drama, 1963), 80, 89–94. Freda Kirchwey to Howard, 29 June, 12 July, 1934, *Nation* folder, Howard Collection.

36. Howard to Polly [Howard], 21 December 1935, Howard to Ann Watkins, 27 December 1935, Outgoing correspondence; Howard, *Diary,* 13 January 1936, Carton 1, Howard Collection.

37. "Preliminary notes for a motion picture treatment of *It Can't Happen Here* by Sinclair Lewis" and "Preliminary Notes for A Motion Picture from *It Can't Happen Here* by Sinclair Lewis," Box 9; Howard to Lucien Hubbard, 5 December 1935, Howard to Sinclair Lewis, 23 January 1936, Outgoing correspondence, Howard Collection.

38. Howard to Polly Howard, 9 January 1936, undated letter [late January 1936], Howard to Sinclair Lewis, 23 January 1936, Outgoing correspondence, Howard Collection.

39. *"It Can't Happen Here* by Sinclair Lewis, Adapted for the Screen by Sidney Howard," Howard Collection (cited hereafter as "Script"), 238, 128, 107, 138, 39–40. Although the script is undated, the references to living Americans, explicit politics, and level of violence make clear that it was an early complete version, finished before systematic negotiations began with the Hays office.

40. Howard, "Script," 206–210, 73, 126.

41. Howard, "Script," 253. Howard to Sam Marx, 23 October 1935, Howard to Lewis, 23 January 1936, Outgoing correspondence; Lewis to Howard, 2 February 1936, Lewis folder; Howard, *Diary,* 27 January, 1936, Howard Collection.

42. Alvin M. Asher to Robert E. Kopp, 4 February 1936, D. O. Decker to Natalie Bucknall, 5 February 1936, *It Can't Happen Here* folder; Robert E. Kopp to Lucien Hubbard, Eckman to [Eddie] Mannix, 5 February 1936, *It Can't Happen Here* interoffice communications file, MGM.

43. Joseph I. Breen to Louis B. Mayer, 1 February 1936, *It Can't Happen Here* file, MGM.

44. Ibid.

45. Howard to Roger Baldwin, 11 February 1936, Outgoing correspondence; Howard, *Diary,* 28, 30, 31 January, Howard Collection. "Script," 121–122, 127, 203–206, 224.

46. Howard, *Diary,* 12, 14, 15 February 1936, Howard Collection. Lewis, "Statement." *New York Times,* 16 February 1936.

47. *New York Herald-Tribune,* 17, 18 February 1936.

48. *New York Herald-Tribune,* 23 February 1936. *New York Times,* 23 February 1936.

49. *New York Times,* 29 March 1936. Will H. Hays, *Memoirs* (New York: Doubleday, 1955), 511–520.

50. *New York Times,* 29 March 1936. Robert Sklar, *Movie-Made America: A Cultural History of American Movies* (New York: Vintage, 1975), 225. Samuel Marx, *Mayer and Thalberg: The Make-Believe Saints* (New York: Random House, 1975), 245–246.

51. "'It Can't Happen Here' Storm Continues Unabated," *Publishers' Weekly* 129 (14 March 1936), 1174. *New York Post,* 25 February 1936. *New York Telegraph,* 28 February 1936. Roger N. Baldwin to Gardner Jackson, 5 March 1936, Arthur Garfield Hays to Cordell Hull, 6 March 1936, Arthur Garfield Hays et al. to Louis B. Mayer, 6 March 1936, Book 277, ACLU Collection, Princeton University.

52. Mark Marvin to Herman Shumlin, 13 March 1936, [Roger N. Baldwin], "Re Censorship Meeting," undated memorandum, Book 878, ACLU Collection. *New York Motion Picture Herald,* 7 March 1936.

53. Howard [Strickling] to Howard Dietz, 13 March 1936, Robert E. Kopp form letter to Dear Sir, 11 March 1936, *It Can't Happen Here* file, MGM. *New York Times,* 3 March 1936. Gardner Jackson and E. P. Higgins to Roger Baldwin, 5 March 1936, Acting Secretary to Arthur Garfield Hays, Book

277, Mark Marvin to Clifton Reed, 31 March, 1936, Book 878, ACLU Collection. Howard, *Diary,* 24 February 1936; Lewis to Howard, 7 March 1936, Lewis file; Howard to David O. Selznick, 1 November 1936, Outgoing correspondence, Howard Collection.

54. *New York Times,* 3 March 1936. Hays, *Memoirs,* 525.

55. "Stage: Lewis Drama Produced Simultaneously in 21 Theatres," *Newsweek* 8 (7 November 1936), 40–41. Hallie Flanagan, *Arena: The History of the Federal Theatre* (1940, reprint, New York: Benjamin Blom, 1965), 115, 120.

56. Flanagan, *Arena,* 116, 119–120. Jane DeHart Mathews, *The Federal Theatre: Plays, Relief, and Politics* (Princeton: Princeton University Press, 1967), 97. JoAnne Bentley, *Hallie Flanagan: A Life in the Theatre* (New York: Knopf, 1988), 241. Francis Bosworth, William Farnsworth, Irwin Rhodes, H. L. Fishel, oral histories, Institute for the Federal Theatre Project and New Deal Culture (hereafter FTP), George Mason University.

57. John O'Connor and Lorraine Brown, *Free, Adult, Uncensored: The Living History of the Federal Theatre Project* (Washington: New Republic Books, 1978), 26. Bentley, *Flanagan,* 193, 241.

58. Bentley, *Flanagan,* 210–219, 234.

59. "'It Can't Happen Here' on the Stage," *Publishers Weekly* 130 (5 November 1936), 829. "An Open Letter to Directors of the Federal Theatre from Hallie Flanagan," 23 September 1936, David Niles, undated release, Box 137, Records of the Federal Theatre Project, Works Projects Administration, Record Group 69 (hereafter RG 69), National Archives.

60. "Lewis Drama," 40–41. Schorer, *Sinclair Lewis,* 523. Pierre de Rohan, "It IS Happening Here—And Everywhere," *Federal Theatre Magazine* 2(2), 7–8. Hallie Flanagan to Bernard Szold, Box 107, RG 69.

61. Bosworth, Fishel, Howard Miller oral histories, Vincent Sherman to George Medovoy, 1 February 1974, FTP. Flanagan, *Arena,* 116, 122. *Variety,* 21 October 1936.

62. Rohan, "It IS Happening," 11, 13. Hallie Flanagan to Leon Alexander, 4 November 1936, Box 151, RG 69.

63. Flanagan, *Arena,* 122. Flanagan to Alexander, 4 November 1936. For photographs of actors and sets, see Rohan, "It IS Happening," 8–17, as well as the photograph and production notebook collections, FTP.

64. Flanagan memorandum, 14 October 1936, Box 107, RG 69.

65. Farnsworth to Federal Theatre State Directors and Project Administrators, 4 September 1936, Box 107; "Instructions Governing Exploitation 'It Can't Happen Here,'" n.d., Box 137, RG 69.

66. E. E. McCleish to Martin Chicoine, 8 October 1936, to W. E. Watts, 19 October 1936, to Lee Norvelle, 24 October 1936, Flanagan memorandum, 14 October 1936, Box 107, RG 69.

67. McCleish to John J. Stein, 22 September 1936, Box 107, RG 69. Flanagan, *Arena,* 117–118. *New York Herald Tribune,* 28 October 1936.

68. Francis Bosworth to All Directors . . . , 1 October 1936, Box 137, RG 69. Flanagan, *Arena,* 119.

69. *Variety,* 28 October 1936. Flanagan to Alexander, 4 November 1936, Flanagan to Ellen Woodward, 27 October 1936, Box 62; McCleish to Farnsworth, 27 October 1936, Box 107, RG 69. Flanagan, *Arena,* 122–123.

70. Hallie Flanagan, "Report on WPA Federal Theatre Project's Productions of 'It Can't Happen Here,'" Lewis Collection. "WPA, Lewis and Co." *Time* 28 (9 November 1936), 21. Schorer, *Sinclair Lewis,* 624.

71. Schorer, *Sinclair Lewis,* 611. "Lewis and Co.," 21. John C. Moffitt and Sinclair Lewis, "It Can't Happen Here: A Play," 18 September 1935, FTP.

72. Moffitt and Lewis, "A Play." Flanagan to Alexander, 4 November 1936, Sherman to Medovoy, 1 February 1974, FTP.

73. *Montclair (New Jersey) Times,* 30 October 1936. Excerpts from reviews in *Motion Picture Herald,* 31 October 1936, as well as "The Critics' Score Board" and *"It Can't Happen Here,"* Box 107, RG 69.

74. *New York Times,* 28 October 1936. *New York World-Telegram,* 28 October 1936.

75. "Critics' Score Board." Audience survey reports from Denver, Indianapolis, Birmingham, Chicago, Philadelphia, New York, Brooklyn, Newark, and Montclair, New Jersey, FTP.

76. Mathews, *Federal Theatre,* 101.

77. Sinclair Lewis, *It Can't Happen Here: A New Version* (New York: Dramatists Plays Service, 1938), 132–136. Schorer, *Sinclair Lewis,* 628, 634, 637–640, 696–699.

78. Sklar, *Movie-Made America,* 244–246. Garth Jowett, *Film: The Democratic Art* (Boston: Little, Brown, 1976), 297–306.

Chapter 6. Is Poland a Soviet Satellite?

1. *The Presidential Campaign of 1976,* Vol. 3: *The Debates* (Washington, D.C.: Government Printing Office, 1979), 99–100.

2. Ibid., 100. "Ford-Carter Presidential Debate," Videotape C3, Jimmy Carter Library. On Carter's campaign themes, see Gaddis Smith, *Morality, Reason, and Power: American Diplomacy in the Carter Years* (New York: Hill & Wang, 1986), 27–30.

3. Walter F. Mondale, interview with author, 28 January 1987.

4. Piotr S. Wandycz, *The United States and Poland* (Cambridge, Mass.: Harvard University Press, 1980), 365. See also Bennett Kovrig, *The Myth of Liberation: East Central Europe in US Diplomacy Since 1941* (Baltimore: Johns Hopkins University Press, 1973), 92–93, 146; Raymond L. Garthoff, "Eastern Europe in the Context of US-Soviet Relations," in Sarah Meikeljohn Terry, ed., *Soviet Policy in Eastern Europe* (New Haven, Conn.: Yale University Press, 1984), 318; and Stephen Garrett, *From Potsdam to Poland: American Policy Toward Eastern Europe* (New York: Praeger, 1986), 68–71.

5. Wandycz, *United States and Poland,* 359. See also Garrett, *Potsdam to Poland,* 4–14, and Louis L. Gerson, *The Hyphenate in Recent American*

Politics and Diplomacy (Lawrence, Kansas: University of Kansas Press, 1964), 218–219, 230–232.

6. Kovrig, *Myth of Liberation,* 244, 247, 249–252, 279. See also Garrett, *Potsdam to Poland,* 4–14; John C. Campbell, "Soviet Policy in Eastern Europe: An Overview," in Terry, *Soviet Policy,* 17, 22; Vojtech Mastny, *Helsinki, Human Rights, and International Security: Analysis and Documentation* (Durham, N.C.: Duke University Press, 1986), 48–49; Henry W. Brands, Jr., "Redefining the Cold War: American Policy toward Yugoslavia, 1948–60"; and A. Paul Kubricht, "Politics and Foreign Policy: A Brief Look at the Kennedy Administration's East European Diplomacy," *Diplomatic History* 11 (Winter 1987): 41–53, 55–65.

7. *Public Papers of the Presidents of the United States: Richard M. Nixon, 1970* (Washington, D.C.: Government Printing Office, 1971), 1:81. See also Kovrig, *Myth of Liberation,* 291; and Garthoff, "Eastern Europe," 327, 353.

8. Kovrig, *Myth of Liberation,* 291. Idem, "The United States: 'Peaceful Engagement' Revisited," in Charles Gati, ed., *The International Politics of Eastern Europe* (New York: Praeger, 1976), 140–147. Garthoff, "Eastern Europe," 316. Andrzej Korbonski, "Soviet Policy Toward Poland," in Terry, *Soviet Policy,* 66–67.

9. Campbell, "Soviet Policy," 29. Garrett, *Potsdam to Poland,* 42–43. Idem, "The Ties that Bind: Immigrant Influence on US Policy toward Eastern Europe," in Abdul Aziz Said, ed., *Ethnicity and US Foreign Policy* (New York: Praeger, 1977), 62–63. Donald Pienkos, "The Polish-American Congress—An Appraisal," *Polish-American Studies* 36 (1979): 17–18, 31.

10. Henry A. Kissinger to Gerald R. Ford, 9 October 1974, Box 42, CO 121, White House Central File (hereafter WHCF), Ford Presidential Library, Ann Arbor, Michigan. See also George Springstein to Brent Scowcroft, 26 September 1974, Jeanne Davis to Warren Rustand, 16 September 1974, Box 41, CO 121, WHCF. All manuscript sources cited are from the Ford Presidential Library unless otherwise indicated.

11. Raymond L. Garthoff, *Detente and Confrontation: American-Soviet Relations from Nixon to Reagan* (Washington, D.C.: Brookings Institution, 1985), 453–468. Garrett, *Potsdam to Poland,* 87–88.

12. Henry Kissinger, *Years of Upheaval* (Boston: Little, Brown, 1982), 1165. See also Garthoff, *Detente and Confrontation,* 472–479; Adam B. Ulam, *Dangerous Relations: The Soviet Union in World Politics* (New York: Oxford University Press, 1983), 140–144; and John J. Maresca, *To Helsinki: The Conference on Security and Cooperation in Europe, 1973–75* (Durham, N.C.: Duke University Press, 1987).

13. James Buckley to Ford, 16 July 1975, Box 14, IT 104, WHCF. See also Grzegorz Rej et al., to Ford, 23 July 1975, Box 57, TR 34-3, WHCF; and Czechoslovak National Council of America, "Foreign Policy Towards the Soviet Union and East Central Europe," 8 June 1976, Box 2, Kuropas files.

14. *Public Papers of the Presidents of the United States: Gerald R. Ford, 1975* (Washington, D.C.: Government Printing Office, 1979), 2:1832–1833.

"A Counterpoint to Cooperation," *Newsweek,* 21 July 1975, 56–57. Ron Nessen, *It Sure Looks Different from the Inside* (Chicago: Playboy Press, 1978), 345. James Burnham, "The Logic of Detente," *National Review* 27 (15 August 1975), 873. See also Ford, *A Time to Heal: The Autobiography of Gerald R. Ford* (New York: Harper & Row, 1979), 297–298.

15. *Public Papers of Gerald R. Ford, 1975,* 2:1030–1033, 1043–1044, 1061–1066, 1071, 1074–1081, 1088–1090, 1092, 1100–1102, 1104, 1110, 1131–1133.

16. Brent Scowcroft to Ford, 16 December 1975, Box 1, IT 104, WHCF. See also A. Denis Clift to Jeanne W. Davis, 25 August 1975, Box 1, IT 104, WHCF.

17. Nicholas Nyaradi to Ford, 22 August 1975, Box 14, IT 104, WHCF. See also Aloysius A. Mazewski to Ford, 2 July 1976, CO 121, Box 1, WHCF; and Czechoslovak National Council of America, "Foreign Policy towards the Soviet Union and East Central Europe," 8 June 1976, Box 2, Kuropas files.

18. Ford to Nyaradi, 29 November 1975; Clift to Scowcroft, 18 November 1975, Box 14, IT 104, WHCF. Scowcroft to Max Friedersdorf, 29 May 1976, Box 14, Kuropas files. See also Ford to Americans of Estonian Ancestry, 19 February 1976; and Jeanne Davis to William Nicholson, 17 February 1976, Box 2, Kuropas files.

19. *Washington Post,* 22 March 1976.

20. Helmut Sonnenfeldt, interview with author, 22 December 1988.

21. Sonnenfeldt interview. See also *New York Times,* 6 April 1976; and "The Kissinger Issue: Whose Alamo?" *Time,* 19 April 1976, 13.

22. *New York Times,* 6 April 1976. Sonnenfeldt interview.

23. *New York Times,* 6 April 1976. See also "Wall Posters," *Newsweek,* 19 April 1976, 48.

24. *New York Times,* 6 April 1976.

25. Ibid.

26. Sonnenfeldt interview.

27. *New York Times,* 6, 7 April 1988. William Baroody to Jack Marsh, 26 March 1976; Kuropas to Scowcroft, 26 March 1976, Box 5, CO 1-4, WHCF. See also *Washington Post,* 26 March, 1976.

28. *New York Times,* 6, 7 April 1976. Kissinger to Buckley, 27 March 1976, Box 5, CO 1-4, WHCF. See also Sonnenfeldt interview; A. Denis Clift to Scowcroft, "Proposed Reply," Box 5, CO 1-4, WHCF; "Kissinger Issue," 13; and "Hot Issue—US A Patsy for Russia?" *US News and World Report,* 19 April 1976, 16.

29. Nessen, *Different from the Inside,* 164. Richard Reeves, *A Ford Not a Lincoln* (New York: Harcourt Brace Jovanovich, 1975), 25–27.

30. Ford, *Time to Heal,* 55–56, 173. A. James Reichley, *Conservatives in an Age of Change: The Nixon and Ford Administrations* (Washington, D.C.: Brookings Institution, 1981), 306, 384.

31. Nessen, *Different from the Inside,* 148–149, 163, 167–173, 208. See also Reichley, *Conservatives in Age of Change,* 307–312.

32. *The Presidential Campaign of 1976,* Vol. 1: *Jimmy Carter* (Washington, D.C.: Government Printing Office, 1978), 80, 216. See also Jules Witcover, *Marathon: The Pursuit of the Presidency 1972–1976* (New York: Viking, 1977), 401; Nessen, *Different from the Inside,* 155, 158; and Robert D. Schulzinger, *Henry A. Kissinger: Doctor of Diplomacy* (New York: Columbia University Press, 1989), 202, 218, 228–220, 227–230.

33. *Public Papers of the Presidents of the United States: Gerald R. Ford, 1976–1977* (Washington, D.C.: Government Printing Office, 1977), 1:892–904.

34. Aloysius Mazewski to Ford, 24 March 1976, Box 5, CO 4, WHCF. See also Istvan B. Gereban to Ford, 23 March 1976, Emilija Cekiene to Ford, 3 April 1976, Box 5, CO 1-4, WHCF; and *New York Times,* 7 April 1976.

35. Buckley to Ford, 5 May 1976, Box 5, CO-4, WHCF. "Hot Issue," 16. "Wall Posters," 48. "Whose Alamo?" 12.

36. "National Surveys—Strategy Book Memorandum," August 1976, 1:2, 20, Box 54, Teeter files 54.

37. "Strategy Book," 22–23, 59–60.

38. "Strategy Book," 35. See also Wandycz, *United States and Poland,* 340; Gerson, *Hyphenate,* 179, 190–192, 217–218; and Malcom D. MacDougall, *We Almost Made It* (New York: Crown, 1978), 47.

39. Ford to Dick Cheney, n.d., Box 17, Cheney files. Betty Glad, *Jimmy Carter: In Search of the Great White House* (New York: Norton, 1980), 293. See also Ford, *Time to Heal,* 412; Kuropas to Michael Raoul-Duval, 20 October 1976, Box 216, FG 431, WHCF; and "Strategy Book," 42.

40. *The Ford Presidency: From an Ethnic Perspective, A Portrait of the First Two Years,* 3, 6, 8–10, Box 10, Kuropas files. *Chicago Sun-Times,* 9 September 1976. See also A. Denis Clift to William G. Hyland, 7 September 1976, Kuropas to Baroody, 7 September 1976, Box 1, CO 121, WHCF; Market Opinion Research, "1976 Presidential Election," Box 62, Teeter files; and Pienkos, "Polish-American Congress," 23.

41. Lloyd Butzger and Theodore Rueter, *Carter v. Ford: The Counterfeit Debates of 1976* (Madison: University of Wisconsin Press, 1980), 22. See also Herbert A. Seltz and Richard D. Yoakam, "Production Diary of the Debates," in Sidney Kraus, ed., *The Great Debates: Carter vs. Ford, 1976* (Bloomington: Indiana University Press, 1979), 110–157.

42. Ford, *Time to Heal,* 405, 414–416. Witcover, *Marathon,* 541–544, 570–574, 577–579. Michael Duval, "Debate Preparation"; Stuart Eizenstat and Michael Raoul-Duval, "Candidate Briefings," in Kraus, *Great Debates,* 105–109.

43. Witcover, *Marathon,* 584–594. Ford, *Time to Heal,* 417–420. Agnes Waldron to David Gergen, 3 October 1976, Box 2, Special files.

44. "Second Debate: Ford Notes on Briefing Materials," and [National Security Council], "Second Debate: Carter on Foreign Policy," Box 2, Special files. See also *Boston Gazette,* 6 October 1976; and *New York Times,* 6 October 1976.

45. Witcover, *Marathon,* 598. *Washington Post,* 8 October 1976.

46. Ford, *Time to Heal,* 428. *Boston Globe,* 7 October 1976. Richard Cheney, "The 1976 Presidential Debate," Box 62, Teeter files. *Public Papers of Gerald R. Ford, 1976–1977,* 3:2444.

47. *Newsday,* 7 October 1976. See also *Los Angeles Times,* 8 October 1976.

48. Ibid. *Washington Post,* 7 October 1976. *New York Times,* 8, 10 October 1976. *Philadelphia Inquirer,* 7 October 1976. *San Francisco News-Examiner,* 7 October 1976. See also *Boston Globe,* 7, 8 October 1976; and *Chicago Sun,* 8 October 1976.

49. Lawrence T. Caldwell, "CSCE, MFR, and Eastern Europe," in Gati, *International Politics,* 193. MacDougall, *Almost Made It,* 63. See also Sonnenfeldt interview.

50. *San Francisco News-Examiner,* 7 October 1976. *New York Times,* 8 October 1976. *Washington Post,* 8 October 1976. *Cleveland Plain Dealer,* 9 October 1976. *Houston Post,* 8 October 1976. See also *Washington Star,* 7 October 1976.

51. Frederick Steeper, "The Public's Response to Gerald Ford's Statements on Eastern Europe During the Second Debate," 3, 7, 9, 11, 19, 20, 22, Box 62, Teeter files.

52. *Public Papers of Gerald R. Ford, 1976–1977,* 3:2457, 2464–2465. *Los Angeles Times,* 7 October 1976. *Washington Post,* 9 October 1976.

53. *Public Papers of Gerald R. Ford, 1976–1977,* 3:2465. *Washington Post,* 9 October 1976. See also Ford, *Time to Heal,* 425; Baroody to Ford, 14 October 1976, Box 5, CO 1-4, WHCF; and [A. James Reichley], "Draft of Presidential Remarks," Box 2, Reichley files.

54. Ford, *Time to Heal,* 424.

55. *Public Papers of Gerald R. Ford, 1976–1977,* 3:2485. *Presidential Campaign: The Debates,* 167. Cheney to Ford, 20 October 1976, Box 23, David Gergen files. See also Ford to Adrian B. Karmazyn, 14 October 1976, Box 2, CO 1A-Z, WHCF.

56. *Washington Post,* 11 October 1989.

57. Sonnenfeldt interview.

58. Richard Cheney, "1976 Debate," 42, 48. Market Opinion Research, "1976 Presidential Election," 24, 28. Patrick Caddell to Hamilton Jordan, 6 April 1977, Box 79, Hamilton Jordan files, Jimmy Carter Library, Atlanta, Georgia. Leo W. Jeffres and K. Kyoon Hur, "Impact of Ethnc Issues on Ethnic Voters," in Kraus, *Great Debates,* 437–445.

59. Leo P. Ribuffo, "Jimmy Carter and the Ironies of American Liberalism," *Gettysburg Review* 1 (Autumn 1988), 746–747.

Chapter 7. God and Jimmy Carter

1. "The 1976 Elections," *Church and State* 29 (December 1976), 4.

2. *The Presidential Campaign of 1976,* Vol. 1: *Jimmy Carter* (Washington, D.C.: Government Printing Office, 1978), 973. Jimmy Carter, *Why Not the Best?* (New York: Bantam Books, 1976), frontispiece, chapters 5, 14.

3. *Washington Post,* 12 March 1976. Jules Witcover, *Marathon: The Pursuit of the Presidency, 1972–1976* (New York: Viking, 1977), 270–272. Betty Glad, *Jimmy Carter: In Search of the Great White House* (New York: Norton, 1980), 331–332. Bruce Mazlish and Edwin Diamond, eds., *Jimmy Carter: An Interpretive Biography* (New York: Simon & Schuster, 1979), 151–155.

4. Richard Quebedeaux, *The Worldly Evangelicals* (New York: Harper & Row, 1978), 4. Mazlish, *Carter,* 67–68. Glad, *Great White House,* 332. Witcover, *Marathon,* 270–272. "Jimmy Carter's Faith Healing Sister," *Humanist* 36 (July-August 1976), 39. Ruth Carter Stapleton, *The Gift of Inner Healing* (Waco: Word Books, 1976). Idem, *The Experience of Inner Healing* (Waco: Word Books, 1977).

5. David Kucharsky, *The Man from Plains: The Mind and Spirit of Jimmy Carter* (New York: Perennial Library, 1976). E. Brooks Holifield, "The Three Strands of Jimmy Carter's Religion," *New Republic* 174 (5 June 1976), 15–17.

6. *Campaign: Carter,* 965, 458, 967, 178, 459, 969, 171, 457, 963. Wesley Pippert, *The Spiritual Journey of Jimmy Carter: In His Own Words* (New York: Macmillan, 1978), 242.

7. *Campaign: Carter,* 969.

8. Mazlish, *Carter,* 162. Kucharksy, *Man from Plains,* 9–11. Leon H. Charney, *Special Counsel* (New York: Philosophical Library, 1984), 197.

9. Glad, *Great White House.* David J. O'Brien, "The 'Catholic vote,'" *Commonweal* (10 October 1980), 550. Mary T. Hanna, *Catholics and American Politics* (Cambridge, Mass.: Harvard University Press, 1979), 117, 152, 163–165, 184.

10. Kucharsky, *Man from Plains,* 42.

11. James and Marti Hefley, *The Church that Produced a President* (New York: Wyden Books, 1977), 112. William Lee Miller, *Yankee from Georgia* (New York: Times Books, 1978), 5, 10, 172. Pippert, *Spiritual Journey,* 238–239.

12. Gerald R. Ford, *A Time to Heal: The Autobiography of Gerald R. Ford* (New York: Harper & Row, 1979), 306–307. Betty Ford, with Chris Chase, *The Times of My Life* (New York: Harper & Row, 1978), 206–207. Rosalynn Carter, *First Lady from Plains* (New York: Fawcett, 1984), 131. Kucharsky, *Man from Plains,* 135.

13. Ford, *Time to Heal,* 417. *The Presidential Campaign of 1976,* Vol. 2: *Gerald R. Ford* (Washington, D.C.: Government Printing Office, 1978), 617, 909. Ford to Dick [Cheney], n.d., Cheney Collection, Box 16, Gerald Ford Presidential Library.

14. Richard Reeves, *A Ford, Not a Lincoln* (New York: Harcourt Brace Jovanovich, 1975), 110, 113–114. *New York Times,* 10 October 1976. Ford, *Time to Heal,* 175. *Presidential Campaign: Ford,* 981, 919, 911. Richard G. Hutcheson, *God in the White House: How Religion Has Changed the Modern Presidency* (New York: Collier, 1988), 91–96.

15. "The Campaign: Into the Homestretch," *Church and State* 29 (November 1976), 3, 8. *Campaign: Ford,* 910, 799.

16. Ford, *Time to Heal,* 412. *Campaign: Ford,* 913, 982. *Campaign: Carter,* 92–93, 455–457, 968. Ron Nessen, *It Sure Looks Different from the Inside* (Chicago: Playboy Press, 1978), 28. Eve Rubin, *Abortion, Politics, and the Courts: Roe v. Wade and Its Aftermath* (Westport, Conn.: Greenwood Press, 1982), 148–150.

17. O'Brien, "Catholic Vote," 551.

18. Ibid., 552. Patrick Caddell to Jimmy Carter, 11 September 1976, Box 4, Jody Powell Collection, Jimmy Carter Library (hereafter JCL).

19. *Campaign: Carter,* 973, 956.

20. Ibid., 956, 963–964.

21. Glad, *Great White House,* 384. Miller, *Yankee from Georgia,* 43. Hefley, *Produced a President,* 139–141, 211. *Los Angeles Times,* October 9, 1976.

22. Gerald M. Pomper, "The Presidential Election," in Marlene Pomper, ed., *The Election of 1976: Reports and Interpretations* (New York: McKay, 1977), 61, 63–65. Albert Menendez, "How Carter Won," *Church and State* 29 (December 1976), 9–14. Clyde M. DeLoach, "Jimmy Carter: The Effect of Personal Religious Beliefs on his Presidency and their Relationship to the Christian Realism of Reinhold Niebuhr" (Ph.D. dissertation, Baylor University, 1985), 125.

23. Hefley, *Produced a President,* 192–193. Kucharsky, *Man from Plains,* 14–15. Pippert, *Spiritual Journey,* 192.

24. Jimmy and Rosalynn Carter, *Everything to Gain: Making the Most of the Rest of Your Life* (New York: Random House, 1987), 190. *Campaign: Carter,* 164. Kucharsky, *Man from Plains,* 31. Glad, *Great White House,* chapter 3. Pippert, *Spiritual Journey,* 231. DeLoach, "Jimmy Carter," 52.

25. Glad, *Great White House,* chapters 4–5. Rosalyn Carter, *First Lady,* 40–45. Hefley, *Produced a President,* 144–148.

26. *Campaign: Carter,* 176. Carter, *Why Not?* 151–153. Mazlish, *Carter,* 151–152, 154. Glad, *Great White House,* 108–112. Witcover, *Marathon,* 270–272.

27. Carter, *Why Not?* 143–151.

28. Pippert, *Spiritual Journey,* 59, 76, 116, 169, 176.

29. Miller, *Yankee from Georgia,* 193. Pippert, *Spiritual Journey,* 77. Garry Wills, "The Plains Truth," *Atlantic* 237 (June 1976), 49–54.

30. Hefley, *Produced a President,* 189. Quebedeaux, *Worldly Evangelicals,* 38. Kucharsky, *Man from Plains,* 23. *Public Papers of the Presidents of the United States: Jimmy Carter, 1980–81* (Washington, D.C.: Government Printing Office, 1981), 1:181.

31. Pippert, *Spiritual Journey,* 17, 155, 200.

32. Quebedeaux, *Worldly Evangelicals,* 38. Miller, *Yankee from Georgia,* 213–214. Holifield, "Three Strands," 15–17.

33. Pippert, *Spiritual Journey,* 174, 164, 168, 173, 180.

34. Ibid., 234, 240.

35. Ibid., 236, 219, 214–217.

36. Ibid., 186, 192–193, 202–204, 164–165.

37. Ibid., 179, 254, 91, 168, 219. *Public Papers of the Presidents of the United States: Jimmy Carter, 1978* (Washington, D.C.: Government Printing Office, 1979), 1:1115.

38. Pippert, *Spiritual Journey*, 245, 293, 244–245, 257–258.

39. Ibid., 242–243. *Public Papers, 1978*, 1:1117.

40. Hutcheson, *God in the White House*, 104.

41. James T. Hefley, "A Change of Mind in Plains," *Christianity Today* 21 (3 December 1976), 50–53. Hefley, *Produced a President*, 212–221, 226, 233–235. "Carter's Church," *Newsweek*, 28 August 1978, 11.

42. *Philadelphia Inquirer*, 23 April 1977. *New York Jewish Week-American Examiner*, 8 May 1977.

43. Marc Tanenbaum to Lipshutz, 5 May 1977, [Tanenbaum], "A Proposed Statement by President Jimmy Carter on the Role of the Jews in the Crucifixion," Box 8, Lipshutz Collection. Carter to John F. Steinbruck, 12 May 1977, Box PP 83, White House Central File (hereafter WHCF), JCL.

44. *Tulsa World*, 18 December 1977. Benjamin Epstein to Lipshutz, 29 December 1977, Lipshutz to Epstein, 26 January 1978, Eizenstat to Lipshutz, 12 May 1977, Box 235, Stuart Eizenstat Collection; Lipshutz to Eizenstat, 30 January 1978, Box 8, Lipshutz Collection, JCL.

45. Hefley, *Produced a President*, 234–239. *Washington Star*, 29 January 1978. Harwell to Carter, 23 June [1977], Carter to Harwell, 11 August 1977, Box RM 1; Carter to Jimmy Allen, 30 January 1978, Box PP 83; Lipshutz to Susan Clough, 20 February 1979, Jimmy Allen folder, WHCF, JCL.

46. *Public Papers, 1978*, 1:78, 1114, 1116, 2:2087; *1980*, 1:181, 275, 2:1750.

47. Doug Huron to John Hanson, 9 June 1977, Box HO 1; Carter to Rosalynn Carter, 13 September 1979, Carter to Father Theodore Hesburgh, 10 October 1979, Box CO 66, WHCF, JCL.

48. Daniel Patrick Moynihan et al., to Harold Brown, 25 July 1978, Box 103, Eizenstat Collection; Eizenstat to Rev. John F. Quinn, 13 July 1978, Box ED 1, WHCF; Hamilton Jordan to Carter, 30 June 1977, Box 30, President's Handwriting file, JCL. Hefley, *Produced a President*, 230. Ronald B. Flowers, "President Jimmy Carter, Evangelicalism, Church-State Relations, and Civil Religion," *Journal of Church and State* 25 (Winter 1983), 113–132.

49. Dave Bruce, *The Rise and Fall of the New Christian Right: Conservative Protestant Politics in America 1978–1988* (Oxford: Clarendon Press, 1990), 42–43. Erling Jorstad, *Evangelicals in the White House: The Cultural Maturation of Born Again Christianity, 1960–1981* (New York: Edwin Mellen, 1981), 106. Frank White to Tom Leney, "IRS and Private Schools," Box 13, White Collection, JCL.

50. "IRS and Private Schools." IRS press release, 9 August 1980, Box 13, White Collection; Carter to Bill and Pam Harmon, 26 April 1976, Elizabeth Abramowitz to Richard L. Holmes, 19 June 1979, Box FG 105, WHCF, JCL.

51. *Washington Post,* 7 September 1979. Rick Neustadt to Eizenstat, 20 September 1979, Box FG 105, WHCF, JCL. Matthew C. Moen, *The Christian Right and Congress* (Tuscaloosa: University of Alabama Press, 1989), 26–27.

52. Skip Works to Jane [Wales], 18 April 1980, Box WE 6, WHCF, JCL. Rubin, *Abortion,* 151–157. Joseph A. Califano, *Governing America: An Insider's Report from the White House and the Cabinet* (New York: Simon & Schuster, 1981), chapter 2.

53. Califano to Daniel Flood, 22 February 1978, Jan Peterson to Costanza, 13, 20 July 1977, Costanza to Carter, 13 July 1977, Box WE 3, WHCF, JCL.

54. *Public Papers of the Presidents of the United States: Jimmy Carter, 1977* (Washington, D.C.: Government Printing Office, 1978), 1:956. Gaddis Smith, *Morality, Reason, and Power: Foreign Policy During the Carter Years* (New York: Hill & Wang, 1986), 66. Pippert, *Spiritual Journey,* 59, 62, 247. *Washington Post,* 3 February 1978.

55. Pippert, *Spiritual Journey,* 94. *Campaign: Carter,* 970. Carters, *Everything to Gain,* 169.

56. Jimmy Carter, *The Blood of Abraham* (Boston: Houghton Mifflin, 1985), 4–8.

57. *New York Times,* 17 June 1978. John Osborne, "Carter and God," *New Republic* 181 (16 July 1979), 9–10. William Greider, "Can a Real Christian Make It as President?" *Washington Post Magazine,* 5 November 1978, 3, 16, 34. "Hustling for the Lord," *Newsweek,* 5 December 1977, 61.

58. Jordan, "Foreign Policy/Domestic Policies," Box 34, Jordan Collection; Benjamin Epstein to Carter, 27 April 1979, Box 6, Alfred Moses Collection, JCL. *Public Papers of the Presidents of the United States: Jimmy Carter, 1979* (Washington, D.C.: Government Printing Office, 1980), 1:580–581, 684–685. *New York Jewish Week and Examiner,* 28 August 1977.

59. Charney, *Special Counsel,* 203–204. Joyce Starr to Stuart [Eizenstat], 6 June 1978, Box 208, Eizenstat to Brzezinski, 2 June 1977, Box 235, Eizenstat Collection, JCL.

60. Smith, *Morality, Reason,* 161, 170–171. Joyce Starr to Eizenstat, 6 June 1978, Box 208, Eizenstat to Carter, 19 January 1978, Box 142, Eizenstat Collection; Mark Siegel to Carter, 8 March 1978, Box 28, Lipshutz Collection, JCL. *Los Angeles Times,* 9 March 1978.

61. Epstein to Lipshutz, 29 December 1977, Lipshutz to Eizenstat, 20 January 1978, Eizenstat to Jordan, 22 May 1978, Box 235, Eizenstat Collection, JCL. "Offensive Christianity," *National Review* 30 (23 June 1978), 763.

62. William B. Quandt, *Camp David: Peacemaking and Politics* (Washington, D.C.: Brookings Institution, 1986), chapter 11. Kellerman, *All the President's Kin* (London: Robson Books, 1982), 223–225. *New York Daily News,* 12 January 1979. *B'nai B'rith Messenger,* 26 February 1979.

63. Edward Sanders to Jordan/Gerald Rafshoon, 23 February 1979, Box 1, Sanders Collection, JCL. Kellerman, *President's Kin,* 224–225. Charney, *Special Counsel,* 212.

64. *Washington Star,* 7 August 1989. *Los Angeles Times,* 2 August 1979. Leonard Silk to Carter, 2 August 1979, Box 16, Sanders Collection, JCL.

65. Gaddis Smith, *Morality, Reason,* 168. *New York Times,* 15 August 1979. *Washington Post,* 15 August 1979. Jimmy Carter, *Keeping Faith: Memoirs of a President* (New York: Bantam Books, 1982), 491. Rafshoon to Carter, 29 May 1979, Box 18, Rafshoon Collection; Edward Sanders to Jordan, 27 August 1979, Box SP 25, WHCF, JCL. *Public Papers, 1979,* 2:1563–1574.

66. Hanna, *Catholics and Politics,* 102. John Deedy, "A Friend at Court?" *Commonweal,* 104 (7 January 1977), 2.

67. *Public Papers, 1980–81,* 2:1164–1169.

68. Allen to Carter, 7 October 1980, Jimmy Allen file, WHCF, JCL. Hutcheson, *God in the White House,* 116–117. Richard John Neuhaus and Michael Cromartie, *Piety and Politics: Evangelicals and Fundamentalists Confront the World* (Washington, D.C.: Ethics and Public Policy Center, 1987), 84–85. Dinesh D'Souza, *Falwell Before the Millennium: A Critical Biography* (Chicago: Regnery Gateway, 1984), 105–112.

69. *Public Papers, 1979,* 2:1235–1239. Carter, *Keeping Faith,* 114–121. Rev. Robert M. Maddox, interview with author, 9 November 1987.

70. Maddox interview. Maddox, *Preacher at the White House* (Nashville: Boardman Press, 1984), 54–57, 62–63, 73–74, 79, 133, 138–139. Maddox to Jody Powell, 6 January 1977, Maddox file, WHCF; Maddox to Rosalynn Carter, 12 July 1970, Box 52, Rafshoon Collection, JCL.

71. *Public Papers, 1979,* 2:1925–1931; *1980,* 1:180–183, 377–379. Maddox to Rafshoon and Greg Schneiders, 27 July 1979, Box 52, Rafshoon Collection, JCL. Maddox, *Preacher,* 162–165. Maddox interview.

72. John Deedy, *American Catholicism: And Now Where?* (New York: Plenum Press, 1987), 30–31. "The Pope Votes Out Drinan," *Time* 115 (19 May 1980), 30. Eizenstat to Carter, 3 October 1980, Alfred Moses Collection, JCL.

73. Gerald M. Pomper, "The Nominating Contests," in Marlene Michels Pomper, ed., *The Election of 1980: Reports and Interpretations* (Chatham, N.J.: Chatham House, 1981), 26, 28–29.

74. Carter, *Keeping Faith,* 492–493. Edward I. Koch with William Rauch, *Mayor: An Autobiography* (New York: Warner Books, 1985), 233–234. Jack W. Germond and Jules Witcover, *Blue Smoke and Mirrors: How Reagan Won and Why Carter Lost the Election of 1980* (New York: Viking, 1981), 152–155. *Los Angeles Times,* 16 August 1980. *New York Times,* 5, 26 March 1980. *Washington Post,* 17 August 1980.

75. Jorstad, *Evangelicals in the White House,* 144–149. Hutcheson, *God in the White House,* 161–165, 171. Garry Wills, *Reagan's America* (New York: Penguin, 1988), 20–63, 234–236, 454–457. Richard V. Pierard and Robert D. Linder, *Civil Religion and the Presidency* (Grand Rapids, Mich.: Academic Books, 1988), 266–271.

76. D'Souza, *Falwell,* 121.

77. Ibid. Jeff Greenfield, *The Real Campaign: How the Media Missed the Story of the 1980 Campaign* (New York: Summit Books, 1982), 159.

78. Ibid., 276. Leo P. Ribuffo, "Liberals and that Old-Time Religion," *Nation* (29 November 1980), 370–373.

79. James Davison Hunter, *Evangelicalism: The Coming Generation* (Chicago: University of Chicago Press, 1987), 147–148. Greenfield, *Real Campaign,* 276. D'Souza, *Falwell,* 123.

80. Ribuffo, "Old-Time Religion," 570. D'Souza, *Falwell,* 125.

81. "Running Against Darwin," *Scientific American* 243 (November 1980), 80. Carter, *Keeping Faith,* 562.

82. Alfred Moses, "New Right Fundamentalists," speech notes, 9 October 1980, Box 10; "Outreach: American Jewish Voters," 9 October 1980; *President Carter's Bold Gamble for Peace,* flyer, Box 18, Moses Collection, JCL. *New York Times,* 10 June 1980.

83. Carter, *Keeping Faith,* 562. *Public Papers of the Presidents of the United States: Jimmy Carter, 1980–81* (Washington, D.C.: Government Printing Office, 1982), 2:1685, 3:2505–2506.

84. Germond, *Blue Smoke,* 203. "Running Against Darwin," 80.

85. Maddox, *Preacher,* 157–159, 170. Maddox interview. Jim Bakker to Carter, 3 November 1980, Bakker file, WHCF, JCL.

86. Wills, *Reagan's America,* 355.

87. Carters, *Everything to Gain,* 69–70, 90–92. Carter, *An Outdoor Journal: Adventures and Reflections* (New York: Bantam Books, 1988), 238, 264–265.

88. Carter, *Outdoor Journal,* 265.

89. Carters, *Everything to Gain,* 23. Gerald M. Pomper, "The Presidential Election," in Pomper, ed., *Election of 1980,* 71. Albert J. Mendendez, "Religion at the Polls," *Church and State* 33 (December 1980), 15–18. Seymour Martin Lipset and Earl Raab, "The Election and the Evangelicals," *Commentary* 71 (March 1981), 29.

90. Mark J. Rozell, *The Press and the Carter Presidency* (Boulder, Colo.: Westview, 1989), 115. On the rise of muscular Christianity, see chapter 3 in this volume.

Index